BANARAS

ADVANCE PRAISE FOR THE BOOK

'What a delightful gift Vertul has put in our hands! A kaleidoscope which, with a slight twist, creates mesmerizing, iridescent patterns. The auteur—both an insider and a detached outsider—tempts the readers to treat Banaras as a film and absorb what the frames depict from multiple perspectives. The pages of this multilayered volume shimmer hypnotically like a rich tapestry woven in the fabulous fabrics the city is renowned for'—Pushpesh Pant, food critic and historian

'Banaras is an ancient city, it is a holy city, it is a modern city. It is a city with a memory and a past; it is a city that celebrates life lustily and death candidly. It is a mythical city, it is a historical city, it is a city that exists half in myth, half in history. A city of intellect and ideas, of debates and dialogues. A city of spirituality and meditation. A city of great temples and shrines, a city of prayers, hymns and adoration. A city of many religions but prominently of Hinduism. A Sanatan city of music, dance, theatre and poetry. A city that sings nocturnally, a city that wails through the day. A city where poetry, philosophy and politics have been coming together and falling apart. A city of joy and jubilation, and equally of sadness and isolation. A city where "purity" and "impurities" jostle for space and mark the human condition. A city that weaves time, plays and frolics with eternity.

'Vertul Singh's book has been written with passion and vision, with rigour and exploration, and is possibly one of the best portraits of a great city, recreating intelligently and creatively its complexity, vibrancy, energy and vitality, its dark recesses and the mystery of its incredible continuum. Today's Banaras is also the Varanasi and Kashi of yesteryear. It is a city with many names and identities. Banaras, through this book, seems to be asserting its plural identity, mysteries, its past as present and invincibility as an eternal city'—Ashok Vajpeyi, poet and essayist

'Audacious, adventurous, objective and also impassioned, Vertul Singh's panoramic reading of Banaras, a city older than history, is a timely academic intervention in this hour of narrow cultural chauvinism. Combining serious scholarship with personal testimony, it brings alive the grandeur and plenitude of the city's undying catholicism'—Geetanjali Shree, International Booker Prize-winning author

BANARAS
A JOURNEY INTO THE HEART OF THE CITY

VERTUL SINGH

VINTAGE
An imprint of Penguin Random House

VINTAGE

Vintage is an imprint of the Penguin Random House group of companies whose addresses can be found at global.penguinrandomhouse.com

Published by Penguin Random House India Pvt. Ltd
4th Floor, Capital Tower 1, MG Road,
Gurugram 122 002, Haryana, India

First published in Vintage by Penguin Random House India 2024

10 9 8 7 6 5 4 3 2 1

ISBN 9780670098408

Typeset in Garamond by MAP Systems, Bengaluru, India
Printed at Replika Press Pvt. Ltd, India

www.penguin.co.in

To my uncle, the late Thakur Madan Mohan Singh, who imbibed in me the cultural-religious ethos of the scriptures and fealty, with specific references to Banaras

and

My mother, who continues to narrate interesting parables and belief systems prevalent in Banaras since ancient times

Contents

Introduction ix

Chapter 1: The Early Days 1
Chapter 2: Rajghat 31
Chapter 3: Alluring Allusions 58
Chapter 4: Kashi 81
Chapter 5: The Yakshas and the Nagas 121
Chapter 6: The Dichotomy of Shaivism and Vaishnavism 150
Chapter 7: The Ghats 177
Chapter 8: The Weavers of Banaras 200
Chapter 9: Art at Heart 220
Chapter 10: Saat Vaar, Nau Tyohaar 248
Chapter 11: Banaras on My Palate 275
Chapter 12: Living Continuities 284
Chapter 13: Perambulating the Idea of Banaras 309

Afterword 317
Notes 319

Introduction

There is a beautiful word in Bengali—*boi*, which literally means a book. The word was commonly used in the vernacular for cinema and later came to be picked up by the Bengali elite while referring to an artsy movie and continues to be used to imply films. It has a deep connotation in that cinema is not just seen, it is also read. While walking through a city, one also reads it. Even after my journey into the lanes and by-lanes of Banaras for close to five decades, I realized I must rely on the metaphors of the city, akin to the proverbial elephant in the room. And well, *a la* the cinematic term 'Rashomon effect', one must carefully draw inference from one's own perception as well, because it is said that Banaras is not what you see; rather, it is what you don't see. The famous Hindi poet Kedarnath Singh succinctly captures this uniqueness of the city in his poem 'Banaras', translated rhapsodically by another great poet and critic, K. Satchidanandan:

> Enter this city one day
> at dawn or dusk
> without announcing yourself
> Observe it unobtrusively
> in the glow of prayer-lights.

For the great poet Mirza Ghalib, Banaras is the place that came closest to the spiritual garden to which he wished to belong. He called this city the 'supreme place of worship . . . the Kaaba of Hindustan'. Ghalib visited Banaras during his journey from Calcutta (now Kolkata) and back during 1826–29.[1] He stayed in what is called the Ghughrani Gali, near Dalmandi, and at a few other places, pouring his heart out for Banaras in his entire Masnavi of 108 verses. Writing to Nawab Muhammad Ali Khan of Banda, his letter in prose form is the best tribute a poet can pay to a city that has the gift of nature's bounties and aesthetics of the built-up space in equal measure: 'Its breeze blows life into dead bodies. Its every fleck of dust has the qualities to pull thorns and needles away like magnets from the feet of travellers. The river Ganga would not have been considered so noble had it not rubbed its forehead at its feet.'[2]

Nirad C. Chaudhuri, on being asked who could possibly represent the real life of India, replied tersely: 'Mountains, rivers and plateaus.'[3]

To paraphrase him in the context of Banaras: they will be the Vindhyas, Ganga and Rajghat. The ancient, medieval and the modern, all orbit around these three chorographical lineaments. Here, the sacred, the temporal and the profane, all reverberate in unison to give this city its uniqueness. That is the reason Jawaharlal Nehru advised his daughter, Indira Gandhi, to 'go to Benares or Kashi, that most ancient of cities, and give ear to her murmuring'.[4]

He further elaborates in his *Discovery of India* poetically: 'At Sarnath, near Benares, I would almost see the Buddha preaching his first sermon, Ashoka's pillars of stone with their inscriptions would speak to me in their magnificent language and tell me of a man who, though an emperor, was greater than any king or emperor.'

I have elsewhere in the book quoted Ralph Fitch, Jean-Baptiste Tavernier, Bishop Reginald Heber and François Bernier. All of them wrote on Banaras—some with inherent prejudices, some in a very patronizing tone and some rather grudgingly accepted the idea of Banaras vis-à-vis Hinduism, but what was common to all of them was that they were overawed.

Lieutenant Colonel Davidson calls it 'the Hindoo Jerusalem'; Norman Macleod, like al-Biruni in 1000 CE, exclaims: 'What Mecca is to Mohammedans, and what Jerusalem was to the Jews of old times, it is the holy city of Hindostan.'[5] Writing the preface to his seminal book *Benares: The Sacred City of the Hindus*, M.A. Sherring epitomizes the city thus: 'The city of Benares represents India, religiously and intellectually, just as Paris represents the political sentiments of France. There are few cities in the world of greater antiquity, and none that have so uninterruptedly maintained their ancient celebrity and distinction. This city . . . has given impulse and vigour to the two religions, which to this day govern half the world.'[6]

To this, I would rather like to add that three more religions draw significant inspirations from this city: Jainism, Islam and Sikhism. They have their own places of worship and votaries to latch on to. By far, the most scathing and condescending comment on Banaras has been made by Fitzedward Hall, an American orientalist and philologist. In the introduction to Sherring's book *Benares*, he points to the rhetorical and fantastical aspects of Kashi and its attendant scriptures, using the phrase 'copious inanities' of Kashi Khand, that only dwells on the Puranic and hearsay when it comes to chronologically maintaining the almanac of the Hindu religion.

I have quoted very often from the Kashi Khand but have made it clear that it is for the purpose of Puranic references and not for historical vindications. Hall then goes on to conclude: 'There is no ground for believing that Benares, in comparison of what we now see it, with its thousand temples, and their concomitants of holy harpies and willing victims, can ever have boasted a larger population, a prestige of greater potency, or more affluent prosperity.' Lord George Viscount Valentia, a Venetian aristocrat, wrote in 1805 that: 'The city of Benares is so holy, that several *Hindoo Rajahs* have habitations there, in which their *vakeel*s (lawyers or attorneys) reside, and perform for them the requisite sacrifices and ablutions. The land is extremely valuable, and lawsuits respecting it most frequent.'[7]

Along with Sherring, another Anglican Bishop, Reginald Heber, describes the life of the early nineteenth-century Banaras: 'I had an opportunity of seeing something of Benares, which is a very remarkable city, more entirely and characteristically Eastern than any which I have yet seen, and at the same time, altogether different from anything in Bengal . . . alleys so crowded, so narrow, and so winding, that even a tonjon sometimes passed with difficulty.'[8]

Mark Twain's famous and now clichéd comment, 'Older than history . . .' is quite popular, but there are many more gems that he has ascribed to the city of Banaras in his book *Following the Equator: A Journey around the World.* From Chapter L to Chapter LIII, he has devoted all his writing to Banaras, and I would strongly recommend the readers who are interested in Banaras to not miss out reading these four chapters. Astonishing clarity sprinkled with, of course, a condescending description of the natives, but justifiable elegiac and vivid description marks Mark! One of them is: 'Benares was not a disappointment . . . . It is a vast mass of building, compactly crusting a hill, and is cloven in all directions by an intricate confusion of cracks which stand for streets.'[9]

Even the bohemian Beatniks, such as the American Beat poet and counterculture icon Allen Ginsberg, have spent years here and written about the city. Why have so many Western scholars and the missionaries evinced such consistent interest in Banaras? The latter, of course, as I have described in detail, wanted to have a slice of the pie, from this ancient seat of religion to be a potent trophy for their claim of victory of Anglican Christian piety on the 'idolatrous infidels'. But from the metaphysical and spiritual point of view, what perhaps genuinely attracted the materialistic Western world to the city of Banaras was their quest for an answer to the primordial question of humankind that wrestled with the idea of birth and death and the strange concept of the transmigration of the soul in Hindu theology. Banaras, for thousands of years, has emerged as a metaphor of finding a meaning to this question. Although Banaras, since ancient times, has been sustained by not one but rather two umbilical cords of trade and religion that enriched it like entwined twins.

So, when Eck and Sherring call it 'The City of Light' and 'The Sacred City of the Hindus', respectively, or when Nilosree Biswas titles her book *Of Gods, Humans and Stories*, there is certainly a multiperspectivity (sometimes also called polyperspectivity), but simultaneously, the singularity of the overwhelming sense of religiosity is incipient in all genres and oeuvres that have been undertaken till now. I could not resist this as well. Three of my chapters deal exclusively with the theological aspects of Banaras. Narratives and myths in Banaras are dynamic in nature; same story told by different classes or sections of the city's social edifice will have different characters and myriad interpretations. Myths are also referred to as *khyana,* i.e., stories. It has been correctly argued that: 'Formulation of a myth, mostly, is an admixture of a factual happening and imagination biased by religious faith. As time passes, the original myth, closer to the actual happening, drifts towards religious belief and connotations. Thus, the form of myth which reaches us today, after a long time, is generally overpowered by secondary accretions.'[10]

It is therefore important to note that the composition of the myth may have been at a later date than its attributed date of occurrence.

My reason to quote from the Puranas and myths is the collective role of imagination in the context of Banaras. For a religious mind, myth and Puran may not be the same as 'Puranic', which is a category that may subsume 'myth' but is certainly not equal to myth. Puranic is a much larger concept or category, which refers to a particular genre in the Indian literary or intellectual traditions. Puranic and *itihas* are two specific but interconnected categories.[11] The contemporaneity of many such discourses is what has given meaning and sustenance to Banaras since ancient times.

Banaras does not like perfection quite like its world-famous *langda aam,* which has—as called *turshi* in Farsi—a slight sour taste. My father usually reserved this term for Madhubala's beauty! Perfection is frowned upon here; imperfection and a maverick attitude are held supreme. The lust and the celebrations of life are unmatched and that is what gives credence and acceptance to the sublime death.

Absorbing this idea of Banaras, I have my own narrative, which I have been perhaps subconsciously listening to quite like Abhimanyu, only to miss the last few tutorials on how to extricate myself out of the *chakravyuha* of the coquettish seductiveness of the cougar courtesan—this city of Banaras. The nuanced ancientness of Banaras that is present in the wider concept of Sanatan Dharma, its eschatological timelines, get merged with the *joie de vivre* of living. Thus, unlike the Islamic *qayamat* and the Christian apocalypse, here, in Banaras, the *shashwat*, i.e., the eternal, is celebrated, where the enactment of the scenes of life and death are *modi vivendi* in the daily grind. But in his novel *Babu Bangladesh!*, Numair Atif Choudhury mentions 'the Tower of Brahma Puzzle'[12] in Banaras: 'There is a story about an Indian temple in Kashi Vishwanath, which contains a large room with three time-worn posts in it, surrounded by sixty-four golden disks of increasing radius from top to bottom—the Tower of Brahma Puzzle. According to legend, when the last move of the puzzle will be completed, the world will end.'

If at all it exists, it likely emerged as a concept in the later sectarian context.

Like all Banarasis, I have traversed that distance where the trajectory of my premise goes to and from, between the scholarly and the empirical, to the personal and the Puranic, where all gets merged, very often with the sudden leap of faith and imagination. Sometimes, it even crosses the abyss in two leaps. To bolster and vindicate myself, I have quoted from diverse sources, using them as primary and secondary source. The study of the pedagogic classical Sanskrit text, in its prosaic and in its banal contexts and interpretations, has been a tough call to take. Over the centuries, the city, being a pilgrimage and a trading hub, has resulted in the sublimation of its untapped energy into a rich cultural tapestry. To be more precise, this cultural fabric comprises religious elements, wherein its metaphors depict 'imagined and imaged God in a thousand ways, that has been adept in discovering the presence of the divine everywhere and in bringing every aspect of human life into the religious arena'.[13]

The vast arena of Hindi literature that has specific mention about Banaras, along with topical Hindi non-fiction on Banaras, have been liberally used by me throughout this book. To mention a few: *Banbhatt ki Aatamkatha* by Hazari Prasad Dwivedi, *Volga se Ganga* by Rahul Sankrityayan, *Kavita Mein Banaras* by Rajeev Singh, *Aag ka Darya* by Qurratulain Hyder, *Kashi ka Assi by* Kashinath Singh,

Kashi ka Itihas by Dr Motichandra, *Bana Rahe Banaras* by Vishwanath Mukherjee and *Neela Chand* by Shiv Prasad Singh. People have time and again asked me what the intended message of this book is, and I have always told them the most important message is that . . . there is no message. Or, to quote the media philosopher Marshall McLuhan, 'the medium, perhaps, is the message'.

My book encapsulates the singular uniqueness and, often, the spectacular rusticity—of Banaras, not just in its definite antecedents but also from its history, which will be interspersed throughout the narrative, to elaborate on its past. It will also be highlighted in the everyday hubbub and the pulsating vigour and liveliness of this living and breathing city. I have intended to project this optimism like I have attempted in my earlier book *Bhopalnama: Writing a City*, with ample inspirations from Maheshwar Dayal's *Dilli Jo Ek Shahar Hai*, where he, while quoting Meer Taqi Meer, '*Dilli jo ek Shahar tha . . . Aalam mein intekhab . . .*', changed the nostalgia of *'tha'* to the presentness of '*hai*'. However, I have now sometimes started having the sinking feeling of a middle-aged man who has spent his first seventeen years in this city, back in the seventies and eighties. Therefore, I can now readily identify with Padma Shri Manzoor Ahtesham, when he wrote, in the preface to my book on Bhopal: 'I have memories of the days when it was not the ghost it has turned into. I live with a number of impressions of the same place, some narrated, others read and many more disappearing and giving way to newer ones that I have watched with wonderment and apprehension. It is a strange mix of a familiar and never seen or imagined future that coexists in the name of my present birthplace.'[14]

Hence, this book is not a *Kashi Mahatamya*. People who want to know Banaras have to perceive this city beyond its reek of drains and the vehicle exhaust to seek the religious olfactory calmness in the fragrance of sandal paste, *dhoop* (incense) and camphor—amidst the sanitized Banaras for the tourists—or in the hum of Banaras in its gullies, in the psychedelic light festivals or in the temple lamps, in the traditional oil lamps on Dev Diwali, the bamboo lanterns of the *akashdeep* (sky lamps) of the Bindu Madhav mandir, or the boutique hotels or the rented rooms of the Brahmins and the

Gangaputras, who have been renting a portion of their house since hundreds of years to the visitors in this city. The dilemmas between the financial need and the violation of their sacred space are an ongoing scenario here in such houses at the ghats, brought out wonderfully in the works of Kashinath Singh's *Kashi ka Assi* and Ajay Mishra's *Pakka Mahaal.*

While meandering through the Byzantine, whispering corridors of this history, I have meticulously gleaned through them to pick up interesting anecdotes and events from the abundant historical material available. Most of these precious vignettes have been overlooked, while the Hindu religion, per se, and its Shaivite past, have always been overtly emphasized. These timeless tales would otherwise, given the current masochistic projection as against the feminine aspect of the city, have languished in the annals of history. However, I am not just dwelling here on the pedagogical aspect, which will form but a minuscule portion of this book. It is more of a manifestation of my love for and, in parts, an academic analysis of the remarkable churnings that this city of gods and stories has gone through just in my own lifetime alone.

Many a city in the world revolves around a single predominant factor, which they can claim to owe their evolution to; a few maybe have one or two reasons for their raison d'être. Banaras, or Varanasi, is, however, the only city that can perhaps rightfully claim that its evolution, growth and longevity have occurred hand in hand with the overall spiritual and civilizational evolution of mankind itself. Culturally and sociologically too, it has been significant as a trading and religious centre, with favourable geography and climate. The eighteenth- and nineteenth-century Banaras was a happening place. I am surprised that in his bestselling book *The Anarchy*, William Dalrymple has completely bypassed the Banaras theatre, where the Warren Hastings and Raja Chet Singh's game of thrones was being staged complete with its own 'Jagat Seths' such as Kashmiri Mall and Gopaldas Sah. Even though his focus was the triangle of Awadh, Buxar and Murshidabad/Calcutta, the Banaras saga was overlooked.

But my rendezvous with the ghosts of Warren Hastings and Raja Chet Singh continues.

Amitav Ghosh, in his book *The Gun Island,* perceptively writes: 'That there is a strange kinship between Venice and Varanasi has often been noted: both cities are like portals in time; they seem to draw you into lost ways of life. And in both cities, as nowhere else in the world, you become aware of mortality.'[15] I do agree, and with this book, my sincere effort is to explore this 'portal in time', without the aid of any easily negotiable order, observe and read it in its essence. Macabre descriptions of 'people coming to the city to die' make an overwhelming sense of mortality grip you. My objective is to present the most shining aspects as well, that make this city 'the City of Life and Death'.

Ghosh also mentions: 'Everywhere you look, there is evidence of the enchantment of decay, of a kind of beauty that can only be revealed by long, slow fading. The kinship of the two cities is nowhere more apparent than in Venice's Ghetto.' The reference to the Venetian 'Ghetto' is what, in Banaras, is the '*Pakka Mahaal*' or '*Shahar-e-Panah*' or the 'Walled City'. It is here that the city resonates and throbs in all its pristine and modern glory. Most of my narrative is built around this place. Having grown up here, my book 'reads' Banaras with a completely new perspective, with analyses and inputs. The ideation is more or less on the personal observations, and also on those that have been recounted to me by seers, cultural personalities, academicians, laymen and common people. Data and research have been taken from modern empirical studies, the veracity of which may only be countered through parallel arguments, where very often history is superimposed by mythology. I will hopefully not go wrong here, as I have delved deeply into the Puranic and mythological tales to bolster my stance. However, as you know, there always remains a chasm between the writer's analysis and the reader's perception. This may possibly be due to ideological compulsions and also ignorance, perhaps. My primary aim is only to lay bare the historical facts that coexist with the contemporaneity of this city. The Hindi and Urdu translations have been done by me; where not done, I have given due credit to the translators. The names of Kashi, Banaras and Varanasi have been used in accordance with their precedence and occurrence in the historical and Puranic narratives.

This book, in its compositeness and inclusiveness, is like the essence of the Banaras that it is. The Ganga did not flow from where it flows now. Since when and how? Was it the Puranic 'Bhagirath Prayas' or a geomorphic freak? *Khuddari*, or stubbornness, coupled with loyalty, is the hallmark of a Banarasi. How and why did a white elephant captured from Banaras refuse to salute the invader Muhammed Ghori, when all other elephants obeyed? Did the exotic Greek sealings that mention the gods and goddesses of Greece have any relevance with Banaras or did the Greeks actually camp at Banaras in the Rajghat area under King Demetrius? How did Shiva emerge as the reigning deity of Banaras when Vaishnavism was the lead religion of the ruling kings, or how did, after almost 800 years, Sanatan Dharma reclaim itself from Buddhism? Do we know that a form of the dreaded Jizya, called *Turushka-Danda*, was levied by the resolute Gahadavala king of Banaras as a retribution, but the same king also went on to establish localities for orphaned children and widows of the invading Muslim armies that still exist?

We all know that Aurangzeb destroyed the sanctum sanctorum but not many know that about 400 years before Aurangzeb, Quṭb al-Dīn Aibak destroyed around a thousand temples, including the ancient Avi Mukteshwar temple and later Adi Vishveshwara temple that predated the name of Shiva as Vishwanath. Razia Sultan restrained any further temple-building at the sacred spot in the thirteenth century CE, by building a mosque—Razia Bibi ki Masjid—that still exists. Very few know that due to this temple-razing spree, no temples more than 400 years old exist in Banaras. Which ones are these and how have they managed to survive? Through compensation and petitions, the Marathas tried thrice to reclaim and rebuild the ancient Sri Vishweshwara temple at the same site of the present-day

Gyanvapi mosque. Why did their efforts fail? A Maratha king drowned himself in the Ganga in Kashi, at the peak of his rule, because of his religious zeal and the prevalent custom. Do we know that the present Vishwanath temple has a Sikh, Christian and a Muslim imprint? It is in Banaras that Gazi Miyan is revered along with Lat Bhairav; that syncretism of a thousand years manifests itself in all its splendour and pride. The first public strike in the subcontinent was in Banaras in the early eighteenth century. Why? Read on to find out . . .

The title of my book also aptly illustrates the approach I have taken to best showcase the myriad facets of the city. The readers will get a kaleidoscopic view of Banaras through its history (although not presented in a chronological order), the quintessential ghats—the number and the expanse of which is the largest and the longest, respectively—the primordial cult of the Yakshas and the Nagas (which resonates even today in its new avatar of Hindu gods and symbols), the present that is present from the past through its living continuities, the lanes and by-lanes of the walled city, and the eateries, some of which date back to over 300 years, serving exquisite and unmatched Banarasi cuisine.

My endeavour has been to try and present facts and interesting anecdotes, to weave a rich tapestry of facts, folklore, legends and myths that draw a whole. Since a lot of the oral traditions, jargon and idioms have been lost in the onslaught of digital and virtual technology, the need of the hour is to collect, collate and preserve them for Gen X to experience or else risk losing them forever. Linguists and anthropologists are unanimous in their opinion that a part of a human being either dies or mutates into a fugue state whenever a dialect or a cultural tradition (here, I mean all-encompassing lifestyle) gets diluted by way of migration or development.

This book has attempted to project the city of Banaras, juxtaposing and incorporating everything that constitutes life in a holy city. I may sometimes digress to a more pedagogic analysis, which I must confess becomes necessary, as has already been mentioned, when one is building an argument on the theological aspects of Banaras. Since the narratives keep changing, the *ghatiyas*, the boatmen and the priests at the ghats, will now point out and tell you that the tilted temple at Manikarnika ghat is Kashi Karvat. They will then weave a fantastic tale around it—this is to mask and sanitize the sanguine history of the original Kasi Karvat near the Thatheri Bazaar that I have mentioned in this book. A prominent writer on Banaras has been led to believe this story, as stories form the most dynamic and inviolable truth of Banaras.

Having lived in this city for close to seventeen years, I have rejuvenated my bond with it every year, albeit with a new perspective, without cutting the embryonic cord that has nurtured, sustained and mentored me throughout my life. As it is, Banaras is unique in its perpetuity as a city that has evolved every day without compromising its intrinsic character. If we paraphrase India for Banaras, then Gopalkrishna Gandhi is not very far in that, he has rightly ingeminated that few places have been as powerfully imagined as Banaras. It has enthralled some, appalled others and has been 'ever ageless in a timeless splendour that does not satiate'.[16] For a visitor who has grown here, witnessing the maddening pace of progress or should one say 'the change' as has been narrated by Manzoor Ahtesham, I second the scrupulous thoughts of the German philosopher E.F. Schumacher, who in his 1973 book, *Small Is Beautiful*, elaborates that 'change is one thing and progress is another, change is material whereas progress is spiritual'. It has sometimes been a matter of pride and many a time, with wisdom dawning, a cause of concern bordering on consternation. Unravelling the present places from the primordial time to the modern din of this city requires a very clear understanding of mythology and history. To get the grain, layer by layer, it has to be separated from its chaff that has grown thicker and thicker with the indoctrination and propagation of a specific idea of Hinduism that tends to negate, often almost violently, the bare facts and empirical research and studies. I have therefore been careful not to hurt the sentiments of those who tend to wear their religion on their sleeve. Gabriel García Márquez says in *Strange Pilgrims*, 'True memories seemed like phantoms, while false memories'—

with the onslaught of development—'were so convincing that they replaced reality.'[17] This is what has inspired me to write this book—to not let phantoms take over the real.

Spending my childhood in a decadent zamindar family house, we were at the cusp of feudalism and the transition to modernism vis-à-vis the Marxist ideology of my father, and the deeply rooted Sanatan moorings of my grandmother, my uncle and mother. Therefore, at times, like a Freudian dream sequence, many aspects of this city take me to a Márquezian magical realism. Like an ageing courtesan, the enchantress that Banaras is, prods me to write about its shimmering Ganga, its ancient and gentle rustic cultural ethos, the reverberating walled city, the enigmatic labyrinthine lanes and by-lanes leading to some of the most beautiful temples and mysterious havelis, the megalomaniac iconoclast who razed Hindu temples and an equally determined Hindu king who ordered to build a thousand temples in a single day. Magnificent dance soirees on the Budhwa Mangal, opulence and decay in a century replete with anarchy—indeed, it's here that the real converges with the ethereal.

As an assistant writer for the dialogue and screenplay of the mega serial *Devon Ke Dev Mahadev*, I did come across the vast expanse of the Hindu belief system but did not realize its metaphysical aspects till I started my work on Kashi, i.e., Banaras, which overwhelmed me. It was also a long journey for the fulfilment of my longing, or to put it metaphysically, my existentialist quest of finding myself and how much of residual elements of Hinduism, my *deen*, is left in me and to know why I am attracted to scriptures in the most profound manner. For this, I am deeply indebted to the publisher of Penguin Random House India, Milee Ashwarya, who gave me this opportunity. The editors, Manali Das and Akansha Rathi, have chiselled and crafted the extensive raw material I presented them with. I am grateful to them both. Thank you, Rachna Pratap, for facilitating me in the legalities of the publication.

The typical Banarasi sense of humour is raw and unabashed. Two jokes on WhatsApp have become popular and have been shared a number of times. The first is: during its heyday, the Nagari Pracharini Sabha, also known as Kashi Nagari Pracharini Sabha, used to lend books. One researcher approached the library, found a guy at the counter and requested him to show him some books on the self-immolation by the Shiv Bhakts who wanted to die in Kashi, like many did in Kashi Karvat. When he realized that the person at the counter was unable to understand, he tried to articulate and ended up saying 'Ways to commit suicide'. The person at the counter looked at him intently for few minutes and retorted after spitting his paan, 'How will you return the book?'. Another one, that I am sure must be based on a true incident, is: a foreigner came to Kashi and visited the Vishwanath temple and all the ghats. Then he bought a packet of *vibhuti* (ash from the crematorium) from a boy selling it on the street. The foreigner asked him, 'What is its expiry date?' The boy looked at him in surprise and replied: 'It's made from expired people and when you apply it on your forehead, it increases your expiry date.'

During the course of writing this book, Tsar left us after being a loyal companion for fourteen and a half years. Pepa took to existentialist aloofness, till the arrival of another furry wonder—a Beagle who is a tsunami named Biscuit. Pepa initially acknowledged his presence with equanimity and poise, but soon accepted him as her younger brother and playmate. Both competed to have my undivided attention. Immediately after his arrival, he paid a devastating tribute to me as a writer. Within a fortnight, Biscuit the Beagle made his mighty presence felt by trying to chew my Mont Blanc pen and thereafter, innocently cuddling up and ensconcing himself in his typical Beagle sploot. He has now left an expensive, indelible imprint on my pen. I am keeping this pen as His Majesty's war trophy. I must accept with a little guilt that Boond, our daughter, had to suffer many lonely weekends due to my pressing commitments. But my thanks are due to Rajesh Nath Shahdeo, who ensured pleasant breaks for us in the happening Ranchi Club. Dr Avichal Gautam has always, as usual, rescued me from the Sanskritized Hindi texts by offering simple translations. His extempore on Tulsidas was an eye-opener. Jema, my wife, during the course of writing this book, has silently and tacitly provided support and kept me free from the rigmaroles of the daily grind. I have dedicated my book to my uncle and my mother, who have nurtured me with their deep sense of ethics derived from the Hindu scriptures and folk tales. Through my book, I also want to pay my tributes to the writers whose seminal works have been my lighthouse in the maze and deluge of information on Banaras. Writers like James Prinsep, M.A. Sherring, Dr Motichandra, Vasudev Sharan Agarwal, Vishwanath Mukherjee, Kubernath Sukul, Diana L. Eck and the erudite editors Sandria B. Freitag and Vidula Jayaswal, who have toiled to bring the best writers and articles in their books, are worthy of my respect and gratitude. Respected Vidula Jayaswal-ji and Meera Sharma-ji of Jnana-Pravah, Centre for Cultural Studies and Research, Varanasi, spared their valuable time to explain to me, how myth and geomorphic evolvements impacted Banaras. Our family friend, the delightful author-activist, Vasanthi-ji (Vasanthi Raman) enumerated her deep insights on the plight of the Banarasi weavers; do accept my gratitude. Author Pranay Lal patiently answered all my queries on the geomorphic origin of Banaras and the brilliant Vyomesh Shukla spared his valuable time to discuss and update me on many concealed and opaque aspects of the city. Please accept my sincere thanks. My dear friend Rajendra Dhodapkar, almost magically, provided me with rare articles and studies on Banaras. Without him, my approach to many analyses in the book would have tottered. My brother Nimish Singh mailed me from the US the original work of James Prinsep along with the biography by O.P. Kejariwal.

My gratitude to Praveen Gothi, Sanjay Singh, Dileep Singh Sisodia, and my brother-in-law Dr Pramod Singh, who have been my amiable company in Banaras, and are the fountainhead of tales and taboos, of ditties and songs, politics and polemics on the city. My taxi driver, Ajai Sau, ensured I didn't get stuck in the notoriously unpredictable traffic of the city. The savoury delights that my cousin Anjali treated me with, also fuelled my brain to perceive the city.

My childhood friends, Mukul Shah from the Shah *gharana*, one of the most respected business families, hosted me in his nineteenth-century mansion and offered me the variable diversities of Banarasi cuisine; Sandeep Wahi, an activist and businessman upholding the tradition of the ancient Banarasi silk products, has given extremely relevant information on the dying art of zardozi and the Banarasi saree; and Santosh Aggarwal, running the most successful jewellery business in eastern Uttar Pradesh, regaled me with anecdotes of the Pakka Mahal. Thank you, dear friends; without your inputs, I certainly would not have done justice to this book. I also express my gratitude to the people of Banaras, who have risen collectively to reclaim the ancient rituals and traditions from the onslaught of cataclysmic changes. I hope that the coming generation will realize their massive sacrifice in upholding one of the most ancient of cultures humankind has ever witnessed.

Chapter 1

The Early Days

The Geographical Expanse, Climate and Early Settlements

No writing on a city is complete without a peripheral description—if not an exhaustive one—of the history of its geography and geography of its history as Kashi-Banaras-Varanasi has constantly changed boundaries. The city has a mythical origin, securing a place even during the primordial Jambudweep period,[1] where life revolved and was vastly impacted by the river Ganga and its myriad tributaries. The extremely congenial climate for the vast variety of flora and fauna with abundance of water made this area a highly coveted site for human settlement. Large-scale settlement took place around 1550–1050 BCE.[2] Further, no other riverine city has generated so much geomorphic and geological studies as Banaras, owing to its primordial existence as a religious hub due to its peculiar geography. As has been the case with most of the riverine civilization, trade has been the most energetic activity throughout its existence. Most of the world's large historical cities are demarcated between 'pre-modern' i.e., the older areas and 'modern' i.e., the newer portions, and this is termed as 'dual-morphology'.[3]

For the scholars who have studied the development of cities, the road network with its typical topography presents a good case study of its developmental morphology. In Banaras, the old city now called the Pakka Mahal or the permanent built-up has labyrinthine lanes and by-lanes and extremely narrow roads. But the still older portion, or the earliest Kashi, was at the confluence of Varuna and Ganga on the Rajghat plateau. In fact, the Jatakas have mentioned about the ramparts that surrounded the city of Kashi, used for its defence. Sherring has also mentioned about the ruins of this wall in the Adampura area near the Varuna river. Motichandra mentions how effective the defence of the city wall was during an enemy attack, quoting a story from the Jatakas.[4]

The layout becomes significant, particularly for this book, as the approach is to perambulate the idea of the city, revisiting the hurly-burlies from a bohemian perspective as well as creating a weft and warp, like the tapestry of the iconic Banarasi saree, of the interesting, facetious and sometimes eye-opening anecdotes. All this while interpolating the template of the city with modern observations. Some interesting mythological stories on the geographical evolution are about the city being the centre of the universe or that the world may be positioned on the head of the Sheshnaag, but Kashi is balanced on the *trishul* of Mahadev, with both the prongs of the trident comprising the north and south of the city, dominated by the Rajghat plateau and the Kedara highland, respectively. The most prominent one of them, being in the centre, was the Mahadeo hill.[5] Interestingly, a similar word, *trishel*, is in the Romani (Gypsies of Europe) lexicon for 'cross'. Through the mythological stories and from the historical analyses, the geography of this city was ideally suited for trade since ancient times. Its religious significance is relatively a later affair. The locus of the city of Banaras is on the left bank of the river Ganga that uniquely flows from south to north in the shape of a crescent. The topographical details of the crescent shape are also very interesting as the crescent moon is entangled in the matted hair of Shiva; its geological explanation is, however, that: 'The peculiar shape of the Ganga river, "crescent-shape like half-moon", evolved as a result of the fluvial process through which the coarser sediments deposited on its western bank between Rajghat in the north and Samne ghat in the south; it also represents "natural heritage".'[6]

Even for an intellectual and religious text scholar like Vasudeva Sharan Agrawala, it was difficult to reign himself in linking the religious metaphor of Kashi while narrating about the river Ganga: 'Ganga actually becomes *Uttarvahini*—northward bound, as if after entering the abode of Shiva, she suddenly remembers his thick locks of hair in the Kailash, and in her anxiety to meet Shiva, she once again takes a northern turn' (translation my own).[7] Sherring has also noted the amoebic nature of Banaras since ancient times. The emphasis on the three forts that he mentions are geo-strategically located as per the erratic tendency of the Ganga to camber at the Barna Ganga Sangam at Rajghat, Shivala ghat and Ramnagar.[8] The third stage of expansion of the urban format of Banaras was in the west of Rajghat, which perhaps lost its importance during the Gupta period. The first fortress, as per Sherring, where the earliest urbanization started, was somewhere in the fourth century BCE.[9]

The Pakka Mahal and the main town of the city is almost entirely located within the two important tributaries of the Ganga: Varuna and Asi. Its natural boundaries encompass the Ganga to the east, the Varuna river to the north and the Asi nala to the south, although the latter now functions more as a stormwater drain. Eck quotes the *Jabala Upanishad*, where the location of the city is explained in a more arcane manner, in which a seeker is told where exactly the place between the Varuna and Asi is: 'It is the place where the nose and the eyebrows meet. That is the meeting place of heaven and the world beyond.'[10] It also has a Shaivite interpretation, as the third eye of Shiva is also at the glabella. In Yoga, it is called the Ajna Chakra: 'It is the command centre, it operates in conjunction with the reticular activating system, medulla oblongata and the pineal gland. Ajna chakra is the third eye through which the whole subtle world can be perceived. It is known as the gateway to liberation.'[11] No wonder then that Kashi is also called Apunarbhava Bhoomi. The western flank was earlier covered by a thick canopy of forest, a detailed account of which can be found in the *Jataka Tales* and novels depicting that era. This forest boasted trees such as *ashok*, *punnag*, *arisht*, *shireesh* and *maulshree*, and flowers and shrubs like *kubjak*, *mallika*, *kurantak*, *naumallika*, *bakul ki veethi*, *sindhuwaar ki pali* and *champak*. These descriptions[12] of the flora of the Indo-Gangetic plains are reminiscent of what existed during the time the Jatakas were composed. The south-eastern side is dominated by the distant Vindhya hills in Mirzapur, which is within the distance of 60–65 km.

In our narration of the city of Kashi, we need to remember that the city and the region were two different entities but got merged with the enhancement of religious order. Thus, by eleventh century CE, we find the city limits divided into *kshetra*s, each having its own religious significance. Eck has distinguished the 'sacred geography of Banaras' from that of the Banaras region or Kashi kshetra. *Varanasi Vaibhav*, the book written by Kubernath Sukul, is primarily a religious description of Kashi from where Eck has built her arguments on religion, particularly the religious importance of Kashi for the Hindus. Sukul states that the area before the advent of the Aryans was nevertheless called Kashi, but sans its religious importance. It was only after the Aryans that its various limits and boundaries got demarcated.[13] He divides the city into nine kshetras, viz. Kashi kshetra, Varanasi kshetra, Avimukt kshetra (Kashi Khand also mentions Anandvan kshetra), Antargrih kshetra (quoted from the *Padam Puran* and *Vaman Puran*), Trikantak kshetra, Avimuktatar kshetra, Gaurimukh and Mahashamshan. However, the 'concept of kshetras relating to Kashi is very well-documented in the Puranas. Often, these kshetras are used as synonyms in Pauranic verses. But this was not so as these kshetras did not denote the same location. It appears that they represented different localities distributed within a geographical unit (Kashi) across time.'[14] Throughout the extensively researched and thoroughly analysed work, *Kashi ka Itihas*, Motichandra has further referred to the Banaras region as ancient Kashi and the modern urban centre Varanasi as its capital. He emphasizes that the importance of Kashi stems from its geographical and trading location. We will elaborate about this in our chapter with the names of the city. However, Eck accurately points out, specifically in the context of the Hindu religion, that: 'The geographical text of the city is supplemented by a revealing art-historical text. The record of artistic and archaeological remains is virtually unbroken since Mauryan times in the fourth century B.C.E, and each era contributes something to understanding the growth of the city and the emergence of its population of divinities.'[15]

The topography of the city plays an important role on the type of occupation and lifestyle its inhabitants will follow. Surprisingly, not much light is thrown on the geographical history of Banaras in most of the earlier seminal books that have focused on it, except works by Motichandra (in *Kashi ka Itihas*) and Rana P.B. Singh (in *Banaras: The Heritage City*). But the most empirically established geomorphic study has been mentioned in the recently published book *Varanasi: Myths and Scientific Studies.* Most of the writers have dwelt only on the three rivers, Ganga, Varuna and Asi, overlooking the description of the interesting and peculiar terrain that Banaras has, perhaps presuming the vast expanse to be a plains of the mighty Middle Ganga valley. The eternal city of Banaras is located on the western side of a crescent-shaped gravel elevation consisting of lime concretion, running all along the Ganga in the northern side till its confluence for a distance of around 7 kilometres. It is situated on a prominent natural levee on the 'concave (left) bank of a meander of the river Ganga'.[16]

In the typical geographical and evolutionary process, the concave bank experiences erosion, while the convex bank, i.e., the eastern side, undergoes deposition. The early settlers of Kashi were smart enough to know this fact and had deep insight into the river channel process.

'To a large extent, no doubt, the city owes its importance to its peculiar site.'[17] Unlike other riverine urban centres, Banaras is situated on a 50–70-feet-high ridge, rendering it to be quite safe during floods. However, it did face a few devastating floods in 1948, 1978 and, most recently, during the last week of August 1982 to the first week of September, and I have vivid memories of this period because of the severe disruptions it caused to our daily life. My mother had enrolled me in a guitar class that was located in the Bansphatak area near Godowlia near the ghats. It had rained and since it was quite common for the streets to get flooded with knee-deep water, owing to the choked drains, I did not realize the gravity of the situation. I recall negotiating my way till Bansphatak and after an hour, when the class was over, I stepped out with my bicycle only to realize that the water had risen till my chest, and in some places, even as high as my chin. That night, the electricity was disconnected till its restoration six days later. All educational institutions were closed as the floodwater had entered the interiors of the city. For the first time in its known history, the Manikarnika ghat was totally submerged in water and no cremations could take place, and the few that did were at a higher altitude, not where they generally take place. This was supposed to be inauspicious as it is believed that the cremation pyre never ceases in the Mahashamshan (another name for Kashi).

The mythical and historical geographies of Banaras overlap with each other, sometimes making it very complex. Mythological stories astonish the reader as to how the scientific evolutionary process finds a mention through the *shruti* (what has been heard)and *smriti* (what has been remembered), later on developing into the textual sacerdotal narrative. In the Puranic and scriptural literature, which was without doubt *belles-lettres* of its era, the origin of the city has many phantasmagorical descriptions. Bizarrely, though, most of the geomorphic and geological phenomena have been mentioned in the Puranas and in the myths. 'Pauranic may refer to time or different orders of time, but its potential lies in its transcending historical time.'[18] Puranic descriptions of Kashi were also perhaps epiphanic revelations through narratives and even have a yogic interpretation of its layout, which deeply affects the social and cultural psyche of the city—an excellent mode to convey the ethics and conventions to a gullible and impressionable mind. For an average Banarasi, he could be a *ghatiya* (dwellers of the ghats, whose profession could range from being barbers and masseurs to small-time priests) or a professor, the mythical origin and location of the city is inviolable—the ultimate truth. For them, the physical and the metaphysical space converge here on all accounts of its origin—the temples, Shiva and the thousands of other deities related to this beloved city. The *Skanda Purana* describes Kashi as *avimukt,*[19] where Brahma directs all gods to assemble. It also mentions that Kashi is established on Shiva's trishul.[20] Additionally, there exists a yogic explanation of the importance of Kashi and its sacred locale in the site histories, i.e., the *Sthala Purana* (*Sthala*, which means any place or region and *Purana*, which means story).This term is associated with the story of any place, or the historical significance of the temple, or the sacredness of the site. The name of any place or temple has historical association with some major event surrounding it. Scholars have written site histories or the *Sthala Puranas* for various places in Jambudweep. These narratives describe the importance and significance of pilgrimages and temples at these locations. It does enable us to have an insight into history in addition to enriching our knowledge on local customs and culture.

Banaras has a symbiotic relationship with the Vindhya ranges located on its south-eastern side, and since ancient times formed a barrier for people travelling from/to the South. In his book,[21] set in the sixth–seventh century CE, Hazari Prasad Dwivedi gives a vivid description of the Vindhya hills through a protagonist who travels from Prayag towards Kashi by boat, with thick and lush forests set on the banks of the Ganga. He calls this area Vindhyatavi, which was the abode of wild elephants and deer, having an ostentation of peafowls, parrots of different colours, eagles, coucals and peacocks. The forest was full of fruit trees and fragrant flowers. He describes the famous Chunar Fort, which existed even then as Charanaadri Durg, enveloped by the Ganga on three sides. The Chunar Fort, since ancient times, has been the key strategic fort to be captured for whoever desired to rule the city of Kashi. In the Middle Ages, its significance rose even more when Sher Shah Suri, after capturing the Chunar Fort, became the ruler of eastern Uttar Pradesh and western Bihar. Humayun had to negotiate with Sher Shah for this fort.[22] The *Skanda Purana* also has an interesting story on why Vindhya is no longer a mountain, but a hill.[23] My grandmother would narrate that story to me, and I also read about it in *Kashi Khand*. The legend is that once upon a time, the Vindhya mountain prayed to Narad Muni (a Puranic character in the Hindu mythology, who has a mischievous as well as a healing side to his personality, almost equivalent to the Slavic character Baba Yaga in Russian folk tales) by offering him *astaggan arghya* (water and eight mandatory offerings: yoghurt, honey, ghee or clarified butter, unhusked barley corns, *durva* grass, sesame seeds, Kush or sacred grass and flowers). Narad Muni blessed him but also shrewdly told him that his competitor, the Meru mountain, had been insulting him. This is another mythical mountain in the Indic religious texts, quite like the mythological Kun-Lun mountains,[24] that is home to the immortals and extends from the heights of the sky to the depths of the earth. Narad blessed Vindhya, but Vindhya was already seething with anger and plotting to put Meru in his rightful place. He decided to increase his height and in doing so, blocked the rays of the sun. The devas,[25] who were heading towards Banaras, approached Brahma who, in turn, asked them to approach Sage Agastya.[26] It was then that Agastya prayed and sought permission from the *dwarpal* (door or gate guardian) of Kashi, Kala Bhairava, to leave Kashi. Thereafter, he left Kashi to proceed towards the southern side. (My mother firmly believes and is quite adamant that even if we cannot visit the Vishwanath temple due to time constraints, it is mandatory to seek permission from Kala Bhairava before departing from Banaras.) Agastya met Vindhya and cautioned him, acknowledging his intelligence and saintly nature. He reminded Vindhya that they were well-acquainted, and requested that he return to his humble small form. Vindhya then recoiled to his original form. Since then, crossing the Vindhyas has never been an arduous effort for the traveller from the peninsular India. Pranay Lal, replying to my email query dated 12 October 2022, agrees that 'the height of the Vindhyas have certainly reduced over the past 500 million years or so'. However, the transformation of this geological phenomenon into a narrative in the *Kashi Khand*, in the form of this particular story, is truly astonishing.

Apart from the proximity to the Kashi kshetra, the Vindhyas have also served as a sanctuary to many rebel kings and their families.

Balwant Singh and his son Chet Singh's frequent escape whenever he had issues with the Delhi Durbar, the Nawab of Lucknow or with the East India Company, is well-documented. Most of the stones for the construction of the ghats and havelis have been quarried from here. Pranay, in reply to my email queries, has mentioned that 'the Chunar sandstone is of a very high quality, and it comprises condensed grain and little space within its matrix. As a result, some sections from this sandstone can be polished vigorously to give it a shine and are also durable. The Chunar sandstone belt is an extension of the Kaimur group'. I looked up a paper on this where the writers have heaped high praise to these sandstones: 'The Mesoproterozoic Kaimur Sandstone belonging to the Vindhyan Super group has been used in several significant heritage structures and as building material due to their variegated colours, stratigraphic thickness and wide exposure, low porosity, hardness, compactness, mechanical durability, and high tensile and compressive strength as compared to other variants.'[27]

The raw materials for various small enterprises and forest products that form the essential daily consumables of the city come from here. The development of my first taste bud for venison and wild boar meat also has a Vindhya connection. During our winter holidays, on waking up, we would find a huge pinkish blob of flesh—a skinned leg of Sambar, in our courtyard, on the hook. This Indian antelope is favoured for its meat, which is prized for its mild saltiness and fibrous texture. K.T. Achaya, the renowned food historian, mentions that venison seems to have had a special place in the Indian perception. Charaka extols *jangalavasa* and its sauce as particularly nourishing and Sushruth lists it among the foods recommended for everyday consumption. The *Vishnu Purana* recommends its use at a *shraddha* ceremony held in the remembrance of one's ancestors. Xuan Zang lists it among the permitted meats, and about the same time, an Assamese work titled *Kamampa Yatra* notes that it is permitted for the upper classes. A favourite food of sages in the forest was rice cooked with deer meat and spices, called *mamsambhutdana*. Elsewhere in the epic, we read of large haunches of venison boiled in different ways with spices and mangoes and sprinkled with condiments. In south India, venison was sufficiently esteemed to be an item of barter, with, say, sugar cane or beaten rice. A dish of venison cut in slices, served to Edward Terry, in the court of Jahangir, was described by him as 'the most savoury meat I ever tasted'. The British in India rated highly the meat of the spotted deer, as that of the antelope was dry and needed basting during cooking.[28]

In those days, the meat was often rubbed multiple times with turmeric paste and crystallized sea salt. Unlike today, in the small towns of the early seventies, powdered iodized salt packets were a rarity. In fact, one of the tasks of the house maid was to grind these lumps, but they were used only as preservatives; the normal salt consumption mainly consisted of the *saindhava namak* or rock salt. There was a Brahmin in my village, who was so offended by the partition of the country that he stopped consuming salt altogether. Rock salt used to come from the salt ranges in north Punjab, which later became a part of Pakistan. The coming days would see a bevy of dishes: kebabs, roasted meat, qorma and deer-meat pulao. A feast for no reason other than the fact that our relatives whose ancestors used to be the petty zamindars of the hilly terrain of Mirzapur were visiting with their large families for a holy dip in the Ganga during Makarsankranti, Ekadashi and the Poos mela. Many times, the meat of exotic birds and rabbit, along with the meat of wild boar,[29] was also brought by them. Now, when I look back, I feel guilty of consuming banned meat, such as that of black partridges, small sparrow variety called Bagheri or lark, jungle fowl, quail and water birds, although I never particularly liked the meat of water birds because of its distinct fishy smell. Our domestic help, Chotka, who had appeared one cold winter evening in our veranda out of nowhere, used to tell us about the indigenous tricks of bird entrapment. Bagheri birds generally move in ascension, particularly in the months from November to February during and after the rice harvest. He used to describe how a long bamboo pole smeared with sticky gum, on which unhusked rice was scattered all along, was used to catch them. The birds, being small, would stick to the pole and that was how they used to be caught. In the early seventies till the late eighties, the market for the sale of these birds was very small and even though it was banned, the sale was generally overlooked by the authorities. I have seen tribals from the Vindhya hills descending to the city with bamboo straw baskets full of Bagheri, partridges, quail and freshly collected mahua and tendu leaves.

What attracted the first settlers of the Kashi kshetra was the open expanse of the Rajghat plains protected by the Varuna and the Ganga, which acted as a natural moat. Even though the Vindhyas were quite far, they also served as a natural impediment. The entire area was covered with thick impenetrable forest.

Motichandra elaborates on the erstwhile topography of Banaras city, where three virtuous rivers are mentioned in *Kritya Kalpataru*: Pitamhastrotika (Brahmanaal), Mandakini (near Madyameshwar),[30] and Matsyodari (near Omkareshwar). All of them transformed into roaring rivers during monsoon. It's fascinating to note that due to the collection of water through the catchment areas, particularly through Godavari rivulet and Brahmnal, which are now major urban settlements (such as Daranagar, Ausan Ganj, Gowdolia and Misir Pokhra), the entire area of the city, from Rajghat to Dashashwamedh, was surrounded with water and the whole of Kashi kshetra resembled a huge *matsyaka* (fish),[31] and bathing in Matsyodari at the present location of Machodari, Kotwali, was considered to be auspicious.[32] It appears that the Godavari rivulet existed till the twelfth century as there is a mention of this by a character called Hiranya Bhadra in Shiv Prasad Singh's iconic novel *Neela Chand,* who elaborates that after crossing Godavari nala, he reached the Vishweshwar temple. And also that he stays in Brahmapuri (the old name of Banaras), which is located behind the Panchganga ghat. The Matsyodary Teerth was, however, drained in early 1800. Motichandra mentions one 'Brahmnal', which used to cut across the city from Machodary to reach till the present Chowk area.[33] Brahmnal is still a prominent lane that connects the ghats from the Chowk area. Till the eleventh century, Banaras was divided into four main areas: Dev Varanasi—the main temple area, Yavan Varanasi—the Muslim-dominated areas, Madan Varanasi—dominated by the ruling elites and Vijay Varanasi.[34]

The scientific approach of mapping was for the first time quite efficiently done by Prinsep, based on his observations, when he drew the cartographical display of important places in a map titled

The City of Bunarus—1822.[35] If we are to closely observe the city's layout, with the help of Prinsep's map and his *The Ponds and Lakes of Kashi*,[36] we will be overwhelmed by the enormous alteration the city has undergone in the last 200 years. Predominantly, it appears that the city was dotted with tanks, ponds, rivulets and natural catchment areas generally named after the sacred rivers of the Jambudweep, many of which also fell on the sacred Panchkroshi Circle.

Eck laments that 'the basins that were once lakes have become city parks, and the running streams have become streets. But knowing something of its ancient geography, it is possible to glimpse what the Forest of Bliss must have been like a thousand years ago'.[37] Till Prinsep's time, i.e., the 1820s, the length and breadth of the city was not more than three miles and one mile, respectively.[38] This was the description till Prinsep laid the underground drainage system that completely altered the topography of the city and which, to a large extent, is still the main sewage and storm water disposal of the Pakka Mahal area of the city. We may reproduce a description of the entire scheme at some length from the family memoir:[39] 'The work excited the astonishment of all classes during its progress and is still pointed out to travellers as an extraordinary effort of skill and successful enterprise. By the drainage thus effected of all these receptacles of filth, space was obtained for new bazaars and chowks, and for other edifices calculated to promote the comfort and convenience of the people.'

There are many such welfare-oriented efforts since the eighteenth century where catchment areas and nalas have been converted and made into roads, both legally and even illegally. Though ill-planned, it has protected the natural levee from being eroded or breached during their peak flow. The reasons for James Prinsep's draining of the tanks may have been philanthropic but with the drying up of tanks, a portion of the city's landscape and culture vanished too. His sketch, later lithographed *Benares from Mundakinee Tulao*,[40] is a masterpiece, if we observe the sacrosanct, laid-back, everyday routine life that thrived around these ponds, where turtles were fed and rituals performed. To me, it seems the sensitive person that Prinsep as an artist was, it must have been painful when he decided to drain the Mandakini pond but perhaps, the administrator in him overruled the artist.

The Mandakini pond still exists but is more of a very small water body amidst the highly densely populated area. Another pond, the Benia talao, was drained in the beginning of the nineteenth century and is now called Benia Bagh Park, where large political congregations take place. Still, even after Prinsep drained many prominent clay-banked and the *pakka kund*s, some still exist, but their existence is under serious threat. The threat to the *pokhra*s (local term for the water tanks) from the ever-expanding city and from the greedy eyes of the builders is portentous. In my lifetime, I have seen numerous smaller ones being deliberately used as waste disposal, their catchment areas being clogged and gradually, the land being salami-sliced and encroached by the small-town criminals. Many of the city's religious, oblatory and ceremonial rituals were being performed around such pokhras. It is not just a criminal encroachment but also an encroachment on the culture and the integrity of an ancient city—an irreparable loss that is heart-wrenching, to say the least. In the *mohalla* (locality) that I grew up in, strangely named Sonia, it was popular because of the clay-banked tank called Sonia pokhra. I have grown up seeing its salubrious and pristine embankments which had old *peepal*, guava, *bel* (wood apple) and *jamun* (jambul or black berry) trees, sacred plants and flowers like *tulsi* (holy basil) and *shami* (*prosopis cineraria*) shrubs, *harshringar* (night jasmine), hibiscus, marigold and seasonal flower creepers. An *akhada*, a traditional gymnasium near the tanks, was also there. Fishing was permitted only during the winter season. I recall a memorable moment when I persuaded my domestic help, Nand-ji, to join me in witnessing a massive fish that was hauled from the depths of the tank. I have yet to see such a huge fish. Very often, I'd find turtles and water snakes slithering around the embankment. All ceremonies and activities related to birth, marriage and death were performed there. The tank and its embankment were zealously guarded by the sturdy *ahir*s, locally called *sardar*s (a martial cowherd clan), who patronized the akhadas. Now, it is half its size, with an ugly concrete construction on its natural catchment areas.

The pond, now, is reduced to a green slimy slush with a stench all around. A sole peepal tree and an emaciated jamun tree are all that is left, and the area is full of the dust of demolished building material.

The entire district of Banaras is spread out haphazardly, measuring 80 miles from east to west and 34 miles from north to south. Since, almost entirely, the area is located 'in the older floodplain of the Ganga valley, which is attested by the numerous ponds formed due to the abandonment of paleochannels'.[41] Since the river was vigorously shifting its channel position, it has deep deposits of alluvial soil, which gets stratified into clay, soft blue gravel, thick deposits of silt and red sand. Due to the undulating terrain, the western side of the district (250 feet above mean sea level) is higher than its eastern side (238 feet above mean sea level). The main rivers of Banaras are Ganga, Varuna, Baan Ganga or Mrit Ganga, Gomti, Nand, Karam Nasa, Gadai and Chandraprabha. The description of these rivers is there in the Puranic sources but most of them have now dried up and only rise up on the occasion of heavy downpours, mainly serving as outlets for catchment areas.

Ganga: It is interesting to note that river Ganga, which originates from Himalayas, from the Bhagirathi glacier, consists of many pilgrimage sites, but the ancient city of Banaras was not on its banks as we find it now. During the course of its almost 2500-km journey into the plains, it was fed by its major tributaries like the Yamuna, Chambal and Betwa, which swelled into one of the major rivers of the subcontinent. This course was carved by the merging of many rivers, between sixteen and eleven million years ago. The Puranas attribute that the course of the river followed the hooves of the horses of the *rath* or the chariot of King Bhaghirath. 'Occasionally, the intensity with which the rivers arrive in the plains is so implacable that they create new paths for themselves.'[42] A detailed paper also sums up the fertile qualities of the middle Gangetic plains: 'The centrally located Ganga Plain is geomorphologically a highly diversified plain showing alluvial features of various scales. The present geomorphic setup of the Ganga Plain is believed to have evolved under the changing conditions of climate, intra- and extra-basinal tectonics and sea-level induced base-level changes during the

Quaternary.'[43] River systems of the Ganga Plain responded to these changes and evolved differentially in time and space. Therefore, the sediments are important repositories of Late Quaternary changes in climate, neotectonics and base-level.

Something very interesting took place in and around the region of Kashi. How the Puranic and the geomorphic evolutions with scientific evidence find relevance in Banaras is best elaborated by the story of the Ganga Avataran. When Prinsep, Sherring and Motichandra wrote their seminal treatise on Kashi and Banaras, they hinted at one very important ancient and mythological event that Banaras was earlier not located on the banks of Ganga. It was a Mahashamshan and Anandvan. Pranay has also indicated that most of the tributaries of Ganga shift their course very often. He cites the example of Kosi that caused one of the 'greatest fluvial disasters in recent history when it shifted course by nearly 120 kilometres'.[44] There was a severe drought that lasted for sixty years in the Kashi kshetra; the Puranas call it the Padma Kalpa period. People started migrating to other places. It was during this time that many kunds and wells sprung up in the Mahashamshan area. Reference of Ishan digging the Gyan Koop during such a spell of drought is there in Kashi Khand.[45] Historically, large-scale migration took place during the post-Kushana time. The discovery of the earliest settlement at Ramgarh–Bairath, 35 km from Banaras, has proved that the Ganga was flowing from that area which is now called the Banganga. 'It appears that Bairath continued to exist till the Mauryan period, but the river Ganga must have changed its course somewhere around the third century BCE.'[46] This also points to one fact that Ganga was not flowing in the same paleo-channel as we find her to be now. Studies have proved that the river emerged at its present location somewhere about 7500 years ago due to tectonic turmoil in the Ganga basin. It continued to change its course vigorously.

The prominent cliff on which the modern Banaras is located, evolved gradually by what the geologists call 'gully activity'. The *avatarana* (descent) of the Ganga, Puranic reference of Bhaghirath or what is called the Bhaghirath Prayas, seems to be a Brobdingnagian human effort to bring the flow of the Ganga towards the city.

According to the story that we have been listening to since childhood is that there was a massive drought in the Kashi region and King Bhaghirath, in order to do the *tarpan* or the libation to sanctify the ashes of his ancestors as Kashi was the Mahashamshan, penanced for many years, and eventually, was granted this boon. Geologists have now conclusively proved that there indeed was this effort to divert the course of the river Ganga. It is a fact that the present course of the river got silted and dried during the peak time of the city being the trading and cultural hub with a significant human settlement. Due to this, the course of the river encountered the Vindhyan outcrop at Chunar and changed its course towards the north-eastern direction. This, however, also deflected much of its waters towards the eastern side from its present location as we find it today. This involved a human intervention to course correct the flow towards the settlement area and that was the mythical Bhaghirath Prayas.

Though author Meera Sharma has conclusively proved that the Ganga-avataran was earlier related to the origin of this river in the mountains and the extension of this myth as to include Kashi was much later, only when Kashi became a centre of religious activities.[47] One interesting fact that emerged is that Shiva stopped the flow of the river just before Kashi, signifying an obstruction, as we now know that it was due to the Chunar outcrop of the Vindhyas that Ganga turned in the northern direction. I have heard this from many older-generation pandits who testified that the Ganga was not where it is now and the descent of the Ganga was not just the story of King Bhaghirath. Ganga, as per the Vaishnav legend, descends from the foot of Lord Vishnu as Trivikrama. She also is the holy water ensconced in the *kamandala* (oblong water pot) of Brahma, through which he purifies the world. All such myths have one central theme that 'is the connection of the ocean and the sky and the channelization of river systems through human effort. Through centuries, they have formed an elaborate ecologically charged myth'.[48] Ganga is deeply ingrained in the folk and in the oral traditions, and that is the reason it becomes an eternal river like the Nile that has become synonymous with the study of the

Egyptian civilization. Thinker Anupam Mishra has referred to rivers as 'the liquid mirror of the society'; that way, the river Ganga or any river also determines the future of any civilization.[49] No city in the world so neatly fits into the definition and ethos of a society as Kashi and Banaras.

How much it has captured the popular Hindu imagination can be gauged by the fact that one of the most prominent monolithic rock relief panels at Mamallapuram near Chennai, carved by the Pallava kings in the seventh century, is on the theme of Ganga-avataran. The most famous of Raja Ravi Varma's painting *The Descent of Ganga (Gangavataran)* is emblematic of the divine grace for mankind, as against the western Darwinian *Descent of Man.* I am compelled to juxtapose these two opposing ideas as something as the Gangavataran—a matter of faith versus the empirically proposed theory of evolution. The scintillating invention of cinema captured this myth most effectively, when the doyen of cinema, Dada Saheb Phalke, made it into a grand mythological spectacle film titled *Ganga Avataran* (1937).

Many mythological stories abound in the Puranas and the *Mahatmya*, i.e., temple hagiographies, about the upheaval and the furore river Ganga had caused when it was brought down from heaven and it was Shiva who finally tamed it through his tangled locks of hair. Some even mention that he stopped the flow with his trident. Pranay has mentioned another quality of the river Ganga which somewhat vindicates its extraordinary importance in the entire corpus of Hindu scriptures. He writes that out of the three mightiest rivers of the subcontinent, 'the Ganga is more efficient than the Brahmaputra or the Indus in mitigating the greenhouse effect because the clayey soil and silt of the Ganga contains more silicates and therefore captures more CO2 within it'.[50] Water from the Ganga, or Gangajal as it is reverentially called, is sold in small pots near the ghats of the city and these are carried by pilgrims throughout the country and even outside. It is presumed that Gangajal does not putrefy. Perhaps the flow of the Ganga is also from those regions of the Himalayan foothills which have a superabundance of medicinal herbs. The presence of bacteriophage viruses in the Ganga water that feed on other bacteria may also be one of the reasons. According to Krishna Khairnar, scientist and head of the National Environmental Engineering Research Institute (NEERI): 'The ability of the bacteriophage to overpower the nuisance bacteria is appreciably high in Ganga water, but we do not know the reason behind it. We are getting into a deep dive into the sediment analysis.'[51] Bacteriophages are viruses that kill bacteria. What a cat is to a mouse, the bacteriophage is to a microbe. The detailed account of the special quality of Ganga water has been quite efficiently described threadbare by K.T. Achaya, who has listed four causes. One, of course, is the bacteriophages; secondly, the efficiency of Ganga water in absorbing high quantity of oxygen from the air; the presence of some heavy metals with known bactericidal properties; and lastly, the trace elements of radioactive minerals like Bismuth-214.[52]

The earliest mention of the river Ganga was in the Rig Veda, where it is referred to as 'Gangeya' meaning 'provider of peace, good fortune and prosperity'. There is another name of the Ganga, as mentioned in the *Kashi Mahatamya*—Jahanvi. The Kashi Khand of the *Skanda Purana* has an exhaustive eulogy and salutations with a thousand names for river Ganga. The river enters the Banaras district from Mirzapur, near the Betavar village and turns towards east, dividing the Banaras district from Mirzapur. After around 11 km, it turns towards north till Saidpur and thereafter enters the Ghazipur district. Fa Hian, the fourth-century Chinese traveller, called the Ganga river, Heng.

Ahead of the Samne ghat in the south, further on the banks of the Ganga, there is a pristine location with very old banyan and peepal trees. The Shooltankeshwar Mahadev temple is located within these shady groves. It is at this point that the Ganga turns northwards, thus making this spot an Uttarvahini Ganga. I visited this place to have a feel of this unique geographical phenomenon of the Ganga. In the research paper titled 'The Riverfront ghats: Cultural Landscapes', Rana P.B. Singh and Pravin S. Rana have an interesting interpose: 'In terms of river ecology, this characteristic is also considered as the unique aspect of energy quantum and direction of the energy flow.'[53] Located approximately 15 km from the city, my interest in this location was also because of the various religious folk tales associated with the taming of the river by Lord Shiva. One of the priests of the temple, Rajendra Giri, mentioned that this temple was established by a sage called Madhav Rishi and this was earlier Madhaveshwar, but I could not verify this from any scriptures. However, the stories told to us by our elders and in various *satsangs*[54] is that when Shiva married Parvati, she objected to the presence of another woman, i.e., Ganga, in his locks of hair, and asked him to release her. When Shiva acted on it, Ganga once again took on her original disorderly rumbustious behaviour and tried to overwhelm Kashi. Shiva then threw his trishul and trapped her. It is this spot, called Shoolkanteshwar ghat, that she was riveted, and it is here that she turned Uttar Vahini to seek forgiveness from Shiva for her unruly behaviour. Shiva did let her go, but only after he had extracted two promises from her. The first one was that she would flow gently and will never overwhelm the Kashi kshetra and second, she will not give refuge to any dangerous aquatic animals who may harm the residents of Kashi. The ghatiyas still assert this by stating that no crocodiles are to be found in the Ganga. In fact, the popular depiction of Ganga Maiya is that of her riding a crocodile (*makara*). The most iconic portray is in a temple in Assi ghat, where Ganga is shown riding a crocodile and in another one, a tortoise. The latter is clearly an attempt by the Vaishnavas to integrate her with Lord Vishnu. Shoolkanteshwar is not a popular religious place and is rarely visited by tourists and that makes it more unique. One can have a feel of ancient Kashi here. It is situated in the southern side of the city and the route passes through serene rural areas.

It is this Uttar Vahini phase that has all the eighty-four ghats and major pilgrimage places in Banaras. The details will be covered in subsequent chapters.

Reading Pranay's insightful book *Indica,* I came across his description of a 'spectacular cousin of the whales' that evolved six million years ago.[55] It is the Gangetic River Dolphin, which is essentially blind, as it has evolved in the opaque and murky waters of the Ganga. Surviving on fish, crabs and other underwater creatures, this species is highly threatened because of water pollution and on account of construction of dams and also large-scale fishing. It is seriously facing an 'anthropogenic crisis', for which it was not at all prepared. Let me add my personal experience with these shy mammals. Generally during our Christmas holidays, elders in the family took us to our postprandial jaunt for boating in the Ganga. During such freezing nights, the movements of boats used to be scarce. I remember, on one such trip, while gently floating on the Ganga, an ambience invariably was created where even the children became silent and introspective. Only the low lapping sound of the boatman's oars travelled across the tranquil river, its soft ripples ruffling the pillars of silhouettes from the tall buildings on the ghats and the radiant silvery column of the full moon. It is a divine and ethereal experience to go for a boat ride on the Ganga on a full-moon night. Suddenly, we saw a greyish black, plump and glistening creature taking a swirling loop in the river. With a shrill cry of excitement, we wondered what exactly that was. A distant cousin who hailed from the interiors of the riverine islands called *diyara*s, described it to be a *soins*, cautioning us to be careful since it was believed that if they puff out their breath on humans, their bodies will swell and they could die. Also, sightings of these dolphins were not considered to be propitious. Our gullible minds were fully convinced with his description. The animal appeared again, almost like a goblin. This time, it was very daring and got quite close to our boat, with three-fourths of its body out of the water and then diving inside the river, taking a long trajectory. That night, after having the traditional seasonal must-have, *magdal*,[56] which is readily available in the gullies along the ghats, I got thinking of what was going to befall us. That night, I had a dream where I was diving deep in the clouded river water and I saw greyish-black, nude, plump, feminine bodies, half-human and half-animal, with grotesque faces, surrounding me. Whenever I'd try to come out, they would pull me down. Thereafter, I woke up in a cold sweat, breathing heavily. Perhaps a Freudian sublimation in a therianthropic form—as the earlier psychoanalysts would term it. The Ganga also must have been teeming with a variety of aquatic animals. But I am surprised that, as if by providence, no aquatic animals threatening human lives are present in the river; the Indian ghariyals are particularly conspicuous by their absence. Pranay has his take on this: 'Historically, the range of the ghariyal would have extended till here but with increased human activity and lack of fish stock, their populations would have dwindled. Otters were also present in mid and lower Ganga until the mid-nineteenth century. Large turtles were also commonplace in the rivers as were large fish, especially giant catfish.'[57]

The Ganga will continue to be a leitmotif for my entire narration.

Varuna: According to Vasudeva Sharan Agrawala and Motichandra, there is a mention of the river Varnavati in the Atharva Veda.[58] Probably, people of that era believed that the river water had the exceptional potential of mitigating the effects of a snakebite.[59] Eck, quoting the *Vamana Purana* says that both the rivers Varuna and Asi originated from the right and left foot, respectively, of the primordial 'Purush'.[60] The Kashi Khand has descriptions of Varuna as 'Vidhnivaran' or the 'Averter'.[61] The origin of Varuna is near Allahabad and it enters Banaras from the west in a village called Sarvan, where it is joined by its minor tributary Bisuhi. *Bisuhi* is a Bhojpuri word, meaning that which heals the poison, giving credence to its ancient Vedic description as a cure for snakebites. It traverses the entire north-western side of the city and finally converges with the Ganga at the Adi Keshava ghat. However, unlike the Ganga, it has changed course many times. It used to run near the present Rajghat fort, where a shallow moat now exists.

Gomti: This river also finds a prominent place in the Puranas with respect to Kashi. However, at present, it forms the northern boundary of the district of Banaras and merges with the Ganga at Kaithi, near Saidpur.

Nand: It is the only tributary of the Gomti that originates near the north-eastern boundary of Banaras, close to Phulpur. It eventually merges with the Gomti, along with its rivulet, Hathi.

Karamnasa, Gadai and Chandraprabha: All these rivers originate from the Kaimur and Vindhya ranges. Karamnasa is the major river, and Gadai and Chandraprabha are its tributaries. They are located in the south-eastern boundary of the district in the Chandauli subdivision, which now is another district. During the Middle Ages, it was widely believed that the water of this river destroyed all sins. Whenever we used to drive down to our village in Bihar, we had to cross the famous bridge on the river Karamnasa that Prinsep had designed.[62] The deep gorge and the mud banks, with very thick bowers overhanging onto the river, the dried leaves and twigs, along with other vegetative dregs—all resembled the paintings of Hodge and Prinsep.

Banaras, as generally in the entire Ganga Basin, has a season with mild winters and hot summers, with humid monsoon and post monsoon. Mirza Ghalib, during his stay in Banaras, has described the weather of Banaras through his Masnavis: 'Be it in spring, or in summer, or winter, the weather here each season is that of heaven. Bowing in respect to the very air of this garden (that is Banaras), the spring breeze wears a *janeu* made of flowers (43).[63]

In geographical terminology, it can be said to have a subtropical monsoon climate—summers start from mid-March and can continue till the end of June and can record the temperature up till 42 degrees Celsius. Winter months are November to February, preceding the autumnal month of October; monsoon starts from end of June till first week of October. In the seventies and till late eighties, when there were no El Nino and La Nina effects on the weather, we as kids also could forecast the weather and the onset of seasons. The seasons were quite predictable with the sights, sound and the smell, which were quintessentially of the season, and were not available throughout the year.

We came to know of the arrival of winter when the household helpers took out winter clothing and the *rajai*s (quilts), which had the acrid smell of naphthalene balls. A very sharp sound, like an *ektaara*, would greet us often in our compound, just before the full-fledged onset of winter. Invariably, a bearded man, wearing a checkered lungi, carrying a wired teasel called *dhunki*, to remove the clotted cotton from old quilts and mattresses, and if need be, add fresh, soft cotton for stuffing would visit us. The man was often entirely covered with powdery fine cotton, like snowflakes, and was quite a sight for us kids, particularly his eyebrows and goatee. The afternoon sun used to be bright and resplendent and half of Banaras used to be on the terrace, escaping the dark alleys and windowless houses, flying kites and pigeons, preparing fresh green peas *googhni*.[64] Summers are generally very hot, and the usual getaway are *bujra*[65] rides in the late evenings, followed by *lassi* and *thandhai* (details in the chapter on food and cuisine.). There is a folk tale on such hot summer days; like Tramontane—the Western Mediterranean winds that bring misfortune—this city also witnesses scalding winds called the Loo. During these times, in some very old settlements of Banaras, children are told stories of the *budhia aandhi* (dust devil) that can blow them away from their homes to a land far, far away, if they don't remain indoors. My discovery of Banaras ironically happened during such long afternoons. The entire city goes into hibernation during the excruciating summer months, also because the lord and the master of the city—Mahadev—migrates from his home to his *sasural* (in-laws' place), which is his abode in Mount Kailash. Some die-hard Shiva *bhakt*s are also found to have complained of his alleged second marriage to Parvati, the daughter of Himalaya, because earlier, he would never leave Kashi when Sati was his wife. By far, the most pathetic season is the monsoon with incessant rains and humid weather, but a Banarasi will enjoy nonetheless, with hot tea and pyaju (onion pakoras) during the heavy downpour.

Coming back to the geographical evolution and the migration of the Indo-Aryans, the Puranas have an interesting way of linking the evolutionary process with the religious characters, of which some are heroes and some villains. Many derivatives can be found in the mythical stories. The Indo-Aryan was basically a cultural group and not an ethnic one. We will not go into the details of the Aryan migration into the Indian subcontinent but will focus on the Indo-Aryan ingress into the middle Gangetic plains from their location in the Kuru–Panchal region.

It is, however, also interesting to note that even though the Puranas are indeterminate to jumble up the chronological dates, and the acceptance of the Puranic etymology has its own pitfalls and difficulties, still, one can find the broad similarity in the historical events. The advent of Aryans and their subsequent subjugation of the Anarya or the aborigines in the Jambudweep is one such case.

Kashi Khand has a mention of an aboriginal tribe of the plains adjoining the Vindhya hills. This has a story, where, in the past, there lived a famous Bhil named Pingaksh in the forests of Vindhyachal. He was the leader of the Bhils. His house was on the banks of the Nirvindhya river. Along with being brave, he was also averse to cruel deeds. He used to kill the robbers who used to rob the wayfarers, even while staying away from the scene of incidence, through his trusted lieutenants. He also protected the inhabitants from tigers and evil, violent creatures.[66] He must have been the one who could have inflicted guerrilla warfare with the Aryans. But what was the probable date of the arrival of Aryans in the Middle Gangetic plains? It is important to lay emphasis on the arrival of the Aryans in the Gangetic plains as it is closely linked with the advent of classical Hinduism and its scriptures. In fact, the later Vedic Aryans started a hierarchical societal set-up that was to become a part of all the rituals and ceremonies in Hinduism, and Banaras was the hub. The racial purity obsession gets murkier in the later Brahminical dominance over the Puranic and liturgical obsessions of rituals. It is interesting to note that not only the ancient Aryans but the Hammurabi's code also 'established a pecking order of superiors, commoners and slaves'. The ancient Chinese, too, believed that 'goddess Nu Wa kneaded aristocrats from fine yellow soil whereas commoners were formed from brown mud'.[67] In the historical, well-researched and chronologically accurate novel *Volga se Ganga*, by Rahul Sankrityayan, who is accredited for his credible narration of the migration of the Aryans, there is a conversation involving a character called Sage Pala Rishi, and another one called Varun, wherein the fear of Aryans mixing with the local aborigines is well-established.

> Pal: All Aryans consider blood mixing very bad.
> Rishi: Yes! But we are not focussing on that. Why? Are Aryas not cohabiting with the Asuras and the Kol women?
> Varun: They do at the borders and our men frequently visit the prostitutes of the cities of the Asuras.[68]

The story of the migration of Videgha Mathava to the east, accompanied by his priest Gotama Rahugana, has interpretation of the first Vedic people moving into the Gangetic plains. The Shatapatha Brahmana describes this migration from Saraswati to the middle Ganga valley in the story of Videgha Mathava, who travels east but pauses at the river Sadanira (Gandak).[69] Motichandra has also mentioned that the first Aryan who made the Kashi kshetra their home came along with Videgha Mathava and were called Kashya, which was perhaps one of the adventurous tribes of the migrating Aryans.

In the above-mentioned mythological bases, some light does fall on the ancient history of Kashi, but from the historical point of view, it is opaque. It is also not easy to specify the exact time of the Kashirajas in the order of historical chronology. After a lot of deliberations, perhaps we can say that the time of the kings of Kashi, who have come in the mythological genealogy, is before 1000 BCE, but determining the number of years before this era is still a challenge.

Here, we want to draw attention to a special point, which is possible with the rise of Kashyas. From the Babylonian inscriptions dating back to around 2000 BCE, we get to know of the Kassi people. They kept on migrating to Babylon as agricultural labourers for about 150 years. They conquered Babylon in the early 1800 BCE and their authority over that country continued till 1171 BCE. The inhabitants of Looristan moved north and east. Most of the Kassis were Asian, but they were occupied by the Indo-Europeans. As a result, we can see a combination of Babylonian and Indo-European deities and beliefs, along with Asian deities and beliefs in Kassi, such as Sanskrit Surya replacing Shuryash Maruta, Marutash, etc. The horse was the divine symbol of the Kassis. The name of the god of the Asian race was Kashsu.

Interestingly, there is also a place in Iran known as 'Kashan' and the residents of this place are also called Kashi. Mirza Ghalib, who has written a Masnavi titled *Chiragh-e Dair* for the city, has spiritually linked the two great cities of the Aryans in verse 86:

When your madness reaches
The perfect frenzy,
Kashan from Kashi
is just a half-step journey[70]

This lends credence to the Aryan migration in two different regions from their place of origin.

Romila Thapar and Peggy Mohan take a somewhat more practical approach: 'The foundation of Indian Civilization was laid by the coming of the Aryans. The Aryans were seen as conquering northern India and pushing the Dravidians into the peninsula and the south . . . leaving pockets in central India'[71] and that 'The attitude of the Vedic Aryans towards the non-Aryans is characterized by a strong hatred toward the non Aryans . . . The battles with the non-Aryans is called *Dasyu-hattya* (Slaughter of the Dasyus)'.[72]

The mythical version of the Ramayana can also be traced to a larger conflict between the agriculturists of the Middle Gangetic plains and the aborigines of the Vindhyas, who were hunter-gatherers. Romila Thapar writes: 'Further east in the Ganges valley, there is evidence of small settlements of people in the transition stage between hunting and agriculture, using a variety of ochre-coloured pottery. These were presumably the people whom the Indo Aryans met when they moved into the Ganges valley.'[73]

In *Volga se Ganga*, the same character Pal is quoted as stating that Aryans are moving into the east like a forest fire and have established a *janpad* (republic). He also mentions encountering an extremely black-coloured people called 'Kol'.[74] At one time, the name 'Kol' was used to identify a group of primitive aboriginal tribes thought to have descended from Negrito and Australoid peoples, who had entered India in prehistoric times. These tribes are concentrated in central India and the north-eastern regions of the Deccan Plateau. They speak related languages, collectively described as Kolarian, which are known today as the Munda languages. Their tribes include the Santal, Munda and Ho. But in modern usage, the term 'Kol' is used in a more restricted sense, to identify a specific tribe among these Munda-speaking peoples.

Kuber Nath Sukul writes: 'The area was formerly inhabited by the aboriginals and was considered an enemy country, as is evident from the Atharva Veda, where it is invoked that Takma (malaria) be driven away to the land of the Mujavans (North Kashmir), and the Vahlicans (residents of Balakh).'[75]

The name 'Kol' may have come from the Mundari word *ko*, meaning 'they'. It may have also originated from *koro* or *horo*, meaning 'men', who dwell in forests as well as in small hamlets. The Pingash Bhil story could have been the tribe Kol, and not Bhil. Even today, Kols abound in and around Banaras.

Kashi, therefore, was an important part of Aryavarta, the land of the Hindu orthodoxy, separating it from the Mleccha desha, or the land of the uncouth and uncivilized, its geographical division being the south of Vindhyas. Aryavarta, however, got distinctly delineated in the orthodox Brahminical texts in around the third century CE in *Manusmriti*, also referred to as *Manav Dharma Shastra.* It broadly lays the boundaries of the 'land of Aryas' between Himalayas and the Vindhyas, and from the eastern seacoast to the western. In *Mahabhasya*, Patanjali offers this answer to his own question: 'Which is the land of the Aryas? It is the region to the east of where Sarasvati disappears, west of the Kalaka Forest (forests near Prayagraj), south of Himalayas, and North of the Pariyatra mountains (Vindhyas).'[76]

Based on the latest linguistic and archaeological findings, both Peggy Mohan and Tony Joseph are unanimous in the arrival of the Vedic people in the middle Gangetic plains: 'The Harappan civilization may have gone into decline by around 1900 BCE, . . . the Aryans arrived around this time or a little later . . . with a pastoral lifestyle, new religious practices such as large sacrificial fire rituals . . a warrior tradition and the mastery over the horse and metallurgy.'[77]

Notably, it was during the Iron Age that the Vedic people moved and settled in the Middle Gangetic plains, and even their most important three Vedas—the Yajurveda, the Samaveda, and the Atharva Veda—were composed around this time. The earliest Veda, the Rig Veda, was composed around 1700 BCE.[78]

Marianne Keppens and Jakob De Roover write:

> From the complex debate about the Aryan Invasion Theory, one point is crucial: in the search for evidence in support of the theory of the foreign origin of the 'Aryans', scholars concluded that a large-scale invasion cannot plausibly have taken place. Instead, many now speak of migration over long stretches of time, which involved interactions between different groups of people speaking Indo-European and Dravidian languages.[79]

But my personal observation is that the movement of tribes from the western borders of India and the Steppes in Central Asia, like the Greeks, Sakas, Huns, Arabs and Mughals, and the splinter movement of the conquered to find new stretches for their settlements, was an ongoing process that continued till the states and principalities stabilized after the British consolidated their hold over India. The process that the Vedic Aryans started, continued till very recent times, though the later tribes of the Aryans were of mixed races. Obviously, the new settlers had to fight their respective wars to settle down. They would have fought pitched battles with the earliest Indians inhabiting the forest and the periphery of Kashi kshetra—the Cheros, a powerful tribal community controlled by their traditional tribal councils, almost like the loya jirga (Pashto for 'grand assembly') of Afghanistan and north-western Pakistan. They later claimed marital status and called themselves to have been originally the Chandravanshi and Nagvanshi Rajputs and ruled most of the areas of the western Bihar and eastern Uttar Pradesh. They worship many tribal deities with exotic names as Dulha Deo, Ganwar Bhabhani and Sairi Ma. There is a temple with an ancient deity now called 'Shayari Mata' in the Gurubagh area of Banaras, that could be of 'Sairi Ma'. (More of these will be covered in the chapter on Yakshas and the Nagas.) They are now in between the tribe and caste interregnum.

My uncle, who was the last zamindar in our family, before the Zamindari Abolition Act of 1954, often narrated stories about how the remnant Parmar Rajputs from Dhar and Ujjain (after the Muslim conquest of Malwa) came to the area of present-day Dumraon and Nokha in around the thirteenth century CE, after chasing the local aboriginal rulers, the Cheros and Kharwars. But some of their deities continue to be installed outside the houses of the ruling Parmar Rajputs who, perhaps, must have been the animist deities of the local aborigines. (More in the later chapters of Yakshas and Nagas.)

Early Aryans knew the problems of settling in the lower regions of the areas around Kashi, as they were prone to marshes and stagnant water, breeding malaria and other vector-borne diseases. It is believed that when the Aryans started settling down in the Kashi kshetra, they shunned their pastoralist occupation in favour of agriculture. The picture of the early settlement is clear from the sixth century BCE. Towns had come up and Kashi emerged as a major centre of industry and trade. The *Jataka Tales* mentions a flourishing trade and caravan routes starting and passing through Kashi. The Buddhist economic and statecraft system that was 'possibly the earliest expression of the theory of social contract'[80] was in full force at that time in Kashi. Since ancient times, Kashi has boasted an outstanding transportation system. The roads from Kashi, since the era of the *mahajanapadas* (great realm, from *maha*, meaning 'great' and *janapada* meaning 'foothold of a people'), criss-crossed major pilgrimage, and educational and business centres of the country. It went to Rajgriha, Vaishali, Patliputra and Taxila (the prototype of Chandragupt Maurya and later Sher Shah Suri's Grand Trunk Road.) The main mode of transportation, however, continued to be the Ganga. In Hazari Prasad Dwivedi's Hindi novel *Banbhatta ki Atmakatha*, there is a vivid description of boats being used in the river Ganga for pleasure travel, goods transportation, as well as public transport. Even the Jatakas mention stories about ferrying goods on the Ganga. In fact, one of the main reasons for the opulence of Banaras has been its river trade. This continued from Calcutta Port to Delhi till the advent of the railways. With the onset of railways, river trade as a main medium of goods transportation gradually became a thing of the past. Motichandra has observed that all anomalies and malpractices that we find taking place in the transportation of goods today, also took place then. He says river pirates looted and the outlaws extracted protection money to let the cargo pass from their areas of control. The traders also at times deliberately submerged their boats to claim insurance money. The government today has restarted the old Ganga route, and a new port has been established in front of the Samne ghat in the southern side of the Ganga at village Salhupur in Ram Nagar. Transportation of goods and pleasure trips has already started in Ganga from Kolkata.

How and where exactly did the early settlement of the Vedic people take place in Kashi kshetra? Since when did the mention of Kashi in the scriptural texts actually start? All this and more will be covered in the next chapter on Rajghat.

Chapter 2

Rajghat

The Palimpsest of Mankind

Much before the most important historical events unfolded in the West, as per Sherring, Banaras was already a flourishing civilization. 'Benares is a city of no mean antiquity. Twenty-five centuries ago, at least, it was famous. She had already risen to greatness, if not to glory.' This is Sherring at his best.[1]

As stated earlier, Puranic etymology and derivations are often very confusing. They have stories where kings and powerful personalities have been exemplified with gods and goddesses. It also derives its source from social mores and popular beliefs. The chronological aspects are generally lost in the narratives. I have been very selective in accepting the Puranic diktats without scientific backing. As Sherring has further wryly reflected, 'Hindu writers have shown a singular neglect of chronology, and an utter distaste for noting and recording historical facts in a simple and consecutive manner . . . and . . . the result is, that this city of Benares . . . is robbed of the glory.'[2] Almost the same sentiments are shared by Colonel James Tod in his exceptionally brilliant treatise on the Rajputs: 'Is it to be imagined that a nation so highly civilized as the Hindus, . . . were totally unacquainted with the simple art of recording the characters of their princes, and the acts of their reigns?'[3]

However, in light of recent archaeological findings and the erudite analysis of the seals and sealings excavated at Rajghat by Vasudev Sharan Agarwal, it is not difficult to accept the description of Banaras as mentioned in these sources. The settlements found in and around Rajghat may be stratified as pre-Vedic, early Vedic, later Vedic, Janpad era, the Kushans, the Guptas, later Guptas and the Gahadavala era. Historians and archaeologists are unanimous in concluding that the ancient city of Kashi was situated on the elevated plains of Rajghat. As the latest paper on the origin and growth of Banaras points out: 'The tree-dwelling humans when they came down onto the plains within the river valleys, one overarching criteria for building their dwellings is "the highest possible ground" with seasonally/annually flooded lower floodplain around it for filling their granaries and the nearest possible perpetual water source.'[4]

Rajghat is located on the north-eastern periphery of the crescent shape, making it the first ghat encountered when entering the holy city from the northern side. As previously mentioned, it represents the first prong of Shiva's trident. The excavations at Rajghat occurred by a stroke of luck when the workers were digging nearby, for the construction of the Kashi railway station in the 1940s. The pottery and few painted wares which were found resulted in the planned archaeological excavation in the 1960s. The clay seals found during the excavations established empirically the antiquity of Kashi other than its scriptural sources: 'Study of material remains of the past, the focus of archaeology, brings forth comparable geo-cultural environments of some of these mythological stories. This exercise is expected to be beneficial for both archaeology and mythology. The former, dealing primarily with the artifacts, has a great quantum of data of material nature.'[5]

A little distance away is Akhta, which has been recently excavated under the supervision of archaeologist Vidula Jayaswal, and the studies reveal the existence of separate settlements of Kashi Rajghat and Akhta from the period between the Janpada and the late Kushan times (eighth century BCE–third century CE). It inaugurated the ancient history of Kashi from 800 BCE. Another startling fact that emerged and has been brought to light by Jayaswal is that Aktha is the oldest-known site of this region (between Rajghat and Sarnath) that was a Brahmin settlement and where the marks and traces of fire altars of the Vedic rituals have been found. Charcoal samples date these findings to somewhere between 1700–1400 BCE, whereas Kashi Rajghat is dated to 800 BCE.[6]

It is almost thaumaturgical that the mention of some of the Shiva Lingas in the Puranas are being verified with the archaeological evidence found at the Rajghat site, which dates it chronologically to the period of the Maurya, Shunga and the Gupta dynasties. These findings generated a wave of excitement in the scholars' community. It was also established that before Banaras became a centre of pilgrimage for the Hindus, it was an important destination for the Buddhists for at least 500 years. I have not dwelt on the Buddhist part, as the genius loci of Buddhism lies predominantly in Sarnath, with very few scattered locations inside the city of Kashi. Discovery of clay tablets with their seals intact has, for the first time, provided a lead towards the Sanatan aspect of Hinduism, as mentioned in the Puranas. Thus, the archaeological discoveries at Rajghat seem to have empirically established the Puranic origins of Kashi, to some extent.

On this Rajghat plateau, there also exists the Rajghat fort, which is 1 mile in length and 400 metres in width. It appears that this site was chosen for the ancient city of Kashi because of its strategic location. River Ganga protected this fort from the south-eastern direction and the Varuna protected it from the north and north-eastern side in the form of a moat. There is a mention of the massive city wall in the Jatakas, the remains of which can still be found if one carefully observes the undulating terrain in Rajghat near the Krishnamurti Foundation and the dirt track that goes towards Chandan Shaheed Road. I could also locate the moat, which is now buried under a thick foliage of trees and shrubs. It is indeed fascinating that this strip of elevated land has witnessed the growth of the Indian civilization and that of Kashi per se, through the ages.

Let us have a short survey of the history of ancient Kashi till 1947, which will be better for us when we traverse the treasure trove of Rajghat and the subsequent chapters in this book. Historian A.J.P. Taylor is correct when he says: 'History is not another name for the past, as many people imply. It is the name for stories about the past.'[7]

The earliest settlers, as has also been mentioned in the previous chapter, were the Aryans called Kashya; a lunar line of kings thereafter ruled Kashi and one of them, kshetra Vridhi (literally meaning, augmentation of area), was the one who started the Kashi branch and his descendants, Kasiraj and Divodas, founded Kashi. Architectural historian James Fergusson has mentioned that a less pure race of the lunar branch of the Aryans reached the middle Gangetic plains around the fourteenth century BCE.[8]

Puranic stories tell us that during the *samudramanthan* (churning of the ocean), among the several priceless objects that sprang forth was the father of medicinal science, Dhanwantari, who was the grandson of Kasiraja. Banaras could have been once a celebrated school of medicine amongst the Hindus. 'The third from Dhanwantari, Divodasa, is still more celebrated; as in his time, Kasi was the seat of a religious revolution, in which the faith of Buddha superseded the worship of Shiva.'[9]

King Divodas, who has been mentioned as Raja Ripunjay in Kashi Khand, must have established the Bairath and Rajghat settlements. Divodas has been a very important ruler of Kashi, and I will deliberate upon him in the subsequent chapters. During my exploration of the antiquity of Banaras, I read an account of a place called Bairath, near Ramgarh village, located 30 km in the north-eastern side of Banaras. I visited this place very often during my summer vacations, as a child. It was my brother-in-law's place, and a small rivulet called Banganga used to criss-cross the area. We would go for fishing there accompanied by the local fishermen called *kewat*s. Even during summers, in the late seventies, the rivulet ran as a shallow stream. As per the stories of the kewats, Shantanu, a character in the Mahabharata, brought out Banganga by breaking the earth on the occasion of Kashiraj's daughter's *swayamvar*. The capital of Kashiraj was Ramgarh at that time, which must have been on the banks of the river Ganga, but based on this folk tale, it can also be said that once upon a time, the Ganga used to flow through Ramgarh. Our bonus fun back then was the elephant ride from the Baba Keenaram Ashram located nearby. Even as a child, I used to wander about a cluster of mounds covered with shrubs of wild *ber*, bamboo, creepers and trees like the *jungle jalebi*, banyan, etc., located a short distance from the rivulet in the otherwise flat terrain. Out of a sense of adventure and curiosity, I implored the mahout and our team leader, an elder cousin, to take us to that location. On reaching there, we started exploring the gradients, and the crevices in the rocks. It appeared to be a mud embankment and the remnant of the ruin of some huge structure. Many a time, we could spot porcupines running around these mud furrows, as if continually keeping watch over our movements. The mahout had told us that the villagers had found treasures from there and that was the place where the Kichak Vadh (a story in the Mahabharata) had taken place. We also started our 'Ancient Hunt', hoping to find some gilded luck. Little did we realize then that we were at the exact location where the Puranic king Divodas had established his second Kashi; but even Motichandra has not been able to conclusively verify that. He, however, does mention, based on the popular folklore, the archaeological evidence and the Puranic references, that the old Kashi mentioned in the Mahabharata was indeed at Bairath. Kashi Khand, though, is silent on the establishment of a second Kashi by Divodas. Motichandra has given some evidence of the existence of a city, as mentioned in the Mahabharata, by quoting the investigations done by A.C.L Carlyle, the famous British archaeologist:

> The ruins of the ancient fort are on the eastern corner of Banganga. The old fort is made of mud but many bricks are also found in it . . . . There are ruins of a big building near the north-east side of the fort. The traces of the moat outside the fort are still visible. Carlyle found many punch marks, struck and cast seals from Bairath. He found seals of Jyeshtadatta and Vijayamitra and some seals of Kanishka in Brahmi script of second century BC.[10]

Vasudeva Sharan Agrawala mentions Jethdatta from the study of the seals as Jethadatasa dating to the first–second century BCE, with the symbols of Nandipada and svastika above and Vaijayanti below.[11]

Along with Rai Krishnadas, Motichandra also collected many seals from Bairath. He found a coin dating back to the Shunga period. Plus, it was written in Brahmi script. Many gems, such as quartz, were also found from here. Kashi also has a good collection of such gems. A large number of pieces of ivory bangles have also been recovered. He also found a piece of stone on which a Shunga-era creeper, similar to Bharhut, has been made. Carlyle also found Stone Age flakes from streams and fields around Bairath. According to Motichandra, these things prove that Bairath's settlement is very ancient. But it certainly was not Vedic.[12]

Coming back to the Mahabharata connection, there is a story that appears in the 'Anushthan Parv' of the Mahabharata that is mentioned by Motichandra. In the same chapter, there is a reference about a king who ruled from Pratishthan, which is the area around present-day Prayagraj, and who was known as Vatsa-Kasisa (ruler of both the Vatsa kingdom and the Kashi kingdom). King Dhandeva must have been the ruler historically (the date is 275 CE as per the Rajghat sealings of king Dhandeva).[13]

There is a legend that Kashiraj Haryashva was defeated and killed by Vitihavyas in the plains of Ganga-Yamuna. Haryashva's son Sudev also was defeated in the battle. Later, his son Divodas established the second Banaras on the northern bank of the Ganga and on the southern bank of the Gomti, but there is no ruin of any ancient city around Kaithi, where Gomti has a confluence with Ganga. After a thorough study and analysis, archaeologists have come to the conclusion that no other place, apart from Bairath, was the site of an ancient city at the time when the original flow of Ganga was from the present Banganga, and Gomti used to flow and join Ganga near Saidpur. With this assumption, Bairath or ancient Banaras used to fall to the south of Gomti, as stated in the Mahabharata. When the Ganga did not change its course, it must have continued to flow near Bairath till the third century BCE, during the Mauryan era. By the

Gupta period, it must have become history. On the establishment of the second Banaras by Divodas and the possibility of its being in Bairath, Pandit Kubernath Sukul writes in *Varanasi Vaibhav*: 'The Bairath ruins are on the south bank of Banganga and not on the left. In this way, the land of Ganga itself becomes a barrier between Gomti and Bairath.'[14] Commenting on the change of course of the Ganga, again, the Ganga flowing in Banganga and the Ganga-Gomti confluence being near Saidpur, Sukul says: 'According to the Mahabharataa, there was a Markandeya Tirtha at the Ganga-Gomti confluence, which is still near Kaithi. Therefore, if the Ganga-Gomti confluence was near Saidpur, then it may have been before the Mahabharataa, not after the third century AD.'[15]

I revisited this place in November 2022 and was surprised to see that a school, a Navoday Vidyalay, has been constructed exactly at that place where the ruins existed in our childhood. The mounds are still visible but have become diminutive and crumbly. Quite possible, the soil from them must have been used for the landfill of the ongoing construction around. A sad metaphor of our utter disregard to a rich and throbbing past. It's a pity that such a site has not been preserved, as it could have shed more light on our ancient culture. With the use of more scientifically advanced archaeological equipment and methods, a clinching and empirical study could have been presented to the world about our glorious past.

Divodas's father, Sudev, was ousted for some time from Kashi by the Haihaya dynasty. It must have been a contested land, most probably fought over by the Kols. In legend, the Kols trace their origins to a Sheori or Savari, calling her the 'mother of all Kols'. Some try to relate the name 'Savari' to the 'Savaras' mentioned in the Mahabharata, but the name most likely comes from the Ramayana. There is a story in which an aboriginal king Nagaraja Dhatratt attacked Kashi, to marry the princess of Kashi Samudraja. The battle and the siege of the city continued for a long time, and eventually, after prolonged and successive raids by Nagaraja, she was married to him. Nagaraja must have been an aboriginal ruler who fought with the advancing Aryans.

During the Mahajanapada period, Kashi was one of the sixteen Mahajanapadas, and held the medial position among them. It was surrounded by the Mahajanapadas of Kosal and Vatsa on its north-western side, and on its eastern flank were the rich Mahajanapadas of Magadha and Videh. The fabled rivalry between Kosal and Kashi, and eventually both being gobbled up by the great Magadha empire, have been historically and elaborately accounted for. We can find some references in the Buddhist and *Jatakas Tales*, but these have not been verified by empirical findings. According to these sources, the rulers of Magadha, till the seventh century BCE, were the Bahrdra kings and Kashi was also ruled by one of the branches of this dynasty called Brahdutt. Since Bimbisar, of the Haryanka dynasty, who ruled during 544–491 BCE, married the daughter of Maha Koshal, the rulers of Magadha extended their de jure control over Kashi, which continued through his son, Ajatshatru (c. 493/492 BCE–c. 462/460 BCE) and descendants, including Nagadasaka (437–413 BCE).They continued their control over Kashi and made it the central hub for trade. A minister of Nagadasaka, Shishunaga, later assumed control, followed by Kalashok and his ten sons, who ruled Magadha for twenty-two years. The rise of the Nanda dynasty (344–322 BCE) that overthrew the Shishunaga dynasty, is slated to be the rise of Vaishnavism in Kashi, as they were the followers of the Vaishnav religion. The rule of Chandragupta Maurya, that lasted during 350–295 BCE, marked the end of the Nanda rule with the assistance of his shrewd adviser, Kautilya. Maurya's most able descendant, Ashoka, who reigned during 268–232 BCE, is well-documented. Kashi, during this time, was fully under the sway of Buddhism. Ashokan edicts and Buddhist stupas were very common in the entire Kashi region, including Sarnath. Over time, some of these sites were converted into Hindu temples and icons. Sherring has emphatically stated that such sites undoubtedly bear Buddhist signs like the temples at Bakaria Kund, Maqdam Saheb, Lat Bhairav and Battis Khambha.[16] Ashoka's realization of the futility of war and the revelation of the ultimate truth that dawned upon him has been eloquently provided by Jaishankar Prasad's play *Skand Gupt*, although not directly in reference to Ashoka, that: '*Adhikaar such saarheen hote hue bhi sabse zyada maadak hota hai*' (The pleasure of power is so intoxicating and so meaningless).

One of the generals of the last Mauryan King, Pushyamitra Shunga, assassinated his king and usurped the throne of Magadha. During his rule, the Greeks, under Dimitrius and Milinda, attacked the Magadhan capital Pataliputra in 175 BCE. The evidence of the Greeks' presence in the Kashi–Rajghat area has been studied extensively by Dr Vasudevsaran. Kashi continued to be loosely governed by the last Shunga ruler Bhagbhadra (114 BCE–83 BCE); and during the reign of Pushyamitra Shunga, there was a shift away from the earlier dominance of Buddhism in the Ashokan era, with a resurgence of the Brahmanical order. He started a virulent campaign against the Buddhist monasteries and tried to destroy some of them.[17] He restarted the convention of *yajna*s (rituals performed in front of sacred fires) and conducted a grand Ashwamedha yajna (horse sacrifice ritual). However, there is no concrete evidence of the destruction of the Sarnath monastery during his rule. Quite possibly, the renaissance of the Brahmanical order was well-received in Kashi during Pushyamitra's rule. Subsequently, during the reign of the Satavahanas and the Kushan ruler Kanishka (c. 127–150 CE), Kashi was administered from Kaushambi. Kanishka again brought the Buddhist sway in northern India but the rejuvenation of the Sanatan Dharma during his reign in Kashi bolstered the Brahmanical hold over the religious space of Kashi. After Kanishka, Kashi was ruled by a succession of local kings from the adjoining area. A local Shaivite dynasty, called Bharshiv, also ruled over Kashi for some time.[18] At present, another backward-caste community, called Rajbhar, in Uttar Pradesh has realigned itself as a political and social group, claiming descent from the ancient Bharshiv dynasty. Somewhere between the Bharshiv dynasty and the rise of the great Guptas, there is also evidence of rulers who had the title 'sena', like the Bhimsena, Krsnasena, Harisena, along with the royal title of 'rajan' found on the seal of Bhimsena, reading as 'Rajno Bhimasenasya'. These rulers governed over Kashi during their time, and their symbol was a bow and arrow that has been studied to establish the chronological sequence of this dynasty.

Coins of such sealings have only been found from Kolhapur and the Banaras–Rajghat region. This justified its feudatory status under the imperial Satavahanas.[19] Agarwal further mentions the Magh rulers from Bandhavgarh, who ruled in those areas in the first century CE. Recently, two huge archaeological sites have been discovered in the Bandhavgarh area of the Umaria district of Madhya Pradesh, which has 2000 years old evidence of a 'modern society'. Few rock paintings and man-made water bodies insinuate the presence of a highly developed urban culture. Two Buddhist stupas have also been found in the area.[20] The dynasty associated with this era was called the Kosam dynasty, whose sealings have also been found at Rajghat. The most prominent ruler of this dynasty was Sivamagha I, who invaded Banaras and defeated King Dhandeva from whence the independent line of Kashi kings ceased to exist, and Kosam kings became the masters of both the Kasi and Vatsa kingdoms. From 305 CE to 530 CE, the great Gupta empire held Kashi under their political and cultural dominance. Subsequently, from 510 CE to 606 CE, the Maukhari rulers ruled over the Kashi kshetra; and it appears that the governance of Kashi alternated between the Maukhari rulers and the later Guptas of Magadha, called the Magadha Guptas. Their two kings, Damodar Gupt and Mahasen Gupt, continued a sustained battle with Maukharis, eventually defeating their rulers Ishanvarman and Avantivarman, respectively. Eventually, the Maukhari kingdom was subsumed by another great king, Harshvardhan (606–648 CE), who ruled from Thaneshwar. As has been mentioned earlier, the famous Chinese traveller Hiuen Tsang visited India during his reign. Around 794 CE, another notable king, Dharmpal, ruled over Kashi, but by 931 CE, the Gurjara-Pratihara rulers held suzerainty over Banaras, and one of the kings from this dynasty, Vinayakpal Dev, is known for giving villages to Brahmins. By the eleventh century, Banaras was conquered by the Kalachuris, a central Indian dynasty. One of the most important and a watershed moment in the history of Banaras occurred during the reign of Gangeyadeva Kalchuri, when the city experienced its first Muslim invasion and plunder by Ahmad Niyal Tigin in 1033 CE. The religious tenor of Kashi thereafter underwent catastrophic moments, but somehow the resilience and the joie de vivre of the Brahmanical order, which later became ritualistic Hinduism, bounced back with much more elan in its puritanical ancient form. Some of the Kalchuri kings were Buddhist but were tolerant of the Sanatan Dharma. Around mid-eleventh century, the Doab region of Ganga and Yamuna witnessed the ascendance of a new regnant power that, by 1090, had established its suzerainty from Kannauj to Banaras. They were the legendary Gahadavalas of Banaras. Their rule lasted till 1194 CE, when Qutb ud-Din Aibak and Shahabuddin Ghori overran Banaras. He handed over the reins of administration of Banaras to one of their *subedars*, Syed Jamalluddin, and as per popular legend, the Jamalluddin Muhalla of Banaras was established by him. After Aibak, when the Delhi Sultanate was headed by Shams ud-Din Iltutmish, many small revolts from the local rajas of Banaras were crushed by him and this way, the Slave dynasty ruled Banaras till 1236. Eck mentions about the oldest temple of Vishwanath that was razed and a mosque was constructed there on the orders of Razia Sultan, the daughter of Iltutmish, which still exists today, by the name of 'Razia Bibi ki Masjid'.[21]

Later, Ghiyas-ud-din Balban (1266–1287 CE) and Allauddin Khilji (1296–1313 CE), during their reigns, did not interfere much in the administration of Banaras and continued the revenue collection in a relatively mild manner. During the Tughlaq rule, from 1320 to 1394, not much is recorded in this regard, except that a mosque was constructed at Bakaria Kund by a loyal subedar of Firoz Shah Tughlaq, a person by the name of Zia Ahmed. This mosque was constructed with the materials of a destroyed Hindu temple. A new chapter in the Muslim conquest of Banaras starts from 1394, when the Sharqi rulers of Jaunpur (1394–1487), a neighbouring district, extended their control over Banaras for about eighty years by revolting against the Delhi Sultanate. After Sharqis, under the ruler Sikandar Lodi (1489–1517) till 1526, the governance of Banaras once again came under the Delhi Sultanate, and the destruction of temples continued. After the defeat of Ibrahim Lodi by Babur in 1526, through a series of skirmishes, Babur captured Banaras on

5 March 1529. An interesting anecdote is mentioned in *Baburnama*, where tigers and rhinoceros were sighted near the forest at Chunar, but Babur was unable to hunt them due to severe cyclone. Chunar happens to be just 50 km away from Banaras. After Babur's death in 1530, his son Humayun continued his eastern conquests. But the governance of Banaras kept on oscillating between the Mughals and, for some time, was under Sher Shah Suri (1538–45) and his son Islam Shah (1545–54). It was only during Akbar's reign (1556–1605) and after his visit to Banaras that finally in 1565, a long reign of Mughals was established in Banaras. Jahangir (1605–27) and Shahjahan (1628–58) had disinterest towards Banaras but Shahjahan's elder son, Dara Shikoh, had great love for Hindu mysticism and ancient sagacity. However, in the cunning and diabolical game of thrones, Aurangzeb became the emperor of Hindostan and his saga of the wanton destruction of temples, specifically in Banaras, is now quite well known. But astonishingly, the Hindu rajas fought on the side of the bigoted Aurangzeb, against the secular and erudite Shikoh. It is one of the great 'ifs' of history that, had Shikoh been the emperor of Hindostan, the history of the subcontinent, decidedly of Banaras, would have been much different and we would perhaps have seen the reticulation of the Islamic piety and mysticism, with that of the pristine Vedic and ritualistic Sanatan Dharma. Aurangzeb's death in 1707 left the Mughal empire in total disarray. Banaras, however, continued to be loosely administered from Delhi and Avadh. The history of Banaras by the 1730s took an important turn with the rise of the local zamindar Mansa Ram, whose descendants continue to be the titular rulers of Banaras. His son Balwant Singh's cat and mouse games with the Delhi and Avadh rulers are still being narrated with relish. After his death in 1770, his son Chet Singh was enthroned. The legendary rivalry of Warren Hastings and Chet Singh forms the staple tales of the old *adda*s of Banaras. Banaras formed an important revenue zone for the East India Company and after 1857, the important infrastructure developments in the city gave it global recognition. The synergistic relationship that Banaras had with the Marathas from the early eighteenth to the late nineteenth century, was remarkable with the development of

religious infrastructure and the revivalism of Hinduism by various Maratha rulers.

After reviewing the brief history, let me give a short account of significant empirical findings at Rajghat and a few other locations in Banaras that underscore the centrality of Rajghat as the palimpsest of humankind. We have thoroughly verified the ancientness of Bairath and Aktha. Now, let us explore the artefacts and the derivatives and analyses conducted by archaeologists and scholars based on these findings.

The books written before 1940s on Banaras generally relied on Buddhists texts, *Jataka Tales* and Puranic descriptions of Banaras to find out about the ancientness of Banaras. It was Sherring who, with his eagle-eye observation, could guess the existence of ancient Kashi on the elevated lands of Rajghat, but his evaluations were also generally limited to Buddhist analogies based on surface reading. 'On the summit of the Barna Sangam ghat, a few remains of an old fort are visible. There is no doubt that, at one time, this fort commanded the city, which was much closer to this spot than it is now.'[22]

After Prinsep deciphered the Ashokan inscriptions, the history of India took its most splendiferous and outstanding turn, with an entire era open for academic research. I have not focused on the Buddhist remains of Sarnath but have focused only on the findings on the Rajghat plateau, as Sarnath does not strictly form the Kashi region. The fort mentioned by Sherring was the old boundary of the city in its early period. These embankments, most of them hardly visible, were till the Tiliya nala and extended on the banks of Ganga till Barna. Banaras was limited within this walled city much before the Common Era. Old bricks and stones having ancient mason markings, seals and broken stone images were often found by villagers before the declaration of this as a protected site by the government. The old annals of Sri Lanka also have testified to a city existing adjacent to Sarnath. In this case, the city existed in the pre-Buddhist era, i.e., before the sixth century BCE. Most of the Muslim shrines and tombs in Adampur, Tiliya nala, and all along this ridge, have used the building materials of the old Buddhist remains, including *kalases*, *architraves*, pillars, a huge slab of stone—presumably a *sinhasan*, quintessential

Buddhist bell-pendants and even carved vases. Remains of a *vihara* (a Buddhist monastery), handsomely carved stone brackets, etc., are also present in the area.

The details of religion, society and the political set of Kashi during the Mahajanapada era, predating the Buddha, has mostly been enumerated and well-documented in various ancient Buddhist and Jain scriptures, as well as in the early Puranas. The origin and forms of Shaivism in Kashi certainly predated Buddhism, which we will discuss in later chapters. Rajghat excavations have brought out many aspects of the Mauryan era. To check the Mauryan level, Shri Krishna Dev, a famous archaeologist, dug two pits in two places below the fifth level of the Shunga period in Rajghat. In one of these pits, about 20–22 feet deep, seventeen pots were found, which were likely used for storing grains. Pieces of polished black or dark brown ware were also found. Such utensils are characteristic of the Mauryan period. There is an inscription Satyavasusya on a Mauryan seal found from Rajghat; he must have been a respectable resident of Banaras during the Maurya period. We also have a detailed description of the Greeks' attack on Pataliputra. Acknowledging the analysis of Motichandra in this respect, Vasudev Sharan Agarwal writes:

> Dr Motichandra, Curator Prince of Wales Museum, Bombay has offered a brilliant suggestion for these exceptional finds at Rajghat. According to him, it was the raid of Demetrius, which brought the Greek Army to Benares where they encamped and crossed the Ganga at the site of Rajghat in the course of an expeditionary march against Pataliputra. The seals are remnants of their settlements.[23]

From the archaeological remains at Rajghat, we have proof of this attack. The bowels of Rajghat have thrown up some seals that have an entire pantheon of Greek gods and goddesses engraved on them. Many ancient objects, including clay currencies were found, which are now mainly preserved in the Bharat Kala Bhavan at Banaras

Hindu University. The figures and heads of many Greek kings and Greek gods and goddesses are marked on some of these artefacts. It is necessary to mention here that, till date, no such seals have been found anywhere in Bihar and Uttar Pradesh. Seals are 'not peripatetic documents like coins' and images. Seals dating back to before the Christian era, with figures of Nike, Apollo, Pallas, Heracles, Eucratides, the king of Bactria, and portrait heads of two kings, Euthydemos and Demetrius, were found. After examining these seals, Agarwal finally comes to the following conclusion.

The earliest known archaeological finds are from the expedition of Demetrius to Pataliputra. There is evidence that indicates that the Greek army going to Pataliputra or returning from there, must have made a stop at this particular site. It is possible that Banaras was at that time under Kaushambi. In about 72 BCE, Devbhuti became the last king of the Shunga dynasty.

What was the condition of Kashi in this era or before, from the few materials found from Rajghat, likely involved the authority of Kaushambi's dynasty over Kashi. In this regard, two currencies found from Rajghat require some elaboration. The first currency was of Jeth Dutta with the name Jethadatasa and on the basis of its script, Agarwal dates its time to the first–second century BCE. There are features of Nandipada, swastik and Vaijayanti on the currency. Probably, this is the same Jethadatta whose coin was found by Carlyle from Bairath near Banaras, bearing an inscription in Brahmi, dating back to the second century BCE, indicating that he was indeed the local king of Kaushambi, and Banaras was under his authority.

Two seals of Gomitra, with the same script, have been found from Bairath. It cannot be said precisely what was the relation of the Gomis inscription with the history of Kashi, but he was probably the king of Kaushambi, whose authority remained on Kashi for a long time. The excavation of Rajghat also sheds some light on the history of Kashi during the Shunga period. Shri Krishnadev found the remains of four houses divided into two circles. Because of the low-quality material, weak walls and simple texture, it appears to be the houses of ordinary people. Among the findings were a seal with an inscribed elephant tusk and a clay seal bearing the name of Balmitas.

Describing the art remains of the Mauryan period in Banaras, reference to some stone wheels found at Rajghat is warranted. Apart from being the best example of Mauryan art, it is also very useful for the religious history of Banaras. Some broken stone wheels of Rajghat feature depictions of a horse near a palm tree in its upper part. These depictions also include a goddess with a bird in her right hand, with an animal with long ears and a short tail, possibly a heron, with a crab-like creature at its feet. This has established that during the Mauryan and Shunga eras, there existed a tradition of the worship of goddesses that still continues in Banaras. Even a private individual seal mentioning the name 'Sasthimitra' draws one's attention to this aspect of goddess worship, as Sasthi was the female counterpart of Skanda as per the Mahabharata, and this seal dates to the early Kushan period.[24]

Clay toys of that era have also been found that are dated to the first and second centuries BCE. The Shunga era sculptures found at Rajghat have broad skulls and the faces are flat with very heavy headdress on women's heads. According to some scholars, the time of the terracotta figurines of such women that has been found at Banaras, dates back to about 40 BCE. A woman's head made of rhinestone, a comb made of ivory, a conch and some ivory bangles that were discovered at Rajghat, prove that during the Shunga era, there was a lot of progress in the businesses of stone cutting, ivory carving, etc. A coin of Ashvaghosha has also been found from Rajghat, which bears the inscription Ashvaghoshasya and a lion couching below it. Even Cunningham and Altekar mention about the coin of Ashvaghosha, before Rajghat discoveries. Although the exact dating of this coin is uncertain, it seems to predate Kanishka's reign over Madhya Desh.

On the basis of seals, coins and inscriptions, as has been mentioned earlier, it can be said that Kaushambi was ruled by the Magha kings of Kosam in the second–third centuries CE. Seals have been found in Vimagha, Bhadramagha, Vaishravana, Bhimavarman, Rudramagh, Satamagha, Vijayamagha, Puramagha and Bhimsen. From this seal, it is confirmed that Rudramagh, with the name inscribed as Rudramaghasya in Kaushan script, was related to Banaras and he used to call himself Mahasenapatisya.[25] Thus, we know that Banaras might have been under the rule of Kaushambi in the second–third centuries CE, that was simply being speculated earlier but has now been testified. The other seals, such as those of Krishnashen, belong to the last era of the Kushan period, as indicated by their script. They also feature inscriptions of Sagittarius, Swastika, Trishul and Srivatsa.

On the seal of Raja Navaa from Rajghat, there is an inscription that reads 'Rajna Navvasya', placed between two symbols, with a bow and arrow above; on the left, there is a depiction of a spear, and on the right is a *yupa*, a trophy inside the *vedika* (platform).

After studying the seals of Navaa, a few scholars like Altekar and Jayaswal came to the following conclusions. The first being that Navaa ruled in the state of Uttar Pradesh. Secondly, his seals were found from Kaushambi, indicating his connection to the place. Lastly, it was inferred that his reign lasted twenty-seven years. According to Jayaswal, the king was the founder of the Navanaga dynasty of the *Nava Purana*. According to him, in the years between 165 and 176 CE, Navaa established the Bharshiv dynasty. However, Altekar, as quoted by Agarwal, remarks that 'since the coins of Navva have only been found around the Kaushambi and Rajghat area—with the distinct markings of the tree within the railings and a Bull, which is quintessentially of Kaushambi rulers, king Navaa was probably a ruler from Kaushambi who came after the Magha kings in 275 CE'.[26]

Motichandra has excitedly elaborated on this: '(W)e would like to draw the readers' attention to a wonderful sculpture from the Bharat Kala Bhavan collection, found in Banaras, which can be related to Bharshivas. Seeing this idol, our attention is immediately drawn to the *Vakataka* text in which Bharshivas are shown carrying Shivlinga on their shoulders.'[27]

Incidentally, a similar tradition is still found among the 'Veerashaivas' or the 'Lingayats' and the ancient Bharshiv dynasty. The Lingayats, a Shaivite sect of north Karnataka, have a practice of wearing a lingam called the Ishtalinga. Even the Veerashaivas share the traditional similarities with the Bharshiv dynasty.

The discovery of many other seals has provided conclusive evidence that Buddhism, Shaivism and several other folk religions were followed in the Kashi region during ancient times. Even though Shaivism predated Buddhism, we do not find much evidence in the archaeological remains because early Shaivism was based more on meditation and was very individualistic, wherein not a lot of idol worshipping rituals were performed. However, Sri Krishnadev's discovery at Rajghat of an ancient structure with a pillared building in the middle, surrounded by hallways from all sides, suggests the presence of religious or ceremonial structures that might be associated with one of these ancient religious practices in Kashi. According to Krishnadev, the ruins indicate that there used to be a temple, most likely a Shiva temple, because all around it is a passageway which could have been the circumambulation path. Sherring, on the other hand, is of the view that it was an ancient Buddhist Vihara,[28] a place of residence for the priests. On the north side, there is a high plinth, and idols of other deities may have been installed in the hallways. The slump in the south-west of the temple may have been used for collecting dirty water and garbage from the temple area.

The presence of other buildings and structures holds significant historical insights. One of the buildings at the temple level has a *mandapa* (pavilion) with five wells. Another house has a lime plastered bathtub; a long courtyard was found in yet another one, in which Krishnadev also found pieces of an earthen pot, which had carvings of lotuses, the moon, leaves and flying swans. Some Greek seals and seals of King Dhandev, with the inscription of 'Rajno Dhanadevasya', were also found. Sri Krishnadeva's estimation was that this level dates to the second–third centuries CE. And since the seals of Dhandev have markings of a sacrificial post called yupa, *caitya*, a bull and a spear behind the bull, and also since the artefacts clearly show a close association with the Vedic religion, it is well-established, beyond any reasonable doubt, that the temple was indeed a Shiva temple and that King Dhandev was a Shaivite king of Kaushambi, who handled the jurisdiction of Kashi.[29]

Till Chandragupta I (305–325 CE), there is no conclusive evidence that Kashi was under the Gupta empire but the substantial findings from Rajghat provide compelling proof that, from the reign of Samudra Gupta onwards, including Ram Gupta, Chandragupta II, and extending into the time of Skandagupta, Kashi continued to be a major player in the sociocultural politics of the subcontinent.

By giving an outline of the history of the Gupta empire, we have tried to link that Kashi and Banaras were a part of the Gupta kingdom till the beginning of the sixth century. At present, we can trace the relation between the Gupta empire and Banaras only on the basis of the inscriptions. The reality, though, is that prior to the excavation of Rajghat, we knew very little about the association of the Guptas with Banaras. 'The religious seals from Rajghat throw considerable light on the educational and religious institutions flourishing in Benares in the Gupta period. The sealings are of exceptional importance for the fact that they provide archaeological evidence of the authenticity of the Brahmanical tradition as recorded in the Kashi Khand of the Skanda Purana.'[30] This is indeed fascinating as the Kashi Khand was only composed and written in the fourteenth century CE. Perhaps the oral tradition has been compiled meticulously and quite accurately. The sources for understanding the religious, social and political history of Kashi during the Gupta period mainly include temples, businesses and the currency used by its citizens. The seals belonging to the royal officials of Banaras during the Gupta era have also been found, and from the related seals used for import–export purposes, it is known that the influence of the Guptas persisted in Banaras until the time of Skandagupta.

Most of the seals found from Rajghat are of four types: passports, seals of Raj employees, traders or the seals of its citizens, and the seals of temples. A deeper examination of these seals of Rajghat shows their widespread use, thereby indicating a prosperous, thriving and a throbbing urban centre of Kashi.

On some other seals found at Rajghat, there are depictions of the bravery of Chandragupta II and Kumaragupta I in their encounters with lions. In one of the representations, Chandragupta is shown shooting an arrow at a lion, while in another coin of Kumaragupta I, a devi is shown riding a lion. Interestingly, on some silver and copper seals, three-fourths of the coin's surface is covered by the portrait of Chandragupta II. Another seal features a side profile of an unconventional portrait with peacocks on either side. The use of peacock imagery was started by Kumaragupta and persisted on the seals of Skandagupta and Bhanugupta alike. These seals have been moulded and cast minted, which shows that the Gupta emperors had their own mint. We still have an area called Taksal (mint), where there was a movie hall by the same name earlier, perhaps started by the Maharaja of Banaras and later by the British. This location too is on the extended portion of the Rajghat plateau.

Dr Vasudev Saran Agarwal has studied many other types of Gupta seals found from Rajghat. Many seals with inscriptions of the name called Amatya Janardhan, have been discovered at Rajghat. These seals date back to the early Gupta era, indicating that during Samudragupta's time, Amachya Janardan was looking after the affairs of Banaras.

A seal bearing the inscription 'Amacha Hastikasa' and depicting a bull seated to the right has also been found at Rajghat. This suggests that Amacha Hastika might have been a minister or official serving under Hastika during the early Gupta period, with the inscription written in Prakrit script.[31] Both of these seals have an inscription of the Taurus, from which the relation of Kashi with Shaivism can be deduced. Many oval sealings have also been found, with depictions of Goddess Gajalakshmi resting on a lotus, with the inscription 'Kumaramatyadhikaranasya' ('of the office of the Kumaramatya') engraved both above and below the depiction. It is evident from the seals that Kumaramatya held an office in Banaras. During the Gupta time, Kumaramatyasadhi-Vigrahik was the chief magistrate or the *mahadandnayak*, minister or *mantri*, feudal lord or *samant* and the governor of the province or *vishaypati*. They also used to work under the princes and the *uparikar maharaja* (provincial governor).

If Banaras's Kumaramatya was the provincial governor, then Amatya probably must have been his consultant. Many circular sealings, bearing the inscription 'Baranasyadhishthanadhikaranasya' ('seal of the office of the seat of the government of Benares'), with Goddess Lakshmi on a lotus, have also been found from Rajghat.[32] It was an office in the main town, which we call the district town today, that could have been an office of a tribunal. If we take the court to mean the tribunal, it may be the seal of the principal court of Banaras. Two more types of seals have been found from Rajghat. In one currency, on one side, there is the impression of a corporation and on the other side, that of the district. There is a domed building on top of the corporation. On another currency, the name of Haridas is engraved and the second impression is of a *nigama* or corporation ('of the city's guild office'). A third impression only has 'Janapadasya', with a seated bull printed on the left. There are two in Kushana Brahmi script, one reading 'Nigamasa' and the other 'Kasthagarikana' ('of the officers in charge of the royal storehouses'). The most prominent one has a 'svastika' in the centre, with marinal legend in Kushana script as 'Gavayaka-seniye' ('of the Gavayaka guild', Gavayaka meaning cattle-herders). From these sealings, we come to know that the two institutions of Banaras, namely the corporation and the district, existed and functioned jointly.

Banaras was probably a corporation from very ancient times, because in the Mahajanapada era and even afterwards, its fame was based on its thriving trade. As we have seen, the seals of the corporation have been found in Banaras, from the Kushan period to the Gupta period. As per Motichandra, the form of this ancient corporation was preserved in the bourse of Banaras, which is now dead. A total of fifty-two persons comprised the managing committee and no new member could be elected without consensus. Only those traders could be elected as members who used to deal in hundi-parts (credit bills) and were involved in the insurance of goods. The members of the *sarafa* (market) had a fixed rate of interest, which was higher than the market rate. Town Shroff (seth) used to be the Chaudhary or head of that bourse, and he commanded much respect in the government and in the whole city.

The presence of the word 'district' on the seals of Rajghat suggests that this institution had a lot to do with the daily hubbub of the city and as a seal shows, it was also related to the corporation; or it may have been an institution like a municipality or a district board. Thus we find an urban set-up, which was not much different from what we have now—truly an amalgamation of the modern with the archaic.

Before the excavation of Rajghat, the evidence regarding Shaivism in Banaras was based only on the Puranas, but the excavation of the many Shivlings, seals and other artefacts has provided historical confirmation to the knowledge given in texts like the *Matsya Purana.* There were eight important Shivlings of the Gupta era, namely, Harichandreshwar, Abharatkeshwar, Jaleshwar, Shriparvateshwar, Mahalayeshwar, Krimichandeshwar, Kedareshwar and Mahabhairav.

The following types of seals of Avimukteshwar from the Gupta era have been discovered at Rajghat: circular soapstone seals with the inscription 'Avimukteshvara Bhattarakah' (Bhattrak means a venerable and worshipful person), featuring a trishul (trident), parshu (halberd) and vrishabh (taurus); seals bearing the image of Avimukteshwar, with vrishabh and Ganga; one with 'Shree Avimukteshwar' inscribed in eighth-century script; and lastly, the naam mudra (currency with a name) with 'Avimukteshwar Bhattarak' engraved in eighth-century script. These writings show that from the Gupta period to the ninth century and beyond, the importance of Avimukteshwar remained prevalent in Banaras. Avimukteshwar Bhattarak's inscriptions also indicate that the Avimukteshwar temple had some *mahant* (chief priest), and this tradition of the superior of the monastery or temple started from the Gupta era and continued till the ninth century. This tradition is still intact and the mahants have a significant say in politics and religious affairs even today. It is also known from the currencies that the main symbols of Avimukteshvara were the trishul, parshu and vrishabh, and the temple of Avimukteshvara was near Gyanvapi.

The following temples of the Gupta period, or a little later, are known from the seals found at Rajghat:

1. ***Shrisaraswat***: This Shivling, according to the *Skanda Purana*, has sealings with Sri-Sarasvata in Gupta script, with a *charan paduka* above it. It is associated with the Saraswata-mahakupa, which is the knowledge well or the present-day Gyanvapi well situated behind the Vishwanath temple.
2. ***Yogeshwar***: The characters found on this seal are: *ardhachandra* (crescent), *akshasutra* (string or rosary of Rudraksha seeds), trishul-parshu (trident and halberd), *kamandalu* (monk's bottle or the pot used by ascetics) and a crooked staff.
3. ***Bhringeshwar***: *Bhringara* (monk's bottle), *akshasutra* (rosary), *ardhachandra* (crescent) and *Tritrashul-Parshu* are depicted on its sealings.
4. ***Pritikeshwar Swamin***: This temple is still situated near the Sakshi Vinayak temple near Vishwanath temple.
5. ***Bhogkeshwar***: Taurus is inscribed on the currency.
6. ***Prajneshwar***: Taurus is ensigned on the currency.
7. ***Hastishwar***: With taurus ensign.
8. ***Gangahwar***: A Gupta era Shiva temple.
9. ***Gabhastishwar***: The letters of the inscription on the seal of this one belong to a seventh-century script, with a symbol of a bull seated to the left, on a pedestal. There is still a temple of Gabhastheeshwar near Mangalagauri.[33]

Kashi was a great centre for learning in the Gupta era. The discovery of seals at Rajghat provides insight into the history of Banaras in the Gupta era and the educational system that existed in Kashi from the Mauryan era to the Gupta era.

The Gupta seals, depicting Sri Chaturvidha (four-fold knowledge), insinuate the presence of an educational system that focused on the teachings of the four Vedas, during that period in Banaras. Similarly, the sealings with depictions such as one with the seated bull with 'Sri-Sarvatra-vidyasya' in Gupta script also appears to have been a religious and educational foundation for the teaching of the Vedas. Possibly, in this school, education was imparted on all the four branches: Anvikshiki (logical philosophy), Trayee Varta (trilogy talks), Dandaniti (judicature) and Shashwati (knowledge related to the earth), with emphasis on omniscience, which is the capacity to know everything. Two seals with inscriptions have been found which indicate that in the Gupta era, there was an exclusive school for the teaching of the Rig Veda, and the teaching of the Samaveda was imparted at the temple of Yogeshwar in Banaras. Some indications from the seals show Vaishnav markings, which also seems to indicate that even some teachers were Vaishnavs, which is a very important aspect. Banaras had a disproportionately large Shaivite domination at that time, as it has now, and from this one can deduce that in Banaras perhaps there was a provision for the teaching of all the three Vedas in one school, within a Shiva temple named Traividya (containing the three Vedas) as well.

It appears that along with Shaivism, Banaras also became an important centre for the worship of Kartikeya, since the time of Kumaragupta. A dancing peacock is seen on some of the seals, which is the *vahana* (mount) of Kartikeya. One seal has the inscription of the image of Shri Mahendra and a dancing peacock on his left. This seems to be the seal of Skandagupta because one of his panegyrics was Shri Mahendra. An interesting continuity is seen on a coin discovered in Rajghat that depicts a devi called Sashthi (the sixth), who is the devi or female form of Kartikeya, as mentioned earlier. As per Motichandra, there were many temples of this devi, and she was duly and ritualistically worshipped during the Gupta era; for instance, the mention of the worship of this deity during the birth ceremonies of King Chandrapida underscores the importance of such rituals in that period. In fact, even now, we observe similar customs, such as the sixth-day worship of the goddess after the birth of a son in a family. The popular Hindi aphorism '*Chhatthi ka doodh yaad dilana*' ('To be reminded of one's baptism') reflects the cultural memory associated with these age-old customs and traditions. It is paradoxical that despite being the rulers of Kashi with predominance of Shaivism during that period, the Gupta kings have been referred to as 'Param Bhagwat' in their seals and treatises, which suggests that they were potentially Vaishnavites. We will cover this aspect in detail in our chapter on 'Vaishnavism and Shaivism'. Apart from religious denominations, many epithetical seals from Rajghat throw light on some interesting and pulsating urban cultures. Seals with names like *rasik* (playboy), *blak* (a mixture of treacle and milk; perhaps a contracted name-form could also mean Balagupta), *suvimal* (perfectly clear or pure), *botil* or *bota* (young and handsome) and *nalshree* (a beautiful man, like the blossom of the sacred lotus) have also been recovered.

Another type of seals from Rajghat form a unique category, characterized by profound aesthetics and remarkable creativity. They contain single indicative markings, such as Garuda holding a snake with its wings spread in the middle of a pillar and a garland, a dancing peacock, a pot-bellied deity seated on a tabouret with a mace in his hand, and Varaha, symbolizing the boar avatar of Vishnu, holding the female form of the earth on his tusks. This, although prima facie appears to be religious, could have other versatile employability.

With this plethora of archaeological remains of the buildings, seals and treatise being discovered and deciphered at and from Rajghat, we have been able to scrutinize and assay one entire millennium. All this evidence has an undisputed imprint of the cultural, financial and religious importance of Kashi during the Mauryan, Kushan and Gupta eras.

Even though Banaras remained an important town from the Mauryan period, it was never made the capital by the ruling dynasties, barring the Bharshiv. After the first Muslim invasion led by Niyal Tigin, a series of Muslim invaders continued to loot the city in succession. The Muslim invasion led to a massive political and religious dislocation and the morale of the Hindus went down to an all-time low. In the northern part of India, there was complete anarchy and mayhem. The harassed Hindus were desperately seeking a leadership, which could take revenge from the Muslims who decimated them culturally and religiously. An en masse hatred for this religion was quite natural. The famous Iranian scholar al-Biruni has also noted in his travel diaries about the condition of the Hindus. It was around this time that a Gahadavala king, Chandradev

(1073–1100 CE) emerged, who not only defeated the Muslim armies but also established Kashi as his capital. Kashi became the capital of the ruling establishment after 1700 years. The rule of the Gahadavalas had been very well documented. The many treatises found at Rajghat provide substantial insights into their rule and governance. The origin of Gahadavalas is aboriginal, perhaps, since the etymology has the reference to *guhar* (a cave-dweller). Some scholars also believe them to be a branch of the Rashtrakuta. Some, like Bisheshwar Nath Reu, believe that the word 'Gahad' means brave, and also that there is a place beyond the Vindhyas in the south that is known by the name of Gahd. Their aboriginal origins were later brought into the Kshatriya clan by the Brahmins, who, mention citing some legends, are the descendants of the great king of Kashi—Divodas. To mitigate the effects of 'Shani' (inauspicious time), they were called 'Grahvar', which later got distorted to 'Gahadavalas'. Colonel Tod has described their antecedents as:

> The Gaharwar Rajput is scarcely known to his brethren in Rajasthan, who will not admit his contaminated blood to mix with theirs; though, as a brave warrior, he is entitled to their fellowship. The original country of the Gaharwar was is in the ancient kingdom of Kasi. Their great ancestor was Khortaj Deva, from whom jasaunda, the seventh in descent, in consequence of some grand sacrificial rites performed at Vindhyavasini, gave the title of Bundela to his issue.[34]

Historians have observed that whenever the relatively lower class of rulers capture power, they try to create a narrative with the help of the Brahmins, of their being descended from a lineage which has had preternatural achievements and have made a niche in the collective subconscious of the masses. Such tales have been passed down as oral traditions. The Gahadavalas were no exception to this phenomenon. They continued to harass and wage a guerrilla war with the petty rulers of Banaras from their stronghold in the Vindhya hills. Later, King Chandradev and specially his grandson, Govindacharya, revived many Hindu festivals and rituals, which were dying down after the overwhelming patronage by the Guptas and the later Guptas. They restored the massive ancient defence at the Rajghat ridge, the remains of which we have discussed earlier. Rajghat, till the present Adampura area and the embankments of the confluence of Varuna and the Ganga, emerged as the city centre. *Neela Chaand* describes a battle near the Adi Keshav ghat at Rajghat, between Rudrachandra, a Gahadavala nobleman, with a local chieftain, Karan, and a Kalchuri General Bhimkarma, whom the Gahadavala nobleman defeated with only ten horsemen.[35] Historically, that is correct as, to finally capture Kashi, the Gahadavalas faced many onslaughts from myriad warlords and the nearby ruling dynasties. A golden period for Banaras unfolded under the rule of King Chandradev, and his successors Madan Pal (1100–09 CE), Govindchandra (1109–54 CE), Vijaychandra (1154–70 CE) and Jaichandra (1170–94 CE). We are quite aware of the deceit of Jayachandra through the popular ballad *Prithviraj Raso* by Chand Bardai, who collaborated with Mohammed Ghori to defeat his arch-rival Prithviraj Chauhan. In the double whammy, Ghori went against his promise of restoring the annexed territories to Jayachandra and had him killed. This led to the end of the rule of the great Gahadavalas in Banaras in 1194 CE. However, a treatise found near Jaunpur mentions the rule of Jayachandra's son, Harishchandra, which continued to be effective around Banaras till 1197 CE, when finally, the armies of Qutb ud-Din Aibak ravaged Banaras to such an extent that the entire city on Rajghat could never really recover from the impact of this invasion. It is disturbing to note that in light of the history of Banaras, the petty squabbles of the four great Rajput dynasties—Chandels, Chahmans, Parmars and the Gahadavalas—devastated the cultural and religious centre of Banaras, in particular, and that of the entire northern India, in general. The Muslim invading armies were quick to grab the advantage of these situations, shaping the course of history. Despite this, the spirit of Hinduism endured. We shall see in detail how Banaras played a consequential and esteemed role in conserving, upholding and disseminating Sanatan Dharma.

Chapter 3

Alluring Allusions

A City with Different Names through Different Eras

Your name hangs in my heart like a bell's tongue.

—Edmond Rostand, French playwright

Banaras is perhaps the only city in the world with many different names that have appellations for various phases of its existence with its growth as an important urban centre since ancient times. The toponymy or the lexicological study of the names of places, in the context of Banaras, is as much enthralling as its ancient past. All these names carry specific insinuations of the activities that were being carried out and its significance was thus gradually established with the onset of various other hurly-burly that an urban centre caters to. This is not very surprising, because in the Vedic texts, as well as in the later Hindu scriptures, like the Puranas, there is a ritual of chanting *sahastra* (100 names of gods and goddesses). Clearly, Banaras has been the centre of numerous scriptural and spiritual rituals and practices of Hinduism since long. The different names that the city has been called by throughout its existence have evolved over the years and are not mere casual references. The etymological connotations have been clearly defined in the Jatakas and the Puranas. Each name has logic and a deeper meaning, and is a result of political, historical and geographical implications and hieroglyphic manifestations of the 'Kathenotheism' (a term coined by Max Muller, meaning the worship of many gods, one at a time) during the early Vedic period. This chapter will go into those details wherein the reasons behind Banaras being referred to by such varying and exotic names will be elaborated.

Kashi

The first reference of the word 'Kashi' is found in the Atharva Veda, which was likely compiled as a Veda contemporaneously with the Samaveda and Yajurveda, around 1200–1000 BCE. This appears in both the Paippalada edition, which was believed to have been lost but a well-preserved version was discovered among a collection of palm leaf manuscripts in Odisha in 1957, and the Shathpath. The *Shatapatha Brahmana*, meaning 'Brahmaṇa of one hundred paths', is a commentary on the sukla (white) Yajurveda and contains detailed explanations of Vedic sacrificial rituals, symbolism and mythology.[1] The name of Kashi has been mentioned in a deprecating manner in which the person who is chanting the mantras says that the disease of malaria should go and affect the people of Kashi and Magadha.[2] It appears that he says so, because at that time, the Aryans had not ventured in the region of Kashi and it was occupied by the 'Anarya'.[3] Even in *Manusmriti*, Kashi was considered outside the pure land of Brahmavrata. On one account, the first settlers of this region were a tribe of Aryans known as the 'Kashya', the mention of which has been made earlier as well. As Fitzedward Hall puts it: 'Among the descendants of Ayus was Kasa, whose son is noticed under the patronyms of Kaseya, Kasiya and Kasi'[4] Mirza Ghalib, while composing his eighty-sixth verse, mentions about another city in Iran—Kashan—whose residents were also called Kashi:

When your madness reaches
The perfect frenzy
Kashan from Kashi
Is just a half-step journey[5]

The emphasis on the continuation of two ancient civilizations is a brilliant attempt to manifest the syncretism that Ghalib felt Banaras was.

The regal successors of Kasi, and equally their subjects, were called 'Kasis'. Though at first a masculine appellation, Kasi, as applied to the city so styled, is feminine.'[6] Motichandra gives reference of a more ancient Babylonian civilization from inscriptions of about 2000 BCE, about the Kassi people. They seem to have conquered Babylon in the early 1800 BCE and their authority over that country continued till 1171 BCE. According to him, the deities and beliefs of the Kassi people have a lot of similarities as well. The horse was the divine symbol of the Kassis. The name of the god of the Asian race was 'Kashsu'. The actual history of the Kassis begins in the 2400 BCE. The Ashurs called them 'Kassi' and the Greek called them 'Kassaioi'.

According to Vasudev Sharan Agarwal, a terrain that was perennially covered underwater had a thick overgrowth of a grass called Kush and Kash, and that is how this region came to be called Kashi. Even now, in the native language, this silver blooming plant is called Kaswar and a subdivision of Banaras exists with this name, too. In the sixth century BCE, i.e., 2800 years earlier, when the king of Magadha, Bimbisar, married the sister of Prasanjeet of Kosal, under whose suzerainty the area of Kashi was, he is supposed to have gifted an area called Kasik to Bimbisar. In Kashi Khand, it has also been referred to as Kashipuri.[7] In the Uttar Kand of the Ramayana, Banaras is mentioned as 'a city in the country of Kasis'.[8] In *Dashakumaracharita*, the expression 'Kashipuri Varanasi' means 'Varanasi, a city of the Kasis'. It also appears that the name of the sacred zone could have been derived from the Sanskrit word 'Kashate', which means 'to shine, luminous and beautiful'. Kashi therefore is also called Kashika. According to Diana L. Eck, 'The word play of Sanskrit continually underlines the relation of the city of light to the light of enlightenment . . . . when it is called the "city of light, which illuminates liberation", Kashi is said to illuminate truth, thus manifesting the real from the implicit.'[9] As per Prinsep, Kashi is indicated in Ptolemy's map.[10] Fa Hian called the kingdom of Kashi 'Kia Chi' and its capital Banaras, Pho lo nai. Hiouen Tsang, another Chinese traveller in the sixth century CE, called the city of Banaras as P'o-lo-ni-sse.

Banaras

The first mention of Banaras is also found in the Atharva Veda as the River Varnavati for the present-day Varuna. Initially, Varanasi was Varuna. Another interpretation is that Varuna is also indicative of a type of tree that surrounded the river. Thus the river came to be called Varanasi, and that subsequently bestowed its name to the settlement that came up around it. In ancient times, many places were named after the popular variety of trees that flourished in that region. For example, from Koshamb to Koshambi, Rohit to Rohitak and so on. One British scholar, M. Julian, has confirmed that the old name of Varuna was Baranasi. The Jatakas and Pali literature mention a Kosala king, Kamsa, who was designated as the Baranasiggaho or the 'conqueror of Varanasi'.[11] Thus establishing the fact that even during the Mahajanapada time, Kashi was known as Baranasi. In the Mahabharata also, the river Varuna has been referred to as Varanasi. Even Valmiki's Ramayana, composed around 700 BCE, has praised the city. In the Udyog Parv of the Mahabharata and in the *Vishnu Purana*, there is a reference of Varanasi being burnt by Krishna. In the Puranas, King Divodas established his capital at Banaras, thus also indicating the Kashi region as a separate entity. In the pre-Buddhist era, Banaras was the capital of the Kashi Mahajanapada and as per the Jatakas, the extent of Kashi Janpad was 300 *yojan*as,[12] which is clearly exaggerated. At one place in the *Jabala Upanishad*, Varuna and Asi have a yogic interpretation. The generally dry bed of Asi is referred to as the *pingala nadi*, Varuna as *ida nadi* and between these, the Matsyodari is the *sushumna nadi*.[13] From the yogic perspective:

> In the spine, there are three major nadis, known as the *ida, pingala* and *sushumna* nadis. Here, *'nadi'* does not mean 'nerve'. It is not a physical channel. Nadi means 'flow', like the flow of electricity

> within a cable. One wire carries the negative force and another carries the positive force of electricity. So, in hatha yoga, ida nadi represents the negative force, the flow of consciousness, pingala represents the positive force, the flow of vital energy, and the sushumna nadi represents the neutral force, the flow of spiritual energy.[14]

The Puranas have elaborated upon a bigger area of Kashi, which is not restricted between the Varuna and the Asi rivers; in fact, Asi is not recognized as a river and is therefore called a 'Shush nadi', meaning a dry river.

Now let us discuss the most popular etymological derivative of the term 'Varanasi'. As per the Puranic explanation, the city that is located within the boundaries of the Varuna and Asi rivers is the city of 'Varanasi'. There is an attempt to make the city appear to get a direction-based dimension, as the ancient linear layout of the city did not somehow conform to a religious place. This emphasis is quite later, as only the Puranas, composed in the medieval times, mention this layout. For example, the Kashi Khand describes the boundary of the liberation (moksha) zone of the city surrounded by the great river Dhuni—the destroyer of the evil in the east; 'Asi'—the sword that destroys the sinners in the south; and 'Varuna'—the remover of obstacles in the north. Lord Shiva then established the Dehli Vinayak to protect the western flank of the city. The *Kashi Mahatmaya* also mentions the same and refers to the river in the east as Jahanavi (Ganga) and in the west as Pashpani Ganesh. Nothing can be farther from truth. We shall see why the history scholars are unanimous in stating that the ancient city of Banaras was located on the plateau of Rajghat with few very old settlements at Bairath, and some settlements spilling across Varuna also, but certainly not in the south towards Asi. Firstly, Asi is not a river and there is no proof that it was a river even in ancient times. Agarwal quotes two ancient texts, where the River Varuna is referred to as Baranasi: one is in the list of the rivers mentioned in Bhismparva (the *Bhishma Parva*, or the Book of Bhishma, is the sixth of eighteen books of the

Indian epic Mahabharata). The other one is, as per Panini's *varanamdur bhavam nagar varuna*, meaning 'the place near the Vauna trees is called Varanasi'. One of the devis that has an aboriginal origin but has been given a very high place in the Puranas is the 'Varanasi devi'; she was one of the many nagar/gram-reigning devis (town goddess). Her nondescript shrine is at the Trilochan ghat within the confines of the Trilochan devi temple. Sherring describes her to be 'the black ugly figure of the goddess Barnasi, presented by Raja Banar'.[15]

Having analysed the above origin of the term 'Varanasi', it can be assumed that, in essence, the city's name is derived from its location along the banks of the river Varanasi or Varuna. The imagination of it being located between the Asi and Varuna is a later affair, and only after its status as a religio-pilgrimage destination got enhanced, that the population moved southwards. Till Prinsep's time, i.e., the 1830s, Durga Kund was a place surrounded by forest and behind that, there still exists a temple of Bankati Hanuman (bankati means a forest that has been cut down). In fact, Prinsep has come to the conclusion that till the early eighteenth century, the Manikarnika ghat was surrounded by a forest. One of the places where Tulsidas lived near Gopal Mandir was on the edge of a forest. However, this explanation of the term Varanasi is strictly limited to scholarly interpretation, which is impossible to explain to an average Banarasi. The most popular and the most accepted explanation continues to be the Hindu tabernacle that is an area between the Varuna and the Asi. A popular story about Pandit Madan Mohan Malviya, the founder of the iconic Banaras Hindu University, is that despite being a staunch Brahmin and an upholder of the ritualistic Hindu order, he refused to establish the university in the sacred zone and the holy limits of Kashi and also insisted on dying outside the Kashi kshetra. Until the Mughal and British rule, the city continued to be called Benaras, and its ancient appellation as Varanasi was nearly lost. Tulsidas has used the name of the city as 'Baranasi', in one of his chaupayees (quatrains): *lok bedhoon bidit baranasi ki badai: basi narnari ees ambika saroophai*, meaning 'the homage to Kashi is avowed in this world and the Vedas: all the men and women of this city are the form of Lord Jagdeesh and Mata Ambika'.

The name Banaras was changed to Varanasi by Sampurnanand, a teacher and politician, during his tenure as chief minister of Uttar Pradesh. He was the state's second chief minister, from 1954 to 1960. It is during this time, on the occasion of the Buddha's 2500th birthday, that he officially changed the name.

In *The Sacred City of the Hindus*, Sherring quotes General Cunnigham: 'Raja Banar is traditionally believed to have rebuilt Benares about eight hundred years ago.'[16] It has been called 'Banaras' since that time. Prinsep and Motichandra have noted that once Raja Bunar ruled over Banaras in 1017 CE. During the raid of one of the generals of Sultan Mahmud Ghaznavi, Masood Salar Ghazi, who was also the nephew of the Sultan, he was defeated. By the above accounts, one of the adaptations of Banaras can be traced to Raja Bunar. Some have also emphasized that it is a corrupted form of Baranasi. If we dissect the word 'Banaras', then, as per Rana P.B. Singh, it's 'always ready', for bana and ras is the juice of life.[17] A typically wry explanation also emanates from the run-of-the-mill street intellectuals, who are worth a dime a dozen in Banaras, is that when the Britishers first came to the city, they found it to be devoid of joie de vivre and called it Binaras (literally meaning 'without any juice'). However, Vishwanath Mukherjee has a facetious explanation of why Britishers called this city Benarus. He says that when they came to this city, they found that all the denizens are mostly busy in straining the juice of bhang (Indian hemp or cannabis) and were also fluent speakers.[18] The British continued to call it Banaras but spelled it as 'Benares'. Sherring has also quoted, though sceptically, one Colonel Wilford, who while mentioning 'the old city of Benares, north of the river Burna', calls it Sonitapura, as mentioned in the Jatakas.[19] Another evangelist called it Pachanadatiratha or 'the quinquennial resort' quoting a Vaishnav term for the city.

In practice, the names Kashi, Banaras and Varanasi are coterminous with each other and are interchangeable. The name also often reflects the segment of society that is using it. Customarily, a Brahmin or a Sanskrit scholar would use the name 'Kashi', the common folk would prefer 'Banaras', while the official 'given name' used in matters of the government and business is 'Varanasi'.

Apunarbhava Bhumi or Mukti kshetra

A less-known fact is that the city has also been referred to by various esoteric and mystical phrases, such as Apunarbhava Bhumi, meaning final beatitude or exemption from further transmigration, and Mukti kshetra, alluding to a place where one retires after renouncing life, in the pursuit of the ultimate freedom of one's soul from the cycle of rebirth—the unencumbered, supremely liberated and blissful state known as moksha. The practice of 'Kashivas', meaning to live in the city, is quite common even now, in times where logic has overtaken the faithscape. One can well imagine its prevalence a few centuries back when faith held a more predominant role. Ralph Fitch describes it rather grotesquely: 'When a man or woman is sick and likely to die, they are laid all night before the idols, either to help their sickness or make an end of them. If they do not mend that night, the friends come and sit up with them, and cry for some time, after which they take them to the side of the river, laying them on a raft of reeds, and so let them float down the river.'[20]

Prinsep has described these places as: 'Further on are situated the rich *Dewuls* on *Munikurnika ghat;* and on the river's edge are seen one or two *Murhees*—chambers into which the sick are removed when at the point of death, that their sins, to the last moment of existence, may be washed away by the holy stream.'[21]

The newly renovated Kashi Vishwanath Corridor has a forty-bedded hospice in Baidyanath Bhavan, known as Mumukshu Bhawan or the house of liberation, specifically for the elderly who want to spend their last days in Kashi under the aura and blessings of Lord Vishwanath.

Our ancestral house was also converted into a kind of tavern, which used to be visited by our relatives from both Banaras and Bihar throughout the year. My father's maternal uncle's place, Baheri, was a short distance away from Banaras and every year, for about four months from November to February, during a week-long consecutive stay, we would have an unusual visitor, whom we affectionately called Baheriwali-dadi (grandma from Baheri) or potliwali-dadi (grandma with bundles). She used to arrive with a myriad of knick-knacks stuffed in assorted packets, often crudely trussed in dirty muslin cloths or old sarees. For some weird reasons, her short continuous sojourn would occur only in the freezing winter months. She would wear a white cotton saree, with a thick blanket wrapped over her emaciated body, a blanket we, as kids, were convinced weighed more than she did. Despite being half bent, having a very garrulous and bossy voice, she was quite agile for a woman of her age (she must have been past eighty years old). I remember her ordering us around for small errands. Her gift to us would be small black ladoos made of jaggery and sesame seeds, locally known as tilwa, which she took out from one of her bundles with great care. She would always carry her ration of mustard oil in a small, rusted tin can, along with *usinachaoor* or boiled rice and makai ka sattu or roasted corn flour. While ostensibly we were told that the purpose of her visit was religious, one of her close relatives once confided to us that she had this wish to die in Kashi, and that a *jyotishi* (astrologer) had told her that she would die in the *sheetkal* months of Ashadh, Paush and Magh (Hindu calendar winter months corresponding to November, December and January). So, she continued to come every winter, decidedly joyous and beaming that she was going to die! Conversely, she would be most dejected when returning to her village in Baheri. Eventually, we came to know that on her way to our house once, after reaching Banaras, she fell from a cycle rickshaw near the railway station and passed away. Our cousins who used to accompany her told my uncle that when she was dying, there was a strange luminous glow on her face, and she was giving her quintessential toothless smile. Similar insistence was made by my uncle, who died peacefully at the ripe old age of eighty-six. He, too, refused to leave the sacred zone after he attained the age of seventy-five. I remember seeing his dead body shrivelled up like a small bird, with a serene glow on his face, and I was told by the caretaker that he, too, gave a beaming smile just before breathing his last. The memory of this old woman and my uncle now makes me realize the fervour and the pious space Kashi kshetra has in the hearts of millions of Hindus.

Avimukt

When once Shiva was perambulating in Kashi, he told his consort, Gauri, that he would never leave the city and since then, as per the *Agni Purana*, the name of the city has also been 'Avimukt', or the place never forsaken. As mentioned in the Kashi Khand, Skand tells Sage Augustya that since Shiva never left Kashi, this place is called Avimukt.[22] As per the *Vayu Purana*, Shiva also confided in Parvati that even if Kashi is destroyed, he will not leave this city.[23] Pandit Kubernath Sukul has elaborated on this Avimukt kshetra with its boundaries described as Pritikeshwar in the east, Lakshareshwar in the north, Magadhaeshwar in the north-west and Kameshwar in the south.[24] As per the *Shiva Purana*, Shiva, after beheading Brahma, came to Avimukt to brood and meditate. Seated on a tiger skin under the banyan tree, facing south, it was here that he revealed to his students and disciples the secrets of understanding and internalizing the mysteries of the cosmos through the practice yoga. It was here that he was honoured as the 'Dakshinamurti'.

Mahashamshaan

In the Kashi Khand, it is explained that during the great flood, this place became a resting ground for all the great intellects and principles (mahatattva). The city witnesses large numbers of people settling here to await death, so much so that one of its names has come to be the Mahashamshan (meaning vast cremation ground). The specific origin of the cremation tradition in Banaras is unknown, but what is certain is that when the city was located in the north, i.e., on the Rajghat plateau and along the banks of the river Varuna, the cremation ground, as per Vaastu traditions, was located in the southern area near the present Meer ghat, earlier called Jalsai ghat. Even when the city extended towards the south, the cremation ground continued to be at the same place. But as per reliable oral traditions, the cremation ground kept on shifting and the oldest one being at Jam ghat, near the Sankhata Devi temple. Presently, the bodies are burnt at the Harishchandra and Manikarnika ghats. The detailed stories on these two ghats will be covered in one of the later chapters. Unlike other places where a passing dead body elicits hushed silence, in Banaras, a childhood hilarious ditty, whenever we saw a dead body being taken for cremation, was: '*Ram nam satya hai, murda beta mast hai*' (translated as: 'The name of the Lord is eternal truth, but the dear dead body is in ecstasy'). It also showed a metaphysical exhilaration with life and death alike.

Banaras, since ages, has symbolized life and death being one, and later, Buddhism and the Sufi philosophical thought also incorporated this ancient wisdom. Owing to the inherent sense of mortality in them, Amir Khusrow's famous *dohae* (couplets) are truly immortal: '*Gori sove sej par, mukh par daare kes. Chal khusro ghar aapane, rain bhaii chahun des*', and '*Kaaga sabtan khaiyo mera chun chun khaiyo maas do naina mat khaiyo mohe piya milan ki aas*'. Even Kabir's '*Chalti chakki dekh ke diya kabira roye, do paatan ke beech mein sabit bacha nakoye*' is a doha that invokes a sense of awe for the transient nature of life. The famous *bol banaav ki thumri* of Banaras, most popular during the late nineteenth century: '*Baabul mora, naihar chhuto hi jaae, chaar kahaar mil, mori doliya sajaawen, mora apana begaana chhuto jaae*', was said to have been composed by Nawab Wazid Ali Shah, who carries the inherent theme of liberation from everything that one beholds dear. Dying in the Kashi kshetra is coveted also because it is the abode of Shiva, who is believed to whisper a mantra known as the 'tarak mantra' in the ear of the dying, which immediately liberates them.

Brahmapuri

Another old name of Banaras has been mentioned by Shivprasad Singh in *Neela Chaand*.

There was an important settlement all along the Brahmnal, as mentioned earlier. It originated from Matsyodari and merged into the Ganga after passing through the present-day Chowk and Manikarnika lane area and it also acted as backwater storm drain during the rainy season. Their symbol of faith was encapsulated in an epigraphic phrase: *Dharm naad tahan paap maand* (Wherever there is a proclamation of religion, sin is subdued). This was the hub of the Brahmins from the southern and western India. Perhaps this also was the harbinger of the settlement that later came up after the Mughal invaders destroyed the Rajghat area. This entire area was called Brahmapuri. The ghatiyas and other locals still use this name to refer to the settlement on the Ganga ridge. There is massive corpus of the legends and folk tales about the Yakshas in Banaras, according to the Atharva Veda. The area inhabited by the Yakshas is called Brahmapuri.

* * *

Some of the most ornamental names of the city we find are in the *Jatakas Tales*, which were composed around the third century BCE–fourth century CE. These include:

Pushpvati: City of Flowers

To reason that a Hindu pilgrimage has to have a thriving flower market is natural. However, Banaras was initially known for being a trading city and much later as a religious centre. As a trading hub, it had its hedonistic aspects and flowers signified much more than being mere offerings to deities. They were extensively used in the perfume industry and in ancient Vedic ceremonies that were not necessarily religious in nature. Even today, a flower market is set up in the veranda of the Satyanarayan temple every day, from as early as four in the morning, which winds up by ten or eleven in the day. It serves as a retail and wholesale hub of flower trade. The wholesalers, usually aggressive and always male, contrast the more aesthetic section of the retail sellers, who are invariably female. The hustle and bustle, along with the tête-à-tête of the flower sellers and buyers, is an interesting activity of the city that reminds one of the paintings by the impressionist era painter Louis Marie de Schryver titled *The Flower Seller, Avenue de L'Opera, Paris*. Since ancient times, the flower sellers, invariably women called *malini*s are known to be flirtatious with their customers. I always found a strange kind of energy here, with the early morning positivity and the fragrance of the seasonal flowers with the melodious, short, lyrical calls of the flower sellers. Malinis are supposed to educate you on what flowers to buy for specific gods and goddesses. They are also a staple subject of folk and mythical stories. They don't have the seller's instinct to somehow sell their flowers. I have found that they maintain a strict ethical value system where, if they know that their customer is heading towards a particular devi temple, they will not sell them the flowers forbidden to be offered to that devi. If they do not have the required flowers, they will direct them to a particular seller who has that flower. This ancient flower market continues to be an integral part of the sacred space of the city.

Brahmavaddhan

The word translates to a place of learning or acquiring knowledge. Since ancient times, Banaras, along with Takshila, has been a seat of learning. As per the Pali text *Khuddak Paath Athakatha*, some of the educational centres of Kashi were older than Takshila. There is a detailed account of the system that was followed in such centres. As per one of the Jatakas, a king of Kashi named Manoj defeated most of the kings of Jambudweep and was briefly crowned as the king of the entire region. He was also honoured with the title 'Aggraja'. It was during his time that the name of Kashi was Brahmavaddhan.[25] As mentioned earlier, owing to the connection that Dhanvantri—the physician of the gods—shared with Kashi, we may conclude the legend insinuates that Kashi was once a celebrated school of medicine. We still have a 'Dhanvantri Koop' (well) in the compound of the present-day Maha Mrityunjay temple near Machodari area, the water of which is known to have high medicinal value.

In the field of art, music and literature, Banaras still holds institutional memories and archives. The extent of erudition was vast and polycentric and was not limited to the conventional Brahmins. For instance, King Ajatshatru of Kashi was known to often impart *deeksha* (a way of religious observance) to the learned Brahmins; and the famous scholar and spiritual teacher Shankaracharya was enlightened by a *chandal* (lowest caste) Jaanitor in Kashi. However, Kashi reached its pinnacle as the cultural, financial and educational centre during the Gupta period and has been a religious seat of learning since the time of the Gahadavalas. Interestingly, Kashi, as a centre of learning, made the most progress in the study and instruction of the Vedas. The seals found at Rajghat serve as an outstanding testament to Banaras's position as a great centre of excellence. The seal mentions Bahvrca-carana, a massive university for the learning of the Rig Veda, and an ashram is depicted on the seal. An acharya with matted hair stands at the centre, holding a kamandal and sprinkling water on the trees of the ashram, symbolizing his nurturing the tree of knowledge. On either side of him, *brahmacharis* (his disciples) are shown standing respectfully, wearing a scarf on the bust and holding a staff in their hands. This was the Brahmavardhan form of Kashi. The universities to promote the studies of all the four Vedas were called Chaturvidya, and for three Vedas, it was Trividya. This 'fostered a much greater catholic spirit than colleges specializing in only one of the several Vedic texts'. College of Samaveda, called Chandoga, was present in the early Gupta period, apparent on the sealing with a seated bull. The combined religious and educational institution that imparted rudimentary knowledge on the aspects of the Shivling, along with studies of several classical shastras, was called Sri-Sarvvatra-Vidya. There was also, during Gupta period, as deciphered from the seals at Rajghat, a college of the Krsna Yajurveda that pursued studies on *caraka-carana*.

During the Gahadavala era, Brahmins used to keep their students with them to impart education, and the state rulers also encouraged this by providing state grants. However, it appears that during the Sultanate period, the educational scenario was subdued along with other religious and cultural activities. The initial invaders always perceived the education and culture of the Hindus intertwined with religion; hence their bigotry was quite apparent. Banaras, however, during Mahmood Ghaznavi's time, became a centre for Sanskrit learning because most of the Brahmins from western India, Punjab and Kashmir started settling down in Banaras. Then, during Muhammad bin Tughlaq's time, Banaras continued to be the centre of excellence for such specific subjects such as metallurgy, alchemy, logic, theatre, astronomy and literature. During the Mughals, however, it bounced back to its early glory and the pandits of Banaras played an important part in the protection and dissemination of the Sanskrit language throughout the subcontinent. Students used to take pride in getting Sanskrit education from Banaras. Dara Shikoh, the heir apparent to the Mughal king Shah Jahan, who was later killed by his younger brother Aurangzeb, stayed in Banaras during his tenure as the subedar of Allahabad. His secular credentials were well known. He translated the Upanishads in Persian and studied Sanskrit from Pandit Ramanand, a great scholar of that era. As per the ex-mahant of Kashi Vishwanath temple, Rajendra Prasad Tiwari, the descendants of the family that taught Dara Shikoh, still live in the city.[26]

I have not been able to verify his claims, but two points are very clear that Kamlapati Tripathi's ancestors have been great stalwarts in the field of Sanskrit education and that Dara Shikoh indeed tried to restore the religious confidence of the Pandits of Banaras. During the time of the British administration, it appears that the donations and patronage from the rajas, rich merchants and the zamindars was not so forthcoming, resulting in the decline of Sanskrit education.

With the Maratha kingdoms taking control of the religious affairs of Banaras as the self-declared *dharma-rakshak*s, the situation improved. The late eighteenth and early nineteenth century saw a plethora of educational institutions being established in Banaras, based on the modern system of education. In 1792, the Resident Commissioner of Banaras, Jonathan Duncan, proposed to the governor general for the setting up of a Sanskrit College. His first objective was to collect Sanskrit handwritten books on various subjects with the help of the pandits and students, and secondly, this would increase the prestige of British among the Hindus, and such pandits would be able to emerge from the college as learned people who would help British in understanding Hindu law. Thus, in 1791, the college began and its first principal was one Pandit Kashinath. Its current Gothic-style building was constructed in 1853 and ironically named Queens College. Even today, we call it by this name or simply Sanskrit University. It is located in Lahurabir. It was declared a university in 1958 and was renamed Varanaseya Sanskrit Vishvavidyalaya, with A.N. Jha appointed its first vice chancellor. Later, in 1973, it was renamed yet again as Dr Sampurnanand Sanskrit Vishwavidyalaya. The C.M . Anglo Bengali College was established in 1898 by Chintamani Mukherjee in the Bhelupur area of Banaras. The first English-medium school, The Anglo-Indian Seminary School, was opened by Captain Thosbey in Banaras in 1830. However, Raja Jaynarayan Ghoshal is considered to be the pioneer of English-medium education in Banaras, starting a small school in 1814 with around 100 students. Udai Pratap College, Varanasi, was founded in 1909 as a high school by the late Rajarshi Udai Pratap Singh Ju Deo, Raja of Bhinaga. This is my father's alma mater, initially established for the children of the Rajput ruling families and later for poor Rajput children as well. The alumni include Arjun Singh and V.P. Singh (former prime minister). There is a saying about Raja Bhinga that he had no issues and was worried about his successor. A wise man advised him to establish a school for the boys of the Rajput community, cutting across social status. That way, he would always have many talented boys to choose his successor from the brightest students. Even Bhartendu Harishchandra took special interest in the field of education, particularly women's education. The greatest contribution to education in Banaras was made by the reformers Madan Mohan Malaviya and Annie Besant. Besant started the Central Hindu Girls School in 1898, which was to become a harbinger later for Malaviya. He proposed and campaigned for an exclusive university from 1904, Indian and to some extent Hindu, in ethos, and finally the university's foundation was laid by then Viceroy Lord Hardinge in 1916, on the land donated by Raja Banaras beyond Asi Nala in the Lanka area. Malaviya was its first VC. Kashi Vidyapeeth was established in 1921 by Shiv Prasad Gupta, a wealthy merchant of Banaras. It was later renamed Mahatma Gandhi Kashi Vidyapeeth. It is located in Sigra. Rajghat Besant School in Banaras, a resident-cum-day school, was established in 1934 by Jiddu Krishnamurti. It is named after Annie Besant and located in Rajghat.

The Church of England, along with the London and Baptist Missionary societies, is actively engaged in conveying the gospel to the inhabitants of the city and neighbouring villages by labouring with more or less efficient means of European and native agencies. The Mission associated with the Church of England was established in 1817 and includes four ordained and two lay missionaries, thirteen native Christian schoolteachers, and six readers or catechists. Additionally, there are bungalows for resident missionaries, orphan institutions for boys and girls, a village inhabited by native Christians, a Gothic church capable of holding around 300–400 persons, two normal schools—one for the training of native Christian young men as teachers and evangelists and the other for the training of native Christian young women as teachers at female schools—a large college, and several girls' schools. 'The normal schools have a catholic basis and admit pupils from all Protestant missions in the neighbourhood, who receive a good education, fitting them for employment in their several missions. The college is situated in the city and is called Jay Naayan's College, named after a native gentleman of rank (Raja Jay Narayan Ghosal), who founded it in 1817 for the education of his poorer countrymen and liberally endowed it. The government also gives a large sum annually to its funds. In 1866, the college had 475 students, and the number of native Christians in the mission was 437'. A new church was erected amid the Hindu population of the city, near to Dasasamedh ghat, now called the Girijaghar Chowk.

Jitwari

In the Vedic texts and Buddhist literature, the Janpad of Kashi has been given importance as a cultural and trading centre, unlike its attestation as a Shaiv Dharma centre mentioned in the medieval Puranas. In the second century BCE, traders referred to this city as Jitwari, which means a place that offers maximum profit. The river trade on the Ganga has been the first and foremost endeavour the residents of Kashi delved into. Not only the river trade, but if the ancient Sanskrit and Prakrit stories are believed, the traders of Kashi also ventured into seafaring expeditions through Tamralipti. This port city, also known as Tamralipta, was also the capital of the Suhma kingdom in ancient Bengal, located on the Bay of Bengal coast, reaching as far as Indonesia. There is still a locality in Banaras, called Sapt Sagar Mohalla (Settlement of Seven Seas), which has a temple where prayers are offered for *'Sapt Sagar Mahadan'* (grand donation to the seven seas). This was a tradition of expressing gratitude by the traders who successfully returned after a fruitful and profitable sea voyage. The Jatakas have also mentioned about the sea trade and specifically mention the use of Disha Kaak by the traders.[27] It's an interesting and quite original method of finding land nearby. In ancient times, sailors on sea voyages would take crows with them called Disha Kaak (direction-finding crows). The presence of the shore or nearby land was detected by releasing these crows in the middle of the sea. If the crows returned to the ship, it was understood that there was no land nearby. In the event of the crows not returning, the boat or ship was steered in the same direction where the crows had gone. Although a well-maintained road, which was later termed as the Grand Trunk Road, existed since the Mauryan times, from Pushklavati (now in the Swat Valley in Pakistan) to Pataliputra (present-day Patna) and then to Tamralipiti (present-day Kolkata), the river trade was considered safer back in the day.

There also existed a very powerful guild of traders called the Naygamya. Coins found from Rajghat testify to this. They bear names of some important traders, who were called Maha Shreshthi. By the Gupta period, these traders became very powerful and prestigious protocols similar to kings were allowed to them, such as riding an elephant. They were likely akin to the Jagat Seths of the East India Company. Prinsep has also done a painting on the Haveli of one Kashmiri Mal.[28] Merchants like Kashmiri Mal even funded the Raja Banaras and the East India Company during their war campaigns. Kashi has boasted a variety of guilds for small enterprises since ancient times. Many of these still exist in more or less the same form. For example, the Gavyak Shreni or the guild of milkmen and cow-herderers, the Varanasi aranayak Shreni, or the guild of the forest-dwellers who lived around the city and traded in a variety of forest products. Similarly, there were guilds for artisans making pottery and clay toys called the Kumbkar Shreni, and those dealing in gems, whose products have been found at Rajghat, called the Manikar Shreni. Another profession that played a crucial role in society was that of the *naat*s (performers). Belonging to a powerful guild, the Naat community, now classified under the scheduled caste category, has historically settled around urban centres. Their traditional livelihood involved juggling, acrobatics and dancing. Their very profession is to entertain people with the gymnastic and flexible manoeuvres of their body, showcasing different postures, walking on ropes and performing different types of stunts. The women among them are beautiful and skilled in performing dances and singing with suggestive gestures. They are also experts in playing different types of musical instruments and have been an important part of the ecosystem of Kashi since ancient times. During my childhood, I remember seeing their performances in the weekly markets. Interestingly, owing to their high mobility and ability to mix with the general masses, they were sometimes employed as spies by various local warlords. Stories of naat and *naatini* are narrated with great delight at the tea and paan shops of Banaras. There is a wonderful description of the rendezvous of a character in *Neela Chaand,* named Krishn Mishra, with an old naat during the Gahadavala era, who visits the hut of the settlement of the naats. We come to know that they had established their settlements at the periphery of Banaras, which was surrounded by the thick forest.[29]

The Naygamya existed until the late Mughal era and eventually converted into a kind of bourse or sarafa. The bills or sureties, known as *hundi*s, issued by these influential sarafas of Banaras were accepted throughout India and became a popular mode of payment for huge amounts. By the eighteenth century, the entire financial system was fully under the control of the Banaras Mahajans, who exercised great control over the kings of Banaras and even on the nawabs of Awadh and Bengal. The banking industry flourished in Banaras and Sherring seems astonished to find the exorbitant rate of interest that the Mahajans of Banaras charged.[30] The bankers of Banaras constitute an extensive fraternity. The habits of borrowing, and then plunging recklessly into debt, are lamentably prevalent in India. As multitudes are ready to borrow, it is a natural consequence that there should be many ready to lend, especially as the rate of interest is enormously high. This pernicious custom of society enriches a few but impoverishes many, and greatly interferes with the comfort and happiness of the Hindu community in general.[31] In fact, Vyomesh Shukla, a writer and resident of Banaras, mentioned in an interview with the descendant of such a family, Rai Anandkrishan, a startling revelation. According to him, the ancestors of the famous Bharat Ratna-awardee Bhagwan Das, gave a loan of Rs 55 lakh to the East India Company in the early eighteenth century. He emphasized that, in today's equivalent amount, this would have to be multiplied by 500.[32] The 'ancestor' referred to might have been Gopal Das Sah, who was not only the chief banker of the East India Company but also of the Nawab of Farrukhabad Muzaffar Jung.[33] The Rajas of Banaras, Chet Singh, and Maheepnarayan Singh, once faced threats from the Mahajans during a financial dispute. The famous Mahajans of Banaras were Seth Gopal Das, Ramchand, Gokul Chand, Kashmiri Mal, Sukhlal Sahu, whose families produced great stalwarts in literature (including Bhartendu Harish Chandra), business, politics, and freedom fighters (like Bhagwan Das and Sri Sri Prakash), archaeologists and historians (like Rai Krishan Das and Motichandra). All of them carried a wonderful harmony of fine taste and sophisticated, nuanced aesthetical sensibilities, along with their mind-boggling riches. Their families still continue to stay in the ancestral houses and localities established by them.[34] Prinsep describes Banaras being the trading hub, because of the large number of footfalls of the pilgrims who, to quote Eck, continue to 'vote with their feet' to establish Banaras as a pilgrimage and a trading hub.[35] His description of commerce articles are saltpetre, indigo, opium, sugar and embroidered cloths.[36] Bishop Reginald Heber, who visited Banaras when Prinsep was the district magistrate, says that Benares is a very industrious and wealthy as well as a very holy city.[37]

Banaras was well connected to Kaushambi through the river and the distance was thirty yojanas. As has already been mentioned, this river trade continued till the advent of the railways. It's again very apt to say that traditions and the ancient trading activities never die in Banaras. There are detailed descriptions of caravans plying from Kashi to different parts of the country in the Jatakas. The trade goods and related practices in Banaras have persisted since ancient times, with very old families still involved in them. The clothes made in Kashi were famous and Buddha's shroud is known to have been bought from Kashi. It was called Kashi Kuttam, Kashiya and Varanaseyak. The Periplus[38] mentions a special type of muslin called Gangetic, which was made near the Ganga, obviously originating from Kashi. The muslin called *tanzeb*, during the Mughal time, was known for its fine quality. It was particularly appreciated for its soft and smooth texture, owing to the excellent quality of cotton yield, well-trained weavers and the soft water in the region. As far as the production of silk industry is concerned, Banaras has maintained its edge and has kept its ancient historical prominence intact. The perfume industry was also renowned and called Kashik Chandan. The banks of Varuna had thick groves of sandalwood trees and this trade was specifically popular during the Mahajanapada era. My grandfather once patronized a perfume shop in the Raja Darwaja area near the chowk, which was claimed to be from the Gahadavalas's time. Even now, the *itr* (perfume) of Banaras has its own savour. The woodwork and the wooden toy industry, the trade in ivory products, especially the famed ivory bangles, are popular even now. There is even a mention of thoroughbred horse trade from Uttarapath (the northern and the north-western trade routes). An ancient ghat adjacent to Dashashwamedha ghat was called Ghoda ghat (ghoda meaning horse), where horse sacrifices were performed during the Vedic period. It also served as a trading port for horses till the late nineteenth century. *Buggies*, *tangas* and *tamtam*s (horse-drawn carriages) were a common sight on the roads of Banaras till the late eighties and at the present Godowlia intersection, there was a huge tanga stand always reeking of evaporating horse urine and dung. The Jatakas are full of stories about the traders carrying cartloads of goods in caravans to Kashi. There is also a huge population of Nishads and Mallahas, who have been involved in professions such as boatmen and fisher folks since ancient times. In the surrounding areas of the Vindhya hills, villages of bird-catchers known as *bahelia*s and small game hunters still exist. They supplied both ornamental and table-caged birds, as well as wild animal meat. References to these communities are found in ancient texts and the Jatakas. Most of them, due to the government's Wild Life (Protection) Act, 1972, have now branched out into different professions, though.

* * *

Let us look at some other names of Banaras as mentioned in the Jatakas. These include: Surundhan (protected), Sudarshan (sightworthy), Rammnagar (beautiful city) and Molini during Ashoka's era, with its capital referred to as Potli for Varanasi. It was this time that Sarnath gained names such as Isipattan (where the holy men landed), Mrigadava (deer park), Ramma (beautiful) and Sudassana (one with a pleasant appearance).The other noteworthy names that the city has been addressed by are Rudravas, Shivpuri and Shankarpuri.

Rishi Augustya, in Kashi Khand, has mentioned Kashi to be the residence of Shiva, abode of the Rudra (another name for lord Shiva).[39] The names Anandvan or Anandkanan are mentioned in Kashi Khand and the *Matsaya Purana*, denoting the time when a thick forest cover flanked the city. In Kritya Kalpataru, the reference word is *udyan*, or garden. It also denoted the convergence of the city culture with that of the forest culture. The *tap-sthali*, as it was also the land of penance, was described as Gaurimukh and Anandarupa, succinctly elaborated by Pandit Kubernath Sukul in *Varanasi Vaibhav*. The deity Vishalakshi is mentioned as residing in Gaurimukh.[40] In the Rig Veda,[41] big settlements were often referred to as *aapnanteerth* (universal pilgrimage). Over a period of time, these eventually became the centres that integrated all human activities. For many years, Kashi was also recognized as an aapnanteerth. In the *Matsya Purana*, Kashi was briefly named after its great king Alark and was called Alarkki Puri, or the city of Alark. In the healthy competition between the Vaishnavites and Shaivites over the hold on Kashi, it was also called Harikshetra (Lord Vishnu's domain) and Narayanavasa (abode of Vishnu).

In the medieval and relatively modern times, the city, by and large, continued to be called Banaras, except for a brief period, when the fanatical Mughal Emperor Aurangzeb destroyed the Kashi Vishwanath temple and renamed the city Muhammadabad, but fortunately that was only for a very short time, until his death in 1707.

The various other locutions that the city has been referred to by has been compiled by Rana P.B. Singh:[42]

City of Light, where every day the sunrise reflects on the crescent moon-shaped Ganga river, and finally illuminates the riverfront;

City of Delight, where high degrees of pleasure and joy are experienced;

City of Plight, where ups and downs always make life full of frequent and sudden changes;

City of Might, which possesses the power of feeling and attraction;

City of Sight, which allows clear vision to emerge where humanity and divinity meet;

City of Right, where all the human deeds are righteously assessed by the patron deity Shiva, who then blesses and curses accordingly.

Chapter 4

Kashi

The Incubator of Hinduism and the Saviour of Sanatan Dharma

Praayah kanduk paten patatyaryah patannapi

The above Sanskrit quote summarizes the fall and the subsequent rise of Sanatan Dharma against all odds. It literally means that a noble person often falls in the manner of a falling ball and rises again. The source of daring confidence that the Sanatan Dharma has manifested over the years comes from such Upanishadic proclamations as *Aham Brahmasmi*—'I am Brahman', as correctly remarked by Nilima Chitgopekar, is perhaps 'the boldest statement ever made by human beings in any age or part of the world'.[1]

We shall see how, amidst the threats and sometimes after almost complete annihilation, facing oblivion, Sanatan Dharma, because of Kashi, continues to have a firm grip on the Indian subcontinent. Moreover, it has preserved its essence in the diasporas to the West, in its more or less the same form as in the Middle Gangetic plains. I vividly recall a statement by the Noble laureate V.S. Naipaul which was widely quoted by leading newspapers and magazines in the political development of the nineties: 'Hindus have never gotten over their subjugation of over a thousand years by alien religions.'[2] Then, of course, my left-liberal leanings were hurt, but now, when

I read the scriptural details of my own religion, I realize the author was not very far from the truth.

Some interesting facts emerge from the Puranas and the Buddhist texts, such as that the city has been the incubator of Hinduism ever since the animist religious doctrines threatened the concept of the puritanical Vedic rituals. I must bring the reader's attention to this rather uncomfortable truth about the evolvement of the present form of Hinduism through the great theologian Ananda Coomaraswamy's sagacious observation:

> In centuries preceding the Christian era, when the fusion of races in India had already far advanced, the religion of India passed through its greatest crises and underwent the most profound changes. Vedic ritual, indeed, has survived in part up to the present day.[3]

The elite, animism, polytheism, the folk, oral and scriptural traditions have all, in unison, thrived in Hinduism and in Kashi particularly. The greatness of Kashi was not only on account of her becoming a holy city—it is rather also because it was a huge trading and cultural hub. The religious aspect was a natural phenomenon that emerged from a prosperous and satiated society. Why did the Vedic seers choose Kashi to be their focus of religious and spiritual quest?

As will be discussed in the next chapter, the overwhelming and almost primeval animist gods are still ingrained in the collective subconscious of the people of Banaras. It was here that we first came across the role of the Puranas in subsuming the importance of animist gods and goddesses and thereby, undertaking assimilation on a gigantic scale that evolved into the great religion of Hinduism. That, despite having faced innumerable challenges and ravages, continues to thrive and inspire billions of people from all corners of the world today. The Puranas are a communication with the masses about complex issues of conventions, thoughts, morals and ethics through stories. 'It appears that through mythology, society is directed to think and act in accordance with the inherent norms and our deep-rooted cultural traditions . . . These stories transmit almost all the thoughts and conventions of our culture to the next generation.'[4] However, while drawing conclusions, scholars and historians are generally careful about the chronological dates, as the Puranas have undergone multiple revisions and rewritings.

A popular story recounts Shiva fighting the Yakshas, until eventually a compromise is reached where all the Yakshas become *gana*s, or followers of Shiva. In the Buddhist text *Mahamayuri*, 'Mahakal' is designated as the chief Yaksha of Varanasi, which shall be covered in one of the following chapters, along with how the Shaivites withstood the Vaishnav cult. Thereafter, we find that the biggest threat to the Vedic religion came from Buddhism and Jainism. Their dominance was so profound that it almost wiped out the practice of Vedic rituals of *karmakand* and yajnas. In spite of these aspects, Kashi continued to preserve and keep alive the original seeds of the Sanatan Dharma. The Jatakas are stories of the Buddha's rebirth as a Bodhisattva (one who is on the way to the attainment of perfect knowledge) and subsequently as the tenth avatar, undergoing metempsychosis as Vishnu. Most of the stories are based on *rinanubandhana* (kinship based on the debt of past karmic deeds).

We also observe the gradual appropriation of Buddha as a family man and his inclusion in the Vaishnava sect as the tenth avatar of Vishnu. This is not only a skilful deconstruction of the Buddhist doctrine, but also a superimposition of trade as a means of livelihood. All the stories are centred on Kashi. Eck has beautifully surmised thus: 'While the "gods" were part of the Vedic and Upanishadic world, and were even recognized in the Buddhist world, they were never the center and anchor of that world. Not until the rise of theism did the gods take a place at the center. Many of the ritual forms of this religiousness came from the Yaksha tradition.'[5]

Vaishnavism has borrowed a lot from Buddhism. The emphasis on vegetarianism and non-violence is one example where the Brahmanical element affirmatively denounced non-vegetarianism and violence, in order to compete with the religions of Buddhism and Jainism. The Brahmins of Kashi are credited with preserving the ancient texts and literature through their *guru-shishya* tradition, sustained by the akhadas and maths, and under which, even a Brahmin householder is expected to be a scholar of the scriptures and rituals of idol worship.

However, the most brutal and violent threat to Hinduism by far had come from Muslim invaders. The details of how Banaras survived this onslaught will be elaborated later. Let me first discuss the origin and development of the Vedic way of life that crystallized into what we now call Hinduism.

The endonym Sanatan Dharma has been used to refer to a way of life and coded rituals, as described in the ancient texts of *Manusmriti* and the *Bhagwat Puranas*. 'Sanatan' means eternal and was later revived in the early nineteenth century by those who did not want to be referred to as 'Hindus' since it has a Persian origin. Scholars now suggest that: '"Hinduism" refers to a body of culturally related traditions rather than one religion and those tribes speaking Indo-European languages migrated to the Subcontinent in several waves.'[6]

Audrey Truschke is also of the opinion that the term 'Sanatan Dharma' was coined in the nineteenth century, during British colonialism. However, the stupendous living continuities that we find in the Santan Dharma quashes Truschke's premise. 'Sanatan' means eternal and 'Dharma' forms one of the four goals of life, and along with *artha, kama* and *moksha*, they are known as *purusharth chatushtaya* (quaternion collection of sutras consisting of four sections) in the Vedic Arya traditions—a concept that is evolutionary in form. According to the Vedic ideology, the foundation stone to make life successful is dharma. The meaning of the word dharma is vast and all-inclusive, and religion happens to be just a part of it, it can also be defined as: 'that whatever is not *adharma* or unrighteous is dharma'. Having a wide array of meanings and interpretations, it can refer to the rites and rituals that an avowed Hindu engages in throughout the sacraments of the life cycle, which is known as *samskara*. It includes *yajna, shasthi, shraddha* and *pinddaan* and *teerth yatra*. Dharma is also the natural law that governs the cosmos, it can be purported as ethics, also in the life of a householder, it can signify *purushartha* (literally, virility) or the just and right way to perform one's duties. However, here, we will stick to its connotation as a religion. In my conversation with Vidula Jayaswal, in her ambient erudite office at the Centre for Cultural Studies and Research, many puzzles on the origin and terminology relating to Kashi were resolved. She is of the view that it would be better to call the earliest form of Sanatan Dharma as Vedic religion, even though the former term is mentioned in *Manusmriti*. She elaborated on the religious importance of Kashi, which was much before the Buddha, who chose Sarnath for his *Dharma Chakra Pravartan*.[7] It clearly goes to vindicate the ancientness of Kashi, both in terms of a trading hub and a religio-spiritual centre that compelled even the most enlightened soul like Buddha to inaugurate his wisdom from Kashi. In Kashi, since ancient times, the manifestation of the divine is always in a perceived idea of a sacred geographical location, what the Romanian historian of religion and fiction writer Mircea Eliade calls the 'showing forth' or the hierophany.[8] In the Kashi kshetra, it is believed that the various avatars descend to interact with humans through an act of '*par-kaayapravesh*', i.e., transmigration, which would be called metempsychosis in religious lexicon.

Over thousands of years of Aryan migration to the east, from their original settlements in the Kuru Panchal region, what now comprises western Punjab, Vedic religion, too, underwent development, and new religious practices and traditions were continuously established. The Aryans in the west of Punjab looked with disdain at the territories of the non-Aryans in the east. However, as the area came under the authority of the Aryans, its prestige kept on growing and Kashi became the centre of Vedic learning. Today, the continuities of the Brahmanical religion that amaze the world should also be considered alongside its many discontinuities for a hardcore Aryan moving from their present location in the Kuru-Panchal region.

The old beliefs of the non-Aryan religions were also influenced by the rituals of the new inhabitants, enabling the transformation of religious ideologies into new forms. Similarly, the Vedic religion, too, in turn was affected by the pre-Vedic settlers' 'vegetative divinities'. The process of forging together an 'entire spectrum of beliefs, practices and experiences', as quoted by Yuval Noah Harari,[9] must have indeed been a very dynamic activity in the history of mankind for the 'horizons of possibilities' that were being unfolded in this era.

As per some theories, when the Aryans entered India, they encountered an indigenous population, whom they ended up defeating in warfare. This conquest allowed the Vedic culture, religion and language to gain dominance over the traditions of the local tribes. And with the passage of time, Vedic religion took on a new form (sometimes being known as Brahmanism).

Another very enthralling ancient philosophy that this land of Jambudweep gave to the world was the philosophy called Charvaka. The Charvaks were unabashedly materialistic and epicurean. They believe in the very rudimentary principles of human existence, equivalent to the philosophy of 'eat, drink and be merry'. Charvaka is also known as Lokayata (meaning 'of and from the people'), an ancient school of Indian materialism and atheism that does not believe in the authority of the Vedas, most likely founded by Sage Brihaspati. They outrightly rejected the existence of the ethereal, supernaturalism, ritualism, and non-perceptible entities like God, soul, heaven, previous birth and reincarnations. They were well entrenched in the land of Jambudweep much before Buddha and perhaps it was the philosophy of the masses, as is evident from its other term 'Lokayat'.

This tradition of religious development dates to ancient times. Both the pre-Vedic and Vedic systems are strikingly similar in their belief in the superhuman order, except that the Vedic religion, in their spiritual quest, propounded some mystical sutras with 'telepathy and extra sensory perceptions' that continues to perplex the scientists even today. As Professor P. Krishna has observed: 'Conscious phenomena like telepathy and extra sensory perception are as yet beyond science; but we cannot say that they are unscientific or untrue.'[10] This syncretism continued to run intact even after, and, as we will discuss, Kashi has a lot to do in this development. In ancient times, Kashi was a large territory referred to by the names 'Kashi State' and 'Kashi Janapada', whose capital was the city of Banaras.

What exactly was the religious structure that was followed by the aboriginal tribes inhabiting the eastern Gangetic plains? The inhabitants of the area, where the ochre-coloured pottery, as mentioned earlier in the first chapter, was found, were perhaps the first aboriginals whom the advancing Aryans encountered. However, Jayaswal is of the opinion that the ochre-coloured pottery was not discovered from the Kausambi region and certainly not from the Kashi kshetra. As she mentioned, the Akhta excavations have pushed the antiquities of Kashi to somewhere around 1800 BCE. Now, this gets interesting here. It means that the Vedic rituals were being followed in Aktha much before the Aryans actually came to this region.[11] When I asked her who were these people who followed the Vedic rituals and if they were the aboriginal people inhabiting the Kashi kshetra, she affirmed that they were, and quite a few of them had come in contact with the Aryans in the Kaushambi region and started following some of their rituals without abandoning their own. This has been verified by the discovery of the Yaksha image in Akhta.[12] Pandit Kubernath Sukul has also emphasized that it was not just the Vedic religion that got affected by the *shishna-deva*s (phallus worshippers). They were also inspired by the puritanical rituals of the Vedic Aryans and started imbibing them.[13] Now this was the organic syncretism of Hinduism, which was mutating and which eventually crystallized in this very region of ancient Kashi from somewhere between 1800 BCE to the third century CE. The essentials of the Vedic religion though, remained confused at this stage as the practice of 'constructing ritual homologies' has long been considered 'the quintessence of Vedic ritualism'. The overwhelming populace in the eastern region beyond Sadanira, was still *anagnidagdha* (not sanctified by fire). According to this Vedic ritual, the fire of *agnihotra* has to be taken from one place to another, in a pot, and this is the fire that is used to make the area of occupation pure or *agnidagdh*.[14] The advancing Aryans came across followers of a strange and complicated animist belief system. They referred to them as *shishna-devas*, *asura*s and *dasyu*s. In *Volga se Ganga*, there is an interesting conversation between two supposedly recently migrated Aryans, where a character says about the asuras or the aboriginals:

'I have heard that they worship phallus and genitals. I do agree that it is a source of enjoyment for the man and the woman and through which we have our descendants; but to worship them in literal form or by making its clay or stone images is purely foolish.'[15]

These tribes had dwellings in caves, tree houses, thatched huts, etc., and worshipped a plethora of animist symbols in stones, trees and hills, to which offerings of fruits, flowers and meat were made. The practice of sacrificing animals had also begun. Subsequently, the worship of Shakti or Prakriti, along with the worship of numerous village deities emerged. These gods and goddesses were different from the present-day gods and goddesses, and sacrificing animals, and sometimes even humans, was a common practice to appease them. The ritual of cremation and burial was largely the same as what is observed in some present-day tribes. Prakriti Devi, or the Mother Goddess, had the most important place. Her worship was also prevalent in West Asia at that time, and perhaps the reference in Quran to the three Goddesses—Al-Llat, Al-Uzza and Al-Manat—called the 'Daughters of Allah' in the pre-Islamic Arabia, also meant the same. In addition, a deity with three faces was also worshipped, around which figures of animals were made.

According to the scholars, this is the contemporary Shiva or Pashupati. The Shivling was also worshipped, resulting in their being condescendingly called 'Shishandeva' by the Vedic Aryans. The religion of the primitive inhabitants of Kashi also had a proper code of conduct, the glimpse of which is still visible among the people living in the Vindhyachal and Kaimur regions adjoining Banaras. Ancient Vedic texts are mostly silent on the religious importance of Kashi, but in the Upanishads, composed around 600 BCE, we do find mentions of the kings of Kashi, Ajatshatru and Dhritarashtra, conducting Ashwamedha yajna before the Shatpath Brahman, composed around 800 BCE. This establishes the fact that the religious importance of Kashi was well rooted and established by the sixth or seventh century BCE, and perhaps this was the reason why Buddha chose to propose his dharmachakra in Sarnath.

According to Max Muller, the time of Shatapatha Brahman is from 600 to 800 BC, but some modern scholars date this period till 1000 BCE. Thus, we can infer that Kashi was captured by the Aryans long before 1000 BC. Initially, when the foundation of the Vedic religion was still evolving in Kashi, only a small group of Aryans, the followers of Videh Madhav, followed the chaste Vedic religion. The religion of the aboriginals continued to be non-Aryan. Despite the absence of a tradition for converting people to the Vedic religion and no set procedure for initiating those from other religions into Arya-dharma, and even though it was considered a blasphemy for a Shudra or a Dasyu to hear the chanting of the mantras, silently and synergistically, the amalgamation of religious doctrines crept in. There was no conflict between them due to religious reasons. However, since the Aryans were establishing new states by snatching the lands that rightfully belonged to the tribals, setting up new anchorages for their farming and cattle rearing in large areas, they destroyed the forests, which were the means of sustenance for the aboriginal tribes. This led to minor battles in which more often than not, the aboriginals were defeated. While some accepted slavery, others continued to wage guerrilla warfare from the adjacent forests and hills. The Puranic tales often narrate the stories about rakshasas who created ruckus and harassed the rishis by destroying their ashrams, and then the kings would send armies to protect the rishis. Eck has a point when she writes that: 'Asuras are frequently called "demons", but we should note that they are characterized primarily by being the "other side" in the cosmic struggle with the devas, or "gods." Sometimes the asuras are not demonic at all, but devotees of Shiva or virtuous observers of dharma.'[16]

However, there is another angle to the story. It is that when the Aryans started occupying the aboriginal lands, they destroyed their forests and conducted mega yajnas that involved *havan*s on a large scale. This directly threatened the way of life and sustainability of the aboriginal tribes who were fully dependent on forests. Even Ravana, as perceived by the Gond and few eastern Uttar Pradesh tribals, 'was against the sacrificial rituals performed by the Aryans. Whenever such rituals would take place, rakshasas would attempt to create disruptions'.[17]

Interestingly, even today in many parts of the country, the tribals are protesting and sometimes taking to arms to protect their lands, rivers and forests. This continued till late nineteenth century in the famous Santhal rebellion of 1855 and the Munda rebellion under Birsa Munda, on which the award-winning novel of Mahasheweta Devi *Jungle ke Davedar* (The Claimants of the Forest) is based. It was revived in the form of Naxalism in the Vindhya hills in the early twenty-first century as well. The adherents of Naxalism were predominantly the lower castes, whom some scholars believe to be the descendants of the aboriginals who were pushed towards the forest and the hills by the Vedic Aryans. As I have mentioned earlier, the living continuities in Banaras never cease to amaze you.

Due to contiguous settlements, it was natural that the influence of Arya-dharma would affect the non-Aryans as well. In times of difficulties and crisis, some Aryans may have even adopted non-Aryan traditions by cohabitation with the Dasas or Dasyus. The non-Aryan rituals and worship were becoming a part of the Vedic rituals. Many lower rung Aryans, particularly the Shudras, were increasingly adopting the non-Aryan rituals and it was getting more internalized due to the matrimonial alliances. A new religion was taking shape. Before the Buddhist era, four types of religious belief systems and practices manifested in the eastern Gangetic plains.

> Pure Arya Dharma, Pure Non-Aryan Dharma, Hybrid Arya Dharma and Hybrid Non-Aryan Dharma. In course of time, the last two religions almost merged and only three types of religions remained. From the point of view of numbers, the number of followers of pure Arya Dharma was not very large, because only the progeny of Aryans were in this class. The pure non-Aryan religion survived only in the forests and Vindhya-mountain regions away from the city.[18]

This was the segment that eventually coalesced to form the single largest chunk of Sanatan Dharma that we more or less follow now. The pure

Vedic Aryans continued to worship their two principal deities, Varun and Indra (lord of the cosmic order and lord of thunder), amongst the pantheon of other deities. While watching the film *Mongol: The Rise of Genghis Khan,* directed by the brilliant Russian director, Sergei Bodrov, my subconscious—or to an extent, the primordial collective subconscious—romance of the Transoxiana overpowered me and I realized the diasporic culture and the genes that overwhelmed the subcontinent through centuries of intermingling. The film has a scene where Genghis Khan is shown to lead the most decisive battle that would catapult him to be the world conqueror by defying the lord of thunder 'Tengri', when he shrewdly realizes that his own troops and his enemies are horrified whenever there is a lightning and start running helter-skelter. He then decides to attack them on a prolonged stormy day but not before he had spectacularly rid his own troops of the fear of Tengri. I was struck by the similarities between the words 'Indra' and 'Tengri', who was also the lord of thunder for the Mongols and the steppe people, as well as the main god in the Turkic pantheon, controlling the celestial sphere. The Aryan god of thunder was 'Indra'. The Serbs also worship Indra, the supreme god of thunder, who battles to defend his heavenly realm known as Svarga Lok. The myth goes to project the worship of nature by the central Asian tribes, including the Aryans who migrated from this very region.

At that time, despite having so much emphasis on the knowledge of the metaphysical aspects of religion or the Brahmagyan, Vedic religion had gradually become very ritualistic. The knowledge space of the Brahmagyan was consigned only to as a subject of discussion by the erudite. The overwhelming plebeians followed their rituals of worship in an orthodox and paroxysmal manner. Some Vedic personalities, including Krishna, are said to have mused on this aspect of religious transformation and after the Mahabharata, i.e., around 1000 BCE. (The original events related by the epic probably fall between the ninth and eighth centuries BCE.) The affectionless and lacklustre worship of Indra was overtaken by the worship of Vishnu and natural symbols. Ferguson is of the view that: 'The Vaishnava faith, on the other hand, arose contemporaneously with the Sivite, on the ruins of Buddhism, but with much less of the appearance of being a local indigenous superstition . . . it found the means of coming to the surface between the eighth and the tenth centuries.'[19]

I presume that idol worship started from this very era. The process of the present form of Sanatan Dharma that we see today, thus, had started since 800 BCE. In the Mahajanapada era, belief in the Mantra and Tantra was widespread. All auspicious occasions and even sundry day-to-day affairs were performed by active consultation of astrologers. Areas believed to be inhabited by ghosts and evil apparitions were sanctified by mantras and people tied a consecrated thread on their head, even carried consecrated sand whenever undertaking a long journey. Motichandra quotes an example of a king of Kashi, mentioned in the *Dhammapada Atthakatha* (1/151), who paid 1000 pieces of gold to a Brahmin to learn some esoteric mantras.[20] During these times, when *darshan* (philosophy and scriptural muse) was the guiding path of Vedic knowledge, a substantial transformation in worship and rituals was underway. Against the Upanishadic era of yajna, havan and sacrifice, the supremacy of Shiva and Vishnu among the deities got fully entrenched. Although the havans remained an essential part of the rituals and without a havan, worship of God was considered incomplete, but animal sacrifice was performed only in the worship of the goddess. A proper code of conduct for the worship of Shakti was the prominent feature of this era. Although some religious scholars, who are ardent Vedic cult followers, like Pandit Kubernath Sukul, have argued that there is a detailed description of the various forms of Parashakti in *Devisukta* of the Rig Veda, from which it is clear that the worship of Shakti was going on since very ancient times. There is, certainly the mention of minor goddesses, but the present Shakti cult has more to do with the tribal and gram devi traditions, I mentioned earlier, predating the composition of the Puranas.[21] He also dismisses that the Yakshas were the aboriginal deities, by quoting passages from the Rig Veda and stating that they were the minor gods of the low-caste Aryans, who were offered flesh and liquor as offerings. Eventually, the Yaksha and the Naga cult were what the Vedic Aryans accepted; it was certainly the cult of the aborigines who worshipped trees and the spirits who supposedly dwelled in those trees, and even netherworld creatures like dangerous snakes. One can imagine when the advancing Aryans entered the thick, forested areas to clear the land for pastoral and agricultural purposes, cutting down trees, clearing shrubs and overcoming various hurdles. They subsequently destroyed the natural habitats of the snakes and other poisonous creatures. Many Aryans must have also succumbed to snake bites and other dreaded tropical diseases like malaria. Surely, the shamans of the local aboriginals must have convinced the more religious and superstitious Aryans to start worshipping the spirits of the forest and the Nagas before venturing to clear the forests. This is how they must have adopted the cult of the local deities. It was also a survival instinct of the Vedic Aryans to adopt and subsume the mores and the manners of their conquered land, much against their stipulations and wishes, that these deities were accepted. From the fifth and sixth centuries of the Christian era, this form of devi worship gained momentum, with the composition of *Devi Bhagwat*. Gradually, the Shakti cult started adopting a lot of Puranic formulations and eventually got absorbed in the great mythological religion of Sanatan Dharma. The famous stories of the sixty-four yoginis in Kashi Khand exemplify how Kashi, the most prominent city, became the theatre of the merger of the Shakti cult. Similarly, by the Gupta era, Yaksha and Naga worship became a part of the Sanatan Dharma ritual. After Shunga kings, Samudragupta and the Vakataka Bharashiv kings performed Ashwamedha yajna, by the advent of the fifth century CE, this form of yajna almost ended. The chasm between the Vedic Upanishad era religion and the religion that we follow today got metamorphosed, and it would not be inappropriate to term it more as a Puranic religion. The present-day Sanatan Dharma is the perfect example of such a paradigm shift.

Hereinafter, it's important for us to observe how Buddhism and Jainism became a threat to Sanatan Dharma which got eclipsed for over a thousand years and, most importantly, how Sanatan Dharma reclaimed its importance in the subcontinent. Some scholars also believe that when Buddhism and Jainism threatened the supremacy of the Brahmins, they codified strict rules by establishing the *varna* system and a Hindu law book called *Dharmashastra* got consolidated.

The Vedic religion lost out on many of its pristine cosmic rituals and succumbed to an elite class of priests. In a paper presented by Marianne Keppens and Jakob De Roover, the argument builds on the elitism of the Brahmins. They write: 'The theological and the racial—were crucial to the speculations about the Vedic people and the rise of its Brahmin priesthood.' Also, according to Keppens and Roover, Rudolph von Roth, an early expert on Vedic philology, traced the name of 'the priestly caste' to the Sanskrit word *brahma*, which he translated as 'prayer'. This etymology convinced him that the caste's origin lay in the growing importance of rituals. Consequently, a distinction emerged between the commoners, who sought refuge in the gods, and the priests, who possessed the knowledge and the authority to perform rituals. When the function of priesthood became hereditary, the families responsible for performing rituals came together as one community and after leaving Punjab they moved southwards. Consequently, conflict erupted among the different kings and their tribes, leading to a power vacuum, which the Brahmins took advantage of to rise to an even higher level by usurping the supreme position in society.[22]

Albrecht Weber, another German Indologist, told a similar story. He characterized the Shudras as the original inhabitants of India, who had been enslaved by the superior Aryans when the latter migrated southwards. These indigenous tribes—'partly black, partly brown of skin, and all of the lowest cultural level'—outnumbered the Aryans, who therefore had to unite their tribes against this 'wild force'.[23] Here, Weber followed scholars such as Müller, who suggested that the warrior-like Aryan people had reduced the aboriginal inhabitants to a state of slavery and degradation and absorbed them as the lower classes of the Hindus.[24] Weber could also access the psychology of the Aryans. He analysed that the constant battle against the indigenous people and the hostile climate had generated tremendous uncertainty among these invaders. They felt a growing need for protection from the gods and, hence, ritual and sacrifice became a crucial aspect of their religion. In this context, the Brahmin priesthood acquired its prominent position by monopolizing the knowledge needed for performing rituals.

However, one aspect that becomes clear here is that the varna system practically manifested a social ideal rather than a social reality. It was at this stage that the Vedas got a canonical status by being intertwined with the varna system.

In this entire dance of religions, the centrality of Kashi or Banaras grew manifold. The religious and philosophical ideology of this era was the natural development and transformation of the Vedic rituals. The masses got extremely disillusioned and disinterested in the Vedic Karmakand. They realized that to attain self-realization or the true nature of the soul or of the supreme spirit, only serious contemplation and knowledge is required and Karmakand, *vedadhyayana* (repetition or recitation of the Vedas) and *daan-dakshina* (alms and donations) are but a clever ploy of the Brahmins to harass and exploit them. The prevailing thought process was that Brahmagyan was far more superior to the yajnas and the *homa*s (votive rituals). Under the leadership of the revered sage of that era, Uddalaka Aruṇi,[25] a movement against the Vedic Karmakand was launched, likely laying the foundation for the tradition of *parivrajak* (shunning all worldly pleasures to be on the move). In the ideology of Aruni, there was more seeking of philosophy than the pomposity and hypocrisy of Vedic religions, and gradually, this ideology started distancing itself from the activities of the Vedic religions. This was the scenario in the Mahajanapada era when we find the luminosity of Mahavira and Buddha emerging on the horizon. There existed another religion predating Buddhism and Jainism, known as Aajeevak Dharma, which was propounded by an ascetic called Makkhali Gosala. Gosala's followers believed in intense penance and stayed naked. They were fatalists and did not believe in good and bad, and considered all forms of life as equals.

The seventh *tirthankara* or *Jina*, Lord Suparshvanatha, as per Jain records, was born in Banaras. Also, 270 years before Mahavira, the twenty-third tirthankara, Parshvanatha, was born in Kashi and made it his centre of dharma. I once visited a temple in the Bhelupur area, which is said to be located at the birthplace of Parshvanatha. The temple still exists there but is of the later Gupta era as claimed by the local seer. It has a black idol and the design is clearly based on the architectural designs of the temples from the post Gahadavala period. Since mostly Jainism emphasized on the penance and cleansing of the soul, its effect on the masses was not too endemic and Sanatan Dharma continued in its own ritualistic manner. However, when Buddha propounded his doctrine of the Middle Path and Ashtaang Marg, or the Eight-fold Path, it inherently contained fundamental differences with the Vedic religion. The masses wholeheartedly accepted this way of life and code of conduct, thereby signalling a threat to Sanatan Dharma quite like the cult of the aboriginal 'vegetative divinities'. Buddha, though he was born in Kapilvastu in the Shakya kingdom and attained enlightenment in Gaya in the Magadha Mahajanapada, he nevertheless intuitively knew the religious and spiritual significance of Kashi. He had been visiting Kashi and, particularly Isipatana, which is modern-day Sarnath, between 535 and 485 BCE. His famous Dharma Chakra Pravartan or the 'Wheel of dharma' sermon was delivered at Sarnath. The Magadha Emperor Bimbisara is known to have extended regal protection on the Buddha whenever he visited Kashi. In one of the legends, Buddha did not have enough money to cross the Ganga when he was visiting Isipatana from Uruvela, present-day Bodh Gaya. Bimbisar thereafter signed an edict, which exempted all ascetics and sages from paying any money to cross the Ganga. The purpose of narrating this incident is that despite having a massive following in the kingdom of Magadha and the royal patronage, the importance of Kashi and its religious-minded people attracted Buddha to choose Kashi for his first sermon. Buddha, through this sermon, gave the unprecedented message of four noble truths. Some of the most prominent personalities of Kashi took the path of *pravrajya* or the life of a religious mendicant. Buddhist literature and texts mentions Yash, the son of the richest merchant of Kashi, along with his parents and his four friends Vimal, Subahu, Purnajit and Gawnpati, who were the first to embrace Buddhism. There is also an interesting reference of a cocotte known as Janpadkalyani Addadhkashi, who was initiated into Pravrajya by Buddha himself. It is said that her one-day fee was equal to half of the earnings of Kashi. After initiation, she was designated as Arhat or the learned.

Another Mauryan king, the great Ashoka, did what St Constantine had done for Christianity. He adopted it and made it into a state religion, with complete coercive power of the state. Clearly, for the orthodox Brahmins of Kashi, this was likely perceived as a direct attack on the very hub of Sanatan Dharma. Thereafter, we find that there was a deliberate attempt by the Brahmins of Kashi to keep Buddhism as a fringe religion or sect—outside the limits of the sacred Kashi zone. They never allowed the Buddhist monasteries to come up anywhere in the sacred zone of the Kashi *teerth*. The choice of Isipatana was perhaps because of its centrality between three very important ancient settlements of Rajghat, Akhta and Ramnagar. Since Sarnath was the epicentre in the initial days of the growth of Buddhism, but immediately after the Magadha Emperor Bimbisara embraced Buddhism, it shifted to Rajgir and the propagation of Buddhism saw cumulative enhancement with the patronization of the emperor. Centuries after the Buddha, his dazzling message only deepened the conflict between these two important religions that continued for 1000 years. Even 500 years after Buddha, Hinayana, signifying 'the narrow path' or 'orthodox Buddhism', continued to flourish. But two new sects in Buddhism—Mahayana, i.e., 'the great path' and Vajrayana or Sahajyana, i.e., 'the spontaneous way'—threatened to implode its very basic tenets of anti-ritualism and anionic form of worship. With the intrusion of the local gods and goddesses, particularly from in and around Kashi, the appearance of many monstrous idols took place. These idols were diametrically different from the earlier calm and composed Buddhist statues. Their appearance was indicative of the decline of Buddhism that was proactively exploited by the Kashi Brahmins, the upholders of Sanatan Dharma. Both these sects increasingly and with the active support of the Brahmins, adopted and assimilated most of the gods and goddesses, including the extreme form of Tantra and Mantra from the new Vedic religions. In the Kushan era, Mahayana became the dominant sect. Many statues of Maitreya Avlokiteshwar have also been found from Sarnath. The popular Tantric deities of Vajrayana, Padhpani, Tara and Pragyaparmita occupied the faithscape in this era. However, till the initial Gupta period, Hinayana—the original Buddhist tenet, of the non-idol worshippers—continued to have its sway. Some of the Vedic gods quietly passed into oblivion and some were being reborn as new gods with additional attributes, as per Romila Thapar.[26]

While the assimilation of religious ideas and rituals was by natural process, the appropriation was by design and with intent. This intent was to save the ancient Sanatan Dharma from being subsumed by the plethora of theological and hieratic movements. When these two new religions—Buddhism and Jainism—did not accept the beliefs of the Vedic religion, such a situation warranted that a proper answer be given to their objections and rebuttals for the survival of Sanatan Dharma. For this work, there was a need to systematize the form of theology of the Vedic religion, in which appropriate answers could be given to the arguments of the opponents. This upheaval between dharma and faith necessitated a cognitive avocation that led to a new thought process that we now term as the Upanishadic ruminations. This arrangement created the six main philosophies of the Vedic religion: Nyaya, Vaiseshik, Samkhya, Yoga, Poorvmimansa and Uttarmimansa (Jurisprudence, Specificity, Statistics, Yoga and Inquiry into or the interpretation of the first or mantra portion of the Veda and Vedanta metaphysics).

The composition started from the sixth century BCE and continued for almost 400 years. Kashi remained the navel of all such metaphysical developments. Right from the second century BCE, when Patanjali established his ashram in Kashi, many, even after touring the entire Jambudweep, came back to establish their ashrams and centres of learning, like the philosopher Adi Shankara in the eighth century CE, theologian Ramanuja in the eleventh century CE, their followers Madhava and Vallabha, the Tantric Gorakhnath cult, Aghoris and many more. The rise of sectarian religious reformations had started by the Gupta period and was consolidated by the end of the seventh century CE.

On the basis of these philosophies, the scriptures of the Vedic religion started moving away from Jainism and Buddhism that continued till the eighth–ninth century CE. The talent of Shankaracharya and Kumaril Bhatta, a Chandal from Kashi who gave Brahmagyan to Shankracharya, devastated the arguments of the Jain and Buddhist scholars and subsequently the sway of Jainism and Buddhism among the masses gradually eroded. During the debates, large public events were organized, and the common man understood the concept of *jaya* (victory) and *parajaya* (defeat). Unlike the Gladiatorial era morbidity of the ancient Roman empire, the duels in the ever-secular and eclectic Sanatan Dharma and its opposing religions were limited to verbal calisthenics by both the parties and it was a display of *shaastrabal* (ethological and scriptural might) and not *shastrabal* (the might of the weapon system). They were the primogenitors of 'the argumentative Indians'.

Kashi was throbbing and reverberating with the chants and rituals of Buddhism, Vaishnavism, Shaivism, Sauraism (sun worship), the Pantha cult (started by a person called Pantha in Kashi), Pushtimarga of Vallabhacharya, and the Shakti cult. It was during this time only that we find the statues of the vegetative divinities taking anthropomorphic and zoomorphic forms. Some were the mythical lion or tiger, *shardula* or *vyala*, the many-winged beast *suparna*s, *makara*, etc. Even aniconic religions such as Jainism and Buddhism started imagining their seers in idols. The present sculptural and the few remaining ramparts of the architectural marvel are the achievements of this era. It was indeed a period characterized by artistic, cultural and at that time by default a religious refinement extending particularly in Santan Dharma—truly a belle époque.

However, from the late Gupta period and establishing its deep roots by the Gahadavala period, a significant aspect within Hinduism was the cult of *jaadu-tona,* i.e., witchcraft and sorcery. We observe that in these years, all the primordial practices of the aboriginals were sanctified and ritualized. The age-old Aryan fear of the Shishnadev worshippers took on a new form through the Shivling and the associated ritualism of tantras in the form of the Shakti cult.

Priest and dharma teacher Rami Sivan has surmised these developments quite precisely:

> In the Vedic period the pre-eminent form of religion was the sacrificial (yajña) paradigm. This elaborate and extremely complex paradigm had nothing for the common folks and was accessible only to the upper elite who had the vast amounts of money necessary to sponsor them. They were secret and exclusive and based on the Vedas - known as NIGAMA. At the same time, there was a parallel system of religion known as AGAMA, which served the needs of the common folk. So today 90% of modern Hinduism is Agama-Purana based with the foundation still being the immutable Vedānta.

The unnecessary trivialities of doctrinal minutiae were squabbled, and long philosophical debates took a back seat by the end of the eleventh century. In Banaras, since that time, the East is somehow connected with jaadu-tona, particularly in the areas of Bengal and Assam. I tried to find out a few instances explaining why Banarasis have such a strong bias against the far-eastern areas. I came across a dialogue between a member of a royal family and a weaver of Kashi in *Neela Chand,* set in the Gahadavala era. When asked by the weaver about the royal member's origin, and he says that he is from Bangbhoomi (Bengal), the weaver shrieks in fear and says, 'Oh my God! I have heard that the sorceresses of the place turn the men into a ram and tie them in their courtyard!'[27] The fear of the East is so potent that the most popular and famous thumri singer of Banaras, Girija Devi, has a thumri rendition: '*Poorab mat jaiho more raja ji . . . goriya ki lambe lambe kesh, ulajh mat jaiho more raja ji . . .*' (Do not venture into the east, oh my darling . . . The fair maiden has long hair, do not get entangled, oh my darling . . .).

With the decline of Buddhism and the resurgence of Hinduism, many Buddhist places of worship were converted into temples along with their statues and bas-reliefs, and their building materials were used to erect new temples. Many such temples have been listed by James Princep, M.A. Sherring and by Motichandra. Even Charles Allen, in his book *Ashoka,* has convincingly postulated that most popular and famous Hindu temples were erstwhile Buddhist structures with an array of Buddhist icons, in the form of deities, images and even lingams. He further challenges the Brahmanical Order, when he says that the most striking evidence of Brahmanical hostility towards Buddhism came in the form of silence: the way in which India's Buddhist history . . . was excised from the historical record.'[28] Nowhere is this triumph of Brahmanical order, or Sanatan Dharma, better encapsulated than in Banaras. We have numerous statutes where a giant Brahminical *yyala* (lion) is sculpted over a Buddhist elephant, deliberately projected to be dwarfed. However, Pandit Kuber Nath Sukul refuses to endorse such archaeological analysis and is of the view, like all Kashi Brahmins, that those places of worship have always been of Vedic and Brahmanical religion.[29] Well, nobody can argue against faith with a Banarasi, after all. There is, at present, a raging controversy in Tamil Nadu,[30] where Buddhism was a dominant religion throughout. Many statues of Buddha are still being excavated from the state. In a small village of Periyeri, the Hindus worship a local deity called Thalaivetti Muniappan, which literally means the headless Muniappan, that is contested by the Buddha Trust to be the statue of the Buddha. The matter is sub judice at present. Incidentally, in the Gurudham Colony area in Banaras, there is a Murikatta Baba, a headless statue of a sitting sage.

Both these new religions were essentially Indian, and they grew symbiotically with the Vedic religions, but after around the eleventh century, a very different kind of religious creed (Aqidah) and doctrinal movement convulsed Hinduism. It was an attack by Islam in my opinion.

> These are the laws and the rules which you must carefully observe in the land that the Lord, the God of your fathers, is giving to you to possess, as long as you live on earth. You must destroy all

> the sites at which the nations you are to dispossess worshipped their gods, whether on lofty mountains and on hills or under any luxuriant tree. Tear down their altars, smash their pillars, put their sacred posts to the fire, and cut down the image of their gods, obliterating their name from that site.[31]

No, dear readers, these are not quotes from the Qur'an; these stanzas are from the fifth and last book of the Torah, containing a second statement of the Mosaic Law (in Judaism), where it is called Devarim and is the fifth book of the Christian Old Testament. In fact, Islam borrowed largely from the already prevalent scriptures of the Abrahamic religions. Kashi had seen many invaders before, but for the first time, a cult of vicious upholders of the faith of Al-Qur'an, under the guise of plunderers and looters, threatened to brutally erode every aspect of the antiquity and sacredness of Kashi. Islamic invaders, in their virulent religious frenzy, have left a festering wound in the collective subconsciousness of the Banarasi people.

The wholesale destruction of sacred shrines in the subcontinent has been dismissed as 'a lust for plunder', unconnected in any way to Quranic injunctions. In a definitive enunciation of this viewpoint, Muhammad Habib declared that the expeditions of Mahmud of Ghazni, in the last half century and more, were not crusades but secular exploits waged for the greed of glory and gold.[32] Habib's assertions were perplexing, given the Qur'an's explicit hostility towards idols and idolatry. Before the Islamic advent, idol worship was widely prevalent in Mecca, as attested by Ibn Ishaq (d. 768–69), the earliest biographer of the Prophet.[33] The Prophet himself led the destruction of 360 idols around Kaaba. Among them were statues of the moon god Hubal, Abraham and Ishmael.[34] It was an assault on the idea and the sacred space of Banaras; loot and plunder was secondary, because since the times of Janapadas, which included the Sakya Muni as well, to 'capture' the sacred faithscape of Kashi meant 'capturing' the whole of Jambudweep and beyond.

Barring a few instances of armed sectarian struggles within Sanatan Dharma, the use of weapons was never there, but the invasion by Islam was dominated solely by the force of arms. Initially, in the subcontinent, wherever the Muslim army was victorious, there was the choice between death or conversion to Islam. The first Islamic attack on Banaras was for plundering and not strictly to spread Islam, which occurred in 1034 CE, led by Ahmad Niyaltgin during the rule of the Kalachuris.[35]

Following this, a general of Mahmud of Ghazni's nephew Masood Salar, Malik Afzal Alvi, along with some soldiers and followers, attacked Banaras but were defeated by the armies of the Gahadavala ruler Govindchandra. Most of the soldiers were killed, but their women and children surrendered and were given areas to settle around the city. These places are still called Salarpura and Alvipura. In this first attack of Muslims on Banaras, the Hindus won. The Gahadavalas in the eleventh century, like even the Marathas later, took upon themselves to protect Hinduism, canonically proclaimed and sanctified by Kashi Brahmins, who had declared that the sunset of Gahadavalas will be the sunset of Hinduism.[36] By this time, they had realized that it's as much a religious war as a war on the most sacred site of the Hindus. After it was declared the capital of the Gahadavala rulers, the centrality of Kashi as a religious and political entity got enhanced. This phase of Banaras saw a supernova-like explosion. After a long spell of inertness, proliferating cosmic debris of culture, trade, pilgrimage and Sanatan Dharma combined together to make Banaras an enviable place to stay in those times. Perhaps the reason for the importance of Kashi as a pilgrimage was also because of the eulogistic texts written by Govindchandra's minister, Bhatt Lakshmidhar. Even though the remnants of Buddhism persisted amongst the elite, the Gahadavala rulers had undertaken the construction of many temples. Govindchandra, whose wife was a practising Vajrayani Buddhist, constructed the Vishnu Adi Kesava temple at Rajghat, and the Karmadeshwar Shiva temple at Kandva village near the city, dating to around the tenth century CE. However, it most probably was built by the Kalachuri kings, as they were strong Shaivites and the Gahadavala rulers followed a Vaishnavite tradition. They could have renovated or built upon the already existing structure. Both these temples still exist and perhaps are the oldest surviving temples of the city. The Gahadavala emperors took pride in considering themselves as the rulers of Kashi. Tenth-century south Indian inscriptions suggest that there was no greater sin than killing a Brahmin or a cow in Kashi of that time. Not known to many, in response to the dreaded tax Jizya, and due to the call by the furious Hindus for retribution in equal measure against the extreme oppressiveness of the Muslim rulers, Govindchandra levied a similar tax on his Muslim subjects, calling it Turushkdand, literally meaning punishment or fine on the Turks. But the Gahadavalas were finally defeated by Qutb ud-Din Aibak, and the fort and Rajghat settlement totally destroyed. It was a time of great distress for the Hindus and for Banaras, where more than a thousand temples were desecrated and razed, and the immense wealth of the city and the temples were carted on 1400 camels to Ghor in Afghanistan. *Taj ul-Ma'ashir*, a contemporary work, claims that after the defeat of Jayachandra in 1193 CE, the Turkish soldiers destroyed nearly a thousand temples in Banaras alone.

Many new mosques and *dargah*s were constructed brazenly using the rubble of the destroyed temples with the motifs, frieze, cornices and carved statues still intact. Some important ones that still stand are Razia Bibi ki Masjid behind the Adi Vishveshwar temple in the Chowk area, Dhai Kangura ki Masjid near Hanuman Phatak, Chaubees Khambon-wali Masjid near Chaukhamhba, Maqdoom Saheb ki Kabr in Gulzar mohalla and other mosques in Rajghat near Palang Shahid.

Aibak, for the governance of Banaras, in 1197 CE, appointed one of his officers, who strictly followed the religious intolerance of his master and made every effort to abolish idol worship. Due to the terror of the Muslim rulers, the broken temples remained as they were. Despite all this, the Vedic rituals continued in low tenor and Hindus became all the more rigid in following the religion. The temples of Banaras were gradually rebuilt by 1296 CE.

In 1302, a person named Veereshwar built the temple of Manikarneswar and, in 1296 CE, one Padam Sadhu built a huge temple named Padmeshwar at the entrance of the Vishweshwar temple. After the death of Alauddin Khilji in 1316 CE, the oppression was somewhat relaxed and the gradual reconstruction of temples once again started in full force. There is no clear mention of the demolition of the temples of Banaras during the Tughlaq reign, but there are a few mentions of mosques being built in Banaras using the ruins or rubble of Hindu temples, especially during the rule of Firoz Shah Tughlaq in the Bakariya Kund area. Sherring, though, is of the view that it was the remains of Buddhist *chaityas*.[37] Firoz Shah was a patron of the cult of Ghazi Mian, who is interestingly worshipped in the form of *lat* (pillar) by both Muslims and Hindus alike, at the Lat Bhairava site located in Idgah. Firoz Tughlaq also reinstituted the dreaded Jizya tax on Brahmins, who had earlier been exempt from paying it. However, when the Brahmins refused to pay and sensed trouble, the prominent, rich merchants and mahajans paid the tax on behalf of the Brahmins of Kashi.

Meanwhile, in 1393 CE, a new state named Sharqi was established in Jaunpur, whose ruler was responsible for the promotion of Islam. He built many mosques in Jaunpur, using stone pillars and other materials from the demolished temples of Banaras. This construction spree continued from 1436–80 CE. After the Sharqi kingdom of Jaunpur came to an end, Banaras was ruled by the Lodis from Delhi. Sikandar Lodi was a staunch Muslim bigot, who was given the title of 'Ghazi'. He, too, continued the destruction of temples and the killing of Brahmins. The Hindu dharma, continued to be a congeries of many faiths and sects. Barring the few spurts of temple construction by the Rajput rulers, who were advisers and ministers in the Mughal empire during Akbar's reign (1556–1605 CE), the later Mughals, by and large, followed a detached policy towards Kashi, and this gave a lot of impetus to the revival of Sanatan Dharma. However, during Shah Jahan's rule, once again, a bigoted attempt was made to demolish Hindu temples. However, two important temples—Vishweshwar and Bindu Madhav—were constructed in response to this. The latter was built by Maharaja Mansingh of Jaipur in 1650, while the temple of Vishweshwar was built in 1585 CE by King Todar Mal on the request of his guru,

Panditraj Bhattnarayan. It is said that Raja Mansingh had vowed to construct 1000 temples in a single day—a mammoth task, which was nevertheless accomplished by sculpting a few holes and prototypes of the temples in many stones. Vishweshwar and Bindu Madhav temples were unique in their time, but by the orders of Aurangzeb in 1669 CE, along with all the temples of Banaras, both these temples were demolished. Aurangzeb built four mosques in Banaras, three of which were constructed on the rubble of the famous Hindu temples of that time. The mosque that was built in place of the temple of Vishweshwar is still known as Gyanvapi Masjid, while the Dharhare-wali Masjid at Panchganga ghat replaced the Bindu Madhav temple. Another mosque, known as Alamgir Masjid, was constructed in place of Kirtivaseshwar temple. More recently, it has also been contended that mosques built of temple parts displayed 'a productive engagement with local traditions of temple architecture'. The reuse of temple columns in mosques required careful architectural planning and conformed to indigenous principles of design. The most elaborately carved columns were placed on either side of the *mihrab* aisle, and simpler columns in the remaining spaces. What occurred was a mere 'translation'; one type of sacred space was translated in terms of another. In the process, a certain degree of communality between the two was also communicated. The most touching account was given by Lord Valentia, in his 1803 book, which he wrote when he visited the destroyed site of Bindu Madhav temple where the Alamgiri mosque has been built. He expresses his feelings in the following manner: 'The mosque with its minars was built by Aurungzeb to mortify the Hindoos. Not only is it placed on the highest point of land, and most conspicuous from being close to the river, but the foundations are laid on a sacred spot, where a temple before stood, which was destroyed to make room for it.'[38] Furthermore, he goes on to propose a solution to it as well: 'I felt myself sufficiently a Hindoo when viewing the lofty minars, to wish that hereafter Government may restore the spot to its original owners, and remove this cruel eye-sore from the holy city.'

In 1809, Lat Bhairava, in the Jalilpur area, saw a fierce Hindu–Muslim riot, in which the entire Lat Bhairava was destroyed and the place violently desecrated. It has been ascertained that the Lat notwithstanding all these attempts, did not fall till they sprinkled it with the blood of a cow and her young, which they had obtained from a garden and dragged them, tied by the neck, to the spot. Like the fallen pole of the Indra festival, the Lat itself is said to have been thrown into the Ganga about half a mile away, whereas the physical probability is that the sandstone largely crumbled under the heat of the fire.[39]

Most of the Western writers and scholars, such as Sherring, Kennedy, Prinsep and Eck, who have written extensively on the Hindu religion, and Banaras in particular, are appalled at the wanton destruction and audacious superimposition of Islamic structures on the temples and at the sacred sites. Even Meenakshi Jain, in *Flight of Deities and Rebirth of Temples*, appears to be partially correct in the context of Banaras. While Somnath was looted for its wealth and no mosque was constructed, in Banaras, the Islamic rulers derived perverse pleasure not only in looting the temple but also in desecrating it. They did it in a manner that made it impossible for any Hindu rituals to take place at that location, leave alone rebuilding the temple.[40]

Aurangzeb later issued firmans for the reconstruction of many temples in Kashi and provided grants to religious scholars, as has been collected by Shree Bishambhar Nath Pande in *Aurangzeb ke Farman.*[41] Yet, in the subconscious memory of a Banarasi, even after 1200 years, the Muslims have not been forgiven for this act of transgression that shattered the faithscape beyond redemption. I have come across many seemingly liberal-minded intellectuals of Banaras, who either maintain a studied silence or more often than not agree that the Muslims did indeed dishonour their sacred city.

The choice to construct mosques on the holiest of temples, like the Bindu Madhav and Vishweshwar temples, seems deliberate in hurting and devastating the core religious sentiments of the Hindus. However, a different analysis is presented by Richard M. Eaton, an American historian, on the allegedly diabolical Muslim rule and the plunder of the city by the victors, often orchestrated by religious zeal and greed. He says that the explanations given for the destruction of temples by the zealous Muslim rulers were the religious hegemony. However, another theory given is that such contestations were religious alone. The Hindu temples were destroyed by the Muslim rulers as 'they serve the repositories of authority used to further their patron political ambitions'.[42]

Due to the violent threat Hinduism faced from the Muslim conquerors, it became more rigid, and that put a heavy burden on the practising Hindus during the Middle Ages. Banaras fought back and became the centre for the revivalism and redeeming of Sanatan Dharma, but at the same time, it also became the centre for all types of religious and social exploitation, being the premier pilgrimage of the Hindus. For once, the Brahmins of Banaras, as mentioned by Jawaharlal Nehru, faltered to save Sanatan Dharma, when the ruler of Kashmir requested them to allow the converted Hindus back to their religion.[43]

The religious gullibility of the masses, particularly of the pilgrims, which is present even now, was exploited by both the Brahmins and thugs of Banaras alike. The belief in 'the sacerdotal order', 'mediators between man and God', existence of *betaal*s (goblins), mantra and tantra, and other forms of black magic pervaded the masses. These types of superstitions were then further exploited by the pandits and the *ojha*s (shamans). The social dogmas are still well ingrained in the gullies and mohallas of Banaras. As children, we have come across many such grotesque forms of social stigmas. In our mohalla, one of our relatives' daughter-in-law was from a noble family of Rewa state. She was very beautiful; we called her 'Cheeni Bhabhi Saheb' because of her slightly Mongoloid features; whenever we used to visit their place, we were told to avoid her and not go near her. Later, we came to know that she was a declared *baanjhin* (women who can't give birth) and was supposedly a 'bad omen'. She was treated miserably and later our cousin married another woman. Even then, they faced fertility issues. In all certainty, it became evident that he had some medical problems, but the absence of advanced medical facilities and the prevailing social malaise of misogyny just exacerbated the situation. In another instance, the wife of a carpenter in the outhouse quarters of our compound once gave birth to a deformed baby boy with an unusually large head and just one eye in the centre of his forehead. The news immediately spread that an incarnation of Shiva was born, attracting people from all over for darshan, but the baby passed away soon after.

Under such a social scenario, a strict form of idol worship commenced that denied entry to all marginalized sections of the society, including some upper-caste women during certain times. Widows were particularly castigated, and we will see how Hinduism, through various movements, reformed to remedy the inherent cancer that was eating up the essence of Sanatan Dharma. The eleventh- and twelfth-century thinkers and religious commentators, like Kshemendra and Krishna Mishra, alerted the masses and religious leaders about the growing maladies in the society and in Hinduism. The Smarta Brahmins had started a codified system of ceremonies for death and marriage, which was reintroduced during this time, but there was no large-scale reformism. During this time, large-scale conversions began since Islam did not have untouchability and caste discrimination. So, by embracing Islam, the Hindus earlier belonging to the untouchable castes found liberation from this social disdain. Like in the past, once again, many religious leaders came forward to save the Hindus from conversion. Sant Ramanand was one of them. Though born in south India in 1299, his education took place in Banaras, where he established his sect and preached equality and co-dining among all castes.

As the literature of the Bhakti Marg expanded, serious efforts were made to strengthen the simpler aspects against the puritanical and doctrinaire insistence on worship. The religious sentiments of the Hindus, which had been flowing since the time of Vallabhacharya, were further nurtured by Surdas, Tulsidas and all the other devotional saints and poets of Braj literature. Banaras, in this area, has also made a huge contribution. Ramanand's disciple, Sant Kabir, carried forward his teachings, but unlike his guru, his preaching was more inclusive and syncretic—there was contempt for religious hypocrites and only love was considered divine. Another important sect, the great Aughar tradition,[44] also got impetus during such religious upheavals. It was made prominent by Baba Kinaram, who accepted only the most downtrodden as his disciples. Unlike Kabir, Ravidas and most of the other Bhakti movement preachers, Baba Kinaram was from the revered Kshatriya class, born in a village close to Banaras called Ramgarh, where he established a huge ashram. His presence extended into the city limits with an ashram in Krim Kund, New Colony, that is a pilgrimage centre for many. I once visited his ashram in Ramgarh and the famous well that is located there, renowned, like the Dhanvantri Koop in Banaras, to have medicinal properties. Surprisingly, even in the era of RO water, I found this well's water refreshingly sweet and energizing. A story that I had heard before from my brother-in-law, Pramod Singh, whose family is a descendant of Baba Kinaram's clan, was recounted again by the chief priest of the ashram that day. It is said that once, Baba Kinaram decided to visit Banaras, so his followers started making all logistical arrangements, but Baba stopped them and asked them to meet him at the Krim Kund in Banaras. He then jumped in this well and appeared at Krim Kund.

Another reformist of that time was Vallabhacharya, who was born in 1477 CE. His early education took place in Mathura. After his father's death, when he was just eleven, he left his home and later came to stay in Banaras, where he composed his commentaries on Vadrayan's *Brahma Sutra* and Shri Bhagavad Gita. The sect of Vishuddhadvaita or Pushtimarg started from Banaras itself. The well-known Bhakti movement in which Kashi holds a special reference is the outcome of this era.

Tulsidas, a staunch Brahmin, was a folk poet who dreamt of a utopian society, an ideal family and an ideal relationship. He brought the extravasate stream of Sagun and Nirgun Bhakti on the same platform, with its attendant ideals that saved Sanatan Dharma from falling in a deep pit, ironically, due to the puritanism of the Kashi Brahmins, during the Mughal era. Tulsidas wrote many of his books in Banaras; he is the product of his social milieu. He composed the *Ramcharitmanas*, for which the puritanical Brahmins threw his manuscript in the Ganga for writing in local language, which was Awadhi, and he was even stoned by the Brahmins whenever he would cross a locality near his residence. The area Bhadaini, near Assi ghat, where he stayed, is named because once when Tulsidas was asked to come from that locality to a place where he was invited, he refused by exclaiming that he could not because that place was *bhay-dayeeni* (a place that creates fear in the mind).[45] Five centuries later, a similar humiliation was perpetrated upon Raja Ravi Varma, when he started painting the popular mythical gods and goddesses and brought them out from the confines of the temple. Tulsidas and Ravi Varma salvaged the Hindu religion at a time when it was heading for disaster. They brought the tenets and icons of Sanatan Dharma to the hoi polloi out from the clutches of the puritanical Brahmins. Just imagine if the Ramayana had continued to be in Sanskrit and the images confined within the four walls of the temples; Santana Dharma would only have survived with the vestiges of the 'elitisque' pomp and splendour. Ravi Varma's biopic *Rang Rasiya*, a film by Ketan Mehta, has a spectacular scene depicting a group of fringe Brahmins destroying his painting exhibition.

Tulsidas also started the festival of Ramlila, involving the masses, but not before venting his extreme anger and frustrations on the prevailing religious and social environment in his another classic *Vinay Patrika*. The practice of worshiping Hanuman became stronger with his reintroducing the *bhakti bhav* or the devotion of Hanuman towards Lord Rama, and it is said that he himself made twenty-four idols of Hanuman, which are established in different parts of the city, including the famous Sankat Mochan Hanuman temple of Banaras. To establish a Vaishnav icon in a predominantly Shaivite Banaras of 'Kashipuradhipati', Tulsidas resorted to an interesting and clever literary device—a genre of narrative technique that is often called 'intradiegetic' narration. In *Ramcharitmanas*, the ruling deity of Kashi, Shiva, narrates the entire story of Manas to Uma, his consort, as a 'heterodiegetic' narrator. Hanuman is the most agglutinative and emblematic deity in the mythological corpus of Hinduism. Hanuman is the best example of the plurality of Sanatan Dharma, where both the Vedic and Agamic traditions of India come together to create a character as rich and diverse as has been in ancient Kashi. He is mentioned in Jain and Buddhist scriptures as well. An avatar of the Vedic Rudra, in Valmiki Ramayana, he is portrayed as a superhuman with prowess and strategies of a soldier, but Tulsidas imagines and creates the character of a loyal devotee, which fits in the Vaishnava Bhakti movement of that era. Hanuman traverses quite smoothly from the most compassionate bhakt to the tantric cults and mysticism. Another style that he introduced to manifest the love for the lord was *kirtan*.

However, some documents prove that Ramlila has been an older tradition and existed in the Banaras region even before Tulsidas. The oldest director of *Ramleela Meghabhagat* directed Ramlila in 1543 and Tulsidas himself has mentioned watching such 'leelas', but Tulsidas certainly made it a more public event.[46] Lilas were associated with the philosophy of the Bhakti movement, which embraced all sections of society, and thus displayed 'positive strengths of their own'. The decentralized nature of Hinduism also ensured that devotees could worship their deities at home when temples were under siege.

The original handwritten manuscript of *Ramcharitmanas* is preserved at the Tulsi Manas mandir, near Durgakund in Banaras. The most revered, Sant Ravidas, again born and died in Banaras, was an untouchable from the shoemaker class called *mochi*, but it is said that his grace was so radiant that even the high-class Brahmins revered his doctrine. Like Kabir, through his simple verses, he conveyed the most complex of life philosophies, his most famous one being *'mann changa to kathauti mein Ganga'* (if the mind is pure, then one can find the river Ganga even in a pot). However, gradually, puritanical Brahmins started perceiving the Kabir Panth and other such reformists as another form of threat to Hinduism. As mentioned earlier, even a pious Brahmin like Tulsidas was harassed by the puritanical Brahmins. Once an acquaintance, who is related to Tulsidas's family from his mother's side, told me that Tulsidas was cursed by the Kashi Brahmins and even now the children born in that family show traces of mental disorder. The fallacy spread by the fringe Brahmins, so much so to protect Sanatan Dharma.

After 1708, with the rise of the Marathas, Banaras suddenly became the cynosure of the eyes of all the prominent Maratha chieftains. The fascination of the Maratha kings and chieftains for Banaras was so great that the king of Jhansi, Raghunath Hari, during the peak of his rule, who was widely renowned for his religious piety, died by suicide by drowning himself in the Ganga in Kashi, in 1794. Colonel Sleeman, his friend, however, has said that since he contracted the disease of leprosy, he volunteered to leave kingship and offered himself to Lord Shiva.[47] Such acts were considered the most devotional at that time. We will explore this more in the chapter on Shaivism.

Culture and Power in Banaras states that: 'While this Maratha desire to exercise direct political control was thwarted when the British replaced Awadh as ruler of the area, the Marathas remained culturally important in the city of Banaras itself . . . Marathas financed much of the eighteenth-century Hindu reconstruction of the city, which encompassed rest houses for pilgrims, temples and feasting to support Brahmin priests.'[48]

Incidentally, Gaga Bhatt, one of the most prominent scholars and a respected Brahmin of Banaras in the seventeenth century, the great-grandson of Narayan Bhatt, is also accredited with accepting the offer for the coronation or the 'Rajyabhishek' of Shivaji. Most of the orthodox Maharashtrian Brahmins and the Kashi Brahmins had refused to perform this important consecration ritual for the imperial crown, considering Shivaji to be of Shudra origin. A religious frenzy in all aspects of life, particularly in the construction of ghats and temples, not seen before, vigorously began in Banaras. After a gap of nearly 500 years, a zealous and uninterrupted development of Banaras started. Despite this, serious damage was caused to the temple building's art and architecture. Lack of royal patronage to construct temples and statues resulted in most of the artists and sculptors either turning towards other sources of livelihood or sculpting cheap statues that could be purchased by all and sundry.

The temple building complex aesthetics was the biggest casualty. Towards the end of the eighteenth century, when the political climate of Banaras had stabilized largely under the British rule, the reconstruction of temples resumed in Banaras, mainly by the Marathas, and this continued till the beginning of the nineteenth century. Although the end of the eighteenth century marked a decline for arts and aesthetics, its impact is unmistakable in the temples and sculptures of Banaras. The temples of this era can be revered but not admired from the point of view of art.

Sherring has mentioned about a Gujarati Brahmin named Gor-ji, who in the late nineteenth century tried to restore the old statues and temples of Banaras and as per Sherring, Gor-ji has done more for the revival of Hinduism in the city, rivalling the Marathas and the Rajputs. His restoration efforts focused on the temples mentioned in Kashi Khand.

Most of the present temples and ghats like the Kashi Vishwanath mandir, Annapoorna Devi, Kaalbhairav, Trilochan and Sakshi Vinayak have all been the contribution of Queen Ahilya Bai Holkar of Indore and the Maratha chieftains. Rani Bhavani and Jaisingh of Amer had also significantly contributed to redevelop Banaras as the hub of Hindu pilgrimage, but more than any royals, it was the people of Banaras who took the lead in safeguarding the religio-cultural ethos of the city. They simply did not bow down to either the dictates of the alliance of the ruler—priestly authority—or to the anthropological speculations about the 'primitive man' and his 'magical thinking'. Rather, as has been argued in the preceding paragraphs, they struck to the age-old hand-me-down version of Sanatan Dharma.

Even though the initial invaders had desecrated and constructed mosques on the ruins of the temples, many later Muslim religious sects accepted the Hindu tenets and its inherent metaphysical rituals of idol worship. This was most profound in Banaras that mid-wifed a syncretic religio-cultural ethos, which gave Banarasi culture a unique flavour and status. The continued amalgamation of worship and rituals at the shrines and former temple sites witnessed the development of a symbolic emplacement that blended egalitarian Islamic ideals with the Hindu scriptural doctrine. Ghazi Mian and Lat Bhairava are some of the examples. Even the Europeans were allowed to enter the temples. The lower-caste Muslim weavers, especially, never forgot their Hindu origin, and their primordial subconscious memory of the Yaksha worship got intertwined with the cult of Ghazi Mian in the worship of Lat Bhairava. When Aurangzeb came to know of the subtle influence of Hinduism on the Mohemmedans, he went on another temple destruction spree and even destroyed the ancient 'Parishad'—educational centres of learning in a decree in 1639.[49]

However, this extreme bigotry was only with Aurangzeb. The sacred and divine quality of the Ganga water was so widely putative that when Muhammad bin Tughlaq shifted his capital from Delhi to Daulatabad in 1340 CE, the Ganga water was brought by his runners by traversing around 1500 km. Akbar always used Ganga water for his daily ablutions and cooking. He believed it to be the water of immortality. Jahangir, too, was highly fascinated by the Ganga water. Surprisingly, according to the French traveller François Bernier, who was also a personal physician to Aurangzeb, the emperor only used Ganga water.[50] Banaras has had a profound impact on many, including Ghalib, who was enchanted with the city's devotional moorings; we shall discuss about him later. Prominent Sufi saints carried forward the spiritual aspect, which had a strong local infusion of belief and rituals. Muslim fakirs, among whom Khwaja Muineeddin Chishti, Alibin Usman Alhajbisi and Shaikh Ismail Bukhar are remarkable, spread the message of love and equality, but according to Pandit Sukul, the spies of Ghazni maintained contacts within their *khanaqah*s and mosques. Their spiritual powers impressed the Hindus, eventually leading some to be convinced enough to embrace Islam.[51] However, no historical evidence is on record on this claim by Pandit Sukul. We will elaborate how the initial bigotry of the Banaras Muslims evolved into respect, admiration and even shared beliefs, underscoring the Islamic influence on popular culture that is quite apparent now.

Ever since the influence of the British started increasing in India, in the last century, a new crisis came to plague the Hindu religion. This was the attempt by the Christian priests to convert Hindus into

Christians. Many Christian missions in India engaged themselves wholeheartedly in this work. They established many schools to promote general education. Along with that, efforts were made to shape public opinion back home regarding the heathens and pagans of the uncivilized world who were seen as candidates to be civilized, i.e., the acceptance of the biblical doctrine. The Bible was taught under the subject of moral science. Hospitals were established by the different missionaries, providing free healthcare to the poor. Large-scale conversion also started. This had a limited impact on the upper classes and similar to the initial phase of Islam, it remained a proselytizing force among the common people.

I remember our days in Smith's Junior High School, where the administrator was a retired Irish sergeant from the Second World War, whom we called 'Big Uncle'. His Indian wife was the principal, whom we called 'Big Auntie'. The school was located in a small enclave of Anglo-Indians, which went by the name of Isayee Gaon (Christian village), with English cottages and beautiful gardens. I remember learning the psalms and participating in the Nativity play. I can still sing all the Christmas carols. It's interesting how certain memories stick with us, despite the school's stance on capital punishment—literally rulers were used to hit us on our palms while spanking and pulling of ears were considered minor punishments. An all-out convent style education, which did not have an iota of inputs from any other religion. We behaved like good Christians in school but when back home, our grandmother and my elder uncle chanted mantras from the Vedas and narrated tales from the Mahabharata and the Ramayana. Hanuman Chalisa was regularly recited, and needless to say, all festivals and pujas were diligently and ritualistically performed. This I narrate because I feel that this kind of schizoid existence can only happen in Banaras. We grew up comparing the stories of the great deluge, the birth of Christ and the cruel Jewish kings with that of the Mahapralaya, Krishna's birth and Kansa's cruelty, respectively. Reading the *Jataka Tales*, *Chandamama* and the likes, kept us rooted, but yes, I also ate my first *bade ke kebab* (buffalo meat steak) sold by an Anglo-Indian hawker, whom we lovingly called 'Harvey Uncle'. He used to sell small burgers with the kebab filling, and he was the only outsider who had an access inside the school campus. While all types of meats were staple for us, consuming the meat of a buffalo, that was considered to be beef, was a big no-no! When my uncle got to know about this, I remember being sprinkled with Ganga water, followed by chanting of some mantras for purification, and this ritual would continue for a few days; but I must confess, I surreptitiously continued to eat those yummy kebab burgers. I have come to realize the importance of religion not merely in a ritualistic and abracadabra manner, as often portrayed in worship. Instead, we were raised to perceive it in its inherent cultural and aesthetic context, which essentially forms the raison d'être for one's personae and the growth of overall sense and sensibilities.

Despite our school being patronized by all the who's who of Banaras, I remember an attack led by some Sanatanis that became violent and damaged the facade of our school. Big Auntie was also manhandled. The group wanted the school to stop teaching the Bible. However, the gentle pull of Sanatan Dharma is so strong that now, when I meet my Anglo-Indian and Christian classmates in Banaras, they follow more Hindu rituals than perhaps even I do, staying out of Banaras now. They visit Vishwanath-ji, Sankat Mochan and other city deities, and of course continue to attend the thinning strength of the Sunday mass with their old parents.

The missionaries found a ready ground to indoctrinate the innocent and deeply religious people of Banaras. Conceptualizing that if the deeply blindfolded religious followers of the citadel of Sanatan Dharma, i.e., Banaras, can be convinced somehow to follow the teachings of Jesus, it will certainly have a domino effect throughout the country. The leading Jesuit and author of religion in Banaras of that era, James Kennedy, wrote that if they were able to have some major conversions in this holy city of the Hindus, then: 'The news would soon spread that Hinduism was drying up at its fountain, and that its power could not much longer be maintained.'[52]

Sherring, for example, eulogizing at the same time, almost acerbically chastises the Hindus of Benaras.[53] However, when he realized that it is very difficult to penetrate the protective armour of the intensely sacred Sanatan Dharma with biblical edicts, he vents his frustration when he says that 'Benares . . . is a city wholly given to idolatory', and mind you, Sherring was a Jesuit missionary first and then a scholar and thinker. He further optimistically says that the chances of Christianity and the teachings of the Gospel are very bright. 'If Christians in India be faithful to themselves and to their Divine Master, the triumph of their cause is certain.'

At the height of British imperialism, this priest got away lightly on such blasphemous statements on the sacred Sanatan Dharma.

A vile and subtle attempt was made by the early-eighteenth-century missionary priests like Van Der Hey: 'Such is the order, which the Creator has determined for that particular thing', which in other words meant: 'Nature is the law and god is the legislator, without whom there would be no law'.[54] He noted that the doctrines of the Brahmins 'clearly show some traces of the great truths concerning the eternal and immutable existence of god, the creation of the world, and the fall of humanity from its original state of innocence and happiness'.[55] The biblical chronology also came in: despite the Hindus being among the most ancient peoples, the author claimed that they appear to have no knowledge or memory of the deluge. In any case, the few traces of truth should not delude us about the idolatrous character of this people: 'While the Brahmins are convinced of the unity and spiritual existence of the Supreme Being, they nevertheless maintain the worship of a multitude of idols of different names and imaginary dignity.'[56] Alas! The dream of all these eighteenth- and nineteenth-century evangelicals, who aimed to replace Sanatan Dharma in Banaras, was shattered. Today, the teachings of Brahmins and other luminaries of the Vedic philosophy are spreading the different aspects of Indian culture, like the gentle lilting Indian classical music, the nuances of Vedanta, sagaciousness of meditation and yoga and the efficacy of organic Ayurveda, to the ever-expanding aficionados in the West and the other Islamic nations. There was another minor threat from within Sanatan Dharma, which was more of a competition with other denominations. This culminated in the late nineteenth century with the rise of the Brahmo Samaj that liberally borrowed from the Jesuits to genuinely reform the grotesque aspects of Hinduism. Other movements like the Arya Samaj, completely negating idol worship, the Radha Soamis and the Ramakrishna Mission also played a crucial role during this time. Even though the aim and preachings of these factions were reformist, they sometimes did create deep schisms in the Hindu society. This dichotomy within Hinduism was similar to the Catholic–Protestant division in Christianity and the Shia–Sunni conflict in Islam, albeit unlike Islam and Christianity, it was more on the *shaastrabal.* Banaras rejected most of these, but it does host a sizable number of maths and establishments of the adherents as it has done since ancient times. Between 1927 and 1930, Dayanand Saraswati visited Banaras six times. Under the symposiarch of the king of Banaras Ishwarinarayan Prasad Singh, a great debate on the relevance of rituals and idol worship took place. Even though no clear consensus of Jaya and Parajaya was established, Dayanand left Banaras almost chastised. In fact, even today, the Gangaputras, i.e., the Nishads, the Kewats and the Nau (barbers) influence the visiting foreigners more to follow the Hindu philosophy of acceptance of death and enjoyment of life than the puritanical Brahmins. We have had ample examples in the world of the religious centres that revived their religio-cultural space even after hundreds and even thousands of years of occupation and superimposition by other cultures.

In Turkey, the old Byzantine yolk was thrown and the Hagia Sophia mosque, which was initially a Byzantine church that was converted into a mosque after the Arab conquest, was reclaimed by President Recep Tayyip Erdoğan recently, after the secular government of Mustafa Kemal Pasha had converted it into a museum in the aftermath of the abolition of Caliphate. Spain is another shining example when they defeated the moors in the Christian Reconquista in 1492 at Ahambara. The Jewish state of Israel was formed in 1948 after the great exodus in the thirteenth century BCE. Although the *Moor's Last Sigh* did not ever take place in India, a syncretic tradition has still evolved but at the same time, without addressing the ulcerated inheritance of loss of a wounded civilization.

Some thinkers do entertain the concept of Akhand Bharat, although whether it will ever be realized is a hypothetical presumption. One thing is certain though, that it will not be a political system; whether it becomes a religious or cultural entity, I think Sanatan Dharma has a great soft power to gradually influence and inveigle those who are yet to embrace its essence. Allen Ginsberg, in one of his interviews, commented on this unusual phenomenon of Sanatan Dharma: 'The greatness of India I saw was the absorption into Hinduism of all the gods—the western ones and the Buddhist ones—and the open space, the accommodation to all varieties of human nature, and I would imagine the curse of India would be this exclusiveness.'[57]

From this point of view, it is closer to being a cultural entity. As this young writer Vyomesh Shukla from his Banaras themed memoir *Aag aur Pani*, elegiacally says: 'The qualities of Nirguna are Rama and Saguna is sleeping in the mosque . . . All the symbols of the identity of Banaras are its lost deities. They stand along with the endless queues of devotees coming out of their temples. Time is sitting in the boat.'[58]

This idea has been wonderfully articulated by Amit Mazumdar in his article in the *Times of India* mentioning about the builders of the magnificent Angkor Wat that even at the height of the Chola empire, they never conquered South-east Asia and the builders were local dynasties, only the idea was transferred. 'The South Asian Kingdoms quickened into feats of architecture were native dynasties. The Indians who transmitted this new dharma were there by invitation. They did not impose it by force. They did not have to. Indian civilization was charismatic enough, even without hard power.'[59] In addition to this, Amit also mentions that 'the challenge for India will be how to maintain its distinctness in an increasingly globalised world. India's extraordinary cultural diffusion has always coexisted with extraordinary cultural permeability'.[60]

This charisma emanates from the patience, determination, confidence and the sense of being a *vishwaguru* (world teacher)—qualities that the sacred geography and by-lanes of Kashi and Banaras have endorsed for ages.

Chapter 5

The Yakshas and the Nagas

A Fable Agreed Upon

Years ago, our house help, Chotka, which means 'the little one'—actually, nobody bothered to find out his real name; he was called Chotka due to his exceptionally small size—appeared mysteriously, as if from nowhere, in the veranda of our house in Banaras, on an insanely cold evening in January. Hungry and shivering uncontrollably, he was wearing navy-blue half-pants and a torn, white terylene shirt. He was scrawny, undernourished, with soot-black glistening skin. His sparkling set of white teeth was the first to be noticed through his permanently grinning face. Much later, we came to know that he was from a tribal hamlet in southern Banaras, near Mirzapur. Chotka was unbelievably agile and ate kilos of steamed par-boiled rice, only with raw onions, green chillies and salt. I must have been around nine or ten years old, and Chotka immediately became my accomplice in the juvenile crime that we both planned and executed with cold-blooded finesse. He was also a good fighter in our mohalla gang fights. The baddies in our locality called him *kareeva moos* (black bandicoot) and had even composed a ditty: '*kareeva moos, billi mein ghoos, le lemonchoos*' (black bandicoot, go furrow in a burrow, dandy on lemon candy). On a particularly hot and sweltering afternoon, on those long, extended summer holidays, when our creative escapades and skylarking were at their peak, Chotka and I decided to go on a bird-catching spree.

The heat was so intense that even the otherwise chirpy and irritatingly energetic bulbuls (nightingales), wagtails, mynahs and harils (green pigeons) had holed themselves in the thicket and the low bowers of the neem and mango trees. This area was in the backyard of my house. We spotted a well-fed haril nestling on a low branch of the neem tree. Thrilled, we were about to catch it, when suddenly I saw Chotka trembling with fear. He grabbed my hand and said, 'Let's go from here, Bhaiji, Barham Baba is resting on this tree.' 'Barham Baba' is the local term for Yakshas. He pointed towards the main trunk of the tree, where I saw a vermilion mark, red threads, a broken earthen pot and a handful of rice scattered on the ground. Adamant on continuing with our adventure, I tried to assuage Chotka's fears, but he would not budge, and instead, dragged me as far away from that tree as he could. Tree worship continues to be a dominant form of worship even today, as we often see in all the prominent temples of Banaras, where the tree is treated as an idol to worship the Yaksha or the spirit residing in that. Most eminently, it is found in the ancient worship of the peepal tree near the Gyanvapi well, adjacent to the Kashi Vishwanath temple. In earlier times, *bali* and *narbali* (animal and human sacrifice) was prevalent, but with the appropriation of the Vaishnav cult, it was gradually ceased and now only vermilion flower garlands, sacred threads and oil lamps are used.

Though I did not realize it then, now, when I read the *Jataka Tales* and am familiar with the animist symbols of veneration mentioned in them, I understand that Chotka's reaction was a result of the folk tales and oral traditions about the Yakshas, passed on by the ojhas, down the generations over the centuries. A trader-traveller in the Jatakas, about 1500 years ago, would have reacted in a similar manner. This chapter will narrate the traditions of these ancient deities, their places of worship and origin of their being subsumed in the larger pantheon of the present form of Hinduism, along with their traditions related to the Yakshas and the Nagas that are still followed in Banaras. *A Dictionary of Mythology* mentions Yakshas to be another name for rakshasas, who were 'beings with some characteristics of the gods, who were violent and malevolent. They had magic powers and could take on any form at will. Kuber was the king of the Yakshas.'[1] Similarly, it defines the Nagas as 'a group of serpents, appearing sometimes with human shape or as monsters, but generally simply as snakes, who were known for their strengths and deception. The Nagas lived below the surface of the earth, in a kingdom of magnificent palaces, temples, and great buildings of all sorts. Their ruler was Vasuki'.[2]

Both these anthropomorphic creatures were presumably pre-Aryan gods, worshipped by the local tribes inhabiting the area around Banaras. Their appropriation in the form of Hindu gods and goddesses constitutes a major chunk of folklore, which later got incorporated into the Puranas as well. In fact, the true fusion of Agamic and Vedic practices can be traced down at least in the Kashi region from the wide expanse of disparate worship traditions and cults.

The traditions of the Yakshas and Nagas are more exuberant and are not as meticulous as the ritualistic worship of the main pantheon of the Hindu gods. The intriguing question of who exactly these aboriginal gods were and how they impacted the worship pattern of the people of Kashi is indeed fascinating. The religion was called Yakshadharma, i.e., the religion of the Yakshas in which many hamlet deities, guardian angels and directional devis all fused together. They included rakshasas, Gandharvas, yakshis and yoginis (the seductresses), Ganas and Ganesh (the troops and their leader) and Bhairava (the fearsome). As highlighted in the previous chapter, the present form of Hinduism is significantly different from the fundamental and core aspects of the Vedic religion. It is much later, and particularly in the epics, that we find the innumerable gods and goddesses and the cult of the localized deities taking deep roots in the religious disposition of Kashi. Among the deities of Indian folk religion, the worship of Yaksha was at one time the most prevalent in the subcontinent. On one hand, Yakshas, as an identity, are mentioned in the Rig Veda, Yajurveda, Atharva Veda, *Brahmana, Upanishad Grihasutra,* Purana, Jataka, *Digha Nikaya,* other texts of Pali literature, Jain Agama literature, *Bhasya, Churni Katha* and poetry of Sanskrit literature, among others. On the other hand, they are worshipped in their most terrestrial form as the form of Bir-Barha that is prevalent even today, especially in Banaras. This 'tree and serpent worship'[3], or more precisely, the Yakshas and the Nagas, are worshipped more in their primitive form as symbols of fertility and rainfall. Later on, they became associated with the deities related to disease.

The word 'Yaksha'—first mentioned in the *Jaiminiya Brahmana* as 'a wondrous thing'—was a 'spirit' associated with Kubera (the chief of Yakshas). Much later, the Yakshas were collectively invoked in the *Grihya Sutras*, where they, with a multitude of other major and minor deities, were classified as Bhutas. It is quite apparent that the Vedic Aryans knew the strong pull of these vegetative divinities and have cautioned their fellow Aryans from even venturing near the Yaksha places of worship. In the Vedic codes itself, 'Yaksha' was celebrated as a wonderful, beautiful, great and priestly deity, the proof of which is found in the Rig Veda. The most remarkable distinction of the Yaksha was his wonderful or unique form. In one of the Mantras, it exhorts: 'My dear strong friend and Varuna, all your subjects are beyond wisdom, in whom neither a miracle nor a Yaksha is seen—Oh friend and Varuna with amazing power let us inculcate the same miraculous and amazing powers of the Yakshas.'[4] This mantra discourages the worship of the Yakshas by elaborating that 'when even you possess such powers, why do we need to worship Yakshas and why should he come closer to us?'[5] The mantra's euphemism suggests that those with undeveloped intellects, still dormant and unawakened, should be inspired from the wonderful or miraculous gods like the Yaksha. However, another mantra contains a strong advice, almost a warning, that: 'If a neighbour or a relative of ours goes to the Yaksha Sadan (Yaksha place of worship), O Agni, do not sneak into his place.' 'Neighbour' here, means the non-Aryan caste, who believes in Yakshas, and 'if any misguided Aryan starts worshiping Yakshas, then Agni, the great god of Aryans, should not mix with him even by mistake'. The mention of Yaksha's house or place is worth noting, where mere entrance could become the cause of being declared a social pariah. In about four mantras from the Rig

Veda, while mentioning the Yaksha deity, there is a clear inkling of avoiding or staying away from the Yakshas and his being inferior to the other deities. But in some places in the Rig Veda, as mentioned earlier, there are mentions of Yaksha being beautiful and handsome. It has been said in the *Grihya Sutras* that a Brahmachari, newly entering the Vedic learning phase, should visit his acharya and should pay homage to the erudition of his acharya and his educational centre, and thereafter wish to cultivate these feelings of becoming as dear as a Yaksha in the eyes of the institution.

यक्षमिव चक्षुषः प्रियो भूयासम

yakshamiv chachhushah priyo bhooyaasam[6]

Even Buddha had cautioned that all the common people should know that Gautama has risen above from such confused and hypocritical practices, such as the Aditya (sun) worship, Yaksha worship, 'invocation' of gods, faith in the burning light in the forest, etc. Quite apparently, many of the Buddha followers continued Yaksha worship and that is the reason we still find a plethora of such deities in the Buddhist literature.

Yakshas, by name, or as a cultish deity, are much more familiar figures in the epics and the Jatakas, always in the form of beings frequenting forests and mountains. The Ramayana mentions worshipping them for 'spirithood and immortality'. The Mahabharata provides an elaborate classification of people based on their different *pravritti*s and *guna*s (tendencies and qualities of the body types) to please the gods for their benediction. Hence, the men of the *Sattavik* (pure) class, worship the gods (devas), those of the *Rajasik* (passionate) class, Yakshas and rakshasas, and those of the *Tamasik* (dark) class, pretas and bhutas. Thus, the Yakshas are ranked below the devas, but above the goblins and ghosts, and this is how they have been distinguished from the bhutas, but very often, they are not clearly distinguished from the devas and the devatas. The Yakshas are sometimes sylvan deities while other times, they become coterminous with the rakshasas. So, even though they share a common origin, the Yakshas are portrayed as having both kind and violent qualities, whereas the rakshasas are always depicted as extremely malevolent, violent and cruel.

In a *Jataka tale*, when the Bodhisattva embarked on his journey from Banaras to Takshila, he encountered a Yaksha who questioned him and then asked him to stay because the Yaksha intended to make him his meal for the day. In response, the Bodhisattva assured the Yaksha that he had trust in himself and then proceeded to attack the Yaksha using all his learned skills with the sword, bow and arrow. Even though the Bodhisattva couldn't inflict even a minor injury to the Yaksha, the latter, feeling remorseful, pondered over how he could consume such a brave man who possessed great confidence and dreamt of conquering the world. Eventually, he let the Bodhisattva go.[7]

In the Mahabharata, there is a dialogue between Yudhishthira and a Yaksha, which is in the form of question and answer. The famous *Yaksha Prashna* (riddle of the Yaksha) features the Yaksha as the questioner and Yudhishthira as the representative of religion who answers. Much before this, there already existed a tradition where the complications of life were resolved by asking questions from the Yaksha. The *Yaksha Prashnottari* of the Mahabharata was an integral part of the folk literature. Some of the questions and answers given in the Yajurveda's Brahmodaya episode, between Hota and Rajamahishi, are those which have been given a place by Ved Vyas in *Yaksha Yudhisthira Prashnottari*. This is a unique and the most significant example of the combination of folk literature with Vedic literature. In fact, Chotka always used to solve some of our childhood problems, like that of finding a lost ball, winning the kite flying competition or the likes by telling me that he is going to put this question to the Barham Baba. Then he would shout and pose the question and wait for the answer. After a few minutes, he would announce that Barham Baba will tell him in his dream. A recent Kannada film *Kantara*, which translates to 'the forest', is based on the theme of the collective subconsciousness and an animist belief system. The plot line involves the revenge of the deity, presumably a Yaksha. The story revolves around a king with a vast kingdom and a happy family, who, despite his success, struggled to find inner peace. So, while searching for the elusive peace, he comes across a stone that is worshipped as a local deity, Panjurli Daiva, who is the protector of the village. He donates land to negotiate for the stone, which is then willingly handed over to him by the villagers. However, the deity warns him that neither he nor his descendants should reclaim the donated land, as it rightfully belonged to the forest dwellers, and if he reneges on his commitment, the deity's companion, the ferocious Guliga Daiva, will be extremely retributive. Over time, the land becomes a bone of contention between the villagers and the independent state. Ultimately, human perfidy is punished by the Yaksha, emphasizing the repercussions of violating the sacred agreement.

In Kashi, the word 'Barham', a local Bhojpuri word for the Sanskrit *Brahm* for Yaksha, is prevalent in the surrounding areas till today. The Kashi Khand narrates the story of Harikesh, the son of a Yaksha called Purnbhadra. Harikesh was an ardent devotee of Lord Shiva, who was given the post of Dandapani (staff-handed policeman) by Shiva himself. He is worshipped as Mahakaal in Banaras, depicted with a club in his hand and a dog by his side. A terracotta toy, found from Rajghat, bears exactly the same features. It is mentioned that since childhood, his playground was the precincts of the Shiva temple and he followed a puritanical lifestyle, unlike other Yakshas, who used to be present at the most haunted places to consume cannabis, flesh and alcohol. Harikesh, on the other hand, only ate the prasad that was offered as *naivedyam* or offerings to Shiva. His father strongly objected to him not following the Yaksha dharma and asked him to leave his house. Harikesh then came to Kashi and, through strict penance and devotion to Lord Shiva, was blessed by the god. Harikesh, in its Yaksha form, is worshipped even today, and has an important place in and around Kashi, renowned by the name of Harsubaram in Chainpur, around 80 km from Banaras. Motichandra and Kedarnath Sukul differ on this. The two aspects of Hinduism are very clear here: Shaivism and Yaksha dharma had a tussle between them, and the Puranic storytelling, particularly in the Matsya Puran, of how

Shaivism replaced or rather embraced the old Yakshadharma. Over time, by the Gupta era, Shaivism became the dominant religion of Kashi. In the Matsya Purana, most of the Yaksha names mentioned have eventually transformed into the Ganas of Shiva in Kashi. Examples include Vinayak, Kooshmaand, Gajtund, Jayant, Madotkat, Mahakaal, ghatakarn, Dandchandeshwar and others. The appearances of some of them were horrendous, some had theriomorphic faces of lion and tiger, some were hunchbacked and dwarfish, but all were moustachioed and with a big belly. In most of the old localities of Banaras, paintings of such depictions find prominence, particularly after the Gahadavala period, adorning the walls, especially after the whitewashing of houses right before Diwali. These are called *chitru rach*, *duar mand* and *chauku poor*. Another example of the ancient Yaksha puja that we find in Kashi is seen in the worship of Bhairava. Banaras had a horrendous tradition of *agnipat* or *agnipatan*, meaning self-immolation—throwing oneself into the fire to please Lord Shiva—and this continued till the beginning of the nineteenth century. Prior to the commencement of this practice, Bhairava, in its most ancient form, was worshipped, and his detailed scroll painting known as *pattachitra* was created. In this painting, Bhairava was studiously depicted as menacing and formidable. He had twenty-five arms adorned with bilboes, shield, prong, wheel, elephant hide, *khaṭvāṅga* (a long, studded club originally created as a weapon that Shiva-Rudra carried as a staff weapon), *vajra* (a thunderbolt or mythical weapon, especially one wielded by the god Indra) and the *damaru* (pellet drum). The Yakshas were extremely short-tempered and vindictive. There is yet another interesting story in one of the Jain scriptures, about the wrathful nature of the Yakshas. A sage named Matang was camping in Banaras, and because of his ethics and manners, he attracted the attention of one Yaksha called Gandi Tinduk, who became his follower. During his preaching trip, the local princess spat on Matang, finding him to be extremely unkempt. The Yaksha got annoyed by the princess's behaviour and possessed her and forced her to marry the sage.[8] In the lanes of Banaras, the traditional Yaksha paintings that adorn the walls are a fearsome depiction of a man with the caption

Bhairava Bhishanamah or Bahirava, the fearsome. However, it is important to note that they were helpful and women desiring children used to worship the two major Yakshas—Manibhadra and Purnbhadra. They also cured people from various diseases. There was another strange belief that Yakshas also made love to women.

One of the names of Kashi was also Brahmapuri. The abode of the Yakshas has been called Brahmapur. In the Atharva Veda, there is mention of Brahmapuri surrounded by nectar and Vapushman Mahakaya Yaksha (*atmanavadayaksh*—the corporeal Yaksha) living in it. It contains a spiritual description of the human body, with symbols culled out from the ancient Yaksha worship. From the philosophical point of view, it has been explained that by controlling the six enemies of lust, anger, greed, pride, attachment and the body, a person attains the happiness akin to that of a Yaksha, while living in his abode of Brahmapur. In ancient times, Brahma was synonymous with Yaksha, and Yaksha puja is called Veer Brahma puja. The unique aspect of Brahmapuri was that it was believed to be the abode of nectar. Yakshas are considered to be associated with nectar; hence, this Brahmapuri is also called Aparajita. Legend goes that there was a treasure of *hiranya* (gold) in this Puri, and the *akshaya kosh* (bountiful treasure) of gold was always considered in place of Kuber. A Yaksha with a big belly used to reside in this Brahmapuri, many sculptures of whom have been found in Rajghat. Kubera is also known as Jambhal Devta in the Buddhist literature and was of non-Aryan origin and is believed to have possessed the secret knowledge of the nectar. Thus, the desire to get the nectar was the strong attraction at the core of Yaksha worship. This likely influenced the minds of the Vedic people, who started to follow folk religion to a great extent. Yaksha idols are shown holding a pot of nectar in their left hand. Due to the association with nectar, the place of Yakshas was called Avadhya or Aparajit, signifying fearlessness in the face of death. Later on, when the rituals of Yaksha were adopted for other deities, Vishnu worship incorporated many aspects of Yaksha worship. In the idols of the Kushan period, Lakshmi is depicted as the wife of Kubera. In the Ramayana, the term Kubera bhavanopamam has been used for the accumulation of wealth. Kubera was the patron of merchants, and it must be remembered that Kashi was more of a trading hub, much before it became a pilgrimage, and its treasures and opulence was widely known. In the Rajghat chapter, we have seen how guilds of traders even influenced the decisions of the kings. The statue found at Rajghat, which is that of a pot-bellied man, no doubt, was a statue worshipped by the traders. Even Ganesha is a Yaksha, going by his big belly and the general character of him being worshipped particularly for pecuniary benedictions. As per the Kashi Khand, Ganesha is mentioned as one of the Ganas of Shiva, who was appointed as 'Dehli Vinayak' (guardian of the boundaries) by Shiva himself. Located in the western part of the city, this deity guards the buried treasure, with a metaphysical interpretation underscoring the importance of the kshetra for attaining moksha. Nilima Chitgopekar agrees to this possibility in the following words: 'There is also a possibility that Ganesha evolved from the Yaksha tradition. The discovery of an elephant-headed Yaksha sculpture dating back to the second century CE in a temple in Amravati reinforces this idea.'[9]

Ganesha's worship as the Vighnaharana (remover of hurdles) further highlights this aspect of him being a Yaksha. However, Ganesha's popularity and his reincarnation with the various pantheons is directly connected with the rise of the Shaivite traditions. The very origin and subsequent myths of Ganesha indicates a very complex interplay between the Vedic and non-Vedic spheres. Many consider Ganesha to be a totem of some Dravidian tribe. It is likely that sensing the usefulness and the physical power of animals like elephants and the bulls, they were domesticated and assigned a divine status. This era certainly predates the Vedic period.

There is also an intimate connection of the Yakshas with water cosmology. The lotus and the conch represent Kuber's inexhaustible treasuries. In the famous incidence of the Yaksha prashna in the Mahabharata, there is a pond where the Yaksha lived, and the Pandavas came there to quench their thirst. Kuber also controls the rains essential to prosperity.

In Banaras, as we shall see, the Yakshas are considered to be the Ganas of Lord Shiva. Most of the ancient pools in Banaras have a shrine in the form of a Yaksha under a tree. Yakshinis, too, were extensively worshipped in Banaras, in the form of the sixty-four yoginis, Shitala Mata and various other devis. They continue to be worshipped almost in their same medieval cultish form. The temple of Shitala Mata is located behind the present Kaalbhairava temple. The yakshi sculptures always share a common motif, depicting them clinging or leaning on a tree—particularly the Ashoka tree, as it has medicinal properties essential for the biological and natural health of women. The *salabhanjika*s, *vrikshika*s, *surasundari*s (the celestial beauties) and the Aranyani (goddess of the forests) of the Vedas—as we have seen that in the ancient names of Anandvan and the Nandankanan for Kashi, the Aranyani becomes significant. Two very insignificant from the Puranic scriptures but extremely popular deities are the Vindhyavasini, who are perched on the Vindhya hills around 65 km away from Banaras, and Mundeshwari devi in the nearby Kaimur hills, who must have been a form of the Vandevi or Aranyani, later integrated as Yogmaya and Narayani, who are the deities symbolizing the cycle of life, reproduction and fecundity. Most of the Banaras citizens visit their shrine for the *mundan* (tonsuring) ceremony of their firstborn child. In her theriomorphic form, Ganga is always shown riding a crocodile. There is a story of Shiva being expelled from Kashi and his re-entry, involving the expulsion of Divodas (in another myth, he is defeated by king Bhadrashrey of the Haihaya dynasty), who, in turn, had a rakshasa expelled from Kashi, hints at intonations of old aboriginal lingam worshippers and followers of Yaksha dharma being expelled by a Buddhist king. However, later, the same rakshasas, known as Nikhumb and Kshemak, are known to have ruled over Kashi, and later in the Puranas, the expulsion of Divodas is glorified by the Vedic version of Shiva. This story is elaborated in the next chapter.

Archaeological evidence from Bairath has unearthed Stone Age tools, insinuating the earliest existence of tribal confederations, but here, it is important to point out how Buddhism replaced the old Yaksha dharma and later Buddhism itself was subsumed with the Vaishnav and Shaiva dharmas. The Jataka stories are one such scriptural example of this. Set in a tight template woven around the kingdom of Kashi, there was a king called Brahma Dutta. His subjects encountered several obstacles from the reigning deities of the trees and forests, as well as the serpent gods of the water bodies—the *vandevta*s and *vrikshika*s. Eventually, all such vegetative divinities accepted Buddhism. The Jatakas are not just imaginary appropriations of the Yaksha dharma but are also a narration of the everyday life of the ancient Banaras.

Banaras does not let its deities go down into oblivion; we still find the residual elements of their worship. The ancient Yaksha images of Nikumbha, Virupaksha, Dandapani and Mahakaal are all worshipped in the precincts of the sanctum sanctorum of Banaras—the Kashi Vishwanath temple. During visits to the outskirts of Banaras, it's common to find such local deities called Birs, who are placed under a sacred tree or on a raised platform. These are similar to the ancient abodes and shrines of the Yaksha known as Chaitya and are quite often located outside the city amidst a cluster of trees or within the niche of the wild grasses. This raised altar is referred to as *veyaddi*. During the aboriginal phase, the sacred places of the Yakshas and other gods were under the open sky and later enclosed by walls. Instead of idols, symbolic representations made from a lump of clay or bricks, akin to the statue of the Goraya Deva, were used. The creation of giant statues of Yakshas in anthropomorphic forms began around the Mauryan period, in around the second century BCE, and in the same style, statues of Vishnu, Shiva and Buddha were also created. The statues from Rajghat and Akhta in Banaras, dating back to around the first–second century BCE, have established these ancient and perhaps the oldest idol worshipping rituals. Yakshamurtis (Yaksha idols) are supposed to be the most ancient of Indian idols. Some scholars, like Coomaraswamy, believe that the inspiration for creating idols of Buddha came from the earliest Yaksha idols. The excavated Yaksha idols have all been found to be well adorned and detailed—wearing a turban on the head, heavy earrings in the ears, a flat *kantha* or ornamented necklace around the neck, a triangular necklace on the chest, bracelet in the arms and an armlet in the hands. Their hands were in a straight standing posture, with a shawl as the upper garment and dhoti as the lower garment. The right hand was raised up and the left one was kept swinging. The imitation of these features can be found in later Bodhisattva and Vishnu idols as well.

Yaksha worship was very ritualistic, and its offerings ranged from various flowers, garlands, incense, lamps, scented offerings to prasad and music. Gradually, the same pattern started for the worship of Brahmanical deities as well. These practices are still identical among the contemporary devotional cults.

The Gita refers to this worship as *Patram Pushpam Phalam Toyam* (leaf, flower, fruit, water). The Vedic method of deity worship was in the form of yajna, but in the end, the methods of the folk religions had their own way. Later sects, including Buddhism, Jainism and Sanatana Dharma, accepted and promulgated almost the same rites, sacraments and solemn observances. In fact, the Jains, Buddhists and Brahmins—all these streams merged openly with Yaksha puja, because religious differences did not affect the masses, who held on to belief systems through oral traditions and rootedness with their land. This weaving of a common thread of their own theological doctrine in every household is quite at variance with Brahminical and puranic sanctifications.

Such a practice of religion is very common in Banaras; the old deities continue to exist in some form or the other and they continue to be worshipped and recognized by the public. In particular, two things are also rarely transformed; one is the religious place of the deity and the other is the fair that is organized for it. The age-old *haat*s and special religious fairs still manage to find space in the ever-growing metropolis, where space crunch is throttling the very existence of the city. Some of the daily vegetable fairs or *satti*s display their wares right on the curbside of the main roads, spilling on to the centre of the road and blocking traffic. The noise and jostling between the stray cattle, hawkers, customers and the traffic is mind-boggling. Astoundingly, though, eventually, everything fits its place and life goes on.

There is a pattern even in the chaos. I have been visiting the Chanua satti near my house since the last five decades and I still find no change at all. The oldest sattis are located in Vishweshwar Ganj, in Pakka Mahal, Kamachha and Maduadeeh. During my postings in Jharkhand and Telangana, we used to visit the local tribal haats, and during my interactions with the people there, one came to know that these are the haats that are being held since ages in the same place. In Banaras, the sattis continue to exist at the same place, irrespective of the creeping modernization of this ancient city. There is also a progressive sequence of development in the fairs of Banaras, shedding light on the ancient origins and evolution alongside the growing religious trends in different periods of Banaras. Among these, four special public events called *lakkha* melas—fairs that attract at least a hundred thousand people—are Nakkatia at Chetganj, Bharat Milaap at Nati Imli, Nag Natthaya at Tulsi ghat and Shiv Barat, a procession of Shiva's marriage. All these are of relatively recent origin and will be covered later. However, I need to mention about some very ancient religious fairs of Banaras that have characteristic attributes of Yaksha, Naga, tree, devi, well, pond and river worship, as well as the remnant of the tribal element associated with it.

1. Daura Dauri Mela: This fair is organized at Maduadeeh, which was once the outskirts of the city but is now the main railway station. In this fair, women sell wares, primarily consisting of forest products. Some of the items include *daura*, *dauri* and *jhadu* (big and small hampers and brooms made from bamboo), many medicinal forest products, fruits and berries found only in the forest.
2. Narsingh Chaudas: This derives its essence from the killing of Hiranyakashyapu, who was a daitya, a demon, by Vishnu, who takes on an anthropomorphic form of a half-lion and half-human. This story has its apparent origin in Vaishnavism, taking on the Yakshadharma.

3. Naag Panchami: This is celebrated in the month of Shravan at Naga Kuan area where the great debate of Patanjali took place.
4. Piyala ka Mela: This is a quintessential aboriginal festival, celebrated on the banks of the river Varuna, Chaukaghat and Shivpur, in the month of Agrahayan, around December. The local deities, known as Kalka and Sahja, are offered liquor and sugary syrups, which are consumed thereafter in humongous quantity by the revellers.
5. Lota Bhanta Mela: This fair was earlier organized in Pishach Mochan, the heart of the city, in the month of Agrahan, but now, it is only held on the outskirts of the city in Rameshwaram teerth in Harauan near the airport. Pilgrims from around the nearby villages of Banaras gather here and eat roti and *bhanta* (roasted brinjal).
6. Katahariya Mela or Shankuldhara Mela: Like the Lota Bhanta, this mela is also quite ancient and was held to honour two birs: Nadwa Bir and Kankarha Bir at the Shankuldhara Kund, which is in the Khojwan area behind the Gurudham Colony. I visited this place and found that it had an idol of Nadwa Bir under a peepal tree, very similar to the Yaksha image mentioned earlier. The fair held here is reminiscent of the ancient Yaksha puja and related festivities. People worship the birs and sell jackfruit along with other forest products. It was celebrated immediately after monsoon, in the month of September, and was patronized by the Raja Banaras, and because of this, all the notable musicians and dancers vied to seek attention of the nobles and the rich merchants adding a ceremonial charm to the fair.
7. Amausa ke Mela: In this mela, lakhs of people gather to take a dip in the Ganga during the month of Magha. Celebrated on *amavasya* or the new moon day, it has ancient roots, paying homage to the dark and mysterious. The belief is that the Yaksha particularly helps people on this day and grants boons and blessings.

Idols of Yakshas and snakes were made in Banaras during the Kushan era, and I found at least two such idols in Bharat Kala Bhavan. Many clay sculptures of Kushan era have also been found from Rajghat. One of these has a mud pond for worship, depicting ugly faces of humans, birds, snakes and a flight of stairs. Such ponds were probably associated with a prevailing religious belief of the Nagas and the Yakshas. In our mohalla in Banaras, even today, two days before Janmashtami, the festival of Lalahi Chhath is celebrated, in which various idols of grotesque snakes, flat-nosed and thick-lipped human figures and ponds are made by mothers desiring long and healthy life of their children. How does one actually observe the ancient forms of worship in and around Banaras?

Walking down the lanes and by-lanes, conversing with the local people, one realizes that the Banarasi disposition has encountered a cul-de-sac and cannot go beyond the descriptions of their city in the Kashi Khand and Kashi Mahatmaya. Even the supposedly erudite Brahmins will complacently date every temple and ritual of Kashi to be at least 5000 years old. Whereas no temple in Banaras exists which is more than 300–400 years old. Only two temples, one in Kandwa village and the Adi Keshav, date back to the Gahadavala era around 1000 CE. Eventually, an observant mind will be able to remove the grain from the chaff and will pluck out the non-essentials, and only then Banaras will open its arms to a visitor, to showcase its mesmerizingly extensive opulence of aesthetics, traditions and commotion. So how does one observe the ancient elements, now?

It is present in the collective subconscious of the people when they worship and celebrate the festivals, which have been elaborated above. It is embedded in their grassroots art, decoupage, craftsmanship, limericks and ditties. It manifests in their ceramic, clay and wooden toys, in their impromptu design of the buttresses and cornices of the buildings, in their knowledge about flowers and fruits to be offered to the deities, and in their oral traditions, although sometimes you may find them to be confused and merging myth with history. It's evident in their numerous Barham devatas, Daitra Babas and birs. Walking down the Pakka Mahal area of

Banaras, one notices the remnants of the Yaksha images in the subconscious mind of a mason. He carves out a waterspout jutting out in the lane, serving as a rainwater discharge from flat roofs, similar to the Western gargoyles, most remarkably seen in ancient cathedrals like the Notre Dame. The mason's gargoyles do not have a body, only the face is attached to a cylindrical casing. Most of the temples and old buildings have buttresses or brackets that are, in fact, like gargoyles, but with a human body and the face of a grotesque creature that cannot be associated with any kind of animals—it's the manifestation of his dream sequence, deep fears, which was passed on to him through his primordial ancestry. In the gaudily painted walls, terrifying paintings of a man with large canine teeth and blood-red eyes, holding a scimitar in his hand. A potter, wedging and moulding his clay pots or toys into the shapes of big-bellied monsters or theriomorphic creatures like birds and snakes, expresses his subliminal anamnesis. A carpenter crafting wooden toys, a toddy-suffused boatman suddenly bursting into the songs praising Barham Baba, a pujari invoking Bhairava with his mantras—all these, and many more, adding to this vivid tapestry of cultural expressions in Banaras. Even now, in the rural belt of Banaras, if a person is believed to be possessed by a bir, a question-and-answer session is initiated with the possessed person by the shamans. Undoubtedly, this is the continuation of the *yaksh prashna* episode of the Mahabharata and its manifestation that Chotka, too, has learnt.

On the outskirts of the city, there are elevated platforms with conical structures and some small, padded clay structures. These are called *Barham Baba ka chaura*—the abode of the Barham Baba. Many similar structures also serve as places of bir worship, known as *Bir ka chabootra*.

It is also interesting to note that nearly all the temples of Banaras have many such minor deities located within the precincts of the temple. Since there is no mention of such deities in the Kashi Khand, it becomes very clear that the birs worshiped in Banaras were folk deities, local deities or village deities. However, the Brahmins of Kashi argue that many ancient Shivlings, whose *ardha* (stead) has been destroyed, have been and are being worshiped as birs. They are invoked in the mantras chanted on the occasion of any Hindu ritualistic worship, establishing their importance in the Hindu pantheon. Tulsidas in *Vinay Patrika* has mentioned bir worship with a doha. Generally, there are two types of birs: Lahura Bir (small bir) and Bulla Bir (big bir), and we have two prominent localities called Lahura Bir and Bulla nala in Banaras. Bir and Barham are amongst the last remains of the worship of Yakshas. However, Barham, bir and Daitra Baba are three different entities. Barham is actually a short jargon for Brahma rakshasa (a Brahmin who dies an unnatural death is reincarnated as a rakshasa), whereas Daitra Baba is the fearsome form of the Barham Baba. They make up whatever is left of the Yaksha worship, and their offerings consist of hemp, liquor and sacrifices in their shrines.

In my village, the ruling Parmar clans of Rajputs, who were hereditary zamindars of the area called Dumraon since many centuries, have been worshipping a village deity of the Paswan community called Goraya Dev. As per our inferences, the Paswans, belonging to the scheduled caste, are likely the descendants of an aboriginal tribe, Chero Kharwars, who once ruled the area in western Bihar adjacent to the Vindhyas boundary with Banaras. The Goraya Dev idol is a hand-made clay idol with a melon-sized spherical ball and a lemon-sized clay ball perched on its top, symbolizing a big-bellied man with a small head. This idol was never brought inside the house but placed in the niche or the hole in the wall called *takha* at the entrance of the house. Before any propitious occasion, like harvesting or embarking on a long journey, it was bedaubed with vermilion, durwa grass, red thread, rice and flowers. The Rajput zamindars (the zamindari system was abolished in India after 1947, but in Bihar, it continued till in 1954) also continued the worship of the other Vedic gods, along with Goraya Dev. My grandfather, who received a portion of the zamindari in this area of Dumraon from his mother, was an ardent Arya Samaji. He destroyed the idol of Goraya Dev from his house, much to the consternation of the local population. Incidentally, Goraya Dev was only worshipped by the upper-caste

Parmar Rajputs and never by the Brahmins, Vaishyas and even the minor Rajput families. Some of the practitioners of the Goraya Dev worship, sotto voce cautioned my grandmother and warned of bad omens and setbacks. Immediately after my grandfather's iconoclastic act, it so happened that a few villages under his zamindari were taken away by the district magistrate and transferred to a rival family of claimants for the zamindari. This became big news, but still, my grandfather refused to reinstall Goraya Dev in our house. This form of worship was also an ancient tradition of the Yaksha worship and accepting the deities of the conquered has been an age-old phenomenon in the middle Gangetic valley.

Now, 'bir' is also a corrupted form of 'veer', meaning brave. It seems that the birs were the village protectors having a Robin Hoodesque personality. In the written text, they are mentioned for the first time in *Prithviraj Raso* by Chand Bardai, which describes a total of fifty-two birs. Still, in Banaras, the phrase *baawan birhona* is used, meaning achieving great tasks. Banaras always had a Robin Hood figure, locally called a *gunda*. Invariably, they were either Kshatriyas or Bhumihars. In the late seventies, there was this famous gunda called Lallu Singh, whom the Banarasi feared and respected, and as kids, we were in awe of him. The prominent Hindi writer from Banaras, Jaishankar Prasad, has written a short story titled 'Gunda' on such a character. Nanhku Singh, the protagonist of the story, is a quintessential gunda, who changes his life's purpose due to unrequited love but still does not compromise on his character. The story is set in the early eighteenth-century Banaras during the reign of Raja Chet Singh.[10]

Prima facie, the birs and Shivling may seem similar, but there are distinct differences. While the structure of the former is larger, ranging from 3 to 5 feet, with a pointed snout, the latter is small and rounded on top. Shivlings are typically surrounded by ancillary deities, whereas in a bir's shrine, there is only the statue of the bir. The religious practices of bir worship and Shiva worship denotes two different eras. In ancient times, the former was prevalent, and much later, the encasement of Shivling worship was added on top of it. People believe that the original birs are those who are in the sacred zone of Kashi, and as per the Matsya Puran, in the fight between the Shiva worshippers and the Yakshas, all the Yakshas left Kashi, but their original shrines remained there. Thus, we find that the original birs who are worshipped by the city dwellers include Lahura Bir and Daundia Bir.

From this anecdote, one may also derive that the Yakshas, in the form of birs, were always worshipped by the lower castes, who were not allowed entry in the temples. In the temples of Baghebir, Tadebir, Kankarhabir, Deodiyabir, Ahirabir and Chamrubir, they are worshipped in the form of Shivlings and at many places, the ramparts and broken statues from the ruins of ancient temples are preserved. We see an ancient tradition of worshiping the remains of old temples by keeping them under a tree, and people often put vermilion, etc., on them and offer water daily and burn camphor. Goats, chickens, pigs, etc., are also sacrificed at places like the Deyodiabir, Daitrabir (Badi Gaibi), Ladhubir (Churamanpur) and Bhangarhabir. Sheetla Devi is worshipped in the Chaitra Navratri, which is known as Basipora. Women also make offerings of water (Gangajal, *panchmeva* and milk) to the temples of such heroes or birs. Shayari Mata, whose temple is located in Gurubagh, is considered as the Shakti Peeth of the birs.

Chotka was particularly afraid of one uncommonly fearsome and awe-inspiring being, whom he would refer to as Daitra Baba. In a prank I played on him, that nearly killed him, the cooking coal in our home was dumped in the backyard, and it generally used to be dark there. On a late winter evening, when Chotka was sent to fetch coal, I tiptoed behind him and covered myself with a used white bedsheet. I gurgled some beastly noises and when Chotka saw me, he started shaking and immediately collapsed, whimpering, 'Daitra Baba . . . Daitra Baba'. After we sprinkled some cold water on him, he came back to his senses but continued to cuddle up and whimper. I got a nice bashing from my uncle that day.

When I analyse this now, I find such deep-rooted fear comes from the Yakshas and the goblin worship in ancient times. There is a temple of the Daitra Bir behind the Panchkroshi Hanuman temple near the university, as well as within the city limits at Chetganj. Here, Hinduism and the religious mien of Kashi, in particular, should take a bow. Especially when we compare the manner in which other ancient civilizations like the Greeks, Romans, and pre-Islamic Arabian and Persian civilizations treated their gods and goddesses after Christianity and Islam made the region their bastion and an area of predominance. Unlike Hinduism, which accepted and incorporated the beliefs of ancient religions, a vicious and violent smear campaign to spite the spiritual powers of the deities and also against their followers went on for centuries in the Roman empire and the Arabian Peninsula. We find the most despicable and vile words like heathens, pagans, pariah, kafir, *but parast*, Satan, etc., as a result of such contemptuous campaigns. One of its major exponents, Augustine of Hippo, agreed that the worship of false gods had as its object 'most vile spirits and malignant and deceitful demons', who had their misdeeds 'celebrated for them at their own festivals'.[11]

Early Christian apologists had drawn upon some biblical passages and classical Greek terms to clarify how false religion worked and held people in its thrall. In brief, they argued that the worship of false gods and idols consists in trafficking with demons (*daimone*s was a term used by the ancient Greeks to refer to some of their deities). This is done by people who have learnt to invoke daemons by charms and incantations and to induce them to do what they wish. On this account the worship of daemons is foreign to us who worship the Supreme God. The worship of the supposed gods is also a worship of daemons. Because of the sacrifices and spells, the demons performed the petitions of those who brought requests to them; by means of magic and formulas, men could enchant them and have them obey. These evil spirits were the minions of their ruler, Satan or Beelzebub, the lord of this world.

Serpent worship is quite common even now as in the earlier times. Kapila Vatsayan calls the serpent symbol to represent the moment of transition: 'swift, silent, limbless and deadly'.[12] The Mahabharata, too, is replete with commentary on the affairs of the Naga race, about the marriage of the two sisters Kadru and Vinata with Rishi Kasyapa. The Kashi Khand also mentions Kadru and Vinata, with Vinata becoming the slave of Kadru. Later, Vinata goes to Kashi to rid herself from Kadru's slavery. Kadru then becomes the mother of 1000 Nagas, who later were considered to be the forebearers of the whole serpent race. The Hindu pantheon is suffused with the references of snakes and Nagas, like the Sheshnaag, Vasuki, Takshaka, Kalia, Karkotaka, Nila and Anilla, Nahusha, etc. Vinata became the mother of Garuda, who eventually annihilates the Naga race. Let us trudge a little bit into how the Nagas came to dominate the religious space of the Vedic people.

The Mahabharata clearly portrays the interaction between the aboriginal serpent worshippers of the Naga clan and the advancing Vedic Aryans. The first mention where the Nagas appear is the burning of the forest of Khandavan, where the entire forest was set ablaze, and all the Nagas are killed except their king, Takshak. Later, some kind of a matrimonial alliance takes place, where Arjuna marries the daughter of the Naga king. It appears and has been argued in the preceding chapter as well, that there seems that there was an extended hand of friendship towards the aboriginal tribes. Much later, when King Parikshit is bitten by Takshak, his son vows to destroy all the agas. Thousands were killed, but the intervention of Astik and the nephew of Vasuki, the Naga king of the Gangetic plains, led to a compromise, and the killings stopped. Here, again, this compromise was likely reached only after accepting the dominance of the Vedic Aryans, as well as, perhaps, incorporating the elements of the non-Aryan worshipping pattern.

Barring a few years of Bimbisar's rule, during which, as James Fergusson has pointed out: 'As a part of the reform which he introduced, ancestral worship was abolished, and the sepulchral tumulus became the depository of relics of saints. Serpent Worship was repressed, and its sister faith of Tree Worship elevated to the first rank.'[13] Naga worship, though, continued to be an undercurrent of the main river of Hinduism. However, Sanatan Dharma adopted the worship of the Naga cult amongst its main pantheon much later, only after Buddhism held sway for about 1000 years. Earlier, Shiva was depicted with a cobra or other venomous snake in his hand or sometimes twisted around his neck, but in all these instances, the serpent was always portrayed as an object of fear and as a weapon, certainly not an object of worship. People believed that the Nagas stay in huge palaces underwater, and can frequently change form, at will, between a serpent and a human, and guard the treasures in the very old palaces. They were like the dragons in South Asian and Western cultures, but with auspicious rather than sinister intentions, they are always hidden away from the outside world and populate the netherworld or the water bodies. At the Kala Bhavan in Banaras, there is a first-century BCE statue of the Naga deity Balaram that was found from the ruins near Adampura. Balaram, later, was arrogated as the brother of Krishna in the Puranas.

I do not know this connection, but I remember always listening to some fascinating stories and accounts of the mysterious Naga devatas during the long spells of rain during the monsoon in the dark of the evenings because of power cuts, when we could not go out to play. These stories were narrated to us by the old nannies or the old servant Nand-ji. Interestingly, the ritual of offering of milk during snake worship has the element of a prevalent folk story in Banaras, about a species of snake called Dhamin, the Indian rat snake (*ptyas mucosa*), sucking milk from lactating cattle. It was very common to spot cow paintings in the old stone houses of Banaras that included our mohalla as well. Among many such paintings, one was that of a very well-ornamented, extremely well-fed, white, lactating cow with her plump udders dangling till the ground. It portrayed a black snake coiling and tying up her hind legs and suckling milk from the cow. The belief that when a healthy cow stops giving milk suddenly, a Dhamin is accused of siphoning off her milk adds an additional element of folklore and mystery to the narrative.

Banaras, being an urban centre for the dairy business, where the second most powerful guild is that of the Ahirs (Yadavs), who are the cowherders, this story is not only believed but measures are taken to obviate such instances of Dhamin milching the cattle. After listening to this story, Chotka and I had convinced a shrewd relative of ours to shift his cow elsewhere from our compound, as the cowshed was restricting our cricket play area, telling him that we witnessed a Dhamin who regularly comes at dawn to suckle milk from his cow.

Nand-ji also told us about some other Naga devatas, the snakes that carry a sparkling gemstone called Nagamani, which they use as a source of light whenever they are out to forage for food. Going back to such stories, I can't think of a better example of Marquezian magical realism, gradually occupying our subliminal cognitive space. The most popular dragons-like snakes also carry with them wishing stones—stones that embody their soul. To capture a dragon's stone is to get all one's wishes fulfilled and to gain control over them.

One of my aunts, who was married in a minor principality in the Vindhya hills, called Baghan Kot—as per her descriptions was reminiscent of the Western delightful Chateau en Espagne (which always reminds me now of the cottages in *A Day in the Country*, a fantastic film by Jean Renoir, from 1936)—located not very far from Banaras. She would often come to our house for her monthly quota of cinema and shopping. We used to call her Ammi. We particularly liked her, as she always slipped in copious amount of toffees and candies in our small pockets.

Ammi was a great storyteller as well, weaving a thrilling account from the seemingly banal occurrences and coating them with Puranic myths and folktales. Her vocabulary was very old-fashioned as she often used the word 'motor' for car. She once told us that her principality was taken away by a 'tommy' (her word for a British) and was later restored with severe curtailments. This, I guess, must be true because in the permanent settlement of the late eighteenth century, many such supposedly independent Rajput principalities in the Eastern United Province and Bihar were reduced to zamindaris. She narrated a true incident, which, according to her, was a recurring event every month on amavasya. This night of complete darkness, among the Hindus, is considered a time of great power and boon granting from the Yakshas, Nagas, bhutas and pishachas. In her huge fortress-like home, which was centuries old, there was a *tehkhana* (celler) that led to a much smaller room with thick iron doors. This room is found in different sizes in every old Rajput and Muslim feudal family's ancestral homes and is called *toshakhana* (Persian for 'treasure house') that functioned as a vault for the safe-keeping of family jewellery, valuable utensils, zamindari and land-related documents and other expensive bric-a-brac. Many a family's exotic heirlooms, which may come as a surprise to the present generation, were also kept there. I particularly remember a silver sickle, called *hansiya*, with a handle made of knotted bronze wire in the toshakhana of our ancestral village. I was told by an elder nanny that it was used to saw off the umbilical cord of the child from his mother after or during the childbirth, at the time when no hospitals were there in the vicinity. This hansiya was used in my family since many generations. I also remember her telling me that Grandfather had the entire wall of the toshakhana layered with an extra wall of tinplate that would make a lot of sound whenever there was an attempt of burglary.

Coming back to the Baghan story: Ammi mentioned that since several centuries, a huge *Gehuan* (spectacled cobra or wheat snake) would emerge from the cellar, on the amavasya of every month, and slither around the entrance of the cellar in the corridor, with a slow and graceful manoeuvre. Ammi described the snake as having gentle eyes, and most surprisingly, it also had a beard that, as per Ammi, grew because of it being hundreds of years old. Its skin was wheatish but dull and showed signs of peeling off. According to her, there was even a symbol of 'Om' on his lore (between the eyes and his nostrils). Thereafter, Ammi added an exotic twist to the story. She explained that when she arrived in this huge castle-like home, the elder ladies of the house asked her to keep a bowl of milk at the entrance of the cellar every amavasya before sunset for the Naga devata. Further, they also warned her that she should not venture anywhere near the cellar after sunset. Ammi was a teenager when she got married, a curious and adventurous child who came from a family of avante-garde police officers. Undeterred by the warning, she decided to snoop and trail the snake. What she described, resonated with the most enduring and very commonly believed myth about the Nagas. She said that she saw the Naga devata spit out a huge *manik* (ruby), which was so bright that she couldn't keep her eyes open. Thereafter, the Naga devata swallowed the ruby back inside, after slithering around it for a few minutes. Ammi followed the movement of the snake and saw it going back into the cellar, and ensconced itself, coiling up and raising its hood in front of the iron gate of the toshakhana—its demeanour being that of providing protection to the entrance of the toshakhana. She also described the process of ecdysis that it underwent just before the day of Naga Panchami. After shedding its skin, only once a year on the Naga Panchami day, the Naga devata is known to give a special darshan—all glistening and glowing, but only to the royal members of the Baghan Kot. The villagers used to be distributed the shredded skin as a talisman, which they use to tie as an amulet on their children to ward off sinister and evil eyes. My cousins from Baghan Kot swore by the story and also whispered that Ammi should not have seen the snake and his ruby, as it was believed in the household that anybody who tries to take a dekko at the Naga devata without consent, encounters bad omens and catastrophe. Few years before I left Banaras, once, when Ammi came to stay with us, she looked gaunt and forlorn, and as usual, after offering my greetings, I expected a small packet of toffees from her. Instead, she held my hand in a firm grip and continued to stare at me with her cold, stony socketed eyes. Then suddenly, she burst out into a scary, hysterical and convulsive laughter. Her laugh was menacing, and we kids, got very scared and were immediately huddled away from there. For the few days that she remained with us, in the dead of night, we would hear her hysterical laughter as she paced on the terrace. Ammi received treatment for her severe mental illness, but later we came to know that she jumped from the ramparts of Baghan Kot and succumbed to her injuries. The family told everyone that during one of her hysterical laughs on the full moon day, she slipped and fell. From my local research, I came to know that before the Rajputs, Baghan Kot was an old mud fortification of the local tribal kings who were Naga worshippers. I presume the Baghan Kot family must have continued to consider snakes as guardian angels, and Ammi was deluged with the staple dose of snake stories passed on by the household retinue of old women and nannies who were her only company in the forlorn chateau. It appears to me now that Ammi's sensitive teenage mind couldn't have handled so many of the bizarre and phantasmagoric tales. She internalized them and accentuated them with her own imagination while narrating them to us. In the process, she started believing in the stories and must have already started slipping into her hallucinations and probable schizophrenia.

In fables and myths, the Naga women are supposed to be very friendly and free with their favours. There is a story in the Jatakas wherein Bodhisattva is reborn as a Naga ruler, who embraces Buddhism after realizing that he needs to be born as a human to achieve the higher realm. He observes *uposatha* on the prescribed days and undergoes penance to transcend his Naga birth. The uposatha, or *upavastha*, is a Buddhist day of penance and observance, marked on the full moon, new moon and days midway; it serves as a day of purification, during which disciples offer food to monks and chant for the cleansing of the defiled mind.

In another story, a Naga princess returns to her own realm after falling in love with an ascetic because she became apprehensive of her own prowess of venomousness and envy. The earliest known Naga worshippers were from the Nagavansh, a branch from the Magadh Emperor Bimbisar's clan. There is mention of a Naga ruler of Kashi, Shishunaga, who ruled Kashi and certainly hailed from a tribal Naga worshipper's clan. Hieun Shang has mentioned that the Buddhist in Kashi considered the three ponds located in the three directions of the Vihar to be sacred, serving as abodes of the Nagas who guarded those ponds. In the *Dhammapada Atthakatha,* as quoted by Motichandra,[14] there was a clump of seven 'Sirisa' (*Albizialebbeck*) trees in Kashi, where the Buddha is supposed to have given a sermon to a Naga called Erakpatta.

Eck and Coomarswamy refer to Nagas as aquatic divinities who occupy the pools and the wells in the sacred zone of Kashi and were worshipped, much like the Yakshas and their motifs of Brahma-Birs, long before the compilation of the Hindu scriptures. They continued to be worshipped, despite the changing and appropriating narratives since ages, because of the sacred geography of Kashi, where their shrines and abode remain. There is an interesting inference drawn by Eck, that since most of the Yakshas and Nagas were guardians of immense wealth and gems, the name Manikarnika ghat, with 'Mani' meaning a gem, must also be associated with some ancient form of snake worship. At Gaiya ghat, the Naga is worshipped as a devi. Here, a temple of Nageshwari Devi takes prominence among all other minor deities. At the Shankuldhara pond, the origin of the word could be linked to Naga worship, as 'Shankha' happens to be mentioned in Buddhist texts, quite possibly referring to a prominent serpent deity of Banaras. At the Chauki ghat, under the shade of a very old peepal tree, there exist different types of stone statues of the Nagas. Also, at a place in the heart of old Banaras, there is a well, called Naga Koop, where the Nagas are still worshipped, especially on the day of Naga Panchami in the rainy season month of Shravana, i.e., July–August.

Vasudev Saran Agrawal adds to this fantastic development in Hinduism, that during the osmosis of the folk into the scriptural, fable into the mantras, the Indian culture has been fusing together all the different elements, accepting the worship of infinite gods and goddesses, like the rivers, trees, mountains, Yakshas, snakes, local gods and the earth. This culture has progressed, and from this churning, has emerged all the great gods or immutable elements that the present Hindus follow. The worship of the Yakshas and Nagas, in its most primitive faith, was not just associated to the powers of fertility and rainfall, and were in fact, as quoted by Coomarswamy, in the words of De la Vallee-Poussin, from '*uncertain fond commun, tres riche, et que nous ne connaissons pas parfaitement*' (a certain common fund, very rich, and which we do not know perfectly).[15] Sanatan Dharma only incorporated the devotional and the extant ritualistic symbols but perhaps omitted many aspects of its inherent metaphysical aspects. The Aryan culture has influenced the local cultures in many ways, and as a result, she herself was influenced by those cultures. On the other hand, dance, song, instruments, leaves, flowers, fruits, sacrifices, etc., are considered ritualistic symbols and are mentioned in detail for worship among the vegetative divinities. Thus, the Hindu culture has moved forward with the seed mantra of harmony. This seed mantra has given birth to the *Abhayamudra*, a sort of gesture of fearlessness in Hindu culture, which has made all aboriginal cultures, small and large, high and low, part of one family, but many a minor deities refused to be part of the larger spectrum of the Hindu faith, like the birs and the Nagas.

Chapter 6

The Dichotomy of Shaivism and Vaishnavism

The Struggle of Memory against Forgetting

The struggle of man against power is the struggle of memory against forgetting.

—Milan Kundera,
The Book of Laughter and Forgetting

I have always wondered how the reigning deity Shiva has found so much prominence for everything that the present city of Banaras boasts of. Shiva, as God, has all the geographical and symbolical elements of the city—the Ganga in his matted locks, the crescent shape of the city all along the Ganga, the crescent moon on his head, the ashes of the Mahashamshaan, the ancient worship of the Nagas' representation with the snake as his garland, the Yakshas as his ganas, the location of the three most ancient lingams on the three hills of Kashi that is in the shape of a trident—the trishul of Shiva, the primordial Shivling as the birs place of worship, etc. Not so long ago, Kashi was not the city of Shiva. Even Kabir, the poet, in his poem, questions: '*Shiv! Kashi kaisi bhai tumhaari, ajhoon ho Shiv lehu vichaari*' (Oh Shiva! How can you say Kashi is yours? Does this still belong to you? Give it a thought). We have seen its presence in the excavations from Rajghat, dating from the fourth century BCE to the early Kushan period, and its rise with the Bharshiva in the second century

CE, only to be eclipsed by Vaishnavism, Jainism and Buddhism, and regaining prominence to reach its peak during the Guptas and the later Magadh Guptas but always facing stiff competition from Vaishnavism. The grip of Vaishnavism was so strong that the novel *Banbhatta Ki Atmakatha*, which is set against the historical backdrop of the rule of the Maukharis in the sixth century CE has a detailed description and worship of Mahavarah with the vedi and the tulsi tree.[1] Kashi has been considered by many religious scholars to have been the oldest bastion of Shaivism, predating Buddhism. One must take note of the fact that no pre Buddhist archaeological evidence of Shaivism has been found to substantiate this claim. However, one must not presume that Shaivism did not exist in the Kashi kshetra. It did exist but in its antediluvian form, in which it was primarily a religious doctrine of austerity, penance and meditation. In that form, it did not encourage any *sangha* or federation and its adherents never attempted to manifest their doctrine either in art or in an image. This could be the reason why we do not find much empirical trace of the ancient remains of Shaivism. Most of the *Smriti* scriptural texts were composed during the Gupta era, but constantly underwent additions and deletions, as per the sociological and religious flavour of the day.

Since the Gahadavalas were Vaishnavites, as well as tolerant towards other sects, we find that Shaivism, in its Puranic exuberance, started occupying the religious space of Kashi aggressively immediately after them. *Krityakalptaru* by Lakshmidhar, predominantly a text of jurisprudence, and even though with prejudice for Vaishnavism and devi worship, still mentions Shiva's presence in Kashi. Kashi Mahatmya, Kashi Khand of the *Skanda Purana*, *Shiva Purana*, all were composed from the eleventh century CE to the fifteenth century CE.

While on a visit to Dholavira, a famous Harappan site in Gujarat, I saw many phallus-shaped structures, which I tried to pass on as another wonderful excavation, not wanting to go into the pedagogic archaeological details that was being told by our guide. As already discussed, the Rig Veda denounced all forms of lingam worship: 'while Harappan artefacts leave no one in doubt that phallus worship was part of its cultural repertoire'[2] but somehow the shape interested me and it remained with me in my psyche. Earlier, while assisting in the writing for the mega serial *Devon ke Dev . . . Mahadev*, a sort of a religious biopic of Shiva, I had only researched Shiva and his myriad interpretations through religious and Puranic sources. Even then, I was not able to correctly understand the reason as to why the Shivling was being worshipped; being a matter of faith, I swam with the flow. Although now it becomes clear that the phallus worship predates the arrival of Aryans. The Rig Veda has castigated the Shishnadeva worshippers, when they met the local inhabitants while moving first from their original habitat, into the Kuru Panchal areas, and later during their push into the Indo Gangetic plains. The religious and cultural realm of the Indus people, however, was always awash with the phallic symbols. In another scholarly inference, a seal excavated at an Indus Valley site, depicting an ithyphallic male seated in a meditative posture and surrounded by many animals, has been found to contain the graphical accoutrements and attributes of a prototype Shiva.[3] In that case, Shiva is the oldest deity, in all its myriad representational forms of worship in the world. We have, in the previous chapter, mentioned in detail, about the conical structures being worshipped as Barham Baba in and around Banaras. Sir John Marshall has stated that 'side by side with this Earth or Mother Goddess, there appears at Mohenjo Daro a male god, who is recognizable at once as a prototype of the historic Siva'.[4] Many ruins from the ancient Greece and Rome have phallic symbols, though not all were depicted as religious symbols, like the most famous image is that of the ithyphallic Priapus, a god of animal and vegetable fertility, or the Avenue of Priapus on the Island of Delos, with columns carved as stone phalluses from the third century BCE, and the bronze statue of the god Mercury with numerous phalluses dating back to the first century CE.[5] As Tony Joseph has argued, that even after the decline of the Harappa civilization, it did not disappear completely, rather, it moved eastwards along with their cultural and religious beliefs.[6] They likely did not reach the areas around Kashi, and as the recent Akhta excavations that date to around 1800 BCE, no connection with the Indus people have been found. Further, it's not conclusively established that the Shishnadeva reference of the Aryans, when they moved towards the present area of Kashi, was only for the Indus Valley people or was it also for the aboriginals from the middle Gangetic plains, which was much later. There are, though, references of Aryans meeting the Kol tribes, who did worship some of the phallic symbols.[7] The point is that phallus worship or the 'lingam' worship of some sort, as we see in the veneration of the conical structures of the birs, was prevalent in the ancient region of Kashi, and eventually, a symbiotic Brahmanical version of lingam worship evolved, incorporating primitive and tribal mores and agamic traditions.[8]

Shiva was not even the prominent deity of the Vedic people, though. His rise from the Rudra (praised as the 'mightiest of the mighty') of the Rig Veda to the Shiva Shambhu of the Hindu pantheon is as interesting as his gaining prominence in Kashi. In the Rig Veda, he is portrayed as physically robust and handsome. For the gods of destructive forces who require constant and elaborate appeasement and worship, he is to be feared; he is the lord of all the beasts—the dark, esoteric and the mysterious. He is the howler, and with his growl and howl, he instils fear among both gods and humans alike. He is the supreme being, who sprang from Brahma's own brow, who eventually also restrains and decapitates him. He is the primordial consciousness, and he is always depicted in a formidable appearance. As James Fergusson rightly observes: 'Siva is occasionally represented holding a cobra or other venomous snake in his hand; serpents are also sometimes twisted round his neck or entwined with his hair; but in all these instances the serpent is a weapon . . . not an object of worship.'[9]

The transformation of Shiva as a deity and in his aniconic and emblematic form of Rudra, along with the emergence of Linga worship, were concomitant and chronologically aligned. Let me briefly arrange the sequence of how Sanatan Dharma came to accept the lingam worship when their most salient doctrine, the Rig Veda, has denounced it categorically and is even, at times, outright censorious. It was a quintessential case of cult appropriation of the vegetative divinities, deities of water cosmology, geomorphic features and genius loci to their further assimilation with the scriptural binaries of the Vedic gods. The evolution of Shiva, for the first time, appears in the Yajurveda, which mentions his *shatnaam* (the 100 names), most prominent being Pashupati (Lord of the Beasts). By the time the *Shvetashvatara Upanishad* was composed, Rudra was merged with the Vedic gods and was assigned an elevated position as the Mahadev (Lord of Lords). In the Mahabharata, Shiva is exalted by his 1008 names, and the famous mythical account of the marriage of Shiva with Uma or Parvati, the daughter of the Himalayan mountain king, Himavaan. In the Ramayana, Shiva is again praised for the origin and the subsequent taming of the Ganga. The ancient Kashi was the centre for this phylogenetic unrolling of the entire corpus of the rise of Shiva from the minor deity Rudra, and the adaptation of the phallus as a symbol of worship, through the epics. Two stories from the Puranas have been culled to explain this. The Hindu religion predominantly consists of the Trimurti (Trinity) of Brahma, Vishnu and Mahesh. Most of the epical lore and their myriad intertwined narratives emanate from them. Brahma is the creator of the universe, Vishnu the preserver and Mahesh, or Shiva, the destroyer.

As a child, I used to accompany my mother to her friend's place in the Pakka Mahal area. The lanes were so narrow that if a cow or a bull, which are a ubiquitous presence in these areas, were to come from the other end, it would be impossible to negotiate the passage. The only option would be to step into the slightly open front door of the nearest house in the unbroken rows flanking these narrow, winding alleys and let the animal pass. Most of these houses belonged to Maharashtrian Vaishnava Brahmins—descendants of the great Shri Narayan Bhatt, who revived Hinduism in Kashi. Although he was a Vaishnavite, he got the Vishwanath temple rebuilt in the sixteenth century. Most of these Brahmins settled in the clearings of the forests on the outskirts of the city. They were called Bankate, a now prominent title of a family of Kashi Maharashtrian Brahmins. During that time, it wasn't uncommon to find a number of tortoises roaming about in the central courtyards of many houses.

Little did I realize then that these shelled creatures were considered the custodians of a Vedic Vaishnav sect that dominated Banaras before the Brahmanicalized Shaivism took root and spread here. The tortoise is considered as one of the ten avatars of Vishnu, who is a salient and sometimes the primary god of the Hindu pantheon. In a classic Western orientalist analysis of the origin of Vaishnavism, Fergusson says that what is interesting is that in all the avatars of Vishnu, we find that the Naga appears everywhere in Vaishnava tradition. He adds: 'There is no more common representation of Vishnu than reposing on the Sesha, as the seven-headed snake is called by the Brahmans, contemplating the creation of the world. It was by his assistance that the ocean was churned and Amrita produced. He everywhere spreads his protecting hood over the god, or his avatars, and in all instances it is the seven-headed heavenly Naga, not the earthly cobra of Siva.'[10] He has also justifiably linked the rise of Buddhism with Vaishnavism, willy-nilly trying to establish the premise of their coevalness with each other. The most common form of Vaishnav adoration, i.e., the worship of the Tulsi plant, and Buddha's subsequent reincarnation as Vishnu is cited among the many common points. Nilima Chitgopekar is also of the opinion that the emphasis on vegetarianism and non-violence, which forms the basis of the Vaishnav doctrine, has been largely and affirmatively borrowed from Jainism and Buddhism, even though the idiom of the Vaishnav sect, as against Shaivism, strictly remains orthodox and Vedic.[11]

Vishnu embodies all the traits considered civilized and pure, and follows the moral code of conduct, but at times, is known for his extreme shrewdness and a gerrymandering. He is bejewelled with gold and precious stones, fresh flowers and sandal paste. His symbols are his couch—a curled-up snake called Sheshnaag; the Garuda—his vehicle, the mythical eagle, which, in its spiritual inference, also means the mantra against poison; Laxmi—the goddess of wealth and opulence who appeared during the great churn of the oceans; Padma—the lotus; the Sudarshan Chakra—the spinning disc; and the Panchjanya—the conch shell. In Banaras, Vishnu worship predates Shiva's Brahmanical version of the lingam worship. Many stories and legends, as well as important religious discourses in Banaras, still remind the Shaivites that once upon a time, Kashi's theological geography was dedicated to Vishnu and still the ancient reliquary has strands of the Vaishnav temples and holy places. The four major temples that still exist are the Bindu Madhav temple (near the original one that was destroyed by Aurangzeb), the Adi Keshava on the confluence of Rajghat, described as Padodkati teerth in the Kashi Khand[12] and the relatively newer temples of Balaji and Gopal mandir. There are temples of Vishnu found at Bakariya Kund[13] which Sherring, through his surface reading of archaeology, calls the Buddhist shrine.[14] In the Bakaria Kund ruins, during the Gupta era, a beautiful statue of Krishna lifting the Govardhan hill has been found that is on display in the Bharat Kala Bhavan.[15] Hiun Tsang has described a statue of a god, most likely of Vishnu, that is over 100 feet. Even today, the cult of Krishna has survived not because of its Puranic references, which most of even the sacred texts of Kashi are silent on, but rather because of the temple artisans who have retained the iconic worship of Krishna prevalent before Shiva, leaving his imprint as a leitmotif on most of the temples. The Gupta period saw the apogee of Vishnu worship and Kashi was certainly considered the centre of Vaishnavism in an era of prolific architectural and scriptural achievements. Ironically, though, the worship of the lingam as a symbol started gaining momentum in the epics during these times as well. Many seals discovered from Rajghat testify to the prevalence of Vaishnavism during this time. Among the later Guptas, Aditya Sen (648–673 CE) was the last ruler to have followed Vaishnavism. In an edict by a local king named Praktaditya, who ruled Banaras for a short duration after the Maukharis in around 650 CE, it is mentioned about him having gotten a Vishnu temple constructed, which was called Murdhishya.[16] After the Guptas, the Gahadavalas of the eleventh century CE were known as the patrons of the Vaishnav dharma. The Adi Keshav temple was renovated and a permanent revenue system, along with appointing a head priest was instituted by Chandradev during that time. In fact, the most famous Gahadavala king, Govindchandra, has been called as an incarnation of Vishnu been sent to protect his favourite abode of Kashi. Kashi was also called Harikshetra and Narayanvasa (Vishnu's abode), but this was also the epochal cusp of Vaishnavism and Shaivism, where the former had to preserve its religious turf from the competing Shaivism. Since Gahadavalas promoted all sects of Hinduism and even Buddhism, the aggressive push of Shaivism, despite the state patronage of Vaishnavism, started to dominate Kashi. Vaishnavism and its theosophical precepts once again gained momentum with Krishna worship during the fifteenth-century Bhakti movement, but by that time, Banaras had become the city of Shiva. A few remnants of Vishnu worship remains, like in the ritual of the Holika Dahan, performed on the eve of Holi. As per this myth, the witch Holika was smouldered to death when she tried to burn her nephew, a Vishnu devotee, Prahlad. It was later Tulsidas, who with his *Ramcharitmanas*, started a neo-Vaishnavist movement, which did not see the light of day till his death in the legendary plague of Banaras in 1623 CE. After Tulsidas, somehow 'Rama' did get his place in Kashi, but it was his disciple Hanuman, who in some Puranic tales, has been presented as another form of Shiva, got a massive foothold in Banaras. He is personified with his maverick attributes of a bull, skull-mace, rattle drum, trident, crescent moon, Naga, matted hair-knot, datura flowers, bel leaves, lingam and a womb base. He is antinomian and does not like the civilized world. His favourite body balm are the ashes collected from the cremation ground, the ash colour consisting of and signifying two powerful and indispensable elements of the cosmos: fire and air.

Obviously, Shiva is, and for all he betokens, diametrically opposite to Vishnu. He is antithetical, symbolically, literally and at variance in the spiritual realm as well. Both originated and gained momentum in the Brahmanical religious ethos almost simultaneously. An ideological confrontation was well nigh impossible in such a scenario. Some Puranic references have stated that Vishnu gifted Kashi to Shiva.[17] This could be a historical example when Bimbisar was gifted Kashi as dowry by a Kosala king, when he married his daughter. It is quite impossible to date the rise of the lingam worship, but its presence in the epics started from the Gupta era. Some anthropomorphic icons and images of Shiva exist that can be dated to around the second century BCE. Many link it to the Vedic sacrificial post, as is evident with the worship of Lat Bhairava in Banaras. The 'Yupa Stambha' of the Atharva Veda is cited as an example. The Shiva–Shakti conjoint is represented later as a phallic symbol placed over the *yoni* or the vulva. Whereas, in its original form, the projecting portion called the *peetha* served a more practical purpose of draining the water poured over the lingam.

In one of the stories of the *Shiva Purana*, that can be inferred to be a launch pad for the worship of the lingam, Vishnu takes on the form of a beautiful female and collaborates with Shiva. The Mohini roop (a seductress) of Vishnu has been incorporated in many Puranas and there is even a mention of it in the Mahabharata. The story is about an ensemble of *rishi*s (ascetics who are allowed to marry) of Daruvan, an alpine resort in the Himalayas, who decided that they have had enough of Shiva, and they should follow the Vedic methods as laid down in the Vedas in their journey to attain the moksha. When Shiva came to know this, he decided to impart them a higher version of religious worship and for this, he requested Vishnu to inveigle the rishis by taking on the Mohini roop and compel them to forsake their vows and compromise their ethics. Vishnu appeared in the ashram of the rishis, and seeing her, they lost their senses and started following her with all their passion and lust, totally out of their control. Mohini led them inside the thick forest not far from their ashram, and Shiva then entered the ashram of the rishis and through his virility and magical yogic strength, he attracted the wives of the rishis and seduced them. The wives started dreaming of gratifying their wildest desires and implored Shiva to satisfy them. When the rishis heard the sighs of their women folk, they returned to their ashram and were aghast to see their semi-nude wives running after a dishevelled vagabond. They decided to castrate the stranger and ran to get hold of him. Shiva then took on the form of Pashupati and vanished in the forest. Eventually, when the rishis lay siege on him, he mockingly displayed his lingam and along with the scrotum, he pulled it out and threw it towards the rishis and said, 'Take it; this is what you wanted.' From the castrated lingam, there emerged a refulgent beam of light. It was then that wisdom dawned on the rishis and begging forgiveness from the lord, they made a statue in the form of the lingam and worshipped it with the *bilva patra* (bel leaves), vermilion and sandal paste.

Two points emerge from this story: one, the compromise made between the Vaishnavites and Shaivites at some point in the Middle Ages, and two, the onset of the lingam worship. The Daruvan story resonates strongly with ancient Kashi; it was located south of the present-day Maidagin. When we take into account the already existing traditions of the ancient lingam worship, Daruvan might as well be the 'Anandvan'—the forest of bliss. We also have references that during and after the Gahadavala period, with the surge of pilgrimage centres and rush for establishment of denominational schools in and around the holy city of Kashi, the tussle and the one-upmanship along with the subsequent compromises must have been quite palpable.

The second story is about the emergence of the *jyotirlinga,* which has a direct connection with Kashi that has been mentioned in the Kashi Khand of the Skanda Purana in great detail, and the rise and entrenchment of Shiva in his aniconic lingam form. Once, Brahma was taking a stroll in Kashi and he saw Vishnu resting on his great couch of Sheshnaag. He asked Vishnu, 'Who are you?' Vishnu got annoyed at the sheer haughtiness of Brahma and thereafter, an argument between the two ensued as to who is great and who has been more instrumental in the creation and sustenance of the universe. From here on, the story branched into two distinct versions. As per one, that is the Kashi Khand, both Brahma and Vishnu called for the Vedas to settle their arguments. The Vedas proclaimed that neither of them is the greatest, and only Shiva is the Mahadev. During their discussion, apparently, a huge pillar of light appeared that dazzled both of them. In some of the Shia traditions, 'the link between god and the Imams is visualized as being a pillar of light descending from heaven upon the Imam'.[18] This light of the universe has been termed by the erudite scholar of comparative religions, Mircea Eliade, as *axis mundi.*[19] The Westerners were appalled with this cultus of lingam worship, which, their Christian sensibilities and Victorian prudishness considered to be obscene, particularly the writings on Banaras by the Christian bishops and priests.

Brahma and Vishnu totally taken aback upon learning that neither of them is the greatest decided to trace the origin of this pillar of light. Vishnu, in his avatar of a varah (wild boar), went on a digging spree and tunnelled inside the earth. Brahma, on the other hand, jets towards heaven, seated on his vahana, the goose. Even after 1000 years, they were unable to locate the source of light. It was then that Shiva emerged from the light. Vishnu accepted the overlordship of Shiva and Shiva, in turn, assured Vishnu that henceforth he would have an equal status as him and he will be worshipped and honoured like him, albeit in a different temple with a different set of followers. Brahma, though, still remained defiant and surveyed the universe with his four heads; he was so full of himself that a fifth head emerged along with the other four to accommodate his ego. Furious at the display of Brahma's arrogance and pride, Shiva, in his Bhairava incarnation, severed the fifth head of Brahma, thereby symbolically annihilating the baser element of a human being.

Adding another twist to the tale, the *Shiva Purana* mentions that after returning from the search, Brahma lies and states that he has found the point where the pillar meets the sky and the ketaki flower becomes his accomplice in dittoing this slander. Through this story, once again, Shiva's aniconic worship and omnipotence is projected over Vishnu worship and the theatre of this action is the sacred pilgrimage of Kashi. The only icon of Vishnu installed in Banaras was in the Mukti-mandap of the Vishweshvara temple. Worshippers prayed here before going to the main deity. This continued till 1669 and later, in the new Vishwanath temple, another statue on the left side was installed, but Pandit Kedarnath Sukul has a different take on this: 'Upto 1669 the importance of this image was very great, but

Royal Studio, Varanasi

Karmadeshwar Kund and the temple, which was built in the twelfth century by the Garhwal rulers in the Nagar style of architecture

Royal Studio, Varanasi

An image of Karmadeshwar Mahadeo

Royal Studio, Varanasi

A close-up of Karmadeshwar Kund

Royal Studio, Varanasi

The Durga temple at Durga Kund

Royal Studio, Varanasi

Tulsi ghat, nearby is the home of the famous poet and thinker Goswami Tulsidas

Prabhu ghat, which is inhabited by traditional washermen or *dhobis*

Royal Studio, Varanasi

Royal Studio, Varanasi

Pakka Mahal standing tall against the scenic Ganga

Royal Studio, Varanasi

Chet Singh ghat, the palace of Raja Chet Singh from where he made his great escape

Royal Studio, Varanasi

A view of Lolark Kund near Assi ghat

Royal Studio, Varanasi

Manikarnika ghat

Royal Studio, Varanasi

The Nepali Mandir at Lalita ghat

Royal Studio, Varanasi

The wrinkled brow of the Ganga: a bird's-eye view

Royal Studio, Varanasi

Sculptures at the entrance of Shri Samrajeswar Pashupatinath Mahadev Mandir at Lalita ghat

Royal Studio, Varanasi

The Tripur Sundari temple

Royal Studio, Varanasi

The exquisite sculptures of the *gandharvas* and *apsaras*, the singers and the fairies, at the Tripur Sundari temple

Royal Studio, Varanasi

Musicians, fairies and dancers at the Tripur Sundari Temple

Royal Studio, Varanasi

Adikeshav Temple at the Adikeshav ghat

Royal Studio, Varanasi

The Garbha Griha (sanctum sanctorum) of Adikeshav Temple

Royal Studio, Varanasi

Adikeshav Temple at the Adikeshav ghat

Royal Studio, Varanasi

The Alamgir Mosque or the Aurangzeb Mosque at Panchnanda ghat

Ashta Bhairav and an ancient statue of Kali behind Kal Bhairav Temple in Shitala Gali

Remnants of the ancient Naga and Yaksha worship, behind the Kal Bhairav Temple in Shitala Gali

Banaras's famous malaiyo, which is basically flavoured milk foam served in earthen vessels and garnished with finely chopped almonds and pistachios, in an unnamed shop in Thatheri Gali

with the destruction of the Mukti-mandap, its worship practically ceased, although tradition maintains that the image of Vishnu installed there was removed and is now placed in the left hand corner temple as one enters the Visvesvara's campus.'[20] Not only this, it is now mandatory for every person to worship him first, before worshipping the Vishweshvara. Until this story, it appears that Hari and Hara (Vishnu and Shiva) were two different entities and coexisted amicably side by side. It was later that they emerged together, as one, as the Harihar. Strangely, unlike the Abrahamic religions, these two myths point to a curious aspect of Hinduism where, the creator of the world in the Hindu pantheon is not worshipped anywhere except in two nondescript places: Pushkar in Rajasthan and Kumbakonam in Tamil Nadu. Along with this, the ketaki flower is never used as an offering to the deities.

In the Kashi Khand, there is, however, a eulogy on Vishnu, but later on, he is again subordinated to Shiva in a very clever story. Vishnu once takes on the *vaman* (dwarf) avatar and enters a yajna mandapa. The yajna was being organized by the demon king Daitya Raja Bali. When introduced to Bali, Vaman requested him to grant him three paces of land for his *kuti* or hut. Bali accepted his request and asked the vaman to measure his land, and this was when Vishnu takes on a superhuman form and measures the entire earth with just two paces but then leaves the third pace because there was no space left. He then recoiled his step but because of the sudden jerk, the universe exploded, and river Ganga emerged from the foot of Lord Vishnu. In some Puranas, he is said to have measured it with three paces. So, until here, it appears that it is a panegyric tribute to Vishnu, but the story ends with Lord Shiva having to intervene to control the flow of the unrestrained Ganga.

Once, Vishnu was asked by the gods, who knew nothing about Shiva, as to where he resides. Vishnu told them that Shambhu resides inside him as Shankara; that they both are united. He then manifested the lingam, ensconced inside the base of the lotus, sheathed in its soft petals. It was then that the totality of it all overwhelmed the gods so much that they heard the cosmic resonations of the Harihara and the blissful experience of the symbiosis of the Sattva with the Tamas. The gods exclaimed:

'एकम् सत् विप्रा बहुधा वदन्ति'
Ekam sad vipra bahuda vedanti

(Whatever is complete and one, the sages
call it by many names)

Chitgopekar elaborates another interpretation of the lingam worship, where a school of thought believes that 'the linga is raised in chastity, drawing up the seed instead of shedding it, that is, *urddhvaretah*. The erect penis demonstrates the yoga of gnosis'.[21] In this interpretation, the widely believed myth of preserving the semen energy to attain the spiritual realm and the raised lingam as an embodiment of *tapas* (penance) is accepted in the yogic world almost axiomatically. This is what is termed as *lingavir bhava* or the emergence of the lingam. This was probably an attempt to mitigate sectarian conflict through the narratives added in the epics. In Banaras, the lingam is worshipped more in its primordial form and not in its metaphysical interpretation. This was another Puranic attempt to complete the peaceful coexistence of the two dominant sects. If we look at it through the lens of science and the theory of evolution, then we must consider the meteorite shower, the aurora lights, lightning and thunder that have given rise to ancient legends and myths. It was considered to be a message from God and the fallen object was revered and worshipped. Many scientists believe the sacred stone of Kaaba to be a meteorite.[22]

The ancient Greeks and Romans were known to worship meteorites. Some famous ones include Venus of Paphos, The Statue of Ceres, The Stone of Delphi and The Needle of Cybele. Greeks also mention the Magna Mater that was perhaps the most detailed example of a stone's worship by the Pagans. The romans meteorite worship included the Ancile—a magical shield, believed to have fallen from the heaven, and the Aegospotami—also an ancient object fallen from sky. The closest that can be correlated to the lingam worship was, by far, the Roman Heliogabalus. It was worshipped in the form of the sun god. According to the Romans, it fell from heaven and is described as 'a large stone rounded on the base, and gradually tapering upwards to a sharp point; it is shaped like a cone. In color it is black, and they show certain small prominences and depressions in the stone'.[23]

In India, in the early nineteenth century, a large stone weighing about 12 kg hit the earth at Daurala in Uttar Pradesh in 1815. The locals made a temple around it and started worshipping the stone, but the British authorities seized it eventually and sent it to London, where it remains in a museum. Similarly, in the village of Nedagolla in Andhra Pradesh, an iron mass with brilliant light and incandescent tail fell with a loud thud in 1870. People started worshipping it and again, it was impounded by the British and sent to London. Another instance is that of a meteorite named Sabetmahmet, which received the ceremonial lingam worship for many decades.[24] Similarly, the jyotirlingas could have been inspired by the falling stars. It must have been that the phenomenon of a falling star and due to its impact, the appearance of a shaft or a pillar of light was likely seen by the early settlers of the Indian subcontinent.[25] Lord Viscount Valentia in his book *Voyages and Travels to India and Ceylon* has mentioned about this phenomenon near Banaras that was told to him by a Qazi: 'Account of the Stones that fell from the Sky on the 20th December,1799, referred to in Related by Cauzy Syud Hussein Ally. On the 20th of December 1798, (ought to be 9) or 27th of Aghun1 206 Fussily, when four ghurries of the night had passed, a great meteor, which in the Hindoo language is called Look, fell from the westward. It gave a great light, and breaking in the air, divided into several pieces.'[26] Quite possibly, after some time, the people likely observed a dome like rock structure and started to worship it. This could have been passed down orally through the ages, crystallizing the subsequent belief in the jyotirlinga. Many rock structures called 'Menhirs' have been revered, used as sepulchers and for astronomical observations by an ancient subcaste of the Ho tribe near a place called Pokaria in the Chaibasa district of Jharkhand.[27] In fact, Pranay Lal has mentioned an instance of faith and of idol worship in his book—on a trip to locate the oldest fossils of dinosaurs in Kamathi village, the area around Adilabad in the present Telangana state. Their local guide informed that a few years back, people here discovered two stones, which they started worshipping, thinking them to be some ancient deities. They even consecrated the supposed idols of the deity and erected a temple, where they, with full pomp and ceremony, held yearly celebrations, along with elaborate fairs and festivity. Pranay writes that: 'The scientists decided to visit the temple and were amazed to discover that the "stones" were actually the beautifully preserved and complete fossils of the primitive reptile, Lystrosaurus!'[28]

However, there are three stories, which, unlike the above, indicate a violent and an aggressive imposition of Shaivism on the followers of Vaishnavism. These are those of Prajapati Daksh, Krishna and Divodas. Both incidentally earn the wrath of Shiva, being pardoned later, because of his first and second wives. In one story, when the Vaishnavites aggressively gain control of Kashi, Daksh, the father-in-law of Shiva, married his youngest daughter Sati, against Daksha's wishes. Prajapati Daksh here is projected as an ideal, civilized, highly ritualistic and puritanical entity, who is also the dispenser of law and an upholder of social order, quite unlike Shiva. Daksh hates Shiva and in some stories, he even insulted Shiva in Naimisharanya, a mythical pilgrimage on the banks of River Gomti, in the presence of other gods and sages. He was particularly miffed at not being greeted by Shiva.[29] In the story, Prajapati Daksh organized a yajna on the banks of Ganga at his native place called Kankhal. He invited everyone, except Shiva, and by that inference, he did not invite his daughter Sati as well. When Sati came to know about the yajna, she decided to go and attend regardless, despite having been advised by Shiva that one should not go to a place where one is not invited. She told Shiva that a daughter does not need an invitation to go to her father's place. When she reached the yâjna location, she realized that no one paid any attention towards her and rather behaved indifferently, let alone standing up to greet her. After all, she was the daughter and wife of the two most powerful personalities of that time. To her horror, her father came to her and said, 'You are not invited here. Why have you come? Go away from this place!' On hearing this, Sati realized that this yajna was organized to belittle Shiva and it was a deliberate attempt to humiliate him and everything he stood by. Sati then decided to end her life, unable to bear such public ignominy. In some accounts, it is mentioned that she jumped into the sacrificial fire, while in others, she sat on the ground and meditated to conjure her inner fire, the *prana-agni*, ultimately setting herself on fire. When Shiva came to know this, he became wild with rage; his body became fervid. In this form he came to be known as Jvareshwar (Lord of Fever) and his face became *virupaksha* (grotesque). Interestingly, in the Skanda Purana, till this time, he is referred to by his Vedic name of 'Bhagwan Rudra'.[30] In his fury, he plucked out a strand of hair from his matted locks and then emerged the ferocious Virbhadra and Bhadrakali. Shiva ordered both of them to ravage and desecrate the *yajna-sthal* (place of the yajna) and unleash violence and terror. They not only caused mayhem and chaos but also massacred the gods. Finally, it was Virbhadra who caught hold of Prajapati Daksha and beheaded him. Meanwhile, Shiva, after reaching the yajna-sthal, was overwhelmed with deep remorse. He chose to forgive Daksha and brought him back to life by replacing his severed head with that of a goat. The yajna-sthal regained its purity and Daksha completed the yajna, this time offering a fair share of the sacrifice to Shiva. It was only then that he was accepted in the Brahmanical pantheon as Shiva, but Sati was dead, and Shiva, overtaken by grief, lifted Sati's body and roamed around the cosmos. The gods became anxious and Brahma implored Vishnu to put an end to this or the entire creation would be doomed. Vishnu then wielded his Sudarshan Chakra and dismembered Sati's body into 108 pieces. Wherever these parts fell, they transformed into *shakti peeth*s, and are now worshipped as incarnations of the Devi. In the grand finale of Sati's dismemberment, the subtle importance and indispensability of Vishnu are highlighted. Despite this, Vishnu's continuous subordination to the omnipotence of Shiva persisted.

While the Maheshwar Khand of the *Skanda Purana* portrays Prajapati Daksh as belonging to Kankhal, near Haridwar, an interesting twist unfolds in the Kashi Khand of the same Purana. Here, he comes to Kashi and establishes a lingam that is called Dakhsheshwar.[31] Banarasi people worship Sati as Shailputri and the daughter of Kashi. They consider Daksh to be a Kashivasi as he hailed from a place near Sarnath. However, Banarasis are also known to connect every deity with Kashi. Daksh presumably must have been a pre-Buddhist Vedic aristocrat, who unknowingly must have humiliated a local aboriginal, a worshipper of the ancient form of the Shivling that preceded its Brahminical version. According to Altekar, as quoted by Motichandra in his book, this narrative appears as an endeavour to reconcile the differences between Vaishnavism and Shaivism, yet it failed to do so.[32] The second story is from the Mahabharata[33] where Krishna is known to have burnt down the city of Banaras. Even in the *Vishnu Purana*, there are detailed references of this destruction. In one of the stories, Kashiraj is killed by Krishna. His son then undertakes a severe penance to invoke the blessings of Shiva. Appeased by this, Shiva is then said to have created Kritya, a *rakshasi* (female demon), who is unleashed upon Krishna's city of Dwarka to destroy it. Krishna then orders his Sudarshan Chakra to kill her. Kritya then runs back to Kashi, with the Sudarshan Chakra following her there, eventually destroying both Kritya and the entire city along with her.

In another adaptation of Vishnu's incarnation, Narsimha, where he annihilates the demon Hiranyakashipu, many consider this form to be a pre-Vedic representation of the folk deities that abounded in the subcontinent, and eventually, Narsimha came to be known as an avatar of Vishnu.[34] In Kashi Khand, Shiva, represented as a superior god, tames a demon called Dundubhi, who is depicted as*vyaghra roopam* (a ferocious quasi-tiger), by firmly holding him in a tight grasp under his armpit. Once again, Mahadev is appeased by the demon and the Brahmins who were witness to this incident, established a lingam called Vyaghreshwar.[35] According to the Shaiva mythology, Shiva killed another demon named Tripurasura on the full moon day, fifteen days after Diwali. The festival, Dev Deepawali, is celebrated to mark the victory of Shiva over the evil demon in Banaras. This narrative, again, bears a striking resemblance to the Vishnu avatar Rama defeating Ravana, suggesting a recurring theme.

The third story is that of Divodas. In the previous chapter, Divodas's story revolved around his rivalry with the two rakshas, Kshemak and Nikumbh. This one, however, is narrated within the context of Vishnu and Shiva. Most of the Puranic stories intricately interweave, creating a fusion that gives rise to another set of stories within the same historical context, featuring the same cast of characters. Divodas, Shiva, Kshemak and Nikhumb, along with the other ganas, Brahma and Vishnu, all appear differently in this shared historical narrative. I will briefly recount all these Puranic episodes. Divodas was a very capable ruler of Kashi, who ruled under the overarching dharma code of conduct, suppressing superstition and ostentation in his kingdom. He not only expelled Shiva and all his ganas from Kashi but also all the false deities of the Brahmanical faith. In response to this, Shiva then sent Kshemak and Nikumbh, and various other gods as spy messengers to convince Divodas. However, Shiva, before leaving Kashi, had secretly established his lingam in an unknown place. A different story narrates the events leading to Shiva's departure from Kashi.

In an alternate version of this story, after Shiva's marriage with Parvati, he was searching for a more habitable place away from the wilderness of Kailash in the Himalayas. He eagle-eyed the entire universe and discovered a picturesque place adorned with refreshing lakes and gentle hills, Kashi. However, it was under the rule of Divodas. So, Shiva decided to eject Divodas from there with the aid of his two ganas, Kshemak and Nikumbh. Nikumbh appeared in the dream of a barber and asked him to establish a temple and conduct ritual worship for him and his entourage of other ganas. He further tells him to ask all the inhabitants to offer their prayers there and in turn, he would grant them boons. The wife of Divodas, Suyash, was childless, so she started propitiating Nikumbh as the peripheral guardian of the city gates, Ganesha, 'Lord of the Ganas' and asked him to grant her a son. Nikumbh did not acknowledge her repeated propitiations, so Divodas got angry and destroyed the temple. Nikumbh then cursed him that his capital city will be rendered desolate, and all his subjects will vacate the city. That is exactly what happened, and then Shiva made Kashi his abode and all his ganas then ruled Kashi on his behalf.

In yet another version, Divodas, as Ripunjay, was the ruler of a very large kingdom, with Kashi as its capital. He had ruled his kingdom with dharma and was highly praised by the gods for his upholding of the religious doctrines. Ripunjay, however, decided to abdicate his throne to do penance in Kashi. The entire social fabric broke down and there was mayhem, and the rule of law completely neglected. Brahma got worried, and hence requested Ripunjay to once again take control of his beloved Kashi. Ripunjay agreed, setting a condition. He said that in his earlier rule, the gods had started mingling with the mortals and were interfering in the affairs of his kingdom, and now if Brahma himself sought his acceptance, he would agree only if all the gods, including Mahadev, along with his ganas, leave the city and return to their original abodes in the heavens and Mount Mandara, respectively. Brahma accepted his terms and requested all the gods and Mahadev to leave the city. It was then that Divodas took upon the nom de plume of 'Divodas', which means 'servant of heaven', in an interesting paradox that can only occur in the Puranas, and started his second innings in Kashi. Shiva, however, was reluctant to leave, as he had already told Parvati that Kashi was 'Avimukt'—never to be forsaken. Around the same time (and I request the readers to bear with me through the intricate layering and overlap of these myths, as it can get confusing), Mount Mandara engaged in prolonged Puritanical tapasya on the divine soil of Kashi. Through his ascetic telepathy, he effectively communicated to Shiva his fervent wish to be regarded as equal to Kashi, urging Shiva to make his own peaks an exalted abode. Shiva granted him this boon. With this small yet significant addition as an alibi of not compromising on the omnipotence of Shiva, the story paved the way for Shiva to depart from Kashi. So, Shiva agreed to Brahma's request, as well as honoured the wish of his devotee Mount Mandara. The rule of Divodas marked the golden era of Kashi. Egalitarianism was practised in letter and spirit and sacred chants reverberated through the city. There was religious pluralism; each followed his own path for salvation in their own manner. Naturally, the gods became extremely cautious and jealous. Their share of the sacrificial offerings, the *havishya* and the *naivadya*, rapidly declined and to top it all, Divodas never appeased even the most formidable ones, those universally considered essential for all kings to propitiate, such as the weather and rain god, Indra, the god of fire, Agni and the god of wind, Vayu. (Note the non-acceptance of the Vedas here.) In response, they all decided to withdraw their extended cooperation from Divodas. This led to a momentary chaos, but Divodas understood the vileness of the gods and through his own ascetic potency, restored the fire, rain and wind in his kingdom. Subtly, this narrative suggests the dominance of another religion, Buddhism, in Kashi.

The following narration is presented in an attempt to establish the validation of the manifestations of all the presently worshipped major gods and goddesses, along with their jurisdiction, sacred days, shrines and the festivals associated with them in the Kashi kshetra. Shiva, meanwhile, grew agitated and yearned to return to his favourite Kashi. He realized that Divodas is no ordinary king. He needs to be dealt with shrewdly. So, he sent the sixty-four yoginis to lure Divodas. These yoginis were drop-dead enchantresses. As charming as they were, they were also endowed with the power of sorcery, along with the divine abstemiousness of yoga. When they came to the city, they were fascinated and established themselves in the heart of the city, corresponding to all the temples of the devis that we find at their present locations. Through their apparitions, they assumed roles as dancers and garland sellers, taking upon various assignments to cast their spell on the king, but to no avail. Since they did not want to face Shiva having been unsuccessful in their task, they decided to make Kashi their permanent home. Shiva, however, continued to send all the gods and deities under his control to expel Divodas. After the yoginis, he sent the sun god, who, feeling guilty of tarnishing the Dharmic ambiance of Kashi, decided to make Kashi his home in the form of twelve Adityas. Shiva then sent Brahma, who, disguised as a Brahmin, appeared in the court of the king and requested him to patronize the complicated and highly ritualistic performance of ten simultaneous Ashwamedh yajnas. Brahma had presumed that Divodas, at some point, will commit some errors during the exacting procedure that will render him unrighteous and irreligious, but Divodas emerged righteously victorious. The place where Brahma is said to have performed the yajna is now called the Dashashwamedha ghat—the ghat of ten horse sacrifices. Brahma then decided to continue staying at Kashi at the Dashashwamedha ghat and established a lingam named Brahmasheshwar. One by one, Shiva sent all his ganas—Mahakaal (beyond time), Shankukara (pointy-eared), Mahodara (pot-bellied), Ghantakarna (bell-eared)—and they all found their abode in Kashi. Finally, he sent his chief gana, Ganesha. Ganesha visited the king's court, taking the form of a fortune teller and approached the chief queen, Lilavati. Impressed, she recommended him to the king. At that time, Divodas was going through a phase of self-introspection bordering on an existential crisis. He shared with Ganesha his ennui of the everyday grind of life, questioning the purpose and how it would help him discover the ultimate truth. Ganesha, without expressing his blithe, told the king that exactly after eighteen days, a Brahmin will arrive in this sacred city, who will answer your query. Thus, Ganesha prepared the ground for the arrival of Vishnu, whom Shiva, on not receiving any message from Ganesha, had decided to send next. Ganesha then split himself into fifty-two forms and positioned the mall around the city, awaiting Shiva's eventual arrival. When Vishnu first came to the city, he bathed on the confluence of the rivers Varuna and Ganga and stayed in an icon there, which later came to be known as Adikeshav and Padokateerth.[36] Wherever he went, his presence at those places became the tirthas, the most famous being the Bindu

Madhav teerth and the Panchnadi teerth at the Pachnanda ghat.[37] From this point onwards, the story takes on the form of Buddhism and openly challenges its foundation of dharma. The many places that I have visited, where sculptures of erotic symbolism are located, at Khajuraho, Ellora, Puri, Konark, etc.—all have a common story behind their origin. All argue that they have been deliberately carved to bring back and remind the people about their duties as a *grihastha*—a householder's life, and to sustain the life cycle, which got severely affected due to the rise of self-abnegation and penance in Buddhism and Jainism. The Vishnu story is all about this, but very subtly, the original message of Buddhism has been subverted with that of the Vajrayani sects of incantations and black magic, which apparently seemed to be prevalent during the composition of this myth in the Puranas.

When Vishnu, Garuda and Laxmi entered the centre of the city, they took on the form of a Buddhist monk, a disciple and a nun, respectively. They started spreading the message that there are no gods and the individual alone is responsible for his own salvation, there are no castes and no sacrifice, even those that are sanctified by the scriptures, need to be renunciated, as violence is forbidden. One should renounce their desires and passions and become a seeker. The nun initiated the dissemination of enchantments and magical spells among women. This resulted in complete anarchy and profanity taking control of the city. On the eighteenth day, he presented himself to the king and told him about the condition of his beloved city, addressing the wayward behaviour of its subjects due to the king's refusal to allow gods in his city. 'This!' he rebuked, 'despite your supreme blessings and your commitment to upholding the rule of dharma.' When Divodas asked how he can expiate for his mistakes, Vishnu suggested, as you might have guessed, to go and establish a lingam and worship Shiva in that form. He further advised him that if he really wants to completely absolve himself of his impiety and atone for his actions, he must invite and reinstate Shiva back to Kashi. Acting on this counsel, Divodas established a lingam called Divodeshwar and thereafter abdicated in favour of his son.

Shiva returned to Kashi and was welcomed by all the gods at the northern border of the city and they all shrieked with joy and reverence when they saw the Vrishabh Dhwaja (flag of Taurus) of Shiva.[38] The story of Divodas has been given a prominent place in the Kashi Khand due to its significant historical connections and has many interconnected stories, quite common in the Puranic narrations.[39] From a historical standpoint, it is crucial to highlight that there were two individuals by the name of Divodas in different eras in Kashi. The first instance, as mentioned, involved the demon Kshemak, who occupied Kashi, leading to Divodas establishing another Kashi in the present-day area called Bairanth, near Banganga in the Ramgarh tehsil of Banaras. This, as per Motichandra, marked the epic battle between the Haihaya and the Kashyas. The first Divodas was the son of Bhimrath, who established the second Kashi, and the second Divodas reclaimed the original Kashi. Between both Divodas, there were three kings, Shtrath, Haryashaiv and Sudev, who ruled over Kashi.[40] Sherring suggests that the second Divodas was probably a Buddhist king.[41]

I resonate with Diana Eck's perspective, as she aptly states: 'In this one myth, then, we can glimpse the ancient Yaksha dharma in Kashi, as well as a time when Buddhism held sway, and we can see the triumph of Shaivism in claiming the city for the "Great Lord," Shiva Maheshvara.'[42] Additionally, it is worth noting that along with Eck's stance, the non-Vedic and non-Brahmanical goddesses also transformed into yoginis. Through this myth, one can unmistakably analyse how systematically Shaivism asserted dominance over the oldest centres of Vaishnavism, arrogating and ultimately embracing the entire Vaishnav pantheon and its theophany of symbols and images. In the concepts of *pravritti* (the desire to procreate and continue the lineage)and *nivritti* (introspection and eventual renunciation), respectively represented by Daksha and Shiva, lies the essential and inherent conflict of moksha, the eternal, and dharma, the temporal. Here, in Kashi, Shiva seems to reconcile both these aspects. As a householder, he is actively engaged, and as an ascetic, he is poised—an ideal embodiment of sattva. This great reconciliation of the pravritti with that of nivritti is the essence of the metaphysical aspect of Shiva in Kashi. To elaborate simply, it is through Shiva that a maverick wanderer is gradually brought into the householder's fold. Quite unlike many other religions, it is through this 'dualistic-dialectic divide' that Hinduism employs as a methodology to preserve and keep intact the regenerative and the creative cycle of the universe.

Reemphasizing the fact that Kashi, before being a religious centre, primarily served as a trading hub. It was, and still is, a city of traders, and traders are not typically inclined to worship maverick and vegetative deities. From the Jataka stories, a recurring theme emerges—the element of 'fear', whenever traders encounter surreal creatures and beings. They rather go for a well-established religious ideology that falls in their preconceived idea of social order and puritanism. Vaishnavism, in its earliest version, and even now, is the main attraction and theosophical bend. In this story, there are subtle implications where Shiva is portrayed as incomplete and incapable of attaining his desires, despite being the Mahadev with a formidable retinue of ganas. When Shiva realized his mistake of having beheaded his own son, he called upon all the gods and ganas to bring the head of the first living creature they encountered. It was Vishnu who promptly flew on his chariot, the Garuda, and spotted a sleeping elephant. He severed its head with his Sudarshan Chakra and offered it to Shiva, who then coupled the dismembered head of the elephant with the lifeless body of Ganesha, bringing him back to life. Initially, a popular myth portrayed Vishnu as subservient to Shiva, stating that Shiva and Shakti created Kashi and then asked Vishnu to practice austerities there. Vishnu even dug a well in Manikarnika and filled it with his own perspiration of frugality and labour, but thereafter, Shiva always required Vishnu's help to achieve his place in the pecking order of the divinities. The ancient Panchteerth ghats of Kashi had strong Vaishnav roots. They manifested the 'microcosmic body of Vishnu'. Thus, the Asi–Ganga sangam was the head, Dashashwamedha the chest, Manikarnika the navel, Panchnanda the thighs and the Varuna–Ganga confluence or the Adikeshav was the feet. Up until the eleventh century, Vaishnavism was the dominant form of worship, practised not only by the Gahadavala rulers but also by early social commentators such as Kshemendra and Krishan Mishra, who denounced the social evils prevalent in the Banaras region through their prose, and proposed and popularized Vaishnavism as the only solution for widespread social deleteriousness and turpitude.[43]

Shaivism always has only one formidable and most evocative glyph of the lingam, although in some Puranas, Hanuman, too, is depicted as an incarnation of Shiva. Vaishnavism, however, has a succession of avatars or the divine incarnations—sort of forebearers of Vishnu, and by inference, the forebearers of the humankind. These avatars, in theriomorphic and anthropomorphic forms, denote the various evolutionary stages of the earth and Vishnu as a saviour, respectively.

Vaishnavism also has a strong patriarchal element with the overarching representational figure of one God, like Rama and Krishna, whereas the inherent concept of Shakti in Shaivism makes it more inclusive with the feminist ideological precepts. While the rest of the country echoes with the resounding 'Jai Shri Rama' in the dominating influence of the neo-Hinduism, Banaras continues to resonate with the age-old 'Jai Siyaram' (Siya is another name for Sita) or the more prevalent 'Har Har Mahadev'. This also points out another interesting aspect of how Vaishnavism eradicated Buddhism by adopting and appropriating the practices and icons into their own fold. Fergusson is of the view that Vaishnavism rose from the ashes of Buddhism and manifests a strong foreign imprint. It appears that it was imported by a remote immigrant race and somehow could not gain ground, owing to the overshadowing presence of the Buddhist faith, and rose to prominence in the sixth century CE. With the chariot of Vishnu, the Garuda, there was a strong connection with the contemporary empire of the Assyrians, whose supreme deity was a hawk-headed god. Fergusson strongly argues that the serpent symbol of the Vishnu is more heavenly than the earthly and poisonous cobra of Shiva. The serpent is used as a weapon in case of Shiva, but for Vishnu, it extends a protective hood.[44] This nails the basic premise of this chapter that Vaishnavism and Shaivism, being competitive religious doctrines, always resorted to myths and legends, to occupy the religious minds of the followers of the Sanatan Dharma. Coming back to Vaishnavism and its connection with Buddhism, it is clear that all the avatars preceded Vishnu's reincarnation as the Bodhisattva preceded Buddha, with the first four being isomorphic and anthropomorphic. The *Vayu Purana* replaced Buddha with Krishna. The statue of the reclining Buddha, popular among the Indian middle class because of the Feng Shui vibes, is another example of the commonality between the Vaishnavs and Buddhists. In Yoga, it is called Anant asana or the sleeping Vishnu pose.

> From a historical point of view they are no doubt correct in this; all the eight preceding avatars refer to events that certainly preceded the time of Sakya-muni, and when we understand them they may point to a long chain of tradition out of which Buddhism arose, and in to which Buddhism fell, which, when philosophically examined, may throw a flood of light on the origin of Buddhism and of Indian religions generally![45]

We also find the predominance of Tulsi in Vaishnavism. The Chakra emblem of Vishnu is also, as per Fergusson, an import from the Buddhist Chakra found in all the stupas. I have quoted Fergusson to present an alternative view on the rise of Vaishnavism, but here we must exercise caution because most of the western writers on religion in the past—and I believe it continues even now—have given an undue advantage to Buddhism over Hinduism, both in their theory of origin and analysis.

In Banaras, Shiva is now the reigning deity, an incontestable lord of lords, but Vishnu, in his many embodiments, continues to be a sort of eminence grise fully present but as an undercurrent of the main river of the Shaiva faith. Many instances of a serious, though healthy, doctrinal *shastrarth* (debate) on the superiority of one sect over the other have been evidenced from the early Vedic period, but in the later Vedic period the clashes between these two sects had become violent. Particularly, in the southern kingdoms, often during the rule of the Chola Shaivite kings: 'The regular clashes between rival Hindu sects like the Shaiva Nagas and the Vaishnava Bairagis over the least pretext such as precedence in taking their sacred bath in the Ganga during festivals like the Kumbha Mela, reflect an underlying ritual paradigm that valorizes death as liberation.'[46]

As late as in the early eighteenth century, a violent clash between the two sects took place in Nasik during the Kumbh. The *Hindustan Times* quoted that incident in its report on the controversy of the bathing precedence in the holy Trimbakeshwar in 2015: 'A bloody conflict in 1790 between sadhus of the Vaishnava and Shaivite sects over who would have the right of taking the first holy dip claimed the lives of 12,000 ascetics. This bloodbath had forced Peshwa Sawai Madhavrao to limit Vaishnavas to take the Kumbh dip in Nashik while Shaivites were limited to the distant village of Trimbakeshwar.'[47]

However, we do not have any documented evidence of the violent sectarian clashes between the Vaishnavites and Shaivites in the Banaras region. At best, a robust debate and mythological narration that incorporates historical events, along with acculturation occurring from the first to the fifteenth century CE, has given the present lord of lords the divine status that we find him in the holiest of the holy pilgrimages of the Hindus around the world.

Chapter 7

The Ghats

Sonatas Set in Stone

The crescent-shaped layout of Banaras city on the western banks of the river Ganga is truly unique in the world. It stretches from the Samne ghat in the south to Namo ghat in the north—a total of eighty-four ghats over a linear distance of about 6.4 km. The original city was on the northern side on the elevated plateau of Rajghat, near the Varuna–Rajghat confluence, which served as the hub for the ancient river trade. The city's expansion towards the south-western side started with its growing importance as a pilgrimage site. Alongside the sacred kunds, the ghats gained prominence, too, for religious ablutions and sacramental rites. These ghats are the cultural and religious identity of Kashi. Built mainly from sandstone, sourced from the Chunar quarry in the nearby Mirzapur, each ghat has a history and a purpose. Every ritual performed on a ghat is followed by merry-making and indulgence. This sensualist aspect of Hinduism is what makes Banaras a city pulsating with life. A disjunction between the sombre and existentialist questions of the great crematorium and the epicurean delights it lays out. It is here that the difference between Shiva, the lord, and Shav, the corpse, is completely wiped out. The ghats are the spiritual and cultural ambience of the city, and the centre of traditional scriptural erudition. They are not just structures but the muse of the city—the very soul of the city is encapsulated here. The holy Ganga, flowing in a crescent shape, lends its shape to the layout of these ghats. For some reason, though, Ghalib, in his Masnavi, has compared the beauty of Banaras with China to describe the crescent shape of the Ganga.

> Someone once compared the beauty
> of Banaras to China,
> And since that day its brow is wrinkled
> With the bend of the Ganga[1]

Most of the important Hindu temples are located along these ghats. These sonatas set in stone are of recent origin, when we consider the antiquity of this city.

It is irresistible for me to not quote James Prinsep here. When it comes to his description of the ghats of Banaras, he is more of a poet than a member of the Viceroys' government. In a letter to his sister, he described his first tryst with Banaras as:

> This is glorious sight to see the ghats of Benares covered with a moving sea of heads, studded at small distances with temples of red and white stone, all minutely covered and adorned with flowers, while from a hundred places, cymbals and drums peel forth their strains of adoration. The time too is generally favourable to the exhibition, namely, at an eclipse of the sun or at the rising of the full moon. As soon as the signal is given by Brahmins, plunge all the bathers and ripple the holy waters for a mile and a half along the shore.[2]

These ghats, over the years, may have undergone a change of name, although travellers like Ralph Fitch and Jean-Baptiste Tavernier were not able to pinpoint and name these obscure ghats. All the same, in the medieval literature on Kashi, a few unfamiliar names of the ghats do appear. This aspect is important for tracing the changing paradigm of Hinduism, whenever it was threatened. This has mostly happened in the last 300 years. During the British Raj, every Hindu ruler wanted to have a slice of this sanctum pilgrimage pie, by purchasing and renaming a ghat or two after his dynasty or the name of his principality. Even the Muslim rulers, most notably Aurangzeb, attempted and were largely successful, in altering the skyline of the sacred crescent ridge of Banaras forever. Thus, we now have ghats that are named Scindia, Darbhanga, Panchkote, Mysore, Vizianagaram, etc. However, the two most prominent and important ghats for Hindus remain the Dashashwamedha ghat and the Manikarnika ghat, both of which record a heavy pilgrim footfall throughout the year. These two most ancient ghats have also been the places where most of the Puranic stories on Kashi are set. Based on lores, particularly in the Kashi Khand, five such ancient ghats are noteworthy: the Asisamved teerth on the Asi–Ganga confluence, the Varuna–Ganga confluence as described in the *Linga Purana*, the Dashashwamedha ghat, the Panchnanda ghat or the Dharmnad, at the confluence called of five mythical rivers: Ganga, Yamuna, Saraswati, Kirna and Dhootpapa. At Panchnad and at Varuna–Ganga confluence 'the Padoka', it is important to note that Vishnu is the chief pilgrimage deity. The last ancient one being the Manikarnika, we have already mentioned about the well that was filled with the sweat of Vishnu.[3]

The number of ghats increased during the Gahadavala rule, while some were renamed and eventually became extinct during the Islamic rule. These ghats were largely verdant and clay ghats. The prominent ones include: Adikeshav, Vedeshwar, Trilochan and Swapneshwar ghats. The others that came into prominence during the Islamic rule, because of the temple construction spree for a very brief period, before Alauddin Khilji and during Akbar's time, was the Vireheshwar ghat, now called the Scindia ghat. Man Mandir ghat was also constructed at that time by Raja Man Singh.

Fitch travelled around 1583–91 and described most of the sacramental rites taking place on the banks of the river Ganga, but there is no mention of the names of the ghats. For example, he writes:

> Numbers of men and women come out of the town to these places, and wash in the Ganges. On mounds of earth made for the purpose, there are divers old men who sit praying, and who give the people three or four straws, which they hold between their fingers when they bathe in the Ganges; and some sit to mark them in the forehead: And the devotees have each a cloth with a small quantity of rice, barley, or money, which they give to these old men when they have washed. They then go to one or other of the idols, where they present their sacrifices.[4]

The names of twenty-five ghats are mentioned in the Sanskrit text *Girvana-padamanjari*, composed in the seventeenth century by Varadaraja (1600–60). Some of these, like the Sarveshwar ghat, Agnishwar ghat, Vridhaditya ghat, Someshwar ghat, Vireshwar ghat, etc., either do not exist anymore or have been portioned off and renamed. In earlier times, the ghats were largely sand and mud embankments, and presented an area like a raw jetty and were sort of a series of sandy dunes. Till Prinsep's time, i.e., till the 1830s, some remained like that. Many have been lithographed by William Hodges in the early nineteenth century.

However, we find mention of stone steps on the Ganga in the travels of Tavernier, who travelled to India six times and has left a wonderful account of his travels in Banaras in 1679. Describing most probably the Bindu Madhav temple and the ghat, he writes: 'The most remarkable thing about it is that from the door of the pagoda to the river there is a descent by stone steps, where there are at intervals platforms and small, rather dark, chambers, some of which serve as dwellings for the Brahmans, and others as kitchens where they prepare their food.'[5]

After Man Singh and before the ghats and temples construction spree that started with the Marathas in Banaras, an interesting Muslim aristocrat, Meer Rustam Ali, is remembered in Banaras for the many contributions made by him. In the earlier chapter we have mentioned how after the initial maniac bigotry of the Sultanate rulers and then after Aurangzeb's rule, Muslims—both the nobility and the masses—were overwhelmingly adopting the cultural, and to some extent, even the religious ethos of Banaras. Mir Rustam Ali is the perfect example of this. When Saadat Ali Khan became the Nawab of Awadh in 1730, he handed over the *bandobast* (administrative and revenue matters) of Banaras to Mir Rustam Ali for Rs 8 lakh. Rustam Ali was also a great builder and in 1735, in between the present Man Mandir ghat and the ancient Jalashayee ghat, he constructed an elevated revetment to prevent river erosion, a stone paved ghat named after him—the present Meer ghat—and a massive fort. Raja Balwant Singh later utilized the material from these constructions to build the Ram Nagar Fort across the river. With the rise of the Marathas, the construction of temples and ghats in Banaras burgeoned. As has been mentioned earlier, since the time of Shri Narayan Bhatt, the Maharastrian Brahmins made a beeline to settle down and contribute their bit to the religious tasks the city offered or they created some themselves. Through the historical documents from the Peshwa's office, specifically a letter written by Sada Shiv Naik, who handled the affairs in Banaras during Peshwa Bajirao I's rule, we gain valuable insights into the early-eighteenth-century Banaras. The records highlight the phenomenal contribution of a Brahmin named Narayan Dixit Patankar.[6] He was a highly learned religious scholar and a social worker in Pune. As soon as he arrived in Banaras in 1734, along with a retinue of 1200 of his followers and family members, he set about establishing a locality exclusively for his clan and his followers. He even purchased a huge plot of land near the present Brahma ghat that had a temple called Brahmeshwar, previously occupied by the Nishad community, known for typically engaging in fishing and ferry services. He constructed two ghats—Brahma and Durga—along with houses for the Maharashtrian Brahmins and for himself. Later, the famous Maratha general Nana Phadnavis also constructed many buildings in this locality. The place is still called Dixitpura.

Narayan Dixit later renovated Trilochan ghat and Harishchandra ghat. At Manikarnika ghat, he streamlined the cremation system that was dominated by the Dom (considered outcastes) community, traditionally engaged in cremation and subsequent body disposal. They had monopolized the ghat and were bullying the people who came there to cremate their dear ones. So, Dixit fixed a stipulated amount as cremation tax. The stone steps in all the above mentioned ghats were his contribution. The famous leitmotif of Banaras and its ghats—the huge bamboo umbrella and a raised pedestal—was entirely his brainchild. This essentially aimed to facilitate the Brahmins performing religious ablutions and rites. He also constructed many cow shelters and the cow-feeding points along the ghats. However, in some manner, the ghats were more a symbol of the display of pride and for *amarattv* (immortality), which is so seductive a desire for humankind. Pakka ghats and the adjoining palaces ruined the pristine scenic aura of the pilgrimage that was Kashi till the start of the eighteenth century. Only one man, Raja Balwant Singh, and before him, the Gahadavala rulers, decided to construct the embankments at the five places where the danger to the city on account of rising water and soil erosion was the highest. The construction of the pakka embankments at Ramnagar, where the Ganga takes a sharp turn from Shoolkanteshwar, at Shivala where it turns again and at Dasaswamedh, then at Panchganga, finally hitting the banks at Rajghat and acquiring a passive flow. Even in the paintings by artists like William Hodges and William Daniell, particularly the famous 1789 depiction of the Budgerow and Morphunki with the Shivala ghat in the background, mud banks dominate the scenery. However, an alternative, perhaps more scientific perspective suggests that 'the entire concave bank as it can be seen nowadays from its top margin to its lowest possible water level is lined up by heavy and large stones creating beautiful stone stairs running along almost 12 km of distance. These steps are fairly of recent origin from the 18th century onwards laid out mostly by Maratha rulers and devotees'.[7] This single great effort of man has stopped further recession of this concave bank and damage to the habitation above it during the last 250–300 years. While this may be true, the science behind the construction of such huge palaces occupying the serene river front was certainly not in the minds of the megalomaniacs and still does not do justice to the ancient city of Anandvan.

Hodges was a famous eighteenth-century British painter who visited Banaras in 1781, along with the Governor General Warren Hastings, and has painted some of the most beautiful paintings of Banaras that were undergoing a feverish pace of temples and ghats construction. Some of his most outstanding paintings include *The Ghauts at Benares*, *Benares on the Ganges*, *View of Benares* and many more. Apart from painting, he also recorded his impressions in the book *Travels in India*, published in 1794. His description is an interesting and authoritative account of the then Benares. He writes:

> It is built on the north side of the river, which is here very broad, and the banks of which are very high: from the water, its appearance is extremely beautiful; the great variety of the buildings strikes the eye, and the whole view is much improved by innumerable flights of stone steps, which are either entrances into the several temples, or to the houses. Several Hindoo temples greatly embellish the banks of the river, and are all ascended to by Gauts, or flights of steps, as I have already noticed. Many are only embankments, to prevent the overflowing of the water from carrying away the banks at the season of the periodical rains.[8]

Travelling in Banaras in 1803, Lord Viscount Vanentia found the ghats quite enchanting and from his description, one can come to know that a number of ghats in the early nineteenth century were metalled, and the steps were paved with stones.[9]

By 1850, steps were constructed, and most of the prominent ghats were paved with stone steps and the stone pedestals at consecutive heights. Prinsep has listed fifty-seven ghats and by 1910, the recorded number had increased to sixty-four. During this period, there were numerous serious fights between the local Brahmins, known as Gangaputras, and the Brahmins from Maharashtra and south India, called the Panchdravida Brahmins. These Gangaputras claimed exclusive rights for the rituals and ablutions performed by the pilgrims and refused to allow the outside Brahmins from sharing the donations and offerings. They not only harassed the pilgrims but also indulged in criminal activities of looting and murder. Hasting is credited with the reform and restructuring of religious activities on the ghats through the enactment of statutory laws and the use of force to restrain these Brahmins. The heavy footfall of pilgrims and the congested construction on the ghats during the early and late nineteenth century raised concerns about health and sanitation for the British administration. Thus, in 1868, the Banaras Municipal Board tried to close cremations on the ghats. However, there was a huge outrage on the mere consideration of such a proclamation being implemented, and that led to its repeal by the district magistrate. The decision was overturned, citing concerns over law-and-order problems and the strong sentiments of the populace.

There was another group of Gangaputras, who were not Brahmins but claimed the same status. They were the *manjhi*s or the *mallah*s (traditional professional boatmen). They had the sole right to be in charge and take care of the ghats and the monopoly over the boat ride business for many generations. In 1817, the collector of Banaras took over the activities of these boatmen and levied a token tax on their profession. He also restored the tradition of free ferrying for ascetics, mystics and sages—a practice initiated by Bimbisar for Gautama Buddha. Many such stories of the gangs of Kashi Gangaputras continuing this tradition, still circulate. These will be further explored in the description of Kashi Karvat temple. In his partially penned novel *Premyogini*, Bharatendu Harishchandra mentions in the poem 'Dekho hamri Kasi':

ghaat jaao te gangaaputtar nochain dai gal faansii
karain ghaatiyaa bastar-mochan de deke sab jhaansii.

(When you visit the ghats, the Gangaputra maul you and hang
you with their stupid logic, swindling you in the process.)

We have already read the passionate description of Prinsep. Like Hodges, he has sketched many ghats and temples of Banaras during his decade-long stay there that were lithographed by prominent artists such as C. Hullmandel and L. Haghe. He perhaps was too overwhelmed to express his emotions in words and had to switch over to the pictorial medium to do justice to the city.

Around 1870, Bishop M.A. Sherring visited Banaras, ostensibly to study the ancient Hindu pilgrimage centre, but the visit was more to explore the possibilities of missionary activities. He, too, has given graphic details about the life and rituals in and around the ghats and temples, and the socio-economic condition of Banaras in the late nineteenth century in his book *Benares: The Sacred City of the Hindus*. Sherring, like Diana L. Eck, later has taken the sacred Panchkroshi route to describe the ghats and its attendant rituals at the temples on the ghats.

Mark Twain visited Banaras in 1899 and in his famous book *Following the Equator*, eloquently describes the riverfront: 'The Ganges front is the supreme show-place of Benares. Its tall bluffs are solidly caked from water to summit, along a stretch of three miles, with a splendid jumble of massive and picturesque masonry, a bewildering and beautiful confusion of stone platforms, temples, stair-flights, rich and stately palaces.'

The famous Chinese traveller of the early fourth century CE, Fa-Hien, and then Hiuen Tsang in the sixth century CE, both visited Banaras and have mentioned about the city of 'Pholo-nai' and 'Polo-nisse', respectively, located on the banks of the river Heng (Ganga) that is three miles long and one mile broad. Both, however, do not mention anything about the ghats and the temples inside the city and have focused entirely on Sarnath. I have deliberately gone into the details of the travellers as it sheds light on the name and importance of the ghats and its emergence on the popular pilgrimage circuit.

By the time of Eck wrote her seminal book *The City of Light*, published in 1981, the ghats numbered just a little over seventy.

The one daily ceremony that is the pièce de résistance is the renowned Subah-e-Banaras (the dawn at Banaras) at the ghats of the city. For us permanent residents of Banaras, visiting the ghats was almost a daily ritual. Festivals and fairs notwithstanding, a visit to the ghats could be for any reason. With relatives visiting from neighbouring villages, after the end of exam, for ogling at women bathers and sometimes for occasional cannabis. Our family boatman was a mallah called Chhannu. No, he was not our salaried employee, but one whom we always hired to take us for a ride on the river. No one could keep Chhannu at his beck and call; he was fiercely independent and lived every moment on his own terms and conditions—very typical of all the Banarasis. His boat was a modest, typical, traditional vessel, likely passed down through generations, a legacy from his forebearers of ages past. The boat had wooden planks as seats covered with jute bags. Chhannu belonged to one of the most ancient aboriginal communities, the Nishads, who used to call themselves the real Gangaputras, the sons of Ganga, and colloquially the ghatias, the people of the ghats. The references of Nishads are in the Valmiki Ramayana, who ferried Lord Rama across the river. For the Nishads, the river is their farm; they live and earn with everything that the river has to offer. They even grow seasonal fruits and vegetables along the reclaimed land along the river. He was short, extremely muscular, with shining black skin. Those were not the days of cell phones but miraculously, every time we or any other member of our family went to the Dashashwamedha ghat, from where he plied his boat, we would find Chhannu waiting for us. As if through telepathy, he had come to know of our visit. It was Chhannu who initiated me and my brother into the realm of the mystical and transcendental through a puff of his chillum, which was laced with the rawest form of cannabis that has seeds and is sold along the ghats as 'ganja'. While gently floating on the Ganga, I had the first experience of doping and we began to float with strange and surreal images, along with episodic, sensual moments. Chhannu regaled us with the stories of his rendezvous with foreigners, particularly those who came starry-eyed in the twilight days of the hippie era in the late seventies, seeking transcendental experiences. Chhanu had a remarkable ability to sell anything to anyone; he could even sell a refrigerator to a man from the Tundra region. He himself once told us how often, during lean days, he would sell cow dung cakes adorned with a vermilion mark to some group of American tourists who were avid souvenir collectors, and even to some unsuspecting south Indian pilgrims.

We took occasional baths with Chhannu always playing pranks on us. We often saw him diving deep to bring coins tossed by the pilgrims. Sometimes, we used to get anxious as he took a long time returning back to the surface. Later, we came to know that Chhannu's part earnings also came from the temples on the ghats that used to get submerged during and quite after some time in the monsoon season. On auspicious occasions, pilgrims would normally give their offerings and fees to the divers who, in turn, would then dive and perform the puja on their behalf for the idols of the deities established inside the temple. Chhannu's boat was always full of half-rotten coconut and fruit offerings. He now reminds me of the Bajau people of South-east Asia who lived in and around water. Both Amitav Ghosh and Numair Atif Choudhury, in their novels *The Gun Island* and *Babu Bangladesh*, respectively, have spun paranormal tales around the Bajau people.

My first encounter of a semi-nude female body during the flush of teenage years also took place on these ghats. For me, it held a rather mischievously seductive allure. The bathers, with cotton sarees sticking to their chiselled bodies, let their long hair drip with droplets that gleamed in the rays of the sun. The display of taut nipples and shapely derriere through their diaphanous long, petty garments now reminds me of the bathers' series of paintings by impressionist masters like Paul Cézanne, Pierre-Auguste Renoir and Claude Monet. Strangely, though, in retrospect, my innocent ogling never seemed to make them conscious. On the contrary, they remained devoid of any self-awareness about their bodies, a quality that Ghalib described as divine countenance: 'Their gestures of bathing grant, each wave the good tidings of honour and their joy stuns the waves (of the Ganga) to stillness. Their newness grants shape to the body of water.'[10] There was a strange and overwhelming calmness of piety and divinity among the bathers, who perhaps submitted their whole being to the sublimity of Ganga maiya (Mother Ganga). I used to watch them taking a dip, unfolding the edges of their sarees, rearranging it and daintily walking out of the water, negotiating the steps. Thereafter huddling together, chirping and laughing while slipping into their fresh clothes. Then, they used to make clay lingams from the stagnant slush left by the retreating river and perform the puja by pouring water, applying sandal paste and making offerings of datura and flowers. Chanting Shiva's names, they would gently place these lingams into the flowing river. All this seems like a distant dream to me now, though, and could very well be sequenced into a film depicting the Banaras of that time. The river water at the ghats was clean but full of organic refuse of flowers, garlands and fruits.

Even for a bohemian wanderer like me, I could never visit every ghat of Banaras during my stay there. That is why this time, I decided to take a deliberate and planned trip to all the eighty-four ghats. I will begin my journey from the Adikeshav ghat and will let the readers know of the brief history and peculiarity of each of them, along with their Puranic importance. I have dedicated a separate chapter to describing the many temples that line these ghats.

Adikeshav ghat: Also called the Varuna–Ganga Sangam ghat, it is situated at the edge of the Kashi kshetra. The Gahadavala rulers used to bathe and offer donations at this ghat. Originally, it was a natural clay embankment, but in 1790, stone embankments were constructed by a Maratha aristocrat of the Scindias of Gwalior. It holds significant mythological importance as the Vishnu teerth.

Khidki ghat: Originally, a verdant and natural river ghat, it evoked the essence of old Kashi. Now renamed Namo ghat, after being renovated with stone steps and some unrelated concrete structures, it doesn't aesthetically align with the spiritual and cultural idea of Banaras. This is the same ancient Vedeshwar ghat mentioned earlier.

Rajghat: Named after the residences of the kings who ruled from here, this settlement dates back to 800 BCE. Serving as the hub and administrative capital of the Gahadavalas, it was paved with stone in 1988. It is also called the Mahishasur ghat.

Sant Ravidas ghat: This ghat was carved out from the old Rajghat in the early nineties. Sant Ravidas used to stay at this ghat.

Rani ghat: Previously part of Rajghat, this area underwent a transformation in 1937, when Munia Sahiba, a queen of a taluqdari called Itaonja, constructed a huge palace named Janki Kunj on the ghat. Since then, it has been known as Rani ghat.

Nishad ghat: It was earlier the settlement of the Nishads. They are the people after the priests who form the chunk of Gangaputras. Traditionally, they were boatmen but now are into all trades that emanate at these ghats.

Prahlad ghat: The famous slaying of the demon Hiranyakashipu by Lord Vishnu, to save his worshipper Prahlad, as per the Puranic story, took place here. The district authorities constructed this ghat at the beginning of the twentieth century.

Naya ghat: The old name of this ghat is Phuteshwarghat, which had a Shiva temple called Phuteshwar Mahadev. In 1940, a rich resident of Chainpur in Bihar, Narsingh Japal, refurbished the ghat and since then, it is called the Naya ghat.

Telianala ghat: This ghat had an egress to the old Telianala, which was blocked in 1988.

Shuka ghat: Stone paved in 1988.

Nandishwar ghat: Constructed in the 1930s.

Gola ghat: Had the grain market, hence the name.

Trilochan ghat: Important ghat during the Marathas. Sherring has mentioned this ghat and the adjoining temples many times in his book.

Badrinarayan ghat: Till the late nineteenth century, it was called Mahta ghat, and was renamed after the construction of the Vishnu temple Badrinarayan.

Gaiya ghat: Famous for being absolved of *gau hatya* (killing of cows) if one takes a dip here. The Malviya bridge crosses the river, constructed during 1880–87.

Hanuman Garhi ghat: It was a part of Gaiya ghat till 1950, and was renamed as Hanumangarhi after a local sage, Baba Shyamdas, constructed a Hanuman temple there.

Lal ghat: Constructed by the ruler of Tijara principality in Rajasthan at the beginning of the twentieth century, this ghat was later purchased by the philanthropist and businessman Raja Baldev Das Birla in 1935.

Shitala ghat: It is named after the Shitala Devi temple situated there.

Bundiparkota ghat: Originally known as the Adi Vishweshwar ghat, it was stone-paved in the late sixteenth century by the king of Bundi, Maharaja Rao Surjan. It holds historical significance as Chaitanya Mahaprabhu is reported to have stayed here at Chaitanya Vat during his visit to Banaras in February 1516.

Brahma ghat: This is the same place where Brahma came to stay after being ordered by Shiva, as mentioned in the Kashi Khand. He also established a lingam called Brahmaeshwar. It has a thirteenth-century Brahma statue, and the ghat was built by Narayan Dixit.

Durga ghat: It houses the Brahmacharini Durga temple. Built by Narayan Dixit in 1740 and renovated by the Uttar Pradesh government in 1958.

Panchnanda ghat: Formerly known as the Bindumadhav ghat, it was renovated by the Maharastrian nobleman Shripat Rao. The original Bindu Madhav temple, constructed by Raja Mansingh, was destroyed by Aurangzeb, but later rebuilt by the king of Audh, Bhavanram. In 1699, the King of Amer, Maharaja Sawai Jaisingh, constructed a Rama mandir on this ghat. On the steps of this ghat, Sant Ramanand stepped on Kabir after which he was accepted by Ramanand as his disciple. It houses the Ramanand math. It is recorded in some Persian documents that Chhatrapati Shivaji, after escaping from the Agra fort, stayed here incognito and took daily baths on this ghat.

Balaji ghat: It was constructed by the Peshwa Bajirao of Pune in the 1830s. In 1864, the British auctioned the huge palace on the ghat, which was purchased by Jiyaji Rao Scindia. He then constructed the temple of Balaji, and since then, it has been named Balaji ghat.

Gwalior ghat: Part of the old Chor ghat, it was renovated by the ruler of Gwalior in the mid-twentieth century, hence renamed Gwalior ghat.

Jatar ghat: Constructed by the Diwan of Raja of Gwalior, Balaji Chimanji Jatar, this ghat has a huge palace and an ornate temple of Laxminarayan. It is also called the Lakshmanbala ghat.

Ram ghat: A Rama temple was constructed here by Raja Sawai Jai Singh I, which was later destroyed by Aurangzeb. However, a new temple was erected by the Marathas in the 1840s.

Mehta ghat: Constructed by a Calcutta resident, Ballabhram Saligram Mehta in 1960, who also built a hospital here.

Ganesh ghat: This was part of the Agnishwar ghat till the beginning of the nineteenth century. Peshwa Amritrao stone-paved and constructed an Amrit Vinayak (Ganesh) temple in 1807, hence the name Ganesh ghat.

Agnishwar ghat or Yageshwar ghat: The old Agnishwar Shiva mandir and teerth is located here. It was stone-paved by the Uttar Pradesh government in 1995 and is also called the Naya ghat.

Bhonsla ghat: Formerly known as the Nageshwar ghat, it has a statue of a coiled Naga and has been historically associated with the ancient naga puja. It has a huge palace and a Laxminarayan temple, constructed by the Bhonsale rulers of Nagpur in 1795.

Ganga Mahal ghat: It was a part of the Sankhta ghat till 1864, when the Gwalior ruler, Jiya Ji Rao, purchased the northern portion of it, and constructed a stone-paved ghat and a huge palace that eventually came to be known as the Ganga Mahal.

Sankatha ghat: It is named so because it houses the famous temple of Sankatha Devi. This temple was renovated by the queen mother of Baroda in 1820. The ghat was stone-paved by the wife of Pandit Vishwambhar Dayal, a renowned Sanskrit scholar, in 1825. It was renovated in 1923 by Maharaja Siyaji Rao Gaikwad III of Baroda.

Scindhiya ghat: The ancient name of this ghat is Vadeshwar ghat, and was established in 1835 by Rani Baijabai Scindia, the wife of Maharaja Daulatrao Scindia of Gwalior. It serves as a stronghold for ascetics from various sects, including Shaiv, Vaishnav, Kabir, Nanak and Dadu. Around this ghat are located their small ashrams and congregational places.

Manikarnika ghat: This ghat happens to be the oldest one, serving more as a teerth than an exclusive cremation ground. An important observation that can possibly only be pointed by an outsider, is that: 'Elsewhere in traditional India, the cremation ground is outside of town, for it is polluted ground. Here, however, the cremation grounds are in the midst of a busy city, adjacent to the bathing ghats, and are holy grounds, for death in Kashi is acclaimed by the tradition as a great blessing. Dying here, one gains liberation from the earthly round of samsara.'[11] In 1623, Raja Vasudev's minister, Shree Narayan Das, donated a piece of land near this ghat, where the famous Chakrapushkarini teerth is constructed.

This was one of the main Vishnu teerth, even before Shaivism encroached upon the religious space of Kashi. By the nineteenth century, it was already partitioned into Scindia, Sankatha, Dattatrey, Siddhivinayak, Manikarnika and Jalashaayee ghats. Much later, the Siddhivinayak and Dattatary ghats merged with it. This ghat was stone-paved in 1730 by Sadashiv Nayak, with the help of Bajirao Peshwa. The exclusive wing for ladies, in the northern side of this ghat, was constructed by Maharani Ahilyabai Holkar of Indore in 1780. It is noted by Dr Motichandra[12] that other than Harishchandra ghat, no other ghat was exclusively designated just for the ritualistic cremation of dead bodies. The entire area, including the Sankatha ghat, was designated as an ancient crematorium. There is a story about Manikarnika ghat becoming a Mahashamshan. Kashmiri Mal, a very rich merchant of Banaras, could not cremate his mother on the Harishchandra ghat due to the harassment of the Dom community. He immediately brought the dead body of his mother to Manikarnika ghat and purchased the entire area from the petty Brahmin landowners. There, he established a cremation ghat, with a stipulated taxation on the Doms. Manikarnika, before turning into a Mahashamshan, was more popular as a pilgrimage centre.

Jalshaee ghat: Also known as the Jalasen ghat, it is believed to be the abode of Lord Shiva in the form of a lingam. This is the same ghat described by William Hodges as the Gelsi Gaut.

Lalita ghat: It is named after the Lalita Devi temple situated on the top portion of the ghat. It is also called the Nepali ghat because of the presence of the temple of Pashupateshwara, the chief deity of Nepal.

Mir ghat: Initially called the Jarasangh ghat, it was constructed by Mir Rustam Ali and was hence renamed after him.

Tripura Bairavi ghat: This has a Tripurari devi temple.

Varahi ghat: It is home to the renowned temple of the fearsome Varahi devi, situated near a small lane.

Manmandir ghat: Formerly known as Someshwar ghat, it boasts of a beautiful Rajput-style architectural ensemble, including a temple and palace. Constructed by Mirza Raja Man Singh of Amer, it later saw the foundation and completion of an astronomical observatory by his great-grandson, Mirza Raja Sawai Jai Singh II (1699–1743). This astronomical observatory, initiated in 1710 and completed in 1737, features a map designed by the royal astronomer Samrath Jagnath and the famous sculptor of Jaipur, Sadar Mahon. Sawai Jai Singh II holds the distinction of being the only ruler, after Bharshiva, to have performed the Ashwamedhayajna and the Vajpeye yajna.

Dr Rajendra Prasad ghat: It was a part of the Dashashwamedha ghat and was known by its ancient name, Ghoda ghat. This fact also has been corroborated by a copper plate inscription by Pravarsen II, who had established a horse stone statue in the northern side of Dashashwamedha ghat, which gave it the name Ghoda ghat.[13] A few scholars, however, have stated that it got its name from the ancient horse trade that happens here. In 1984, the Uttar Pradesh government renovated this ghat and named it Dr Rajendra Prasad ghat, after the first president of India.

Prayag ghat: This ghat was constructed by Maharani H.K. Devi of Potia, Bengal, in the beginning of the nineteenth century.

Dashashwamedha ghat: Its antiquity can be gauged by the fact that Bharshiv emperors performed the Ashwemedha yajna at this place. This is the most important ghat of Banaras, and all seasonal and religious bathing rituals take place here. The famous Ganga festival and the daily Ganga aarti are also performed here. While idol immersions once took place here, government regulations have led to its relocation near the Mandakini kund. Formerly known as Rudrasar, the ghat earned the name Dashashwamedha after Brahma's yajna. Historical records affirm that the triumphant Naga Bharshiv, after defeating the Kushans, performed the Dashashwamedha yajna at this very site. In Vedic rituals and mantra recitation, Rudra is invoked and the name Rudrasar often comes up during the puja ceremonies.

Sheetla ghat: This ghat was also a part of the Dashashwamedha ghat and is located in its southern side. It was constructed by Maharani Ahilyabai Holkar of Indore in the mid-eighteenth century and houses the famous Sheetla Devi mandir.

Ahilya Bai ghat: As the name suggests, it was constructed by Maharani Ahilyabai Holkar in 1785, along with the adjacent grand palace. Its ancient name was Kewal Giri ghat. It also has a huge monastery, a barnyard and a Hanuman mandir, all built by the maharani.

Munshi ghat: Named after Shridhara Narayana Munshi, the minister of the Raja of Nagpur in 1812, who built this ghat, the palace and the temple next to it.

Darbhanga ghat: This ghat, along with its greatly embellished palace, was also the initiative of Shridhara Narayana Munshi in the same year, 1812. It was earlier a part of the Munshi ghat. In 1915, the Raja of Darbhanga, Rameshwar Singh Bahadur, purchased the palace and since then, it is called the Darbhanga ghat. Currently, it has been leased to a hotel group.

Rana Mahal ghat: Constructed by the Raja of Udaipur, Rana Jagat Singh, in the late seventeenth century, there is an exquisite Rajasthani–Rajput style palace here that houses the sixty-four yogini temples.

Chausatthi ghat: This is adjacent to the Rana Mahal that has the temple of chaunsath (sixty-four) yoginis, hence the name. It was constructed by Raja Pratapaditya of Bengal in the sixteenth century and was renovated by Raja Digpatiya.

Digpatiya ghat: This ghat was also constructed by Raja Digpatiya in the mid-eighteenth century.

Pandey ghat: The ancient name of this ghat was Sarveshwar ghat. It was constructed by Mr Babua Pandey of Chapra, Bihar, in the mid-nineteenth century.

Rajaghat: The ghat and the palace were constructed by Peshwa Amritrao in 1807. It also houses the Annapurana monastery. Until recently, it was known as the Amritrao ghat.

Narad ghat: The ancient name was Kubai ghat. After the construction of the Shiva temple, Naradeshwar, in the mid-nineteenth century, it was renamed the Narad ghat.

Mansarovar ghat: It has a pond called Mansarovar, which, as per the belief, has the same hieratic benefits like the Mansarovar lake in Mount Kailash. This was built by Mirza Raja Man Singh of Amer.

Kshemeshwar ghat: The association of Kashi with the demon Kshemak, is prominently revealed by this ghat, as it is believed that the Shivling that he established was located at this place.

Chauki ghat: Built by the Kumarswamy Mathin in the mid-nineteenth century, this is also the seat of the ancient Naga Puja.

Kedar ghat: This ghat has the famous third Kedareshwar temple of Kashi.

Vijyanagram ghat: It was constructed by the Rajasaheb of Vijayanagaram in Andhra Pradesh, who donated the huge palace located on this ghat to a sage called Swami Karpatri.

Lali ghat: This ghat, also sometimes known as the Lalli ghat, was also stone-paved by Raja Saheb Vijaynagram. It has the residence and now shrine of Saint Lali Baba of Champaran, Bihar. He had established an *akhada* (cirque, arena), called Gudad Das ka akhada, which still exists as a holy place.

Harishchandra ghat: Also called the Adi Manikarnika or the ancient Manikarnika, this is the most ancient crematorium of Banaras. Legend has it that Raja Harishchandra sold himself here to a Dom. The story of Harishchandra, as told to us by our grandmother, encapsulates the essence of King Harishchandra being a true *satyawadi* (the truthful one). As per the story, he once was asked by Sage Vishwamitra for a religious donation, and Harishchandra, displaying an overzealous magnanimity, donated his entire kingdom. Vishwamitra then decided to test the ethical and religious commitment of the king and asked for some more. To his surprise, Harishchandra decided to sell his wife, son, and even himself to an undertaker of the Dom community, at the cremation ground. It so happened that his son died due to a snakebite and his wife brought the dead body to be cremated, and Harishchandra refused to accept the body without the mandatory fee. The gods were pleased with his extraordinary commitment, and he was honoured with the return of his kingdom, along with the restoration of his son's life. An electric crematorium has been constructed here, but the religious-minded still prefer the traditional methods and rituals to honour their dead. This electric crematorium was built in 1986.

Mysore ghat: Earlier, apart of the Hanuman ghat, this, along with the temple and the inn, were built by the Raja of Mysore, Karnataka. It is also called the Karnataka ghat.

Hanuman ghat: Renovated by the Raja of Mysore, this ghat has the famous eighteenth-century Hanuman temple. The statue of Hanuman was established by Goswami Tulsidas. This is the bastion of the Vaishnavites. The thirteenth century reformer, Ballabhacharya, resided on this ghat, and a group of extremely prosperous ascetics have their akhada here, which is called the Juna Akhada. It is said that a gambler named Nand Das constructed the steps of this ghat from his one day's earning. It also has a statue of a 'Ruru' dog, Bhairav.

Dandi ghat: It is home to a sect of ascetics known as Dandiswami, who carry a staff or stick, lending the name to the ghat.

Gulariya ghat: It is named after the huge Gular tree or the Sycamore tree that exists here.

Shivala ghat: Constructed in the eighteenth century by Raja Balwant Singh, it was once a huge ghat that has now been proportioned. The ghat has a massive palace built by the Raja of

Nepal, Sanjay Vikram Shah. The northern part is still recognized as the Shivala ghat and houses a Shiva temple. It serves as the citadel of the Aiyaar Brahmin and the Telugu-speaking Shaivite community of south India.

Mahanirvani ghat: Associated with the Mahanirvani sect, it houses a monastery and a cirque. Reportedly, the Buddha used to bathe at this ghat.

Niranjani ghat: It is home to the ferocious Naga ascetics of the Niranjani Akhada. These Nagas and the gosains of this akhada are the same warriors who fought against the armies of the East India Company, along with the armies of Shuja ud-Daula. William Dalrymple, in his book *Anarchy*, writes that 'perhaps Shuja's most feared crack troops were a large force of 6,000 dreadlocked Hindu Naga Sadhus, who fought mainly on foot with clubs, swords and arrows, ash-painted but entirely naked, under their own much-feared Gossain leaders, the brothers Anupgiri and Umraogiri'.[14]

Chet Singh ghat: This has its own historical importance, as both the ghat and its accompanying fort were constructed by Raja Balwant Singh with the advice of his engineer Baijnath Mishra. The locality is called Shivala, hence the name. His son, Chet Singh, lost the battle with the British and abandoned the fort. Thereafter, this entire property remained with the British for about 125 years. It was only in 1895 that Chet Singh's descendant, the then Maharaja of Banaras, Prabhunarayan Singh, got back the property of Shivala ghat, and this portion of the original Shivala ghat is now called Chet Singh ghat.

Panchkote ghat: We spent our childhood holidays in the Panchkote palace and on the ghat, which was constructed by the Raja of Panchkote in around 1800. This principality in Bengal was where my paternal aunt was married. We had access to its massive living room and bedrooms, all opening towards the ethereal Ganga. There is also a tastefully constructed temple of Kalyaneshwari Devi, the *kul devi* or the guardian deity of the Panchkote family. It still continues to be the private property of the descendants of the raja, who have now converted a part of the palace into a home stay and a boutique hotel. Ruchi, the wife of my late cousin Vikram Singh

Deo, has innovative plans chalked out for her business. She, along with her daughter, has embarked upon a novel idea of a residence cum city tour of Banaras for her predominantly Western guests.

Prabhu ghat: Constructed by a rich merchant from Bengal, Nirmal Kumar, in the mid-nineteenth century, but named after the Raja Benares Prabhunarayan Singh.

Nishadraj ghat: Has a huge settlement of Nishads.

Jain ghat: Constructed by the Jain community in 1931.

Vachchhraj ghat: Built by a famous Jain merchant, banker and philanthropist, Vachchhraj of Banaras. It is also the birthplace of the seventh Teerthankar Suparshvanath.

Mata Anandmayee ghat: This used to be a clay-banked ghat, called Imiliya ghat and Rai Baldeo Sahay ghat. In 1944, the well-known preacher Ma Anandmayee bought this ghat from the British and established her ashram and also stone-paved the ghat.

Janki ghat: It was stone-paved in 1870 by Rani Kunwar, the maharani of Sursand state in Bihar, who named it Janki ghat.

Bhadaini ghat: Named after the locality Bhadaini.

Tulsi ghat: Constructed by Balaji Peshwa in the early eighteenth century, it hosts the yearly Ramlila and has gained fame for the enactment of Krishna killing the Naga Kaliya during the Nag Nathaiyya festival. As per the myth of the snake Kaliya being overpowered by Krishna, re-enactment of Krishna's overpowering of Kaliya is staged inside the Ganga on the boats and a Kadamb tree is planted every year near the ghat. This unique festival, initiated by Tulsidas, is now organized annually by the chief priest of the Sankat Mochan temple, Shree Virbhadra Mishra's family. They have their ancestral house here, along with a laboratory to test the pollution level of the Ganga. The ghat is also home to Tulsidas's *khadau* (wooden slippers) and a Hanuman temple.

Rewan ghat: Its old name was Lala Misir ghat, and was purchased by the Maharaja of Reewan, along with the palace, in 1879.

Ganga Mahal ghat: This ghat has a huge palace constructed by the Raja of Banaras, Prabhu Narayan Singh, called the Ganga Mahal, and this is where the ghat gets its name from.

Assi ghat: Located at the confluence of the Asi rivulet and the Ganga, it has undergone beautiful renovations, offering a spacious and uncluttered environment, unlike the other ghats. The evening Ganga aarti happens here and a musical soiree called the Subah-e-Banaras begins at day break, featuring upcoming singers from Banaras. The atmosphere during these early morning promenade concerts must mirror what Prinsep experienced in the early nineteenth century, when he said, 'The soft melancholy cadence of Hindoostanee music accords very agreeably with the languid influence of an oriental climate.'[15]

Nagwa ghat: Although this does not feature in a religious scripture, it is famous as it has the house of the philanthropist Shivprasad Gupta located here.

Samne ghat: Home to the renowned institution Gyan Pravaah, it was this ghat that served as the only connection to Ramnagar Fort through a pontoon bridge, which is dismantled during the rainy season. Presently, a four-lane bridge connects Ramnagar town with Banaras. This ghat, too, is not mentioned in any religious text.

This was the general survey of the ghats, as they stand today, reflecting a blend of ancient traditions and the grandeur of the structures paved with stones. The magnificent and grandiose palaces and temples atop these ghats signify the Hindu resurgence, a reclaiming of their sacred spaces from the late sixteenth century to the early twentieth century. This compromise between the ancient Sanatan Dharma of Kashi and the evolving landscape shaped the essence of the medieval and modern Banaras.

Chapter 8

The Weavers of Banaras

'Jheeni Jheeni Beeni Chadariya'

While gallivanting around the Chowk and Raja Talab areas of downtown Banaras, one often encounters a bearded, painfully thin but agile man, wearing a lungi, half-kurta and a skullcap, carrying a rectangular cardboard box under his arm. Whether his name is Jumman Mian, Lukman Ansari, Noor Mian or something else entirely, he represents the famed and quintessential *kimkhwab* weavers of Banaras. The box that he carries, contains a single piece of the iconic Banarasi silk saree, its price ranging from anywhere between a few thousand to a few lakh rupees. He ventures to market his unique, handwoven product to one of the numerous retail saree shops dotting the place. Kimkhwab—the art of exquisite gold thread embroidery—is a niche and specialized style of nimble and painstaking needlework with roots tracing back to the Mughals.

The Banarasi cotton and silk industry has been thriving since the Mahajanapadas of the Mauryan era, when weavers, too, had their own guild. They gained fame in the Jataka eras and were called *kasseyak* and *varanaseyyak*. Vasudev Saran Agrawal has pointed to the textile design of such garments, observing their representation on the covering of the Dhameka stupa at Sarnath, which were transferred on to stone with great fidelity: 'A colorful specimen of the ornamentation used in their decoration, that is still an object of adornment on the cover made of stone slabs of Dhamekh stupa in Sarnath. The countenance with intertwined vines and with their auspicious markings is a testimony to its stellar beauty with Yakshas, birds and animals, and many kinds of geometrical patterns.'[1]

Because of its popularity since ancient times, this art of fine-cloth weaving is still famous throughout the world. The Jatakas and the Buddhist literature is full of descriptions of the Kashi textiles and fabric and has lauded the exclusiveness of this fabric that was also called Kashik vastra, Kashi kuttam and Kasheeya. The commentator of the Buddhist text *Mahaparinibbana Sutta* remarks on the buttoned fabric made in Kashi, stating that the dead body of Gautama Buddha was shrouded in the same exquisitely woven fabric, which was so fine that it could not even absorb oil. It is also mentioned that the cloth had iridescent colours of blue, yellow, red and pearly white. The commentator also eulogizes the Kashi cloths, because, as per him, the Kashi region has an excellent yield of magnificent quality cotton, skilled weavers and thread makers, and the high quality of the soft water in Kashi is extremely favourable for laundering the processed fabric.

It appears that women were the main bulwark of this profession, right from protecting the cotton farms, ginning, spinning the yarns and thereafter creating bales of cotton. Apart from the cotton fabric, the weavers of Banaras were also experts at weaving full-length silk and woollen cloths. The silk and woollen fabric for the warp and weft were used by the Kashi weavers to prepare luxurious blankets, regarded as a royal honour bestowed by the kings. It must be the same as the *mirzaee*, a long-quilted coat that was given by the Timurid rulers to honour the nobility, and from this has come the title of 'Mirza'. Jeevak Kaumarbhritya, the great physician of the kings of Magadha, was honoured with such a blanket called the *addha kasiyan* by the ruler of Kashi. The cost of such a blanket was estimated to be 1000 *karshapanas* (ancient Indian coins made of gold or copper). Till date, a very fine variety of linen is called *addhi* in the local parlance of Banaras. There is also a reference of the fine needlework of Kashi in the Jatakas, called the *kasik-soochivath*.[2] The popularity of this cotton and silk mixed cloth from Kashi during the Mauryan era is evident in the references by Kautilya and Patanjali in their ancient texts *Arthashashtra* and *Mahabhashya.* During the Shunga era, the assessment of the fabric of Kashi was based on its fine work and craftsmanship rather than in mere size. It is recorded that despite being smaller in size, Kashi fabric was preferred and was more expensive than the one produced in Mathura during that time.

Even in the Kushan era, the finest clothes were crafted in Banaras, and they were referred to as Kashivastra and Kashikanshu. In the Buddhist healing texts, it has been said in many places that the Kashivastras were very fine (*sukshmani jalani cha samhitani*). There are also mentions of the wearing and manufacture of exceptionally fine fabric from Kashi (*kashikvastravarambaran*).[3] The Periplus mentions that in the first century, the best of Indian muslin was called 'Gangetic', indicating that it was made on the Ganga. Clothes were also exported, and many ancient cities had showrooms dedicated only to the clothes made in Kashi and were called Kashikavastravari. Bullion existed for such trade and was called *nigamsya.* We now have traversed the ancient scenario, where weaving formed an honourable and important art and profession. It was at its zenith during the Gahadavala period, attributed to the overall stability and peace of that time. The cloth trader was called *kapadi* or *karpatik*. Jute cultivation was also prevalent, which is now primarily used for producing rough fabric for bags and durries. Cotton wool was processed through ginning and willowing. The term *kapad jhung* has been recorded for the warp spread. Traveller Ralph Fitch has also emphasized that Banaras is 'a large town in which great quantities of cotton-clothes are made, and sashes for the moors'.[4]

The *katan* cloth, woven with such ethereal finesse, is known to be so delicate that it is said to be shredded by the touch of even the gentlest moonlight. So when Ghalib visited Banaras between 1826 and 1829, he had this fine Kashikvastra lingering in his thoughts as his muse while composing the following Manasvi on Banaras:

I complain to my friends
As if-
The katan cloth will be washed
In moonlight only to be ripped.[5]

However, the first name that strikes anyone regarding the weavers of Banaras is the famous poet and saint Kabir. Volumes have been dedicated to him and his poetry. Kabir was born into a Muslim family of the Julaha (weaver) community in 1398. He received his spiritual initiation in the mystical world from Sant Ramanand and the Sufi fakir Sheikh Taqi of Allahabad. Most of Kabir's mystic poetry was in the form of distich, and was profoundly grounded, as he used metaphors of the daily grind, including some from his own profession. His most famous one, sung by all prominent Indian classical musicians, is:

Jheeni jheeni beeni chadariya,
Kaahe ka tana, kaahe ki bharani,
Kaun taar se beeni chadariya?

(Subtly, delicately, He wove this warp!
What is its warp? What is its weft? With what
fibre was this woven?)

Another one goes:

Chadariya, jheeni re jheeni,
ke Rama nam ras bhini.
Astah kamal ka, charkha banaya
panch tattva ki puni

(Weaving, smaller than small,
dipped in the essence of Rama's name.

A lotus flower with eight petals made the spinning wheel
loaded with five elements (to make the thread))

Even today, what was once the village of Narharpura, now located within the city limits in the Kabir chaura area, preserves the loom of Kabir, along with the room and the grave of his parents Neeru and Neema, known as Niru tila. He started the movement known as Nirgun Bhakti, which was shorn of any pomp and pageantry, as it believed in the formless worship of the divine. His teachings have been integrated into Sikhism, and a sect called Kabir Panth, which is the leading sect to practise his preaching.

When Tavernier visited Banaras in the seventeenth century, he was struck by the deluge of merchandise, particularly the fine cotton and linen that he documented in his travel diary. Tavernier, though, quite unlike a French aesthete, did not describe the types of cotton and velvet that he found in Banaras. The seventeenth-century Venetian traveller and writer Niccolao Manucci, in his *Storia do Mogor* (Account of the Moghuls), has stated that Banaras was the centre for the fine work in gold and silver threads that was exported to around the world. From a 1720 Persian *roznamcha* (daily diary) *Khulasat-ut-Tawarikh*, it is concluded that the main types of Banarasi cloths were called *jhoona* and *mihirgul*.

Over the last three centuries, and more broadly over a millenium, there has been a remarkable surge in the number of artisans and their specialized craft in Banaras city, and their colonies have sprung up at Kotwa, Jalalipur, Alaipur, Lallapura, Rewari Talab, Madanpura and Bazardiha, and in the adjoining areas of the Lohta village. All these areas still continue to be central to the artisans and weavers of this fine art. The production of rugs and carpets in Bhadohi, just about 40 km from Varanasi—formerly part of the Banaras district and now a separate district in an adjoining rural area—began relatively late but evolved into a hub for the carpet export business in the eighties and early nineties. The carpets of Bhadohi were particularly exclusive because of the close-knitted knots that were predominantly done by children, as their small fingers had better dexterity. Bhadohi faced a crisis when the ethical practices of their business were raised in various national and international forums. One of the exporters that spoke to me in the early nineties, as I recall, who had returned from Germany, after attending a meeting with the International Carpet Classification Organization, was horrified to find that everywhere at the official venue and even in the town, they had billboards and posters showing a blood-dripping hand of a child, denouncing the employment of small children in the carpet industry in Bhadohi. Of course, it was another business trick in favour of the mechanized carpet weaving. Here, every single household is engaged in the task of weaving the world-renowned Bhadohi carpet.

The Mughals introduced the renowned zardozi and kimkhwab styles of needlework. In *Dekho Hamri Kashi*, Hemant Sharma notes that while this form of needlework has ancient origins, the Atharva Veda mentions that the cover of the palanquin of a newlywed was adorned with a golden artwork known as *kalabattu*, which actually was a silken thread covered with the golden or silken wire mesh. During the Gupta period, kalabattu was prepared by dipping these threads in a liquid mixture of gold. He also mentions an apparel that was called *hiranya drapi* (golden dress).[6] I found two similar words in Sanskrit that have the intonation of this drapery: *hiranyatvac* (having a gold covering) and *hiranyatvacas* (having a golden caparison). In their current forms, both these art styles were introduced with the Mughals, who also patronized the weavers through liberal grants and encouragement. Later, the Mughal kings and nawabs of Awadh further improvised the art by bringing in skilled artisans from Iran.

In Banaras, a variety of patterns were traditionally employed for brocade, initially intended for the sarees, but now creatively used for most of the ceremonial garments. They include the patterns of rosettes, poppy, pinecones, *jangla* works, etc. The rating of the garment is determined by the gold and silver used in it. Presently, most of the work involves plain silken threads, with some pieces retaining intricate patterns to preserve their heritage significance.

Zardozi, literally *zar* meaning gold and *dozi* meaning embroidery, refers to any form of embroidery using metal threads. The prevalent patterns of zardozi are the flora and fauna of the subcontinent. The Mughals and later, the Awadh nawabs, are known to have invited the artists from Iran who were called *zardos*. The zardozi workers in Banaras celebrate a festival called Huzur ki Miraj, which was started by their patron-saint Hazrat Yusuf Alah-e-Salam.

Describing the city and its wealth, Lord Macaulay, even though he was the greatest bête noire of nationalists, wrote about the city's fabulous fabric commenting that: 'Commerce had as many pilgrims as religion. All along the shores of the venerable stream lay great fleets of vessels laden with rich merchandize. From the looms of Benares went forth the most delicate silks that adorned the balls of St. James's and of Versailles.'[7]

Since the eighteenth century, when the Marathas and other Hindu royals were pouring their wealth in Banaras, this art form gained rapid momentum. The massive construction of ghats, temples and palaces, with their accompanying social ceremonies, many priceless garments of the idols of the deities, following large-scale religious ceremonies, involved the employment of a considerable workforce of weavers. The rush of the Hindu royals to Banaras also popularized this art form and the end products of the Banarasi weavers, to the rest of the subcontinent, bolstering the trade. Sherring, too, noted the weaving activities: 'Silks and shawls are manufactured in the city; and Benares is especially famous for its gold embroidered cloths called Kincob (Kimkhwab) and for its beautiful filigree work in gold.'[8] It was also at the same time, certainly not a coincidence, that the troika of the ruling elites of Banaras—Gosain priests, merchant bankers and Raja of Banaras—all gave liberal patronage to the weaving industry. Prinsep, in a letter to his sister in 1820, describes the costumes of Banaras as: 'The dress of the natives here is far more elegant than in Bengal. Instead of the universal white muslin drapery, we have here the gaudiest colours and costumes displayed.'[9] Despite the policies of the East India Company, unlike Bengal, the silk and cotton industry in Banaras continued to ascend. The reason for this was its status as a traditional trade centre with liberal and active merchant bankers, a well-oiled business nexus and infrastructure for riverine trade and road transport, its role as a pilgrimage site and a retirement home for the royals and the super-rich. It was also because of the ingenuity and adaptability of the weavers and designers with the market forces.

Owing to the international recognition of the quintessential Banarasi weaving art, especially the Banarasi saree, large-scale production started in the early nineteenth century. The artisans involved in this traditional profession also evinced a lot of interest and scholarly studies on their community. Since it could be preserved for hundreds of years, it became a sort of family heirloom passed down from mothers, mothers-in-law and grandmothers to their favourite children or the daughters-in-law. It also served as a kind of security deposit for women. There has never been a system of reselling Banarasi sarees. The most agonizing part of using Banarasi sarees as a security deposit is their destruction. Let me share a personal experience.

A *thikana* or a retreat in Banaras was always considered to be a *symbole de statut* by the numerous zamindars, minor feudatories and business families. My grandfather, along with many of his relatives, had invested in land and houses in Banaras. Over a period of time, apart from our huge joint family, we had many relatives who were settled in the city. I must have been in the ninth class, brimming with social curiosity and a fascination to visit the neighbourhood. Often, I would barge unannounced into the ladies' chamber of the house, where my younger cousins were invariably kept secured and confined during the peak summer afternoons. This portion was usually at the corner of the rectangular courtyard that also opened towards the back door, providing access to sweepers and other female house helps. This was the happening passage where the *churiwallah*s (bangle sellers), sellers of exotic bric-a-brac for the ladies' trousseau, perfumes and attars, sometimes street savouries like golgappas and aloo tikkis, short durational seasonal fruits like badhhar and phalsas, pungent wild berries and many such articles, gathered. That afternoon when I entered the house, it had an acrid smell of burnt cloth and metal instead of attar or the aroma of savouries. I also saw a few burnt pieces of sarees, still radiant with their beautiful colours, scattered in the huge courtyard. There was a hushed silence among the ladies of the house whom I always found chattering and giggling like teenagers. It was then that I saw a spherical skein of blackish-golden wire (I came to know later) the size of a football being handed over to a trader by my distant cousin sister-in-law. From the attire of the man who was squatting on the floor, I could make out that he must have been a minor retailer of jewelleries. My sister-in-law, who always had the mien of a garrulous and proud lady from nobility, looked forlorn and broken with grief. Her face was swollen, and apparently, she had cried. A smidgen of kohl and teardrop markings on her white cheeks exacerbated her sadness. There was a hush and a gloom which disconcerted me. She was horrified to find that I saw this entire dealing. I rushed back home and narrated it to my mother, who confided in me that their family is going through a severe financial crisis. The gold was taken out from supposedly a very old and heavy Banarasi saree and was being sold to that retailer. This also reminded me of Satyajit Ray's classic *Jalsaghar*, which shows the twilight of a decadent zamindar, who projects and tries to uphold the family prestige in the face of economic adversity. The zamindar, Huzur Biswambhar Roy, played brilliantly by Chhabi Biswas, reminded me of this matriarch sister-in-law of mine. Certainly, losing a piece of heritage and family heirloom steeped in happy ceremonial memories, is not a pleasant experience to have.

This profession has a predominance of Sunni Muslims who trace their settlement to the urban setting of Banaras for the last 900 years, with the advent of the Islamic rule in northern India. Some even refuse to accept the tag of the converts and claim that their ancestors, who emigrated along with the armies of the Islamic invaders in 990 CE, brought this original art form with them. However, this claim of immigration is reportedly passed down as oral tradition, not uncommon with upcoming communities. The most well-researched account of the daily life of the weavers of Banaras has been vividly described by Abdul Bismillah in his award-winning novel *Jheeni-Jheeni*

Beeni Chadariya.[10] We are exposed to this destitute and disease-ravaged world of weavers with the help of Matina, Aliman and little Iqbal. We come across diverse characters like Basheer, Najbuniya, Altaf, Roufa Chacha, Kamroon, Naseebun Bua, Rehanash and Latif, who remain strong even when they are completely broke. They do not compromise with their art and the traditions that they have inherited; instead, they want to fight and change them. In this process, we also come to know the internal dynamics of this very strange world of the Banaras weavers. We find that the author has laid bare the entire network of exploitation of these *mastmaula* (bohemian) artists very closely, by *girasata*s (rich weavers) and *kothiwala*s (merchants dealing with the weaving industry), and, on the other end, the corrupt political gimmicks and the so-called welfare schemes of the government. At the same time, he has not ignored the unhealthy traditions, social evils, religious fundamentalism and communal attitude of the weaver fraternity, which helps in their being economically exploited.

Bismillah says that the weavers here believe that they are the descendants of Hazrat Ayyub Ansari and the weaving profession that they adopted en masse was because of Chittan Baba, on whose name a locality of weavers exists in Banaras, known as Chittanpura. It is said that he used to weave *ijaarband* (rectangular cloth belts used to fasten pyjamas). Once, when it was seen by a Nawab from Lucknow, he called the merchant who had supplied this to the Nawab and through him, he invited the weaver of the ijaarband, Chittan Baba. He was extremely pleased with his fine weaving and gave huge pieces of land in various areas of Banaras to establish the Julaha *basti* (weavers' colony). Chittan Baba gathered all his relatives and caste brethren and established five areas of weavers, becoming their 'Sardar'—the chief. This tradition continues, with the hereditary nomination of the head of the guild of weavers. Now, every weaver colony has its own Sardar, also called 'Mahto'. Currently, there are the *Chaudahvon* (the fourteen), the *Bayeesi* (the twenty-two) and the *Bavanoh* (the fifty-two). However, the head of the *Pancho* (the five), is the *primus inter pares.* Still, when the chiefs of the above three are elected, the *pagadi* (turban) is placed by the head of the Pancho, but since his status is hereditary, the Sardar adorns the pagadi himself. This *biradari* (the weaving commune) extends from Chhitanpura to Pathani Tola, to the now very famous areas of Jaitpura, Kamalpura, Ladanpura, Jalalipura, Bakaria Kund, Dosipura and Kaji Sadullapura. Their presence beyond Godaulia, Madanpura, Pitarkunda and Bajardiha is also substantial. In the words of Bismillah: 'Their customs and policies are and may be somewhat different. The spoken language is also slightly different. But all are one. Men's feet are on the loom and women's hands are on the charkha.'[11]

In all probability, they were mostly the converts from the lowest rung of the caste hierarchy and were equated with the likes of the Chamars (belonging to the leather profession community), Doms (undertakers), Bhangis (sweepers) and Dhobis (washermen). They have shunned their earlier tag of 'Julaha' in a revivalist movement within their community in the 1930s and now proudly sport the title 'Momin Ansari'. This can loosely mean to be the helpers of the Prophet, pure-hearted, and a profession dedicated to the Prophet. The importance of these three terms alluding to the weavers' community has been succinctly threshed out by Vasnthi Raman:

> The terms 'Julaha', 'Ansari' and 'Momin' signify important aspects of both the social reality and the social processes of the time, with 'Julaha' meaning just a menial, an ordinary weaver, the term 'Ansari' connoting a Muslim weaver with some standing and 'Momin Ansari' referring one who has, in addition to standing, also attained a degree of spiritual worth.[12]

As a community, they were also formally recognized by the All India Jamaat-Ul-Ansar.[13] The term has become so identifiable with the weavers that even some financially higher-placed Muslim owners of the weaving firms use this title to further their business interests. Additionally, a minuscule number of Pathans and Muslims from other professions who have strayed into weaving also use it. They continue to remain a closed community of urban poor who do not have any land or financial stakes in the villages and are solely dependent on the whims of the urban textile business controlled by Hindu businessmen. In 1931, a commentator on the business scenario of Banaras wrote that:

> In Benares the Mahomedan population is nearly entirely dependent upon the Hindus . With the exception of a few members of the old Mahomedan aristocracy, who are now in straitened circumstances, the entire community lives a hand to mouth existence . . . . The weavers are without exception dependent on the good will of their Hindu employers. The two communities are therefore closely bound to each other by economic ties.[14]

The Hindu traders extended the credit facilities, depending on the trust quotient with the weavers and also marketed and brought in fresh orders for production. The total interdependence of the Muslim weavers with their Hindu traders changed somewhat in the 1940s, peaking in the 1970s with the entry of the Muslim master weavers. Some, with entrepreneurial abilities, also doubled as the *gaddidar*s (middlemen) and *girisata*, eventually carving a niche for themselves in the national and international market.

The lexicon and vocabulary of the weavers are an intermix of Persian, Arabic, Bhojpuri and Awadhi. Some of them are:[15]

Sakaadh: A bamboo stick that is used in weaving.

Taeesa taar: Golden thread, which is also called *kalabattu*.

Dharki: This is the basic and the original instrument of weavers, which comes in two types: *teeridaar* and *makodaar*. The former is used for only *kalabattu*, while the latter is used for normal threads.

Nari: An instrument used in weaving that is filled with thread.

Phalli: The first portion of the woven cloth.

Phoo: Showering or sprinkling of water from the mouth on the woven cloths with a the 'phoo' sound.

Perani: Sameez or short shirt.

Baton: That piece of cloth that is used to cover the loom.

Reja: Unfinished saree or the one which is still being woven.

Ijaar: Shalwar or the lower garment.

Laag: The empty space between two woven flowers in a saree.

Naulakha: A spherical structure made of *lakhauria* bricks that is hung near the loom with a thread.

A typical order placed by a firm or through the initiative of a group of weavers goes through a complicated process of quality and design assessments by middlemen who are called the gaddidars. They can fix the price depending upon the market trends. An ordinary Banarasi saree would take anything from fifteen to twenty days to make and sometimes even months! The weaver is placed at the mercy of the gaddidars, who then sell the products to wholesalers and large retail garment showrooms. The many other factors that affect their earnings are fashion trends, their own mood swings and health, closure of the workshops during both their and Hindu festivals, and law-and-order problems.

Most of the researchers have noted the relaxed nature and positive ambience of work, a certain stoic attitude and a fatalist approach quite common among Banaras weavers. The work and leisure attitude, often termed as *phakkadpan, masti* and trips to *bahri alang*, resonates with Ansaris as much as with the Hindu hawkers, *panwallah*s, rickshaw pullers, Gangaputras, etc., of similar social status. The Ansaris have subsumed in their cultural and professional milieu the very essence of Hindu Banaras and the predominantly Hindu religious metaphors associated with the river Ganga and the syncretic Ganga-Jamuni *tehzeeb* (syncretic culture). With the philosophy of *tana-bana* (warp and woof), their ownership of the Hindu Banaras is as invaluable as their Muslim identity. It is interesting to observe that, perhaps because of the secular and eclectic approach of Kabir, many in the Julaha community today exhibit liberal views. As noted above, they embody more Banarasipan than an orthodox Muslim.

In the early 1980s, the district magistrate of Banaras emphasized the 'inseparable blending' of the Hindus and Muslims in the lower-class communities, cautioning against attempts to 'disunite them' lest it constitute 'a new arrangement'.[16] The paper by Elizabeth Chalier-Visuvalingam and Sunthar Visuvaligam from 1991 suggests—which perhaps may not always be true in the present situation, but has a point regardless—that:

> Stripped off its specifically Hindu references and ritual notations, the 'ideology of freedom' still dominates the lifestyle of the poverty-stricken Muslim artisans of Banaras, who have no doubt reinforced it with the overtly egalitarian inspiration of their own religious tradition. This all-Banarasi 'ideology of leisure,' which had powerfully reconstructed so many lives among an entire generation of pan-chewing Western hippies in the seventies, is perhaps above all the aesthetic refraction if not resolution of the dialectic of transgressive sacrality that pulsates through the very heart of Hinduism.[17]

The Wahhabi wave that swept the subcontinent from the early 1980s has failed to impress upon the Ansaris its ideological impact. In fact, even the two strongholds of the Wahhabis, the largest madrasa in the city, Islamia, and the new college, the Salfia Dar-ul-ulum, have miserably failed to attract the weavers' community.[18] They rather visit the shrines of their patron saints, pirs and shahids on specific days of the week. Some of them are very specific to that particular locality, where they have their *karkhana*s (workplaces). Two of them that I visited are located in the most prominent centre of silk and brocade weaving in Madanpura: Malang Baba Mazar and Amba Shah Ka Taqia. The latter doubles up as a community centre and a shrine of the Sufi saint Amba Shah. Malang Baba shrine is dedicated to the Sufi saint Malang. The weaving community continues to revel in their typical Banarasi pastimes, such as visits to the *bahri alang* (outside the city limits) for picnics, at places like the Rajghat, Chunar and Sarnath. The *urs* celebration of their favourite saints holds a very special occasion for them. The quintessential leitmotif of the weaving community in Banaras is a living example of the evolution of a syncretic composite Banarasi culture that has borrowed from every aspect of human activities. As Sandria B. Freitag has noted: 'Muslims in Banaras pursued, through ceremonials, simultaneous goals of reiterating their Islamic identity and reinforcing their ties with other Banarasis, particularly those power holders interested in the reinvented Hindu culture that came to characterize Banaras.'[19]

Even the two major riots of 1991 and 1992 did not dent this syncretism, barring a few areas where tensions prevailed, but the international and national events, particularly the Kandahar incident and the 9/11, saw the rise of Wahhabi elements and concomitantly the crystallization of neo-Hinduism. This sounded the death knell for the weaving industry, as no longer a weaving locality referred to as *bunkar basti* (weavers' habitation) but rather *musalmanon ka mohalla* and *miyan basti* (the locality of Muslims) and sometimes derisively as 'mini-Pakistan'. The ghettoization continued, further deteriorating the healthy working relationship within the garment industry.

Whenever I have visited the Madanpura area and the outskirts of Kotwa and Bhadohi, I have always found in those Byzantine lanes an overwhelming sense of joie de vivre and a close-knit community life, a common design of the house with a karkhana, places of worship and the dress. Weavers have, since ages, worn a lungi and a half-kurta with a *gamchha* (a kind of towel); this is without exception everywhere in eastern Uttar Pradesh, worn by this community almost as a uniform. Only after going through Nita Kumar's article on the weaving community did I realize the practical aspects of choosing this dress by the weavers. She says:

> A lungi suits the postures demanded by the pit loom, which does not explain why prosperous Ansaris who do not themselves weave, habitually wear the lungi at home. It is perhaps a carryover from their weaving days, but more, it is closely associated with the Ansari identity. All other artisans dress also in lungi and gamchha,

> though in knee-length lungis as opposed to the Ansari ankle-length version. The preference for this choice of clothes is articulated not in Ansari but in Banarasi consciousness. Clothes are supposed to emphasize your simplicity, your inner wealth, and the absence of need to make any kind of external show. Material display is vulgar and indicative of little but poverty, weakness, and shallowness of character. Ansaris and all other artisans dress the way they do, not simply because they are poor or because it is convenient, but because it is an idealized way of dressing.[20]

However, the weaving and the concomitant garment industry saw a temporary decline after the initial scramble of temple and ghat construction by the royals and their having only occasional visits to the city. By the 1880s, the weavers started feeling the pinch as the number of persons and families had multiplied, but the orders were declining. Thousands of weavers in 1891 petitioned the district magistrate for subsidized grains due to the lack of orders for their products. It seems the industry was adversely impacted due to a number of consecutive famines since the 1880s lasting till 1900. An initiative, most probably by some able British administrators, saw the opening of a weaving school in 1915, and grants to support the weavers were instituted. Post-Independence, the All India Handloom Board was set up to look into the problems facing the weavers in the 1950s. Much later, after this board revived and brought the handloom industry into the mainstream, Pupul Jayakar, 'India's 'czarina of culture', who played a key role in the cottage industry revival, exhorted a leading artisan called Jagganath to innovate and experiment with designs. Encouraged by her, he made tents from the hand-woven silk, which became a big attraction.[21]

Torn between the unpredictability of weather conditions, the growing excesses of the zamindars and the sheer multiplication in the number of mouths to feed, a large number of farmers in the early twentieth century shifted to the silk industry and took up weaving, with some even specializing in the traditional craft of kimkhwab. Some Yadavs also left their dairy business and joined the bandwagon of the weavers. Due to the growing demand of silk sarees and quick money in weaving as opposed to farming, the weaving community saw the rise of Hindu OBCs (Other Backward Castes) who are called called *patve* or *patika*s. There were many weavers from places such as Jessore, Khulna and Mymensingh (in present-day Bangladesh) who are called *tanti*. All had adopted the dress and the lifestyle of the urban Muslim weavers. Among the many Hindus who took up saree weaving, abandoning their traditional professions as farmers or as daily-wage earners, the family of the National Award-winning weaver Jagannath Prasad is one such example.

By 2010, there were 95,439 weavers in Banaras, with around 31,300 handlooms. Ironically, the number of weavers who were self-employed declined, and the corresponding number of weavers working under master weavers increased. The master weavers' employability was a little over 5000 in 1995 but shot up to over 1,50,000 in 2010, reflecting the decline of the overall weaving industry.[22] This institution is now on the verge of shutting down, since most of its functions have now been taken over by the local administration and the Central Governmental Policies on Handlooms.

The survival of this ancient art is, ironically, due to the lack, or one may say availability, of mechanization in this sector. The changes that we find in the traditional weaving firms are more cosmetic, saving the weavers some time, but the core activity has not undergone any major transformation and is used more as a labour-saving contraption. Many weavers in 1928 shifted to Jacquard machines without actually deviating from their fundamental approach to weaving. The approach to power loom, that arrived in Banaras in 1950 by the weaving industry of Banaras is also quite different from the other textile towns of Bombay, Surat and Ahmedabad. Here, most of the weavers looked suspiciously at the power loom, competed with them, and some reluctantly adopted but continued to work on the handloom as well. The power looms in Banaras have been made by the recycled parts of the machines from Surat. Surprisingly, the weavers of Banaras, even when working with such jugaad technology, have kept intact their uniqueness and the exquisiteness of the Banarasi saree, mimicking exactly the one created on a handloom. Yet, there remained a tacit understanding between the two, largely because when the power loom was launched in Banaras, there was a lull in the market and many weavers were rendered jobless. Power loom absorbed most of these weavers. Strangely though, whereas the poor weaver looked upon the power loom sector as an alternative source of earning, the traders and the large traditional weaving families bemoaned the loss of conventional and quintessential weaving patterns of Banaras. The plight of such weaving families who held their family business even through the rough and tumble of the industry was ameliorated to some extent by the intervention of the All India Handloom Board and with the heritage tag to the kimkhwab and zardozi.

Some weavers, however, continue to brave extreme poverty and hardships to keep this unparalleled medieval art alive. The complex and time-consuming work of the weavers is further under attack from the tech- and business-savvy fashion designers of urban India. The multi-tiered, interconnected and highly interdependent weaving industry is today seriously debilitated by the advent of power looms and the effects of unmonitored and unlimited import of silk and silk goods from China. These include the China-made Banarasi silk sarees with chemical-laden ersatz fibres and colours, unlike the organic fibres of silk, wool and cotton that impart lustre and iridescence to a Banarasi saree. The cost of such man-made yarn is just a fraction of that of pure silk yarn. A self-employed artisan weaver has more reservoirs of creative ideas than an employed one. Unfortunately, the market forces have divested him of his entrepreneurial abilities due to successive delays in payments and a lack of loans. The writer, Vasanthi Raman, in this regard, has concluded that: 'The changes that have swept across the Banarasi silk industry are not confined to the internal dynamics of the industry alone. They encompass the very identity of the city with its emblematic *tana-bana* weltanschauung, characterized by a kind of fluidity, a mingling of social categories and relations based on good faith and trust.'[23]

That definitely doesn't paint a very encouraging picture, in my opinion, but my observation is that in the past, the weaving industry has seen many cyclic reversals of their fortune, most notably during the East India Company era when an act called the Calico Act was passed that curbed the use of cotton and thereafter, the Industrial Revolution brought the forcible imposition of the Manchester textiles that were unleashed. Even during and for some time after the communal riots of 1809, 1930 and 1991, the business declined due to the marginalization of this particular community. The morale is certainly low, but at the same time, the picture is not so bleak; there is a silver lining with the dictates of the fashion industry that has rejuvenated the traditional baroque and intricate Indian apparels for marriages, religious ceremonies, festivals and birthdays. Apparel and fashion designers like Sabyasachi of Kolkata, Mumtaz Khan and Nilofer of Bhopal, and Tarun Tahiliani and Meera Ali of Delhi and Mumbai, respectively, are increasingly getting their muse and inspiration from the medieval kimkhwab and zardozi, along with the ancient needlework and weaving techniques employed in the Banarasi silk designs. The present generation is cautiously, yet affirmatively, moving towards traditional forms of celebration, aligning with the concepts of *Bhartiya Asmita* (Indian identity) and *Atm-Nirbhar Bharat* (Self-reliant India). This shift is also a response to the sociocultural paradigm shift witnessed in the last decade. The parvenu's greatest desire is to take refuge in the glory of the past, even when not inherited; one can always purchase a piece of history. My point here is that with the resurgence and integration of the traditional into the mainstream, the weavers and their leaders have reasons to grab this opportunity and flow with the tide. The only thing that can hinder the revival of handloom is the atrophying of skills. Saree creation, like any other traditional Indian art form, relies on the passing down of skill sets within the families with the exclusive *guru–shishya parampara* (teacher–student tradition)—both of which are extinct now. These weavers and their craft have also survived with the help of some entrepreneurs in Banaras, who still support them, not just for profit, but with the noble aim of keeping the looms spinning, and therefore, keeping the warp and weft of this ancient industry—and by that interpretation, of the city as well—from going extinct.

My friend and ex-classmate, Sandeep Wahi, is one of the crusaders of the 'Save the Weavers of Banaras' campaign and belongs to a very prominent merchant Khatri family of Banaras. He continues to fight for and support the weavers and their industry. He has held many senior positions within the government, serving as vice chairman of the Indo-American Chamber of Commerce (2014–15), member of the Handloom Board, Ministry of Textile, Government of India (2013–15) and the president of the Eastern UP Exporter's Association (2000–01). During our conversations, Sandeep mentioned about the current state of affairs and the general direction of the silk, cotton and zardozi business: 'Banaras is truly the city of magic, where master weavers skilfully weave zari with silk and cotton threads on traditional pit looms, creating exquisite sarees and fabrics for the "bride-to-be", aligning with the customs and tastes of Indian tradition. It is an "adoptive and secular" industry in its truest sense, that has seamlessly absorbed various cultural movements from time to time.' To add to this thought-provoking message from Sandeep, I would like to conclude this chapter with a Hindi quatrain by the poet Hari Mridul:

Kashi mein ek mila julaha
Bola:humko jara batana
Jo kameej pahni hai tumne
Kya usmein nahin tana-bana

(Found a weaver in Kashi
Said he: tell me
The shirt that you are wearing
Does it not have the warp and weft)[24]

Chapter 9

Art at Heart

Literary Giants, Maestros and Artists of Banaras

Apart from being a trading hub and a pilgrimage destination for at least three world religions—Hinduism, Buddhism and Jainism—Banaras has been, for centuries, a great centre for learning, art and culture. The cultural blueprint that emerged in the ancient times continues to be the same even today but is also evolving and metamorphosing at the same time to embrace the changes with the passage of time and people. Even before the time of Buddha, it was a distinguished seat of learning that offered a confluence of many different spiritual as well as religious ideologies, more specifically, the ideology and the lexicography of Hinduism and the Hindi literature. This chapter will briefly touch upon the lives and achievements of these great men and women and discover their connection with the city.

'For one who really wishes to understand Kashi, writers and artists of Kashi still are the best bet.'[1] This has been true in not just the last century but since the time Banaras became a political entity under the Gahadavalas. Apart from the scriptural writers and composers, who composed various religious mythologies in Kashi, the city became a hub of literature in the beginning of the eleventh century, during the rule of the Gahadavalas. Even prominent social commentators of that time, like Khsemendra and Krishan Mishra, whose progeny was Mansaram who established the hereditary tradition of 'Raja Banaras', made Kashi their focus to denounce the perniciousness and malpractices in the social and religious aspects of life, respectively. Krishan Mishra composed his *Prabodh Chandroday*, in which he has described how, under the guise of being erudite Brahmins, many notorious thugs used to rob pilgrims and common people. Another prolific and recondite writer, Bhatt Laxmidhar, was the *sandhivigrahika* (a minister who decides upon peace and war) of the great Gahadavala ruler Govindchandra. He was the archetypical *kuleen kshotriya* (high caste) Kashi Brahmin, who was not only a great intellectual but also a shrewd war strategist, compassionate administrator and a farsighted politician. He authored *Krityakalptaru*, which is one of the finest treatises on the jurisprudence within the ambit of Sanatan Dharma. It revolved around Banaras of the twelfth century. If we consider the development of the eastern Hindi language, its harbinger was the prose written during this era. The dialect was called Koshali. We do not, however, know much about the ancient folk literature, other than the fact that Banarasi Bhojpuri evolved from Koshali during these times. However, sufficient oral and folk proverbs, colloquial sayings and the *ukti-vyakti prakaran* (figure of speech) of Damodar Sharma, written in the early twelfth century, provide enough material to deduce that in Banaras, literature in Koshali was thriving. Damodar Sharma was another Kashi Brahmin, whose work in the grammar of folk language is a valuable document to study the development of the Hindi language. Nothing could be further from the truth if one were to believe that Banaras only harboured puritanical Brahmanical literature. It not only gave ample space to a diametrically opposite perspective but also saw a major surge in the number of followers of that standpoint. Regarding the rise of Bhakti, it is often quoted that '*bhakti draavidii oopajii, laae raamaanand*' (even though the Bhakti movement started in the South, it was brought by Ramanand). Ramanand was one of the earliest devotional cult poets. His poems manifested the essence of Bhakti and pluralism with the inherent message of humaneness, like: '*jaati paanti poochhai nahiin koii/hari kaa bhaje so hari kaa hoii*' (no one is asked about caste or class, anyone who chants the name of the Lord becomes His). Ramanand was from Banaras, residing at the Panchganga ghat. He initiated a tradition that was continued by his disciples Kabir and Ravidas. Banaras is not only the birthplace but also the workplace of these unforgettable Bhakti-era poets who unsparingly challenged the theoretical space of all sects and major religions of their time. Their non-conformism was once perceived as a threat by the clerical segment of Banaras. Kabir, born in 1398 into a low-caste Muslim weaver family, served as a vinculum between modernity and spiritualism, whose poetry traverses the profane and sacerdotal, embodying a realization that picks up its symbols from the humdrum of everyday grind. In Banaras, his birthplace has been visited by Gandhi, Tagore and followers of a diametrical approach to the freedom struggle like Bhagat Singh and Chandra Shekhar Azad. His poems convey the essence of our collective consciousness and spiritualism. His sardonic and nimble poetry questioned and challenged both the ruling and religious elite.

Ravidas, born two decades earlier in Banaras, also belonged to a low-caste cobbler family and, like Kabir, contributed to the Bhakti movement through his mystically inclined poetry. He, too, was the disciple of Ramanand. There is a popular story about Ravidas, where his mystical life was manifested to his admirers. Once, when he was soaking a piece of hide to soften it in a wooden bowl called *kathauti*, his relatives and followers urged him to be a part of *Ganga pujaiya* (worship ritual of the Ganga). It was then that he composed his most famous adage: '*man changa to kathauti mein Ganga*' (if the mind is pure, Ganga will emerge in one's own house). It is said that people actually saw the waves and heard the gentle burble of the river Ganga in that huge wooden bowl of Ravidas. Kabir's and Ravidas's mystical poetry form a major spiritual portion in the Sikh scripture, the Guru Granth Sahib. It was here that the great Tulsidas composed his *Ramcharitmanas*.

In Banaras, till the early twentieth century, most of the Hindi literary compositions that were addressed to the common people were in Brajbhasha and Awadhi, both being the dialects of the languages Shaurseni and Ardh Magadhi, respectively, whereas the folk language was Banarasi Bhojpuria—a dialect of Magadhi and ancient Koshali. From the Sultanate period, a new language called 'Hindavi' was also in use in Banaras among the elite, which later gave birth to Urdu, also known as Rekhta. Sanskrit and Arabic continued to be the languages of religion, while official work was carried out in chaste Farsi. I remember visiting courts in the early eighties with my uncle in connection with the 'Zamindari Bonds' that were given to all male inheritors of the zamindars by dividing the total revenue valuation of their zamindari after the abolition of the zamindari system in 1954. The declarations and agreements, although written in Devanagari script, were heavy with complicated Farsi words.

Educationist and reformer Raja Jainarayan Ghosal of Khidderpore, in Bengal, way back in the early nineteenth century, started a magazine from Banaras that had a few portions in Hindi. Based on his own observation of the Budhwa Mangal festival, he also composed, in 1857 (Banaras was not affected by the great war of Independence), a highly ornamented poem on the Budhwa Mangal festival in the local dialect:

bad bad paatalite panvariya naache, bhaura chhokara
bhaand kat kaachakaache.
tabala saarangee baanshee setaar muchang mandara rabaab
veena tamboora mrdang

(Many courtesans and young boys dance on these huge budgerows and the environment is intoxicated with the sweet sounds of the tabla, sitar, mridang, flute, etc.)[2]

Hindi, however, as a modern language of literary prose and fiction that we know today, emerged in Banaras from a mishmash of Khadi Boli, Brajbhasha, Urdu and Awadhi. Its originator was the famous Bharatendu Harishchandra, who hailed from a rich merchant family. Born in 1850 and dead at the young age of thirty-six, he left a rich legacy in many genres of creative works. His oeuvres included plays, poetry and contributions in the field of education, particularly women's education. He wrote under the nom de plume of 'Bharatendu' and is the founder of modern Hindi literature as well as Hindi theatre. He was a prose writer, poet, dramatist, satirist and journalist. Having edited the magazines *Bal Vibodhini, Harishchandra Patrika* and *Kavivachan Sudha*, he launched many young Hindi writers and published the works of many great scholars of that era, introducing many new dimensions in Hindi plays that were not present in the popular Parsi theatre of the day. Incidentally, one of the actors of Parsi theatre was one Raunaq Banarasi, who was also a pioneer of intellectual property rights during the early recordings of the songs by Frederick William Gaisberg. Sandria B. Freitag observing his improvisation writes:

> Bharatendu's theatre was moving in a clear direction: away from the open ended, improvisational, stylized, multivalent theatre of the Svang and Parsi stage, and toward a controlled, unambiguous, realistic, morally edifying model of theatre. Not only was the social milieu of theatre now pervaded by values of civility and refinement; the means and ends of theatrical representation were purged to eliminate all that was vulgar. Theatre was henceforth an unabashed arena of instruction, whether its actual locus was the schoolhouse or the parlor.[3]

Svang was another form of musical theatre akin to operatic performances in the Western world that came to Banaras from Hathras and Kanpur in the late nineteenth century and became a strong movement against the elites. It is sung by male singers with husky, full-throated voice with *nagara*s (kettle drums). In eastern Uttar Pradesh, it came be called *nautanki.* The development of svang in Banaras can be attributed, strangely enough, to the wide availability of printing presses and lithograph workshops. Unlike other folk genres that relied heavily on oral traditions, svang was typed and written text of poetry, as it had its origin by some folk poets. The sangeet element in it is still available in archives. Eight svang plays were published in Banaras between 1868 and 1885, by Munshi Ambe Prasad, Munshi Shadi Lal and Lala Ghasiram. Out of these, five are religious texts, namely *Prahlad, Gopichand Bhartari, Raja Harichandra,* and two versions of *Dhuruji*, one is a family war, called *Raghuvir Singh;* and two are romances: *Raja Karak* and *Rani Nautanki*. Bhartendu was highly influenced by the svang but his theatrical improvisations were more towards eliminating the ills of the society with a messianic zeal and a reformist spirit.

Bharatendu coined a term for the Hindi language that he developed with the 'Nagri' script—*Nayi Hindi* (new Hindi). He was also one of the founders of Nagri Natak Mandali in 1909. Mrinal Pandey writes: 'He coined the term Nayi Hindi, and rooted for a multi-textured Hindi free of the Sanskritized Hindi of Varanasi Pandits and also the Khadi Boli . . . It was he, who allowed the common man's Hindi to mingle, develop and run with Urdu and dialects like Braj Awadhi and Purabiya.'[4]

Bharatendu is also credited with reviving a popular thirteenth-century genre of poems called Kahmukri, which earlier was chiselled by Amir Khusrao. Bhartendu's contemporaries in Hindi literature included literary stalwarts like Baba Deendayal Giri, Sardar Kavi, Lachhiram Kavi, Pandit Durga Dutt, Pandit Ishwar Dutt, the great aesthete and educationist Raja Shivaprasad C.S.I. Sitara-e-Hind, Chaitanyadev, Ramkrishan Verma, Kartik Prasad Khatri, Mahamahopadhyaya Pandit Sudhakar Dwivedi and Babu Radhakrishan. They all lived and developed their literary muse in the lanes and by-lanes of Banaras.

Bengali literature and the intellectuals of Banaras have had a strange connection, which has played a major role in the development of Hindi prose writing. But the story writer who started this was a Bengali woman. Even Bhartendu's play writing career started in 1867 with the translation of a Bengali play *Vidyasundar*. Rajendra Bala Ghosh, born in 1882 in Varanasi, hailed from a zamindar family of Bengal whose ancestors had settled in Banaras. She wrote the story with the penname of 'Bang Mahila'. She was the pioneer of the Hindi prose and short story genre. Her stories include 'Chandradev se merii baaten', 1904; 'Kumbh men chhoti bahu', 1906; 'Dulaaiivaalii', 1907; 'Bhaaii-bahan', 1908; and 'Daliyaa', 1909.

'Dulaaiivaalii' was published in the first Hindi journal *Saraswati* (part 8, number 5). It becomes clear from the very beginning that the foundation of Hindi prose writing is deeply entrenched in culture, gradually progressing into a colossal form by the century's end. It transcended boundaries such as caste, religion, state, region and gender divide, creating its own separate, autonomous national form. The tradition of Hindi prose not only bridged the past and the present but also paved the way for the seamless movement of ideas from all directions at a global level.

At the dawn of the twentieth century, Banaras became a citadel of Hindi literature. Noteworthy contributions in prose were made by Kishori Lal Goswami, Babu Shyam Sundar Das and Ramnarayan Mishra. There was one very low-profile person called Mr Wahi, who has been credited with the renaissance of the Hindi literature for developing the idea of the iconic 'Nagri Pracharini Sabha' in 1893. The idea was given a solid impetus by Babu Radhakrishan Das, who also constructed the building of this great institution. It was founded to promote Nagri as the popular script against the Brahmanical Kaithi script. It enlarged its sphere of activities to foster Hindi literature among other endeavours. This institution is still thriving under the active presidency of Vyomesh Shukla, who is trying very hard to bring it back to its pristine glory. Encouraging many non-Hindi speakers to learn Hindi, the mystery novel writer Devki Nandan Khatri was from a prominent merchant family in Banaras. My father's friend, the theatre director B.V. Karanth whose mother tongue was Hindi and hailed from Udupi in Karnataka, was one such example of a non-Hindi speaker's love for Hindi. The Neelkanth locality in Banaras, located near the main Chowk, was a hub of literary activities. The writer Ramkrishan Verma's Bharatjeevan Press, the first-of-its-kind publishing press that performed yeoman service for the development of Hindi literature in the early twentieth century, was located here. It served as a conclave for writers like Dr Shyamsundar Das, Acharya Ramchandra Shukla, Kishorilal Goswamy, the last poet of Brajbhasha, Jaganath Prasad Ratnakar and Devkinandan Khatri. The discussions between the French indologist Sylvain Lévi and Dr Shyamsundar Das also took place here, in a sub-locality of Nepali Khapda, during the early twenties. These discussions revolved around which script, the newly adopted Nagri or the Roman, could be written more quickly. Banarasis believe that Dr Das who was advocating for Nagri, emerged victorious in this discussion. The Lamhi village in Banaras gained international prominence as the birthplace of the iconic writer Premchand, who depicted rural decrepitude and poverty through his short stories. Ironically, Munshi Premchand went to Bombay to try his luck with film scriptwriting, but was not accepted there, so he returned back to Banaras, where the family of Bharatendu Harishchandra provided him with a house in the Ramkatora mohalla near Godowlia. In Banaras, the family of *sunghni sao* (snuff traders), in the area of Govardhan Sarai area was renowned in the pre-Independence era for being great patrons of literature and culture. They were also known for their generous donations. The creator and epoch-maker and of Chhayavaad (Romanticism) in Hindi literature, Jaishankar Prasad, was born into this family in 1890.

One of the greatest short stories ever written, 'Usne Kaha Tha', is the contribution of Banaras. It was here that the writer Pandit Chandradhar Sharma 'Guleri' composed this classic in 1920 while serving as the president and principal of the Oriental School in Banaras Hindu University. In the literary criticism of this era, Acharya Ramchandra Shukla is credited with evolving the tenets of Hindi literary criticism. He started the first Hindi department in India at Banaras Hindu University. Earlier, Hindi was not taught as a separate language and did not even have a standard syllabus. His contemporaries were the luminaries Acharya Keshav Prasad Mishra, Lala Bhagwan Deen and Shyamsundar Das, all of whom have significantly contributed to the development of Hindi language and literature. Among the prominent modern Hindi literary critics, the late Chandrabali Pandey, Hazari Prasad Dwivedi, Vishwanath Prasad, Ramavadh Dwivedi, Jagannath Prasad Sharma and Shantipriya Dwivedi were masters of their subjects. Trilochan Shastri, Chandrabali Singh, Namvar Singh, Vijay Shankar Malla and Bachchan Singh are some other literary giants who have played a significant role in the development of the modern higher education in the eminent universities of the country. The prominent figure in the later tradition of Sathottiri storytelling, who was also a recognized fiction writer, Vijaymohan Singh, along with the brilliant storyteller and Sahitya Akademi Award-winner Kashinath Singh, still continues to add to the rich literary traditions of Banaras. A very sensitive and observant signature of modern Hindi poetry, poet Kedarnath Singh, was also related to Banaras. He not only completed his studies here, but also wrote many classics. The proponent of the modern lyrical poetry, Shambhunath Singh, who was also a powerful orator, held a respected position in Banaras, bringing the modern Hindi verse in the arena of the troubadour.

Hindi literary movements that reshaped the vision and trajectory of Hindi prose and poetry writing, commenced from Banaras. The *pehli parampara* (main tradition) of Ramchandra Shukla and the *doosri parampara* (second tradition) of Hazari Prasad Dwivedi, followed by Namvar Singh's *Tar Saptak*, laid the foundation for notable developments. Thereafter, the post sixties *Saathotari Kahani* movement, featuring four young Turks, Kashinath Singh, Gyanranjan, Ravindra Kaliya and Doodhnath Singh, was brought to the limelight by my father Vijaymohan Singh's book *Saath ke Baad ki Kahaniyan*, contributing to the enrichment and mainstream recognition of Hindi literature alongside other Indian language literature. The new book *Kavita Mein Banaras*, edited by Rajeev Singh, has listed poets from all eras and genres, beginning from Kabir, who poured all his soul in his compositions of the verses on Banaras.

Banaras has such a magnetic allure that captivates all poets, drawing them again and again to express and discover themselves through their verses in praise of the city. Apart from the prominent poets mentioned earlier, there are other notable ones—including Krishnadev Prasad Gaud, Bedhab Banarasi, Shamsher Bahadur Singh, Trilochan, Prabhakar Machwe, Shrikant Verma, Permanand Shrivastava, Rajesh Joshi, Narendra Pundrik, Nilay Upadhyay, Rajula Shah, Upasana Jha, Animesh Mukherjee and Gargi Mishra—all contributing to Hindi poetry. Some Farsi and Urdu poets like Mirza Ghalib, Nazeer Banarasi, Sheikh Hajin, Wali Daccani, Nawab Wazid Ali Shah 'Akhtar', Akbar Illahabadi, etc., have been astonishingly clairvoyant on the spiritual importance of the city. Even Ghalib, during his three-month stay in this city, in 1827, was enchanted by its myriad temples, gardens and lanes. This culminated in what is known as his greatest oeuvre in Farsi, *Chiragh-e-Dair* (Temple Lamp), following *Divan*, an anthology of his verses. Temple Lamp is a Masnavi that is a Persian genre of poetry characterized by a long narration, a conversation with his own spiritual self through the lens of an iconoclast. Full of Persian and Islamic symbols and images, juxtaposed with the scenes of Banaras, it serves as an important composition to gain insights into the city life of the early nineteenth century.

The post-Independence India of the late 1960s witnessed an influx of Beat movement hippies who thronged to Banaras in search of a rustic, bohemian lifestyle that supposedly made India 'downright cool'. Before the Beatles, the mysticism of the genius Maharishi Mahesh Yogi attracted the famous American poet and one of the founders of the Beat movement, Allen Ginsberg. He chose Banaras to start his journey as a seeker—'a veritable Columbus in reverse'. He stayed in Varanasi, along with his partner Peter Orlovsky, for a couple of years and wrote a number of poems dedicated to the city. Ginsberg is a heavyweight in American literature, influencing an entire generation of Americans, through his poetry and more so with his non-conformist approach to life, remaining a kind of 'cult figure'. Some even call him an 'American Beat Yogi'. His anthology of poems *Howl* and *Kaddish* are timeless American classics.

My father had met him in Banaras in October 1963 and described many subsequent meetings with him in his article 'Ve Doosre Allen Ginsberg The' (He was a different Allen Ginsberg), in his book *Bhed Kholegi Baat Hi*. He first met Ginsberg in the famous sixties restaurant called 'The Resturant' near the old tonga stand in Godowlia. The owner, Badri Babu, encouraged all anti-establishment and maverick artists to converge there. It was a kind of an *adda* (meeting spot) for all Banaras writers, poets and artists. My father was introduced to Ginsberg by the famous Hindi poet Trilochan Shastri. Ginsberg looked more like a fair-skinned Indian than an American, terse in conversation style. He told my father that he would be interested in having a detailed conversation with him only if he (my father) could meet him at his room the next day. Ginsberg and his partner, Peter, had rented a room at the Dashashwamedha ghat with a balcony overlooking the Ganga, where they stayed for almost fourteen months. Even now, the owners of buildings near the ghats rent out some portions of their houses to international visitors. Some interesting anecdotes regarding the cultural tug-of-war with certain respected Brahmin families have been described in Kashinath Singh's famous fiction title *Kashi Ka Assi* and in *Pakka Mahal* by Ajai Mishra.

The description of this incident and the subsequent meeting with Ginsberg is historic. In this article, my father mentions the famous 'Indian Journal' that became a classic in the American Beat literature. Ginsberg asked my father to go through the content of the journal till he finished writing letters to the district magistrate of Banaras and the American ambassador. When asked why he was addressing the letters, Ginsberg explained that he has been asked by the authorities to leave Banaras within forty-eight hours. Later, I came to know that Ginsberg was accused of being a Central Intelligence Agency (CIA) spy by the Government of India. He mentioned this fact in an interview when questioned about the veracity of the charge, saying, 'Yes. I don't know why. I think *Blitz* newspaper said that we were CIA spies. India was then at war with China over a border dispute.'[5] Ginsberg even offered my father a cigarette stick filled with charas. Despite my father's refusal, he engaged in a lengthy argument, explaining the benefits of taking narcotics using a wire mesh that could be given any shape. According to him, since our minds are conditioned to see the world in unidimensional form, drugs open up all those obscure shapes and dimensions, allowing us to perceive the diversity of life, the world, language and thinking. Ginsberg later openly discussed his own experimentation with bhang, ganja and LSD in many public forums. The myriad colours of the iridiscent flames of the pyre at the ghats elicit transcendental comments from Ginsberg, where he candidly admits overcoming his sense and fear of mortality. In February 1963, he penned a poem 'Describe: The Rain on Dasaswamedh ghat',[6] which would later become a kind of cult poem, attracting a lot of seekers and hippie adventurists from the Western world to Banaras. The poem reflects a dark, ruthless and Eliotesque perception of life in Banaras, intertwined with his knowledge of the Indian philosophical weltanschauung. An article in the *American Literature and Intercultural Discourses* has a valid comment that 'Ginsberg domesticates Indian gods and goddesses to castigate American capitalism. After bringing American poetry out into the streets, Ginsberg takes refuge in the Indian cultural heritage, and contemporizes its religious myths "to return to America to confront the nation at war".'[7]

The last meeting my father had with Ginsberg was in 1985 at Bharat Bhavan in Bhopal, and apparently, he had indeed transformed into a different Ginsberg with the times, now a middle-aged man dressed in suit and tie, exuding the civility of a CEO. When my father reminded him of his days in Banaras, he gently smiled and said: 'Those times were different and then, I, too, was somebody else.'

Recalling the intellectual scene of Banaras during the mid-1970s, the 'Hungaria' generation was waning but the same lot had also taken to resisting the Indian State. It became trendy to be a rebel and align oneself with the leftist movement. The atmosphere in our house was very stifled. My father's entire generation was brought up on the liberal Nehruvian dream and against the apocalyptic backdrop of Vietnam and Cambodian War. We lived amidst our feudal house at the cusp of embracing modernity. I remember the thin, choleric, bearded, kurta-wearing friends of my father arriving always after dark. Their meetings took place in our living room with only a forty-watt yellow bulb—a scene reminiscent of any movies by Ray, Ritwik ghatak or Mrinal Sen depicting the Bengal of the 1970s. I have heard about some of them: the painter Anil Karanjia, Deepak Mallick, Namvar Singh, Trilochan Shastri and an elusive Bengali gentleman called Chanchal. During those days, my father was also part of the editorial team of the magazine *Pratipaksh,* started and owned by the fiery opposition leader George Fernandes, along with Girdhar Rathi. I remember, during the Emergency in 1975, there was a lot of tension in our house because everyone associated with the magazine were arrested, and somehow, my father's name was excluded; still, he left Banaras for a few days.

Renowned painter Ram Kumar and Syed Haider Raza have garnered worldwide acclaim for their series of paintings depicting the ghats on the Ganga. Raza's *Untitled (Benares)*, painted in 1943 with watercolour on card, expresses tunning dawn hues featuring the Darbhanga House, the minarets of the Bindu Madhav mosque and the shimmering landscape of boats silhouetted in the river. Another Banaras painting from 1947 by Raza is also a typical depiction of the four prominent white shikharas of the temple at the ghats and two minarets. Ram Kumar's *Benaras Series* was an expression of an altogether different perception, though, devoid of human figures but rich in the depiction of the city's stark distress and agony.

His first visit to Banaras was with M.F. Husain in the 1960s, but he continued to visit in the 1990s and then again in 2007. These visits culminated in his phenomenally expressive abstract paintings—the *Banaras Series*—while he was living and absorbing the city like a hermit. Apart from British artists like William Hodges, Prinsep and Thomas Daniell, the early-twentieth-century paintings like Nandlal Bose's *A Boat at Rajmahal*, modern paintings like Manu Parekh's *Evening at Banaras* and *Evening Lights*, Husain's *Varanasi I* and *Benaras Ghat* stand out as remarkable impressions of Banaras by these great artists. Banaras also has its own class of painters, who are famous for their unique styles and techniques, including Anil Karanjia, Kedar Sharma, M.N. Chaddha and the nationally renowned cartoonist Manoranjan Kanjilal.

Just as these painters have left indelible imprints on the city, there have been the greatest of musicians who have created and curated an intricate rhythmic tapestry that echoes the melodic symphony of Banaras. The musicians who have emerged from the egalitarian and the folk traditions of Banaras, with amazing depth, brought the style of *gayaki* (the form of singing), and their instruments in the main genre of Shashtriya Sangeet (Indian classical tradition), popularly known as the Banaras Gharana. What Tulsidas did with the Valmiki Ramayana written in Sanskrit and with his Ramcharitmanas written in folk Awadhi, these artists have done just the opposite. Unlike Tulsidas, who brought the scriptural rendition of the Ramayana from the elites to the folk, these musicians from Banaras have brought the folk musical instruments and the forms of singing of the common people into the realm of the elites. Percussion instruments like the tabla, which has almost replaced the classically approved pakhavaj—except in the solemnity of Dhrupad singing—are because of Banaras. It was Ram Sahai, disciple of Maudu Khan, who brought the distinctive Banarasi baj style in the tabla. Similarly, the shehnai, which was considered a very humble instrument and ranked lower in status as compared to sarod and veena, only played in marriages, has now acquired a classical status because of Bismillah Khan and his disciples. Bhaiyyaji Ganpat Rao brought the hitherto anglicized harmonium as an accompaniment in Hindustani classical music. The flute, always considered a folk instrument and mythically connected with Krishna, never gained classical status, until Pannalal Ghosh and later Hariprasad Chaurasia made the instrument popular in the classical music performances. Hariprasad Chaurasia, although born in neighbouring Allahabad, started learning vocal music from his neighbour, Rajaram, at the age of fifteen. He later switched to playing the flute under the tutelage of Bholanath Prasanna of Varanasi for eight years. Legendary exponents of Hindustani classical music, like Badi Moti Bai, Siddheswari Devi and Girija Devi and the musicologist Jaidev Singh, hailed from here. The artists' cartography of Banaras is coalesced in an alley in the old Banaras. There is even a lane in the Kabir chaura area known as Padamshree Gully, which houses many eminent artists who have been conferred the eponymous honour. Icoinc Kathak dancers like Sitara Devi and Pt Birju Maharaj, the shehnai maestro Ustad Bismillah Khan, tabla player Gudai Maharaj, etc., are from this locality. Bade Ramdas and Chote Ramdas of Kashi are counted among the top singers of India. Rasoolan Bai, Siddheshbari Devi and Girija Devi hold the topmost slots as lead Thumri singers. Their gurus, Jagdeep-ji and Moizuddin Khan, were at one time called the kings of Thumri, who started the Banarasi style of Thumri and gave it an urbane status from the rural folk areas of Banaras. Shiva–Pashupati of Banaras has been a magnifico duo of their times—excellent Dhrupad singers. With the other phenomenal singers Dhamar, Khayal and Tappa, Banaras has been the hub of *poorvibaaz* (eastern) artists.

The famous tabla player Kapte Maharaj, whose magical rhythm even prompted Ustad Faiyaz Ali Khan to kiss his hands in overwhelming emotion, was the progenitor of the Banarasi style of tabla playing. Ashu Babu was not only a master of tabla but was also a great scholar of the prevalent forms of music in the Banaras region. Much before them, a relatively low-profiled tabla player, Ramsahay-ji, made astounding contributions to the evolution of the Banaras Gharana or the Purabi Ang. He has advised and trained students of music across all genres, breaking free from the stifling codified Gharana traditions. It is said that Nawab Wajid Ali Shah was so impressed by his performance that he presented him with a reward of Rs 1.5 lakh and four elephants.

Kishan Maharaj is probably the finest trope of the living continuities of Banaras, where he embraced the musical legacy passed down through three centuries of his ancestors in the codified school of guru–shishya tradition. Having lived and honed his skill in Banaras, he left a rich legacy of innovation in tabla playing and an extremely talented and creatively vibrant group of disciples including Kumar Bose, Sandeep Das, Shubh Maharaj and Sukhwinder Singh Namdhari. Kishan Maharaj played a pivotal role in elevating the independent identity and status of the tabla as a musical instrument in its own right. In fact, the solo and the Jugalbandi tabla performances, integral to the contemporary musical performances, bear a significant imprint of the personae of Kishan Maharaj.

Pandit Samta Prasad, popularly called Pandit Gudai Maharaj, hailed from a very poor family, and has not only played the table with the greatest maestros like Baba Allauddin Khan of Maihar and Faiyaz Khan but has also left a short but very distinct mark in film music. The tabla solo during the chase of Basanti by Gabbar Singh in the film *Sholay* (1975)—'*chal dhanno chal*', Hema Malini's famous line, and the background music with the sound of horse's hooves—is an example.

Lachu Maharaj lived in Nagwa, near the Banaras Hindu University, yet walked every day to the heart of art—the Dalmandi locality—to do his *riyaz* (practice). His first guru was his father, Pandit Vasudev Singh. Later, he continued his training under Pandit Biru Mishra. Lachu Maharaj proudly announced that he is from the legendary tradition of Vishwanath Sahay, who is considered part of the oldest lineage of tabla *vadak*s (players) of the Banaras Gharana. Kumar Bose, the disciple of Kishan Maharaj, is presently the most promising star of the Banaras Gharana who follows the rudimentary code of conduct of the Gharana.

The most prominent metaphor for everything that Banaras represents is a devout Muslim who, after offering his gratitude through his five daily Namaz prayers, chooses to do his daily riyaz in the precincts of the most nondescript temple of Balaji at the Panchnanda ghat—a deity not so important in the Banaras assemblage. There was a certain *je ne sais quoi* in Bismillah Khan. Profoundly grateful for everything that he had achieved in the city of Banaras, he would play at all the major Hindu festivals of Banaras and was an important performing artist at the Naubatkhana of Vishwanath mandir. Bismillah Khan is the glittering diamond in the paan and symbiotic culture of Banaras. Rather than pursuing the more lucrative musical opportunities, he stuck with his humble shehnai, which, by and large, has been the most adaptable musical instrument, fitting for all occasions and closely modulating the human emotions. It has an earthy ruggedness and sensuality. He deserves all the credit for elevating this folk instrument to its significant importance in the vast pantheon of classical instruments. The uniqueness lies in the fact that it is only with the shehnai, particularly, with the trademark versatility of Bismillah Khan's style, that an artist can caper the folkish Thumri, and its sub-genre like Chaity, Savani, Ganga Badhaiya and Kajri, as well as play the toughest nuances of *meendh* (gliding from one note to other), *aaroh* (cadence-lower to higher), *avroh* (cadence-higher to lower) and *alaap* (a musical rendition without words) that is inherent in the musicality of Shashtriya Sangeet. This has influenced the entire gamut of subcontinental music. Though born in the neighbouring district of Shahabad in the erstwhile Dumraon state in 1916, he accompanied his uncle Ali Baksh to Banaras and stayed here forever, contributing to the evolution of a unique synthetic musical tradition. He developed and tuned his shehnai to the primordial rhythm of Shiva—the Anhad Naad—along with the sonorous Azaan (Muslim prayer) and the symphony of the temple bells of Banaras. Bismillah Khan's shehnai infused immortality in the famous numbers of the late fifties films, such as 'Dil ka khilauna hai toot gaya' (*Goonj Uthi shehnai*, 1959), 'Ghar aaya mera pardesi' (*Awara*, 1951) and 'Chod babul ka ghar' (*Babul*, 1950). He also played a minor role in the film *Kinara* (1977).

Like the musical instruments, Banaras has popularized Thumri, Tappa, Chaiti, Kajri, Savani and Birha, which now constitute a major segment of the Indian classical and quasi-classical musical performances. The most outstanding aspect of the Banaras singers was that they all were highly versatile singers and were as much at ease with the folk genre of music, like Tappa, Hori and Thumri, as much with the heavy gravitas influenced Khayal, Dhrupad and Dhamar.

Pt Channulal Mishra, a quintessential Banarasi, learnt the nuances of music from the musicologist Thakur Jaidev Singh. A self-made man, he has given the Banaras Gharana his bassy and countertenor voice that carries the hallmark and aroma of the lanes of Banaras and the sonorous gurgling of the Ganga. He loves his khichdi and practises since 4.30 in the morning. A great friend of Sankat Mochan Mahant Virbhadra Mishra, together they have made Banaras a place where the music gets merged with its everyday mystical existence. Singers like Rajan and Sajan Mishra follow the same tradition and have imparted music lessons to a vast number of their disciples. All of them are committed to upholding the ancient tradition of Banarasi Sangeet in the new world order.

Kashi city, since ancient times, is famous for its *nrityakala* (dance as a performing art). Although Kathak came from Lucknow when Banaras was under Awadh rulers, this art form of court dance developed quite distinctly in Banaras. In contrast to lilting sensuousness, it acquired some aspects of religious symbolism with traces of Bhakti element, quite common in Bharatnatyam and other temple dance forms. There is one spectacular family in Banaras upholding this tradition of Kathak. Shukdev Maharaj and his son Krishna Prasad have made singular contributions to training the dancers across the country. Famous dancers like Sitara Devi, Alaknanda, Birju Maharaj and Gopi Krishan followed the same Kathak style. They have choreographed some of the best dance sequences in Bollywood films. Sitara Devi, in particular, is credited with teaching the nuances of Kathak dance to a bevy of film actors.

Our mohalla in Banaras had a predominance of a community called the Ahirs or the Yadavs, whose main profession was dairy farming. In most of their functions, we used to listen to a raucous series of songs, where a male singer, using a long iron contraption called *kartal*,[8] would perform with all his zeal. He would keep one hand on his ear and would blast out Bhojpuri folk numbers. This was Biraha, developed in the late nineteenth century, as a folk music genre, more specifically to the 'cultural and geographical entity' in the Bhojpur belt of eastern Uttar Pradesh and western Bihar. The earliest-known work on Biraha has been done by G.A. Grierson, who mentioned Biraha to exist as an isolated village folk genre in the 1880s but rose to prominence by the 1960s and '70s. It got its stronghold in the city of Banaras, particularly because of the large percentage of the Yadav community. The development of Biraha has been solely attributed to the efforts and creative instincts of one man named Bihari Lal Yadav, who went by the nom de plume of 'Guru Bihari'. He is credited to be the founder of the modern Biraha, which was so gross and highly folkish that has been referred to as 'Khari Biraha'. He gave a protective cover to Biraha by integrating it with the popular Kajri in the urban ecosystem when he moved to Banaras. He also invented the sine qua non element of Biraha, the kartal. The usual performance lasts for around five to seven hours, where the lead singer stands, while the accompanying chorus, consisting of five to six people, sit on the ground below him. The two special occasions on which it is performed in Banaras are weddings and temple festivals, with the former being more popular on the rural edges of Banaras. The evolution of the Biraha can be credited exclusively to the accommodating and creative temperament of Banaras when it comes to a novel genre of music. As Scott L. Marcus, in his article 'The Rise of a Folk Music Genre: Biraha', has rightly remarked that: 'Biraha 's development from relative obscurity to its present position of popularity has been accompanied by changes in virtually every aspect of the genre: song structure, performance context, the concept of ensemble, the use of musical instruments, economic circumstances, and so forth.'[9]

Just like serving as a crucible for the many artistic innovations, Banaras has also witnessed the forging of some relentless freedom fighters, adding yet another layer to the city's rich narrative. Even though the 1857 Revolt did not affect Banaras, one of the Banaras-born freedom fighters is now a torchbearer and the perfect example of women's power and stubbornness against all odds. Jhansi ki Rani, Laxmibai, born in the house that was almost a part of the huge palace of the younger brothers' family of the last Peshwa, Baji Rao II. Moreshwar Pant, from this family, married a noble woman, Bhagirithibai, and became an important part of the quasi-administrative Maratha circle of the early nineteenth century Banaras. They were blessed with a daughter on 21 November 1835, whom they named 'Manikarnika'.[10] As a child, I always used to wonder at the crumbling citadel which had a rusting iron plaque, announcing the birthplace of Rani Jhansi. I visited the same place near Assi ghat recently where the legend was born. The house has been demolished now and a statue of the Rani with her horse has been erected—a symbol of defiance and obduracy. Other freedom fighters like Pt Madan Mohan Malviya, Lal Bahadur Shastri, Dr Sampoornanand and Bhagwan Das, were all from Varanasi.

Kashi that is Banaras, has been the city of gods, humans and stories. So, let me narrate a small story that elucidates how Banaras has served as an ethereal enclave for enchantresses from time immemorial. In the era before Divodas ousted all the gods and goddesses, including Shiva, the city had its own set of entertainers and danseuses—the Gandharvas and the Apsaras, who were called upon from heaven to perform in the city of Kashi. The gods desperately wanted to come back to this beautiful city. It was then that Shiva sent the sixty-four yoginis from his abode in Mandara[11] who were mavens in all the art forms and proficient in yoga and *maya* (sorcery) to distract the king and thereby find loopholes in his moral demeanour. The sixty-four yoginis, though, could not distract the king; on the contrary, they themselves got so enamoured with the city that they made Kashi their permanent abode.

During the Janapada times, Buddhist literature has recorded that one of the first to be initiated into *pravrajya* (monkhood) was a courtesan from Kashi named Adadhakashi, whose fees for one day was equivalent to half the income of Kashi. She adopted Buddhism and was granted the exalted status of an Arhatpad.[12] Amrapali was another *ganika*, courtesan, whom the Buddha admitted in his Vihara. According to Kautilya's *Arthashastra*, at that time, courtesans were also used for spying or gathering specific information.

From the fifth-century treatise *Padtaditakam*, we come to know of the head of courtesans named Parakramika, whose breasts were tightly clasped by a flimsy upper garment and her lower garment was worn in the manner which displayed her taut buttocks prominently.[13] In a Gupta era rock inscription, the lanes of Kashi are called Varramabhirama (meaning the lanes occupied by harlots; *vararama* in Sanskrit means a harlot). In the *Matsaya Purana*, Kashi has also been called Gandharvasevita (abode of the Gandharvas) The best description of the courtesans of Kashi among the ancient texts is found in *Kuṭṭanī-Mata*—the advice of the procuress. It is a long poem composed in the eighth century CE by Damodar Gupta, who was the minister of the King of Kashmir, Jayapeed (779–813 CE). In this poem, an old courtesan, Vikrala, advises Malati on how to seduce influential and rich clients to get maximum benefit from them and then also on how to get rid of them! There was a religious ceremony that used to be organized in the temple of Shiva known as Vrishabhdhwaj. An integral part of this ceremony was an elaborate dance sequence. In the book *Kuṭṭanī-Mata,* there is a character of Prince Samarbhatt, who was surrounded by courtesans after his puja performance.[14]

During the Gahadavala era, the golden period of Banaras, city life was teeming because of the presence of the best and the most beautiful courtesans. The Kashi courtesans were most popular and the kings and minor feudatory chiefs of the adjoining area were their revered clients. Religious life in Banaras is still closely linked with the dances of the courtesans. Locally called Bai-ji, they are always present, for example, in the old Adi Vishweshwar temple near the Satyanarayan mandir in Chowk. The courtesans, on the day of Gopashthami (generally falls in the month of November) perform for free and offer their dance to the presiding deity.[15] Similarly, in front of the Vishweshwar temple at the Manikarnika ghat, every year after Holi, during the Chaitra Navratra, the courtesans dance at the Mahashamshan to please Lord Shiva.

Two stories are popular in Banaras as to why the dance of the *tawaifs* (courtesans) is performed at the temple precincts. One is purely based on the Hindu Karmakand and has a strong Brahminical implant, suggesting that they dance on this day to get rid of their debased life in their next birth. The second version is that, after he constructed a temple at the Manikarnika ghat during the great temple building spree by Raja Man Singh, a function was organized where the city artists were invited but none turned up to dance in the cremation ground. It was then that the courtesans decided to perform. Since then, the tradition of courtesans dancing at Manikarnika has continued.[16] The 1936 edition of *Hans* magazine, edited by Munshi Premchand, has a reference to the courtesans in Budhwa Mangal Festival and in *Tawaifnama*, Saba Dewan has elaborated on the late twentieth century aesthete Babu Bachchu Singh who, by way of thanksgiving, created a whole chaplet of verses *Veshya Strota* or the

Ashtottari Mala, naming 108 major courtesans and female singers of Kashi.[17]

During the famous Budhwa Mangal, well-known courtesans once sang specially composed musical bandishes for their patrons in the police, like one Meer Rustam Ali or a bouncer named Data Ram Nagar. The city courtesans wore pink dresses and pink jewelleries.

Three types of *mehfil*s (gatherings) were organized in the heydays of Banaras: Gajra, Jhoomar and Dangal. The great singers of those days used to be Tauki Bai, Badi Maina, Dusna Bai, Jaddan Bai, Janki Bai, Gauhar Jan, Rajeshwari Bai, Kashi Bai, Rasoolan Bai, Kamleshwari, Durgesh Nandini, Choti Moti, Champa Bai, Siddheshwari Devi, Shahjahan Begum, Bhaunphati Kesar, Panna, Juhi, Ratna, Vidhyadhari, Husna Bai, and Badi Moti Bai, who were rich and famous singers and dancers of their time in Banaras. These were household names in the late nineteenth and early twentieth century. Husnajan, Wazirjan and Sheokanwar Bai of Banaras were even selected by the W.C. Gaisberg team in 1906–07 who shortlisted them for recording.[18]

They lived and practised their art in areas like Nariyal Bazaar, Raja Darwaza, Dalmandi and the Chowk. With the advent of Islam, the Arabic word 'tawaif' came to be associated with the women who performed in public. The Arabic word 'taifah' means a group of artists and performers, especially a group of singers, and the dancer involved in this troupe has been called a tawaif. They were also referred to as *ghudchari*s or women who ride horses, perhaps because of their ancestors initially coming from the families of Nats and gypsies. There is a village near Banaras called 'Basuka', which is inhabited by gypsies called *godnewali*s or tattoo makers. *'Godna'* was the term we used to hear since childhood, and it was supposed to be a taboo for the upper castes but quite prevalent among many lower castes in Banaras. Nat also means dancer and even now, womenfolk perform acrobatics, rope-walking and many such public performances for which the gypsies in Europe are famous for. But their connection with music has been an evolution with the advancement and refinement of societies. As late as the eighteenth century, they were also referred to as *deraydar*—the ones who moves from one *dera* (place) to another. Generally, they never indulged in the prostitution business but were the upholders of some of the most ancient forms of dance and classical singing. They had their select patrons and some even chose to be the concubines of kings and rich merchants. In the Middle Ages, *mujra* (a dance performed by courtesans) was performed in the homes of nobles and landlords in marriages or other festivals. This tradition continued till the early 1990s. To entertain the *barat* during my cousin sister's wedding in the mid-1970s, which was held in my ancestral village in western Bihar, dancers were called from Dalmandi and we, as children, were thrilled to go and watch *Bai ji ka naach*. Hemant Sharma, in his book *Dekho Hamari Kashi* has also penned a vivid account of Champabai in this regard.[19] The dress of the tawaifs used to be Peshwaj, in which the upper part of the body is covered with an *angarakha* woven with the golden and silver threads of silk, along with a satin or velvet churidar pyjama as the lower garment. *Benares Illustrated* and *Tawaifnama* have a description of their dress as: 'Their trowsers are of coloured silk: the full petticoat of striped muslin, with silver or gold embroidery; and the *do-putta* or folded scarf is of stiff crape, with a border of silver brocade.'[20]

Film afficionados must have seen the same dress worn by Meena Kumari in *Pakeezah* (1972) and by Rekha in *Umrao Jaan* (1981). Incidentally, Umrao Jaan spent her last days in Banaras and has her grave on the Fatman Road in the same graveyard where Ustad Bismillah Khan is buried. The famous actress Nargis' mother, Jaddan Bai, was from Banaras; she was a great singer of Tappa and Thumri. Bismillah Khan's debut musical film song 'Dil ka Khilauna', it is said, was originally composed by the Banaras tawaif singer Brijbala. Even Bharatendu and Jaishankar Prasad were regular visitors to the locality in Banaras called Dalmandi. Mallika, a Bengali tawaif, served as the lover and muse for Bharatendu, and was highly skilled in letter-writing and etiquettes. Banaras, along with Lucknow, was the centre of music and dance, though Kathak and Thumri originated in the Awadh region. In Banaras, it acquired a distinct flavour because of its uninhibited and sultry coquettishness. The myriad forms of folk singing subgenres like Hori, Dadra, Chaiti, Kajari, Jhula, Savani and even Kathak, cumulatively, underwent refinement due to their highly cultured patrons among the tawaifs, who were proficient in arts, culture and literature. Here, it is apt to mention that the musical style renderings, cultural settings and social changes have all contributed to the above-mentioned musical genres, which 'opens up the cantomeric studies on the model of Alan Lomax',[21] the American ethnomusicologist. Their creativity was lavishly appreciated and popularized in such cultural centres of the nineteenth-century India as Calcutta, Pune, Patna and Muzzafarpur. They were mentored by Thumri legends and exponents like Ustad Maujjuddin Khan and Jagdeep Jee Mishra. Thumri is generally known as the 'feminine voice' and in Banaras it is worded in Braj, Bhojpuri, Awadhi and Khari Boli. The bol banao Thumri of Banaras or the *purab ang* is now a highly specialized form of singing. The Lucknow style of Thumri or its earlier much more serious bandish Thumri like the one of Nawab Wazid Ali Shah 'Babul mora naihar chhoto jaye' has more gravitas and is *raga*-based classical, whereas bol baant or bol banao Thumri has a lilting erotic undertone of sexual longing and flirtation but sometimes even devotion.

Typical words of bol banao Thumri would be 'Bisraiho na balam hamar sudhiya' (Never forget the sweet memories my love) and the devotional would be 'Mohika dagar chalet dinhi gaari re, aiso dhitho banwari mori guiyan, binti karat mein to haari re' (He flirts with me while I am walking, oh this Krishna is so stubborn my friend, I am tired, imploring him). The tawaifs were the most ardent devotees of syncretic forms of worship. They symbolized pluralism and a symbiotic social contract where art alone was considered supreme.

The biggest blow to the profession of tawaifs came from the British, who categorized them as 'Nautch Girls' with the tag of prostitution. Even a liberal and highly sensitive Prinsep calls them 'Nach Girls' and writes about them, that: 'The witching influence of the arts and graces of these women is as much acknowledged and as powerful as ever . . . some of the best houses, and the handsomest temples of the city, have been erected by ladies of dancing notoriety.'[22]

Dewan writes that: 'Colonial writers like Buchanan routinely described women who practiced a vast spectrum of female sexualities that existed outside marriage as "'prostitutes". This representation was informed as much by Victorian morality as by Hindu and Muslim laws newly fashioned under the company rule to administer justice to the natives according to their separate religious cannons.'[23]

Thus, in one stroke, the highly respected *devdasi* tradition in south India and the acceptability of courtesans were associated with flesh trade and brothel activity. The nationalist anti-nautch movement of the nineteenth century and the restriction of this profession to a specific public locality further diminished the artistic image of the tawaifs. In the 1827 census of the city of Banaras, a total of 500 Muslim and 260 Hindu nach girls were recorded by the administration. The Kashi Sangeet Samaj is one of the oldest music society that was started in 1905. It was a direct reaction to the popularity of the tawaif and their ustads in the classical music genre. It was to wean away the rich and middle-class youth from the *kothawali*s to the more Vedic Khayal and Dhrupad style of singing.

Some illustrious singers of the late nineteenth century and the early twentieth century who were brought up in the nuanced and urbane tawaif culture have become an integral part of the rich musical tradition of India. Some of them are:

Shivkunwar Bai: Learnt music from the sarangi player Bachau Mishra, specializing in the Khayal, Thumri and Tappa styles.

Badi Malka: Although famous as 'Badi Malka of Calcutta', she was an Armenian of Jewish descent, named Edilian Victoria Imangus at birth and married to an engineer, William Robert Yeoward, posted in Azamgarh, a town near Banaras. To pursue her musical talent, she moved to Banaras and fell in love with her first ustad, Khursheed. Later, she underwent training in music from stalwarts like Bhaiya Saheb Ganpat Rao and Ustad Maujjiddin Khan. She is credited with developing the more simple and erotic style of Banarasi Thumri. She was the mother of the legendary singer Gauhar Jaan.

Badi Maina: Star performer of the Budhwa Mangal festival, she was patronized by the Kashi Naresh Ishwari Narayan Singh and

Prabhunarayan Singh. It is said that once a smitten lover of Maina Bai tried to gatecrash the royal mujra organized by the Raja of Banaras to demonstrate his love for her renderings but was arrested. In an equally magnanimous gesture, the Raja pardoned him and accepted this ardent connoisseur of music to participate in the mehfil.

Vidhadhari: Born in the Khajuri village near Banaras, which has produced some of the best musicians. She was known for her Tappa, Khayal, Sargam and Tarana styles. She was also an ardent nationalist and composed songs like 'Bharat watan humara, Bharat key hum hain bachche; kar do zuban bandi;jailon mein chahe bhar do; mata ke vaste hai sir katana.' (India is our country, we are the children of India, you can try and silence us and throw us in jails, for our mother's freedom we will sacrifice our lives).

Husna Bai: Referred to as 'Sarkar', she was trained in music by Thakur Prasad Mishra and sarangi player Shambhunath Mishra. Her Tappa style of singing became very popular, and it was further refined by Chhote Ramdas-ji. She shared her deep interest in literature with Bharatendu, engaging in discussions on poetry and prose. She undertook some philanthropic endeavours like the construction of many dharamshalas, a Sri Krishna temple, well-digging and planting orchards—all in the memory of her Hindu lover. Actively involved in politics, she founded a 'Twaiif Sangh' (Courtesans' Federation) during Gandhi's visit to Banaras, aiming to collectively address their demands and problems. Her most famous couplet is another example of a tolerant and syncretic Banaras of those days:

Mandir mein hai chhand chamakta, masjid mein hai murli ki taan
Makka ho chahe Vindravan, hote aapas mein qurbaan

(The moon shines in the temple the flute of Krishna sings in the mosque. Mecca and Vrindavan are ready to sacrifice themselves for each other.)

Jaddan Bai: Apart from being a great singer, she was the mother of the famous actress Nargis.

Tina Bai: She, too, was highly literate and took great interest in Urdu and Hindi literature, particularly close to Jaishankar Prasad. She received her musical initiation from Kashinath Kinnar and was an expert at the Tappa, Thumri and Tarana styles.

Moti Bai: One of the greatest of all singers in the early twentieth century, who learnt singing from the famous music maestro Mithai Lal Mishra.

Kashi Bai: Very ordinary looking, Kashi Bai's velvety voice deeply affected the aficionados of music. It is noted that once during a musical Dangal, in which even Begum Akhtar from Lucknow and Roshannara Begum from Pakistan had participated, Kashi Bai stole the show and since then, she has been known to capture the hearts of millions with her style of Chaiti, Kajri and Thumri.

Sidheshwari Devi: One of the prominent founders of the Banaras Gharana and also the first to popularize the folk elements of Thumri, Hori and Tappa nationally and internationally. Even though her training was in exclusive classical and serious style of Khayal, Dhamar and Dhrupad, she has given voice to some immortal bandishes of Thumri. She came from a family of musicians and had a natural affinity towards music. Her talent was further refined by the sarangi player and musicologist Siyaji Mishra. She also held an important position in the Bhartiya Kala Kendra at New Delhi.

Girija Devi: Having heard Girija Devi countless times since the early 1980s, I can ascertain that it's not just the music that one hears, it's the ancient Kashi and modern Banaras that reverberate within the soul. Her guru in the initial years was 'Sarangi Sagar' Pandit Sarjuprasad Mishra and later, Shrichand Mishra. She represented the Banaras Gharana at Calcutta's Music Research Academy. Somehow, my entire collective intellectual muse has been shaped by her songs. I associate her thumris from the Sankat Mochan Music festival to a remote corner on the India–Pakistan border near Bikaner, during my days in the army. Particularly in the cool desert evening, sitting in my tent with a tape recorder connected to an army signal equipment battery, and listening to 'Kaari badariya barse', the ambience created was that of *saawan* (monsoon), with Old Monk rum and the thumris transporting me to a distant magical land of Meghdoot. I was privileged to be a part of the select gathering of Girija Devi's, perhaps her last public performance, in Bharat Bhavan in September 2017. She had the same grace, same pitch and *kashish* (allurement), and the latent joi de vivre whenever she rendered a Thumri or Hori, or Tappa, for which she is so well known.

Rajeshwari Bai, Rabi Bai and Choti Maina Bai: All three learnt music from sarangi player Sarju Prasad Mishra and sang all types and forms of Gayaki.

Chapter 10

Saat Vaar, Nau Tyohaar

Festivals and Foods

In Banaras, Time present is contained in Time past. It is said that a festival or a tradition never dies here. There is an adage in Hindi: '*Kashi ka adbhut vyavahaar; saat vaar, nau tyohaar*' (The amazing tradition of Kashi: nine festivals in a seven-day week). Nowhere else are such elaborate ceremonies conducted during festivals. Every festival in Banaras is celebrated for at least two days. The first day of any festival, with its attendant rituals, is celebrated by the Shaivites, who carry forward the trace elements of ancient vegetative divinities. The second day, termed as Udya Tithi, is the day for the Vaishnavites to celebrate it through the performance of Vedic rituals like havan and and daan-dakshina. Banarasis observe both the denominational rituals with equal aplomb. Festivals and melas (fairs) are inextricably linked and have been a part of Kashi's culture long before the Vedic people came here. Breaking down the etymology of the Hindi word 'mela' reveals that it means 'to meet' or 'to get together'. Generally, there are two types of melas that are organized, where religion and amusement are part and parcel of the entire celebration. In Banaras, there is always an overlap of these two. The colonial administration, with their Victorian morals, could not fathom the merry-making and rituals being so ostensibly linked. In the melas, the colour of the apparel is important and is generally the ones worn during that season, for example, the paddy colour, *dhani*, for monsoon; red during the two spring festivals of Navratra; pink and light yellow during the sun festivals; and so on. In the specifically religious-themed ones, generally, white and pale-yellow costumes are preferred. Some festivals evolved before and during the Mahajanapada era and some were conceived as a reform to counter the social malaise of their time, but one thing is certain: traditions never die in Banaras. Seasons, especially the solstices and eclipses, are deeply ingrained with customs, religions, offerings and worship. They are organically intertwined with festivals, cuisines and celebrations. During our childhood, the taste, smell and the sound of festivals heralded the onset of seasons, as they have always been placed concomitantly for ages. Festivals in Banaras are entwined with the onset of seasons and specific cuisines, where particular food items are prepared and consumed only on those days and never in any other months of the year. Even in the fast-paced life of the twenty-first century, the energy and passion of the people of Banaras during festivals are palpable. There is a ceremony for every part of the day. Banaras, being a typical centre for trade, has planned all these festivals to sell products from nearly all sections of society. Gold is a must-buy on Akshay Tritiya, utensils and silverware on Dhanteras, and major electronic or vehicle purchases on Diwali, specific fruits like wild *ber* (Indian jujube) and dried figs on Basant Panchami, among many other customs. Let me list some festivals that are rarely celebrated outside Banaras, and some important ones also have a Banarasi twang and quirkiness to them. It may sound preposterous and a colossal wastage of time and money for the sensibilities of the younger generation, but these are the customs of Kashi and Banaras—the cradle of Hinduism, that is continuing since thousands of years. The eclectic involvement in celebrations, cutting across race, caste, religion and financial status, is the life blood of the city. From childhood till the onset of teenage years, festivals were an important phase of our formative and growing-up years. It calibrated our aesthetic sense and ingrained in us the value of cultural, social and individual interactions. Here, I am listing them beginning with the New Year of Banaras, which starts from the first day of Chaitra. The festivals and melas mentioned in earlier chapters have not been included in this. Further, most of these melas, barring a few, have little or no attendance now—but the tradition continues.

Festivals and Melas in the Summer Months of Chaitra, Vaisakh, Jeyestha and Ashadha

In the first half of April, a small customary ritual called Sattuan is organized, generally falling on 14 April, marking the harvesting season. The summer progresses with its typical heat wave pattern called loo. This festival, sans any puja, is celebrated by starting the *sheetal* (cold) and sattvic *aahaar* (diet) or the coolant cuisine to be consumed throughout the summer season. Reminiscing my childhood days, I fondly recall the first sight that would greet us upon returning home from school: the rows of durries in the shaded veranda of our house. Family members sat on the ground, each with a brass plate with *sattu* (roasted barley and Bengal gram powder), green chutney made of onion and garlic scallions, mint leaves, coriander leaves and lime juice, a thick paste of jaggery and milk, cucumber and ringed onion with homemade *jamun sirka* (blackberry vinegar), *aam ka panna* (smoked or roasted green mangoes made into a sherbet with roasted cumin seed powder and black salt). Eating with our hands, we first mixed the sattu with the green chutney and a little bit of water, then with jaggery and milk paste, making a bolus out of it, and gulping it down with the sherbet or sometimes with buttermilk! Siesta time began immediately after meals, coinciding with the Chaitra Navratri period. In Banaras, these nine auspicious nights are involved with worshipping the nine Gauris or Durgas on specified designated days. The Navratra Mela takes place at the Durga Kund, historically featuring animal sacrifice, where many animals like the male buffalo calves were slaughtered; this practice is now banned. In our house, the consumption of non-vegetarian food would be stopped during this time. On the ninth day, the

Ramnavmi Mela takes place at Ramghat—started by Tulsidas in the early seventeenth century. The business community, particularly the Marwaris of the old business district of the 'Pakka Mahal', celebrate Gangaur—a festival that began in the sixteenth century after the settlement of the community. Followed by the Narsingh Chaudas Mela in quick succession, which marks the celebration of the saving of Prahlad after killing of Hiranyakashipu, it involves the performance of a drama at the Bada Ganesh. Gazi Miyan Ka Mela also takes place at Lat Bhairava in the downtown Adampura area, which is mostly attended by Muslims and the lower-caste Hindus; songs of martyrdom of Salar, also called Pir Alim or Saint Alim, are sung by the singers called *daffali*s, and women get possessed, predicting the future with their oracular messages. Interestingly, a marriage ceremony between the Lat Bhairava and the well that exists in the precincts of Kapalmochan is also of historical traditional significance. A fair with mock fights between the Kols and Bhils used to take place but has now been discontinued.

The traditional marriage of Lat Bhairava with the well involves the metal *mukuta* (crown) of Bhairava being kept in the house of Bhageluram Tokedar, one of the trustees and a major patron of the festival. This crown is actually a huge moustached head with two faces like that of a warrior. Although of recent origin, it is said to be made of a consecrated mixture of *ashtadhatu* (eight minerals) as per the Kashi Khanda'. On the full moon day in the late afternoon, this crown is carried by some devotees on a red palanquin from the house at Visesvarganj in a procession to Kal Bhairava, who is considered the younger brother of Lat Bhairava. The modern temple is located in the Kotwalpuri district amid the maze of lanes between Chaukhamba Lane, the 'Main Street' of the premodern Banaras and Maidagin Park. Although the procession does not enter the Kal Bhairava temple, it halts in front for one of the Kal Bhairava temple priests, the lone Gosain among the Brahmin priests, to perform the aarti with vegetarian offerings before the crown. The Gosain is the solitary vestige of an earlier ritual organization when the Kal Bhairava temple was in the hands of the Nath ascetics, the successors of the skull-bearing Kapalikas. Just adjacent to the temple, in his house, the capital of the Mahashamshan Stambha is still preserved and worshipped as the 'discus-handed' Chakrapani Bhairava. The festivities conclude with kite-flying competitions.

Akshay Tritiya is another auspicious occasion, marked by the purchase of gold jewellery, typically for sisters' trousseaus. This is also the time when, back in the day, we would have visitors gracing our house to perform the 'Panchkroshi Yatra' around the ancient boundary of Kashi. The month of May–June witnesses the celebration of Ganga Saptami, celebrated at the Panchganga ghat, featuring shehnai with Bismillah Khan's performances. It is celebrated as the birthday of Ganga, traditionally accompanied by day-long musical gatherings.

In the Mahajanapada times, the festival called Jalutsav (water celebrations), marked by the tenth-day tithi, is essentially the taming of Ganga by Shiva's matted locks, and is called the Ganga Dussehra. It is noticed that on this day, the water turns placid and increases in volume per flow, possibly due to the melting snow in the higher regions of the Himalayas. For us, this was a time for long, leisurely boat rides in the cool nights. I recall our uncle taking us for the darshan of the mysterious appearance of a saint called Devrahwa Baba on Ganga Dussehra. Later, my uncle and aunt would take *deeksha*, abstaining from most of the Rajasic and Tamasic foods. A strange custom in Banaras is that girls from respectable families, after having bath in the Ganga a day before Ganga Dussehra, perform a*visarjan* (dispersal in water) of their dolls and avoid touching any toys for four months. Strange indeed! This peculiar tradition reflects the basic metaphysical aspect of *nashvarta* (mortality) and cold detachment from the most beloved objects, engrained in Hindu *mimansa* (epistemology). Some scholars believe that this is a tradition brought by the traders and later incorporated in the form of river worship.

Celebrated during the hot and humid days of summer, the festival of Nirjala Ekadashi in Banaras holds a significance place as a test of endurance, perseverance and will power. According to a popular folk story, on this day, Bhim, the superman of the Mahabharata, had fainted due to thirst, after fasting on this day, and could only regain consciousness after being pushed into the water. The ritual involves having a bath by swimming across the Ganga, applying sandal paste on bodies—hence also called 'Chandan Ekadashi'—and participating in mock fights. There is a statue of Bhim at Ramghat, at the location where he is supposed to have fainted and has been made from the silt and sand collected from the ghat steps. On the Ekadashi day of every month, my uncle observed a fast, having only one meal consisting of boiled rice of the Tinni variety and lentil soup made from a pulse variety called Boklas. These two specific choices were allowed to be consumed because they were not cultivated through ploughing; rather, they grew wild or were scattered in the fields if sown for commercial purposes. These nuances in Hindu religious rituals are intriguing, to say the least. My mother informs me that, in Banaras, this fast is also called 'Savitri Vrat', which is accompanied with an integral ritual of 'Snanyatra', in which Lord Jagannath is bathed. This essentially serves as a preparatory ritual for the most famous Rath Yatra festival and mela. The *rath* (chariot) of Jagannath is ceremoniously pulled by a rope starting from Assi ghat and brought to the Rathyatra Chowk.

Closing the summer festivities is the mela called 'Bataspariksha' or the Patparikshan Mela, a pragmatic celebration, related to wealth and prosperity. On the Guru Purnima in the month of Ashadha, the *jyotish*s (astrologers) predict the health of crops, harvest and weather conditions, after determining the direction, flow and intensity of the wind. For us kids, after the festival of Sattuan, our role was only to follow the elders in their various visits to temples and the performance of petty rituals. There used to be a lull for the entire months of May, June and the first half of July. Thereafter, the back-to-back festivals would begin, only taking a brief hiatus in late October during the Pitru Paksha (inauspicious time).

Festivals in the Rainy Months of Shravana, Bhadra, Ashwin and Kartika

Banaras in the rain is the worst place to visit, with its hot and humid weather and the stagnant waters. Earlier, however, ancient Kashi was the most sacred of all pilgrimages during these seasons when the backwater of the Ganga and Varuna formed a fish-shaped island called the 'Matsyodari Yog'. Now, the focus of the festivals shifts from the ghats where the water level consistently starts rising, to the higher locations of Pakka Mahal and the more interior and outskirts of the city. The Shravan month is the season of the reigning deity, Shiva, and has a retinue of Shiva-related festivals. The first Monday is especially auspicious. I remember attending just once this special darshan of the Mahadev at the Vishwanath temple, and the crowd was unimaginable in the cramped *garbha griha* (sanctum sanctorum); they were rowdy, yelling '*Har Har Mahadev*', carrying pots of milk and Gangajal. As a kid, I had to be lifted by one of my relatives but only after I got drenched in the spilling water and milk from the worshippers' brass *lota*s, and my dress tinged with *haldi* (turmeric) and vermilion. The overwhelming reek of human sweat, crushed bilva leaves, stale milk, sandal paste and the strong smell of the burning dhoop, along with the hot and humid sultriness inside the unventilated cramped space, was choking. I read an account of the same situation described by a Christian priest, James Kennedy, way back in the early nineteenth century while on his visit to the temples of Banaras: 'The whole scene is repulsive. The place is sloppy with the water poured out by the worshippers and is littered by the flowers they present. The ear is assailed with harsh sounds.'[1] This is the scene in most of the temples in Banaras, but then this is what makes the sanctum sanctorum the place that Hindus yearn to visit. Rev. Kennedy's Christian sensibilities were unable to take the chaos and sounds that is a *de rigueur* of a Hindu temple. Sometimes, when the rains used to be particularly merciless starting from mid-afternoon, during this heavy pitter-patter, another very earthy food combination for dinner was prepared—dalbhari puri and kohada ki tarkari. Dalbhari puris were rolled-out circles of wheat dough stuffed with boiled chana dal (split chickpea lentil) paste, spiced with powdered black and green cardamom, pepper, cumin seeds and asafoetida, then pan-fried in an iron griddle with ghee. This is paired with a stew of green pumpkin called kohada.

Vridh Kaal ka Mela: People bathe from this well called the *'vridh kaal ka kuan'* for health benefits. This *koop*, or well, is also called the Dhanvantri Koop, where the great *vaid* (physician), Dhanvantri, is said to have dropped his bag of medicines. There used to be a kund nearby, called the Amrit Kund, which is also mentioned by Sherring.[2]

Fatman ka Mela: Started since the Islamic conquest, it is now very eclectic. The city's tawaifs used to attend this with all their pomp and pageantry, every Thursday of the Shravana month. Most of the prominent Muslim tawaifs and musicians of the city are buried here in the nearby grave, which also holds the grave of Umrao Jaan Ada and Bismillah Khan. Similarly, a Durga ji ka Mela is also held every Tuesday in Shravana, attended by the tawaifs, who were idol worshippers. In the early nineteenth century, this was in the outskirts of the city and full of gardens; close to 30,000–40,000 people used to attend this. Now, the crowd gets distributed in the nearby temples of the Manas mandir and the Sankat Mochan, adopting a dour religious demeanour against the revelry and promiscuousness of yesteryears.

Naga Panchami: People bathe in the Naga kuan—the deepest and the oldest well in the city. Its waters spring forth from Pataal Kot, the netherworld, reminiscent of ancient serpent worship. Hiuen Tsang has mentioned such wells and ponds in his travelogue during his visit to Kashi and Sarnath. According to the Kashi Khand, it is called the Karkotaka teerth.[3] During our childhood days, we would be awakened by the harsh piercing shouts early in the morning around five: '*Bade guru ka, chote guru ka, Naga lo bhaiya Nag lo*' (Buy the Cobra patriarchs—elder one's and the younger one's). These were the hawkers selling the black and white as well as coloured images of various mythical representations of the Nagas on recycled sheets. They used to be drenched, but all their wares were carefully layered with used plastic bags and dirty plastic sheets. The entire sheets, featuring images of Nagas and the concerned gods, like images of Krishna dancing on the hood of Kaliya, the nag coiled around the Shiva Linga, an ancient form of a single erect nag, and intertwining two Nagas . . . all these starkly remind one of the sectarian fusion of Vaishnavism, Shaivism and the ancient Naga worship. Symbolically, the bade guru and chote guru represent Patanjali and Pannini. The Naga Kuan area was where Patanjali is said to have been born. On this occasion, a *dangal* or *kushti* is also organized. Historically, the tradition of Naga Puja was never followed in our family, but it started after a minor incident with my twin brother.

This occurred a few days before the rains on a peculiarly hot and humid evening, when my twin brother and I were around six or seven years old. We were sitting in our veranda, which had *roshandaan*s (skylights) on which various birds like sparrows, doves and even squirrels made their nests. All of us were sitting lined up against the wall, awaiting our dinner. Suddenly, a snake, around three feet long, fell from the skylight with a slight thud on my brother's shoulders and wriggled towards the courtyard where a house help was preparing rotis on a coal stove. Everybody panicked and the house help, whom we called Champa Dai, flung a hot roti on the snake, landing it precisely on its head. The snake started to coil up and writhed in pain, till my father squished it with a hockey stick. The snake must have crawled up the roshandaan from the creepers hanging outside in search of bird eggs. My concerned grandmother then made all of us kids eat raw black pepper and repeatedly asked if it tasted bitter. Apparently, she believed that if a snake bites, a person's taste buds are affected first. Even though the snake was not a cobra, it was decreed by my grandmother that elaborate Nag puja will be performed every Nag Panchami day henceforth.

Rakshabandhan: This festival was a great event for us, as my brother and I became the centre of attention and were quite sought after. In our joint family, including neighbourhood relatives, the number of girls far exceeded the boys. As was the case in most of the earlier families, the preposterous desire for a male progeny led to an increase in the number of females till, if the couple was lucky, a son was born. In our house, the sisters tied a *rakhi*—a coloured and highly gaudy piece of silk or cotton string, some adorned with currency notes fanning out from it and decorations following the latest fashion trends. Brothers were treated to sweets and, in turn, they were expected to offer token gifts and protect the sisters from any untoward incidents. For many years, when my eldest uncle was present, a trio of three elderly men from our village would descend to our house in Banaras, which included a Brahmin chief priest by the name of Ganesh Mishra (whom we called Narad Muni because of his propensity of creating mischiefs), a Maulvi named Haji Karimuddin with an orange beard and a dark, pot-bellied person called Rajaram Sah. Ganesh, Karimmuddin and Rajaram were the chief priest, maulvi of the only mosque, and the top grocer of our village, respectively. They used to tie rakhi on uncle's wrist after performing the entire customary rituals of *tilak*, sprinkling of rose water and the aarti. This festival also greatly honours the benefactor.

Janmashtami: Amidst the monsoon rains, this festival of Janamashthmi takes the centre stage, celebrating the birth of Lord Krishna, with the Gopal-ji mandir in the Chaukhambha area being the focal point. In our neighbourhood, a competition of creating bright tableaus depicting the scenes of Krishna's birth, called *jhankis*, was held. We looked forward to it eagerly and the concept of the jhanki and the materials to be collected for it were decided much in advance. We were also supposed to fast that day, but I remember sneaking into my relatives' house where I gorged on the dishes being prepared for this special day. Customarily, on this day, a special combination of food called phalahari (essentially meaning fruitarian) was prepared, which included prasad called panjeeri—prepared by roasting together powdered coriander seeds and sugar. The halwa—a sweet dish prepared from water chestnut flour and ghee, along with deep-fried puris made from buckwheat flour and sautéed vegetables (a mix of potatoes and pointed gourd), completed the festive fare.

Haryali Teej: Also called Kajri or Hartalika Teej, this tradition was started by the king of Kantit—a village in the district of Mirzapur—who established it for the benefit of women. The mela was earlier exclusive to women, who used to bathe and fast at the Shankudhara near Khojwan and Isar Gangi pond, located in the Jaitpura area. In my locality, I have always seen a procession of beautiful women clad invariably in light-green-coloured sarees and carrying on their heads clay casseroles containing moist earth with barley sprouts. These sprouts are gently plucked and put behind the ears of their brothers; it was also a way to pay obeisance to respected elders in their family. The procession ends at a pond where the earth, along with the remaining barley sprouts, is dispersed in the water. The pre-Vedic deity Vindhyavasini Devi is worshipped on this day. With the barley sprout as a symbol and the worship of a pre-Vedic deity, this festival resonates with aboriginal worshipping traditions that have taken on a Puranic form.

People offered baksheesh (small amount given as a tip) to the professional women singers called *gaunharin*. In Banaras, the term 'Gaunharin' was generally used to refer to a lower-class tawaif. Girija Devi's famous Kajri '*Nahak laye Gawanwa*' brings out the inherent pathos and the social customs related to the Gauna system. In this system, a girl child is married but continues to stay at her parents' place, and only after attaining puberty is she sent to her husband's place. Generally, in the zamindar and other well-to-do middle-class families of eastern Uttar Pradesh and Bihar, two or three maid servants would accompany the bride to her husband's place and stayed there forever. These maid servants were also called gaunharins. They later turned to singing and played an important part in the festival rites.

Dhela Chauth: The word *dhela* means a small piece of stone. This is another entertaining festival that still continues, although ending sometimes in minor scuffles leading to court cases. People believe that if they happen to see the moon on this day, they will certainly incur a series of misfortunes. To ward off this *bhavishya vritha dosh* (future wrath of the gods), they encourage people to pelt stones in their house. Fasting and Ganesh Puja are also a part of this festival.

Lolark Chhath: This is again an ancient form of worship where offerings are made to the Sun God at Lolark Kund at Assi ghat. Traditionally, the gaunharins would sing Kajri, which was supposed to be a sacred act to offer them baksheesh. It is the day when couples bathe in the Kund and pray for a male child.

Vaman Dwadashi: Celebrated at the old Vishnu teerth at Varuna sangam, a play is enacted in which the dwarf Vaman avatar of Vishnu is shown measureing the entire length of the earth in three steps.

Anant Chaudas: After the ritual bath in the Ganga and paying homage to Vishnu, people cross the river to attend the famous Ramlila that is organized at Ramnagar.

Sorahiya Mela: This festival, along with the mela, goes on for a month and is celebrated at the Lakshmi Kund near the Laksa area. People purchase clay statues of Goddess Lakshmi and different coloured cloth threads are tied to the trees at the pond. This one, too, is symbolic of the appropriation of the Yaksha and Naga rituals performed by the Vaishnavs. Ritualistically, sixteen kinds of grains and sixteen kinds of flowers are offered to Goddess Lakshmi; my mother, however, told me that eight types of grains, fruits, dry fruits and flowers, along with eight different colours of clothes are offered.

Jitiya: The concluding days of this season witnesses this festival of Jitiya—a corrupted form of the Jivit-Putrika Vrat, observed for the long life of the male child. It is usually passed down by mothers-in-law to their daughters-in-law on the eventuality of the latter's ill health and the inability to observe the fast. We looked forward to this festival only because a special kind of crispy sweet bread called *thekua* was prepared on this occasion, eaten with a spicy, sweet and sour mango pickle. Thekua is prepared by kneading the dough with melted jaggery, wheat flour and ghee, which is then rolled into small circular shapes deep-fried in an iron deep skillet.

Durga Puja: This is a very popular festival for the Bengali community. As for the Banaras area in north India, this period is marked by observing fasts or simply refraining from eating non-vegetarian food. Many avatars of Durga, Chandi, devis and gauris are worshipped on set tithis for each. The nine gauris and the nine Durgas have specific temples. Most of the mohalla clubs and religious institutions sponsor a huge statue of Durga and the massive pavilions called pandals, which are consecrated, beginning from the sixth day called the Shashthi. Heavy presence of pilgrims at such makeshift worship places and the temples of the great Kushmanda Durga at Durga Kund, Vishalakshi, Lalita, Sankata, Annapurna and Mahalakshmi, all located in the Pakka Mahal area, enhances the general ambience of gaiety and enjoyment that marks the nine nights—the Navratras—finally culminating in Vijay Dashami. In Shakti tradition, this is the day Durga vanquished Bhainsasur, the bull demon. Our early morning visits to the nine durgas with our mother included her narrating the myths and stories related to all the nine gauris and nine durgas enroute to these temples. In the evening, we visited the nearby Bharat Seva Ashram Sangha, which offered many wonderful small plays, mock fights and sword drills by the monks of the Sangha. During these Ashwin Navratras in October, the evening prasad and the sacred smoke of the dhoop of this place had a distinct divine flavour and fragrance, which still lingers and titillates my taste buds and olfactory glands, respectively, wherever I am.

Ramlila and Bharat Milap: This festival, showing the exile of Lord Rama and his subsequent victory over the demon Ravana, was started by Tulsidas in the late seventeenth century in Banaras, and was later adopted by the king of Banaras for the grand display of royal patronage. The mise en scène involves sequential enactment from the stories of the Ramayana, specifically that of Rama's exile—an incident that occurred in 1868, as quoted by Vishwanath Mukherjee and Pandit Kubernath Sukul.[4] An incident that is still talked about is when a British officer was watching Ramlila. The scene being enacted was Hanuman's going in search of Sita—across the ocean—to Lanka, and the place was the Chauka ghat near Varuna. Some missionaries residing nearby could not take the commotion and the noise. One Reverend Macpherson requested Collector Bax, to stop the Ramlila.

When Bax, along with the Reverend, visited the place, he jokingly asked the person Tek Ram who was in the role of Hanuman, if he had heard that Hanuman crossed the sea in one leap, and if he could jump across this river Varuna. This challenge was accepted by the theatrical Hanuman, and he jumped across river Varuna only to collapse and die the next day at Bharat Milap. There is a *mukut* (frontlet) of this Hanuman still preserved in the Narharipur temple and is worshipped before the commencement of the Ramlila near Varuna.

Specific anecdotes of the Ramayana that are staged in Banaras are famous for their place of enactment, like the Lanka dahan of Ramnagar Ramlila, Phulwari and Dhanush yajna of Laksa, Nakkattaya of Chetganj, Khojwan and Kashipura, eventually ending with the Chaukaghat Vijayadashami mela and the Bharat Milap at Nati Imli. The entire Banaras becomes a huge stage, and thousands of people attend this play in the moving stage all around the city. In 1987, the famous German regisseur directed plays based on the Greek trilogy in Bharat Bhavan, Bhopal. He improvised the entire Bharat Bhavan Complex into a stage. This was hailed as the most innovative attempt at using the outdoor space as a theatre stage. Vyomesh Shukla mentions about an act of Ramlila in which the man playing the role of the mythical bird Jayant Pakshi is stoned by the public.[5]

Dussehra: During my time in Banaras, a Ravana effigy used to be burnt near our locality in the Kashi Vidyapeeth Stadium. We find some trace of the festival of Dussehra in a Mahajanpada era festival called Chattramangal and Hastimangal. The city used to be beautifully decorated and the king's convoy would pass the city, culminating at his well decorated palace. There, he would occupy the throne, wield the sceptre under a white umbrella, and grace the courtiers and Brahmins while taking a dekko at his subjects. In Hastimangal, Brahmins used to recite the *hasti sutra* (the mantras for the correct handling of elephants), and a hundred elephants with perfect tusks were covered with golden ornaments. Quite possibly, this day was chosen for the coronation ceremony or even as a victory day, similar to the old princely states of Mysore and Bastar on Dussehra or Vijaya Dashmi. The next day, the famous Bharat Milap, signifying

Rama's reunion with his brother Bharat, takes place at Nati Imli, a downtown locality near the Sanskrit University. The duration is only five minutes, but the attendance can be of close to 4,00,000 people. The Raja of Banaras offers a *ginni* (gold coin) each to the performers. The sami tree is worshipped on this day, and it is considered a good omen to catch sight of the nilkanth or blue jay. Every year, after Dussehra and before Diwali, we were woken up at three in the morning and taken to the corner of our lane, where we huddled together with the crispy fresh dawn breeze nibbling lightly at our cheeks, to witness this colourful procession of Bharat Milap passing by. This used to be particularly thrilling because we got to savour the season's first hot nankhatai (shortbread biscuit). Why nankhatai was prepared for this very day? This connection between the nankhatai and Bharat Milap procession was never discovered by us!

Dhanteras: Banaras, being predominantly a traders' city, celebrates Dhanteras on a grand scale, marked by extensive shopping for jewellery and utensils. The centre of old Banaras used to be the Thatheri Bazar, but now, most of the shopping is done in the newly constructed malls. Still, the old-timers continue to patronize the traditional hubs for festival shopping. This day is also dedicated to the wealthy Yaksha Kubera. In the bright autumn sun, the curb-side shops and the impromptu stalls display festival wares. Villagers and potters sell clay statues of Ganesh, Lakshmi, clay dishes for lamps, coloured fancy bulbs, strips of lights, piles of kheel (puffed rice kernels), batasha (bubbled sweets), strange shapes of small dolls, pot-bellied males and females, birds, animals and flowers made from edible crystallized sugar, cotton wickers, and many kinds of household decorations.

Narak Chaudas: This is celebrated on the birthday of Lord Hanuman between Bhaidaini and Mir ghats, two days before Diwali. Most of the Yadav community and the Gangaputras celebrate this. People get their bodies massaged with warm mustard oil and camphor and have a hot-water bath before going to pray at the Hanuman temple.

Diwali: In Banaras, the tradition of Diwali dates back to the early Mahajanapada era when it was called 'Deepmalika'. The city was decorated like Indrapuri—the city of Indra, and women used to dress in saffron colour. As per Jain scriptures, when the king of Kashi learnt about Mahavir's death, he ordered the city to be lit with thousands of oil lamps because he believed that the light of wisdom and knowledge had died with Mahavir, but the memory would be kept alive by the lighting of the lamps. The Aughars and the Tantriks of Banaras celebrate Diwali at the Manikarnika ghat during this Mahanisha (the great dark night). The rituals are quite macabre, involving a human skull, liquor and raw flesh of sacrificed animals; all part of these rites and perfumed sitting on the partially extinguished pyre. Many people confirm this that during the *pretkaal* (the hours between midnight and 2 a.m.), a tall silhouette of a man with long matted hair and a trishul in hand, along with a woman wearing a garland of human skulls, have been seen on this night in the Mahashamshan. For us, Diwali day used to begin with the strange early morning muhurta and ritual called *Daliddar Bhagana* (literally meaning 'kicking the poverty out'), which generally falls between three and four in the morning. The entire household used to be up by the sound of a bassy *dhub-dhub*, but everybody remained inside their rooms. Only our eldest aunt would be present to supervise the ritual. This was the day when a hunchbacked old woman used to arrive in the dead of the night. The sight of this woman whom we called Kubadi Budhiya was avoided throughout the year and she was ridiculed and made fun of by the mohalla women, chased by the kids, and perceived to be a bad omen, quite like the character of Quasimodo, played brilliantly by Lon Chaney in the classic 1923 film *The Hunchback of Notre Dame*, but for this special early morning day of Deepavali, when she became an important player in the game of rites and rituals, we were not allowed to step out, but as a kid, the curiosity to see what was going on once overpowered me and I slipped out of my bed, climbed the windowsill and peeped out from the half-open window. I saw this old woman half-bent, tottering in the gallery and circling in the courtyard, hitting a tattered winnowing basket called *soop*, with a stick and along with this dhub-dhub sound, she was taking out a muffled sound by clicking her tongue. This is a ritual, again quite likely to have made its way down from the days of the vegetative divinities and the Yaksha puja. All the more reason that we find the Yakshas and the peoples' deities, Kuber, Ganesha and Hanuman, being worshipped on this day along with Lakshmi. Our favourite pastime on the Diwali day used to be to search every nook and corner of the house for a mole, as spotting one on the night of Diwali is considered auspicious. According to belief, its appearance means that the financial crisis of the house is about to go away, and the stuck or spoiled works are going to be completed. Ceremonially, Diwali dinner used to be suran ki sabzi (elephant yam curry) and puris.

K.T. Achaya has mentioned in his book about the prasad prepared in Vishnu temples from sweet tuber called *korai*, to appease the Mahavarah avatar of Vishnu. It is quite probable that Lakshmi, being the consort of Vishnu, this vegetable *sooran*, which is also a root vegetable, is consumed.[6] A picnic under a gooseberry tree is mandatory on this day! Similarly gambling, known in Banaras as the game of *Solah Pari ka Naach* (the dance of the sixteen fairies), is a must. Earlier this game was performed outside the Annakut temple by the tawaifs. Otherwise, the belief is that the person who does not gamble on this day will be reborn as a mole in their next lifetime.

Annakut: Annakut is celebrated a day after Diwali. The two adjoining temples of Vishwanath and Annapurna, on this day, witness a prototype of palaces and temples constructed by the different varieties of food, sweets and the harvested crops that are neatly arranged. One important reminder and a marker of ancient worshipping traditions that continues in Banaras is that on one day in Magh, in this temple, sprouted rice crop is offered, and the devotees receive paddy as prasad. Annapurna Devi is the epitome of abundance and prosperity. Prinsep describes the devi as: 'Unna-Poorna is the name of the consort of Shiva, typified as the Goddess of Plenty; from similarity of her name and attributes, it has been suggested that she is identical with the Anna-Perenna of Roman mythology.'[7]

Yam Dvitiya: Sisters pay respect to their brothers and perform tilak ceremonies, and the brothers are fed by the sisters. Celebrated at Yama ghat, on the second day of Kartika month. This festival has reference to the mutual attachment and bonding of Yama and his sister Yami.

Kartik Purnima: On this full moon day, an auspicious bathing ritual is done at the Panchganga and Durga ghats that starts as early as about four in the morning. In a playful enactment of the traditional rivalry, a mock fight takes place before the bathing ritual, precisely at a particular muhurta, between the original Gangaputras and the later settlers and owners of the ghat—the Maharashtrian Brahmins.

Dev Diwali: This is the most captivating festival celebrated in Banaras. According to the Shaiv mythology, Shiva killed a demon named Tripurasura on the full moon day, fifteen days after the Diwali festival. Dev Deepawali is celebrated to mark the victory of Lord Shiva over the evil demon. All along the ghats, thousands of oil lamps are gently pushed inside the river, creating a surreal scene with the pillared reflections of the lights on the ghats. I attended last year's Dev Diwali in Banaras, and I must confess that despite a grand display and a humongous expenditure, I was saddened by the ersatz ceremony. The ghats on Dev Diwali were flooded with psychedelic lights, laser beams and almost projected a discothèques atmosphere. Gone were those flickering yellow wickers of the floating oil lamps or the larger yellow electric bulbs revealing the dancing penumbra of the buildings and temples in the shimmering Ganga. However, the most scintillating spectacle that remains intact is at the Bindu Madhav temple at the Panchganga ghat, where throughout the month of Kartik, cane or bamboo baskets containing small oil lamps are hung atop a bamboo pole. These lamps are called akashdeep. These towers cover the entire stretch of the ghat and are a sight to behold. It is the symbolic lighting done for the departed souls to find their way to be united with their ancestors. Prinsep was also fascinated with this festival, which he called Dipadanu. He has written: 'The lanthorns suspended from bamboos, indicative of the Dipadanu ceremony in honor of Ananta, an incarnation of Vishnu, prove the time of this view to be October; and it will be seen that the accumulation of the sand of the rainy season has not been cleared away from the ghats.'[8] The Kartik month also witnesses the 'Nag Natthaya' leela at the Tulsi ghat.

The Festivals and Melas in the Winter Months of Agrahayana, Pausha, Magha and Phalguna

Makar Sankranti: Falling on the thirteenth or fourteenth day of the January month, Banaras witnesses a massive footfall of pilgrims from all over the world. Bathing in the Ganga is considered highly sacred during these days. Since the sun moves in *uttarayana* (the period of the sun's progress to the north of the Equator), there is also the symbolic fulfilment of the urge to touch the sky. No wonder then that the most popular sport on this day is the kite-flying competition. I still identify the colours and their permutations and combinations with the colours of the kites. *Patangbaazi* is not native to India, though, and most likely has been brought by the silk route travellers.

> The earliest written account of kite flying, from 206 BCE, mentions that Heuin Tsang had flown a kite to overawe the army of Liu Pang. Various sources suggest that by 169 BCE, kite flying was in place under the Han dynasty, and that the Chinese general Han Hsin had 'a kite flown above a besieged town to calculate the distance his army would have to tunnel to reach under the city wall.[9]

In Banaras, however, it was made popular by the Muslim nobility and later picked upon by the Rajput and Bhumihar zamindars. Now, it is mostly patronized in the Pakka Mahal area along the ghats by the traders' community. In our days, the kites were always hand-made and rhomboid-shaped, varying in size with distinct names. For example, 'Dhaara' and 'Mattha' were large kites, while 'Addha', 'Chilgozia',

'Sugga', 'Chandrika', etc., were medium- and small-sized kites. All of them had thin bamboo spines with a bow-shaped horizontal one and a thin strip dividing it vertically. My subconscious association of colours have been influenced by the colours of these kites. In the adjoining Aurangabad area, there was this most popular and famous kite shop, which did not have any formal name, but everybody knew it by the name of '*Chote Sardar ki Dukaan*' (the shop of the young Sardar). The owner was indeed Chote Sardar, an extremely arrogant and choleric man who was very difficult with us kids, never getting up from his throne and ordering us to pick up the stuff we wanted to buy ourselves. Despite his demeanour, he had the most amazing collection of kites, *pareta* (a kind of bobbin with wheels and a handle used to wrap the strings of the kite), *manjha* (the kite thread covered with pounded glass) and *saddi* (cotton thread). Much before Makar Sankranti, also called 'Khichdi', boys from the neighbouring carpenter's mohalla used to start preparing the sharpest of manjhas by first pounding the broken pieces of bottles, ink pots, etc., into a fine powder and then mixing it with the paste of boiled rice. They would then make many rows of saddi and layer it with this paste. Manjha was only used in the initial length of the thread, and the rest of it consisted of saddi, which, a deft kite flyer dexterously used to slaughter the other kites. Many ethics and unwritten rules were followed stringently, like no flyer can attack another flyer from the saddi stage and confronted only from the point from where manjha is used, and no one was allowed to use metal wires, with the violators being publicly thrashed. Lately, the traditional and local kite industry, like many other products, has been overwhelmed with the cheap and durable Chinese kites and other products. The *Times of India*, a decade ago, lamented this in an article titled 'Kite changes its shape to fly with changing times'. The day was special to us because of the exotic lunch preparation of tehri and jaoor or bakheer.

Panchkroshi Mela: This festival and fair revolves around the ancient tradition of welcoming the travellers. In the past, people from the city would travel to the north-western side, a place called

Shivpur, where the forest area began. They welcomed the visitors with flower garlands, clean water and mishri (crystallized sugar). However, this custom has now faded away.

Nagar Pradakshina: The Nagar Pradakshina fair, held at Chaukha ghat and Barhiya Tank, involved pilgrims circling around the city, completing the journey in two days. They rested on the first night at Chauka ghat, where the Krishna Leela was performed. However, for some reasons, this fair and the city perambulations have been discontinued.

Ganesh Chauth: At the Bade Ganesh temple, especially considered very fruitful for students, a small mela is also organized, where 'Kajli' song books, marigold garlands and small idols of Ganesha are sold.

Ved Vyas: Ved Vyas, the composer of the epic the Mahabharata, is honoured in a Shiva temple at Ramnagar Fort. It is said that once he cursed Banaras, when he came along with his students and was kept hungry for four days. He cursed the Annapoorna deity who inturn cursed him that he has to leave Kashi immediately. Since that day Vyas ji along with his son Shuk Rishi resides in a temple at Ramnagar.But since this curse was on every citizen of Kashi, to free oneself every Banarasi is required to worship him on this day.

Basant Panchami: The spring season is short but overpowering, the breeze heady with the fragrance of *mojar* (mango blossoms), neem and the drumstick blossoms. In some leafy areas of Rajghat, the campus of Banaras Hindu University and the gated areas of Diesel Locomotive Work, the scent of the mahua blossoms is intoxicating and nudging the mortals towards sin. With the onset of the perfect Gandharva days, when the Hindu mythological cupid—Kamadev—strikes with his sugar cane arrows, the festival of Saraswati Puja offers an aesthetic and religious sublimation for all such amorous urges. Small mohalla clubs install a statue of Saraswati, the consort of Brahma and the goddess of wisdom and erudition. People wear yellow-coloured clothes, and students offer their books and other study materials for blessings. It is an important festival for the Banaras Hindu University, which celebrates its foundation day on this occasion of Saraswati Puja. While not very popular in the downtown Banaras, it thrives in the Bengali community-dominated areas of Bengali Tola and Sonarpura.

Shivratri: This celestial celebration in Banaras transcends ritualistic bounds to transform into a cultural extravaganza, where bhang is consumed in copious quantities and the main puja is held at the Vishwanath temple. In all the Shiva temples, the attendance increases by leaps and bounds, but Shivratri in Banaras became more conspicuous and a 'looked forward to' kind of festival later, because of an interesting incident. The Shiv Barat, literally the marriage procession of Lord Shiva, had begun in 1983 and has now become one of the most attended festivals of Banaras and competes healthily with the ancient Ramlila and Nag Nattaya festivals. I met and spoke to the founder and convener of the Shiv Barat Samiti, Dilip Singh Sishodia, who told me that he had realized long back that there is no major epical enactment related to Mahadev, who is the reigning deity of Banaras. He then narrated an extremely engrossing and worrying background of this festival, highlighting the role of the most hard-working and energetic committee member—a Muslim gentleman whom they referred to as 'Mydear'. With childlike enthusiasm, he narrated the following account:

> Kashi, the oldest city in the world, existed much before even the word 'history' was not in vogue. Without Shiva and Ganga, this very ancient city does not exist. In Banaras Puri, the morning of Kashi is famous worldwide. Even before the break of dawn, people leave for Ganga and bathe with the slogan: *Har Har Mahadev Shambhu, Kashi Vishwanath Gange.* The daily routine of the people here starts only after the darshan of Baba after bathing in the Ganga. The people of this place have an unbreakable relationship with Ganga and Baba Vishwanath. This is the reason that whenever there is an injury to the honour or respect of Mother Ganga or Baba Vishwanath, every Kashi resident comes out on the road. This happened in January 1983 when gold plates were stolen from the *Argha*

(the hollow where the Shivling is installed), which was installed by Maharani Ahilya Bai Holkar, and the whole city came out on the road to protest against the theft. Protests started in their own way, in some places there were nook meetings, while road jams in others. Protests and demonstrations became an order of the day. The entire city was in the grip of this spasmodic movement, so some Banaras is decided to create a movement in a novel way to create additional pressure on the government and the administration. The main problem, though, was its expenses. When it came to financial expenses, the philanthropist income tax advocate, K. Anand, took upon this responsibility for all the expense on himself. As a young and active social worker, the responsibility of preparation and direction was entrusted to me, and a committee was formed among the associates with the writer Pandit Dharamsheel Chaturvedi, businessman Kailash Nath Keshari, Mohammed Ikram alias Mydear of the Muslim Majlis, Journalist Sushil Tripathi, and journalist Amitabh Bhattacharya. It was decided that, following the Shiva procession described in the Puranas, we planned to take out a procession that included ordinary people dressed as ghosts, pishachas, demons and all gods and goddesses. We even included all types of animals, eunuchs, magicians, snake charmers, courtesans and thronged the streets of Banaras. When it was announced, the whole city started sending messages to participate in this protest. The administration and the government got worried and started trying to prevent this procession from its very inception. The administration did not leave any stone unturned, but the more pressure the local authorities put on the organizers, the more people resolved to make it happen. The whole city got united and ready and gave a message to the administration that instead of stopping the journey, spend all energy in catching the thief and recovering the gold. The effect of this was that the entire government machinery got activated and the thieves were caught even before the declared date of Mahashivratri for the procession, and the gold was recovered. It was found out that few members of the upper-caste Hindus, who were regular to the temple, were the conspirators in this theft. Immediately, the whole anger turned into excitement, and Baba's gold was found. In massive euphoria, the whole city started preparing for the celebration. It appeared that instead of the procession of the organization, it was the procession of the entire city of Kashi. Hindus, Muslims, Sikhs, Christians all started preparing, and the protest march now transformed into a congratulatory march. In this way, with the inspiration of Baba Bhole Nath in Kashi, a new festival started in the city. The administration and the government also participated in this festival with full determination. In this way, the first Shiv Barat of this era started from Kashi! The popularity of this Shiv Barat can be gauged from the fact that more than 10,000 Shiv Barats are now taking place all over the country. Now, Shiv Barat has started taking place in foreign countries as well. Kashi is a city of festivals, where not only Shiva but also lord Rama is celebrated in equal enthusiasm. The world-famous events related to lord Rama include Bharat Milap and Nakkataiya, along with the Ramlila of Ram Nagar, Nag Nathaiya and Krishna leela, which kept happening at other places but there was no event related to Baba Bhole Nath. In the name of 'events', there was just darshan at the temples, so when the first event related to Baba Kashi Vishwanath happened, all Kashi residents started making it their own and accepted the event in no time. They joined the Lakhi Mela, which a hundred thousand people of Kashi attend. The poorest of the poor and the richest of the rich participate in the Shiva procession of Kashi. In fact, the relation of the people of Kashi with Baba Bhole Nath is not that of God and devotees, not even of king and subjects, but that of father and sons, that's why the people here do not need garlands, flowers or mantras, and only a bel patra is enough for Baba. It happens! We do not know when Baba Bhole Nath was married, but it is believed that he was married on Mahashivaratri, that is why we, Kashi residents, carry out Shiva procession every year on Mahashivratri to make our father's marriage anniversary unforgettable and memorable.

Indeed, a fascinating account!

Holi: It is celebrated like in any other city but with certain added peculiarities. It is hilarious to read Bishop Sherring's highly prudish account on Holi and the subsequent Dharaddi Mela that was organized at Dashashwamedh ghat. He has written: 'This festival is chiefly noted for obscene representations, and the use of abusive language. No woman can venture into the streets, on these days, without being exposed to insults. The grossly indecent festival is immensely popular in the city, and on this day the people cast upon each other the ashes of the Holika pile burnt on the previous day, and then wash themselves, and change their coloured clothes.'[10]

Banaras continues to celebrate Holi even now, after 175 years, in the same manner as described by Sherring. The celebrations span four days, starting with Rangbhari Ekadashi, which is playing Holi with Shiva. Additionally, it also marks the arrival of the New Year in the Hindu calendar. At Mirghat, a mock religious crusade takes place, sometimes resulting in injuries for some.

Before Holi, the household activities would generally include ordering new clothes, preparing various snacks, preparing *ubtan* (body scrub), and most importantly, shopping for 'Holi essentials'. In our house, the enticing aroma of mathari (refined flour rusks), sevda (crisp and salty, deep-fried lentil flour noodles), besan ke laddu (Bengal gram flour sweet balls) and gujia (a kind of sweet empanadas stuffed with khoya or thickened milk and dry fruits) remains confined for days, as mostly the cooking was done in the corridors leading up to the kitchen. A day before Holi, our bodies were scrubbed by a very Banarasi ubtan paste that is made from mustard seeds and Bengal gram flour, by grinding it on a grinding stone, to which a ladleful of fresh cream is added. After it dried up, the yellow peel from the exfoliated dollops was then collected and consigned to the Holika fire that evening, as per the prescribed rituals. We were five siblings of almost the same age. So, in the early 1970s, during days of high scarcity, it was a common practice to purchase an entire length of cloth for such occasions. Thus, all of us would have identical patterns and types of new Holi dresses:

kurta-pyjama for boys, and kurti-salwar for girls. Despite being a festival of free-for-all, with a carnival-like gaiety and frolicking, one discipline that is always maintained with stringent regularity is the rigorous imposition of no water colours after noon. So, exactly by twelve in the noon, in the entire city of Banaras, water colour spraying would stop. Twelve to four is the time for bathing, cleaning up, gorging on scrumptious meals and resting. Even now, the siesta on a Holi day is refreshingly somniferous.

On a Holi day, one shop that remained open was the mutton shop in Aurangabad, next to a small mosque and the graveyard. Jammu, as Jamruddin Miyan was called, was a proprietor who did brisk business on this day. We always accompanied our uncle and Nand, our household help, in the early morning visits to this shop, where my uncle educated us on what part of the *khansi* (castrated goat) to purchase. Additionally, customary delicacies are prepared for lunch and dinner, like raw-jackfruit spicy curry, puris, tamarind sweet and sour sauce, saffron rice and puas (deep-fried sweet of wheat or rice flour mixed with jaggery and raisins).

In the evening, a Kavi Sammelan (Poets' Meet) used to be held at the Assi Chauraha, and this Kavi Sammelan was typical of Banaras, where poets used to recite their most obscene, highly vituperative, and laden with no-holds-barred sexual innuendos composition. It was attended by the who's who of Banaras. Since the last few years, it has been completely stopped. The iconic novel on the cultural mores of the Assi locality and Banaras *Kashi ka Assi* by Kashinath Singh, has a facetious description of this custom of abusive poetry narration.

Budhwa Mangal: Traditional customs made it mandatory for the Hindus to visit the temple of Durga on the first Tuesday following Holi. This festival, also called the Bada Mangal, is celebrated on the second Tuesday after Holi and has an interesting history. It was initiated by Mir Rustam Ali, an administrator representing the Nawab of Awadh. Ali was an aesthete and a staunch supporter of the Ganga-Jamuni culture and envisioned the Budhwa Mangal Festival in Banaras with the ancient traditions of Chattra Mangal and Hasti Mangal in mind. Despite his intent, the exuberance and revelry of these occasions made him introduce public performances of tawaifs. The tawaifs sang the popular Hori, Chaiti and Thumris on huge boats called *bujra*s (colloquial term for a double decker budgerows) in the Ganga. Many such boats of the rich and other feudal zamindars also congregated there. To me, it must have been something like the famous 1881 painting by the French impressionist Pierre-Auguste Renoir, *Luncheon of the Boating Party or the Le Déjeuner des canotiers*. Mir Rustam gave a popular Thumri called 'Hori' in the local dialect that is still sung by the local singers in his name. The lyrics are: 'Kahan gayo mero holi ko khelaiya, sipahi rustam ali banko sipahiya' (Where have you gone, my companion for Holi celebrations, Oh! Rustam Ali, the handsome soldier). It has an inherent erotic element that is present in most of the songs sung during the Holi festival. It was a very favourite and sought-after rendition by most of the tawaifs of Banaras, particularly in the festival of the Budhwa Mangal. I have heard Thumri often during the Sankat Mochan Music Festival in Banaras, sung by the local singers. Many also relate this festival with Chet Singh, who may have refined it. He used to organize a procession, much like the ancient Chattra Mangal festival. This festival has now taken a religious form and the gaiety and frolic attached to it has now given way to a dull and dour religious ritual performed at Durga Kund. The Budhwa Mangal festival was temporarily halted as a form of protest by the Banarasis, after the Jallianwala Bagh massacre. However, it continued till the beginning of the early 1960s and gradually faded into oblivion due to a large number of anti-social elements that took control of the event. During the early nineteenth century, it was likely a grand affair. Till the famous Banaras Gharana singers Siddheshwari Devi and Girija Devi were alive, they continued to perform regularly on this day. However, the celebration is in its emaciated form at present, with only picnickers and revellers participating, and has taken on a rather religious tenor.

Chapter 11

Banaras on My Palate

Foods and Cuisine

The nouvelle cuisine and the gastronomical hybridity of street food in Banaras can be traced back to the Silk Route travellers till it took its present form during the twelfth century CE. The food and cuisine of Banaras are a melting pot of world cuisine because the city has been a trading centre and eminent pilgrimage destination for thousands of years. Some of the eateries here are more than 300 years old and take pride in serving the exact same recipe over the years. In fact, every single ritual of Banaras is intertwined with a particular kind of dessert or savoury dish. Many *Jataka Tales* have elaborate descriptions of food, and novels such as *Volga se Ganga* have even mentioned a staple diet of barley sattu—a commonly eaten food in various forms in eastern Uttar Pradesh and Bihar, often mixed with honey. As per food historian K.T. Achaya, the term 'sattu' has been derived from the Sanskrit *saktu*, which originally referred to the coarse flour obtained by grinding parched barley and later parched rice.[1] The experimenting with different cuisines continues even today in Banaras. In a wedding or religious banquet, it is very common for the *halwai*s (traditional ceremonial cooks), who specialize in local cuisines, to include in their list pasta, Chinese sauces and vanilla essence. Even the humble dosa has a Banarasi spin to it. The cartographical food trail of Banaras can lead one to some of the most nondescript shops, which open only for a few hours and specialize only in a few fares.

The dishes that are mostly prepared in Banaras today started taking roots from the Gahadavala times and consolidated their hold over the Pakka Mahal area for the last 300 years. Rice was the staple crop in the twelfth century, as it is today. Puris were also greatly relished, and some aphorisms associated with puris at that time were *poli panch* (prepare the puris) and *poli ulat-palat* (deep-fry the puris). Sattu was consumed by mixing it with ghee and jaggery, and another proverb advises, *sattu van ta puni san* (if the sattu is not properly mixed, mix it again). Khichdi (dish made of rice and lentils), kheer (rice pudding), chana-chabena (a mixture of roasted grains) and several other types of sweets, like today, formed part of the regular meal plan of even the twelfth-century residents of Banaras. Banarasis, however, did not simply consume vegetarian fare. Meat of various animals and birds was prepared and aphorisms to that effect were in vogue. For example, a popular saying cautioned: *Jaalen lage paali dhankan handi mansu chud*, meaning to simmer the meat by covering it with a lid on fire. Consumption of a mixture of rice, salt, mutton and ghee has also been aphoristically described. Amazingly, till now, a popular assumption was that meat pieces on skewers called seekh kabab came with the Islamic invasions but going by the popular precepts of the twelfth century, *salai masu griha,* which means pleaching the meat on the skewers, one could safely assume that it was a popular dish much before. By the early eighteenth century, mentions of exotic dishes, vegetables and spices are found in *Girivan Patmanjari* of the Varadaraja and *Girvana Vangamanjari* of Dhundiraj. These food items are quintessentially Banarasi even now. In one conversation, a Brahmin directs his son to shop for supplies from the Chaukhambha market for the scrumptious preparations for a guest. He says: 'First go to the Baniya's shop and buy two and a half seers of ghee, white sugar, gram flour for puran poli, asafoetida, cumin, ground turmeric, betel nut, cardamom, clove, catechu, nutmeg, mace, camphor, kasturi (musk), saffron, gorochan (cow bezoar), khus (resin incense)—also known as Sunganghwala and Dasang Dhoop—*kappadchhan* (perhaps a brand of that time) flour, dhuvaans (coarse black lentil) and chauretha (rice flour).' Then, he further directs his son to go and buy vegetables like suran (elephant yam), white and red kanda (tuber), cucumber, elderberry, mustard, pumpkin, yellow pumpkin, pointed gourd, brinjal, ivy gourd, bitter gourd and jackfruit. He then specifically directs his son to purchase ripe and unripe bananas, banana bunches and flowers from the shop near Annapurna temple. After taking the magahi betel leaves, he should proceed to Kal Bhairav market to buy the greens like fenugreek leaves, chaulai, poi, chakwad (all varieties of greens called saag) and Indian nightshade called brishti bhanta, red and white taro root leaves along with tamarind, ginger and banana leaves.[2] Important markets like the Chaukhambha, Kal Bhairav and the lanes adjoining Annapurna temple mentioned above, still cater to these things and are really coveted. In *Girivan Patmanjari*, there is an exhaustive description of food items that has been served to a student monk. The monk then describes in detail and lists out food dishes and their sequences of serving. Let me briefly touch upon the description. The student monk firstly elaborates on a large banana leaf and sal leaf bowls, pickles of raw mango, tamarind, kabak (a kind of mushroom pickle), lemon, lime, orange and wood apple. Then rice combinations of dahi-bhat (curd rice), urad-bhat (black lentil rice), khatta-bhat (sour rice), ghee-bhat (clarified butter rice), pulses and sweets.

There is a more elaborate description of this food in *Girvan Vangamanjari* of Dhundiraj, though. The Brahmin directs his wife how to serve sequentially all the food prepared by her to the guest: after greasing the banana leaves with ghee and serving salt, serve the pickles of mango, lemon, ginger, elephant yam, plum, brinjal, cranberry, gooseberry, radish, myrobalan, bamboo shoot and Indian nightshade. Then, serve a salad mishmash of banana blossoms, bottle gourd and muskmelon, followed by the vegetables of bitter gourd and carrot. After this, pure urad dal vada (vada is coarsely ground and fermented pulses fashioned into various shapes and deep-fried in ghee), fenugreek puffs, tilbadi (sesame seed puff), kohendauri (spiced white pumpkin puffs), aambari (mango puffs), pumpkin seeds puffs, black lentil puffs in curd, and papad with currant sauce. Thereafter, laddus of chickpea gram flour with ghee and curd, fenugreek seeds with jaggery. After all this, a very fine variety of boiled rice is to be served with pigeon pea soup, followed by puran poli, millet laddus, sweet rice flour breads, puris, pancakes of rice flour and chickpea, khoya puris, sesame laddus, bean lentil laddus and milk sweets. He directed her to serve seven types of kheer made of wheat, rice and tinni, and spicy decoction for digestion with a green chilli to be served at the end. The betel quid is customarily served when guests are leaving. The entire description and types of food are still in vogue in Banaras, with the same extensive and minute details. Raja Jainarayan Ghoshal, a great connoisseur of fine taste himself, while describing the Budhwa Mangal Festival in 1857, listed some mouth-watering savouries of Banaras:

> *matichoor paanitooya khaaja aadanrasa,*
> *magdal besan laadoo sangan pachhand,*
> *peda baraphee bundiya michharee cheeneekand*
> *chhoharee kachauree puree sab dravy taaja*
> *morabba aachaar shaak tarakaaree bhaaja*[3]

Banaras has this quality, which it has retained even now, that if you want to eat a particular sweet or snack that is available only in, say winter, you will never get that in summers. Even today, when everything is available all through the year, frozen and preserved, the Banarasi cuisine will never compromise on the seasonal ingredients. Even average households relish the seasonal preparation. Banarasi sweetmeat-makers are called *karigar*s (artisans), which shows how much respect they are given. Otherwise, the commonly used word is halwai.

In the *Matsya Purana*, a shloka places special emphasis on *mishthaan.*[4] Let me give a few examples of such unique practices in Banaras. The most famous Banarasi paan also comes in different flavours through different seasons. A typical Banarasi paan essentially has five constituents: paan (betel leaf), kattha (catechu), chuna (lime), supari (areca nut) and zarda (tobacco leaves), which can be sada (plains) or zafraani (with saffron). For example, the kattha has saffron in winters and khus (essence of the vetiver root) or kewra jal (an extract of pandanus flowers) in summers. Similarly, the exotic paan shops, patronized by the rich, essentially have secret ingredients. Owners of these paan shops recognize their customers even if they arrive after a long absence, remembering the specific type of paan each person prefers. This reflects a very egalitarian aspect of Banaras, where even the common folks take pride in patronizing a paan or a tea stall.

The predominant cuisine of Banaras carries a flavour from all over the country, predominantly Brahminical, and includes snacks and dishes influenced by traders like Marwaris and Gujaratis. Some of the winter savouries of Banaras exclusive to the city are chura matar (beaten rice with green peas) paired with longlatta or magdal (sweetmeat) and the famous Banarasi malaiyo (saffron-flavoured 'milk cloud'), made by churning whole milk early in the morning during winter months and then left overnight in large earthen vessels called *paraat* to soak up the winter nip and the dew. Additionally, the traditional Banarasi breakfast of kachori-and-jalebi undergoes a seasonal metamorphosis. The stuffing in the kachori may change from moong or urad to fresh sweet green peas. The jalebi will essentially have saffron and is served with hot milk in winters and curd in summers. The iconic chaat shops, once located inside the campus of Chitra Talkies in Chowk and Kashi Chaat Bhandar in Godowlia, also adjusted their chaat offerings with the changing seasons. Unfortunately, both have closed down, and a new 'Haldiram' variety is threatening to gobble up the small *rehdi*s (vendor stalls) and corner shops.

Many dishes made their way to Banaras during the reign of the Awadh nawabs, who were known for their gastronomical experimentations. In our house, this culinary influence came from the gaunharis—ladies who accompanied my eldest grandmother from her father's place, Prithviganj state, a taluqdari in Awadh. It included foods like nimona (spicy soup of fresh green peas), tehri (a kind of rice pilaf), besan ki sabji (curry made from flour of Bengal gram), aaloo ka pareh, besan pisan ki litti (bread of Bengal gram flour and wheat flour) and a special type of kheer called *jaur* made by boiling rice for hours on low heat with fresh cane juice. Green jackfruit stew, bajka (a type of fritters made of green Bengal gram with a mix of rice flour and besan), green Bengal gram halwa sprinkled with saffron and green cinnamon and tempered with finely sliced almonds, rose petals and pistachio. These were seasonal delights only lasting for a few days. The word *tehri* has its origin from *Teh* in Persian, meaning layer, and it also translates to 'pure and unsullied' in Arabic. Tehri, nimona and green jackfruit stew were perfected by the Hindu taluqdars (people belonging to high status, owning many ancestral lands and property) of the Awadh region around the seventeenth century, some of whom were strictly vegetarians or their womenfolk disliked non-vegetarian food. All these dishes mimic pulao, mutton curry and keema (minced meat) curry, both in terms of spices used and the slow cooking process. Generally prepared on Makar Sankranti, using only the ingredients available in winters, it involves soaking the fragrant fine rice with saffron and curd. Seasonal winter vegetables, like the fresh crop of potatoes with jacket, cauliflower and green peas, are sautéed in ghee and then either layered or mixed before being slow-cooked. In contrast, nimona is prepared by frying mashed green peas with spices in ghee, served with a kind of spicy, crispy pickled vada called adauri. The aaloo ka pareh dish is crushed boiled potatoes and coriander leaves stew with fresh lemon juice. Besan pisan ki litti are biscuits made from wheat and split chickpea flour, heavily loaded with leek and garlic, shallow-fried in mustard oil and invariably served with pickled garlic and cane juice vinegar sauce. Another typical vegetable stew available in Banaras during the Holi months is gular ki sabzi (sycamore fruit stew). During the peak summer months, particularly in the afternoons when temperatures could soar above 48 degrees centigrade, the sing-song rasping voice of hawkers would begin to reverberate through the lanes and by-lanes, advertising their offerings of fruits, which included juicy dark-violet berries—phalsa (black berry or *grewia asiatica*), the contorted-shaped and unattractive dirty yellow fruit—badhhar (monkey jack or monkey fruit) and the bright yellow berry with milky juice—khirni (Manilkara hexandra fruit). All these fruits have a brief window time of just a few days in the scorching summers. The place of these fruit vendors is thereafter taken over by the tinkling of bells from pull carts, where sellers offer kairi aam panna (a tangy raw mango drink) with a Banarasi secret spice mix that only the vendor knows. One also finds kulfi-faluda (iced frozen thickened milk dessert with soft thin vermicelli noodles); the name 'Kulfi' is derived from the conical metal casing that is called kulfi.[5] Another Banarasi innovation is the specialized preparation, in which a clay pot piled up with freshly grated ice from jute bag-covered ice slabs, topped with one's choice of coloured syrups of roohafza (herb and rose sherbet), rose, khus and lemon. All these pull carts are extravagantly decorated with huge brass pots gleaming and partially covered with an invariably red cotton cloth competing with the many other blingy trinkets and ornaments that adorn these carts. For the upper middle class and the rich gentry, exclusive thandai (a refreshing drink) and lassi (sweet buttermilk) shops at Bansphatak and the Godowlia chauraha offer a refined and nuanced variety of summer drinks. The most famous among them being the Thandai Ghar, which was often visited by my eldest uncle with us hangers-on, located near a lane in Bansphatak. It is oil-painted in a vibrant vermilion colour; in fact, every article in the shop, right from its walls and furniture to the serving jugs and glasses adhere to this singular colour theme. Thandai is a milk concoction made with ground almonds, muskmelon and fennel seeds, peppercorn, rose petals, poppy seeds, cloves, saffron and a very small amount of hemp leaves. For the patrons, the shop owner also adds the extract of herbal aphrodisiacs like shilajeet, musk and ashwagandha. Similarly, the renowned lassi shop Mishrambu boasts a lassi with some secret divine ingredients. For its patrons, instead of sugar, the buttermilk is topped with a thick layer of fresh cream, laced with honey and finely sliced pistachios, pine nuts, almonds, resins and kewra water (extract of pandanus flowers). It would be a disservice not to mention the internationally renowned Banarasi breakfast of kachori, sabzi and jalebi. My mother told me the different ways the famous shops at Kachori Gully, such as the Rambhandar and the Madhur Jalpan sweetmeat sellers, prepare the typical breakfast they offer. I double-checked this from many of my friends and their wives whose ancestral houses are in the Pakka Mahal area of Banaras. The kachori dough is a blend of wheat flour, coarsely ground black lentil called dhunvaans, soaked overnight, ghee, asafoetida and a little bit of sooji (semolina) to add that crusty upper layer to the kachori. Unlike at other places, Banarasi kachoris are not stuffed with urad dal and are deep-fried in ghee instead. The accompanying vegetable curry is very spicy with two common ingredients—potatoes and Bengal gram—along with seasonally available vegetables. The aftertaste and aroma of this curry, as I was told sotto voce, is from the last-minute garnishing with the exotic spice called patthar ke phool (edible lichen or black stone flower). The jalebi, again, unlike its popular method of making with fermented refined wheat flour, is made from fermented black lentils. The pale-yellow colour is achieved by liberally tempering with soaked saffron water.

The Banarasi chaat and golgappas of Kashi Chaat Bhandar and one that was located inside the campus of the now-closed 'Chitra Talkies' served authentic mouth-watering arrays of chaat—an Indian spicy snack combination. The city specializes in its unique tamatar chaat and samosa chaat. Banaras caters to the requirements of its most cherished and pampered class of clients—the international tourists, many of whom stay in this city for months. While kachori and jalebi might be palatable for a few days, their sensitive tummy cannot take much of it. The American Beat poet, Allen Ginsberg, though, confessed in an interview, saying: 'And I remember getting really hung up on puris and potatoes.'[6] A more befitting breakfast for an international traveller, Banaras has offered them 'Malai Toast'—an indulgent and thick spread of fresh cream with sprinkled sugar goes well with spiced tea. The most renowned 'Laxmi Chai Wale' in Godowlia is particularly famous for this.

Banarasi sweets, like Bengali sweets, have earned widespread fame and have been influenced from a variety of sources. This shows the emphasis Banarasis place on sweets that play a role in every possible function and occasion in Banaras. Sweetmeats like the magdal and the malaiyo are seasonal and appear only for about a month each year. Magdal is a lightly sweet, patted dough of boiled black lentil mixed with cashew, mace, nutmeg, ghee and saffron. The Ram Bhandar shop in Banaras is known for introducing sweets made from vegetables, with the most famous one being made from pointed gourd. During the Independence movement, Ram Bhandar added another innovative manner to espouse the cause of independence. The owner, Mr Sah, had prepared a special barfi, with its top layer made of saffron, the middle one white from cashew and then the bottom green one with pistachios, using khoya as its base. He named it Tirangi Barfi (tricoloured sweet), resembling the Indian flag. As a child, I've heard this incident recounted ad nauseum by all my elders whenever this barfi was served on any special occasion—certainly, a matter of pride for all Banarasis.

Another seasonal sweet, called lowanglutta (clove-pinned syrupy quid folds). Both magdal and lowanglutta are paired with chura-matar (flattened rice with green peas), which is a classic Banaras innovation where the chura is soaked with milk before it is pan-fried with spices and peas. While the list is exhaustive, I have only listed the exceptionally popular cuisines of Banaras.

Chapter 12

Living Continuities

Social Mores, Customs, Places of Worship and Ditties

Banaras is *sui generis* in its very concept. The hubbub of the city is interwoven with the weft of the past and the warp of the present continuous, layered by veneers of religious doctrines and beliefs. The ideas of Banaras, in its various avatars, have been discussed in the preceding chapters. Let me enumerate some strange customs that are followed in Banaras even now. I repeat this 'even now' because the metamorphic transition that the world and India, particularly, have seen in the last two decades has eroded and compromised a lot of its cultural and social mores. The contemporaneity of customs and traditions may be on the decline; nevertheless, the spirit and the residual elements still hold the social fabric of Banaras together. Another very important trait that permeates all walks of life in the city is that it is a great leveller. Despite being a cradle of an orthodox form of Hinduism, the caste system is not prominently manifested in many of its public places, with only a few exceptions. This characteristic comes from the deep-rooted egalitarianism in Shaivism. Shiva is not choosy about anything and is not ritualistic. His followers are his ganas, who come from all types of class, fields of work and profession, and many who are considered outcastes. A typical Banarasi is a blend of Shiva himself and his ganas. From Shiva, they draw pride, self-respect, frugality and a 'couldn't-care-less' attitude. The very term *'ka raja'* (what's up, king?) symbolizes that, like himself, he considers all his peers as kings. From the ganas of Shiva, they have imbibed the metaphysical aspect of being subsumed with the elements from which he has been born and sustained. These traits might appear oxymoronic, but together, they constitute the elements that create a typical Banarasi. There is a generic term of endearment for people of all castes. For example, Ahirs are called 'Sardar', Brahmins 'Guru', Thakurs 'Babusaheb' and traders 'Sethji'. An incident not very old, often recounted to underscore the frivolous attitude of Banarasis, involves the Arya Samaj leader Dayanand Saraswati attempting to impose his brand of Hinduism on the people of Banaras. He was not invited to the city, so he challenged some of the pandits of Banaras for a debate. The writer and playwright Bharatendu Harishchandra accepted the challenge and even sent a long questionnaire. A public debate was organized, chaired by the raja of Banaras. Bharatendu was a man of letters and an actor, but hardly knew anything about the scriptures. He was doomed to lose the debate against the knowledgeable and profound orator Dayanand. But à la Shiva, he came to attend the debate with a huge crowd of followers comprising writers, poets, actors, singers, courtesans and nearly all the vagabonds of Banaras. Whenever it was perceived that Bharatendu was losing, his followers would start catcalls and beating kettle drums. The serious and sagacious Dayanand got so irritated that he left the debate midway, and the raja of Banaras declared Bhartendu, the winner.[1] The quirky tradition of Banarasi *phakkadpan* (the easy-going-ness) emerges from frugality, gratitude and satisfaction. The epithet of *Ashutosh*, another name for Shiva, is inseparable from a Banarasi, along with an element of an *aughar* (bohemian). A component of *amour-propre* as the greatest virtue is manifested here even in the everyday business dealings, where practicality is the buzzword. The Daksha–Shiva story, as mentioned earlier, is a mythological imprint on the Banarasis. Some say that in Kashi, this element of self-resect is even present among the animals. An interesting tale about the powerful ruler and famous traitor Raja Jaichand is popular in Banaras. Jaichand had hundreds of elephants, but his favourite was a white elephant, who was very loyal to him. After Jaichand died fighting the forces of Muhammed Shahabuddin Ghori, all the captured elephants were paraded in front of Ghori and were ordered to salute the emperor. All obeyed the command except this white elephant. It simply refused to salute the invader in deference and in memory of his master, Raja Jaichand. A tale of an inherent self-esteem that is the very essence of Banaras.

Banarasis live life to the fullest, their famous *mauj-masti* (fun and enjoyment) can sometimes border on crookedness. They often resort to that, but with full pride and self-honour, which they think is their right, because in the subconscious mind, they know that this is their moment to live, and know fully that whatever they do, they will attain moksha from here. After all, death is celebrated in this city.

The two metaphors of Banaras—Ganga and Shiva—are so deeply ingrained in the mind of an average Banarasi that an outsider in the postmodern world is sometimes stunned and sometimes feels that it is as if the masses have indeed been doped. Take away these two metaphors from the idea of Banaras and it will be a zombie city with its lost 'Banarasipan'. A Banarasi takes delight in hurting our modern cosmopolitan sensibilities by offering exquisite opportunities for social embarrassment. That reminds me of the typical pastime of the Banarasis—of consuming copious amounts of bhang and cannabis and defecating *ganga paar* (across the Ganga) or in an open area. This is now largely controlled, not by any strict order, which in any case was already in place, but because of the space crunch.

Picnics seem to be an ancient pastime of Banarasis, much before the Western concepts of fête champêtre, dining alfresco, picnics and luncheons—wonderfully depicted by impressionists like Monet, Renoir and the neo-impressionists like Georges Seurat. For a Banarasi, a picnic means packing the raw cooking materials along with the utensils and preparing their favourite food outside the city. Around Banaras, three places were very popular: Sarnath, Rajghat and Ramnagar across the river. Most of my childhood picnics were at Sarnath and Vindhyachal. Banarasis call such places *Bahri Alang* and *Nichhadam* (the countryside). What, then, is a Banarasi culture? Pandit Kubernath Sukul is spot on with his explanation:

> If one were to sum up the entire gamut of Varanasi culture in one or two words, they would be Mauj and Masti: two words which seem to have no parallels in the English language. The former epitomises all that goes by the generic term enjoyment, and even recklessness and wayward obstinacy. Varanasi culture as represented above was in full form till fifty years ago, and synchronising with the discontinuance of the famous Burhwa Mangal and Gulabbari festivities—two most typical illustrations of the Varanasi culture as it existed in the eighteenth and nine–tenth centuries.[2]

This was the analysis of the late sixties and early seventies. Since then, Banaras has been encapsulated by many. Having quoted Kedar Nath Singh in the Introduction, let's know the mind of the present generation represented by the young writer Vyomesh Shukla from his Banaras-themed novel *Aag aur Pani* who writes almost lyrically: 'Banaras has a throbbing habit of holding your hands and compelling you to sit with him. When you look at him, he also looks at you with his thousand eyes. Banaras is an impossible place. It's difficult to measure it. It is on this side as well as on that side. It is in ashes, and it is also in the sands.'[3]

Many writers clearly define the city by referring to Kashi as the hub of erudition, enigma and deferential divinity, as well as liberation and detachment. Banaras is symbolized by the succulence of its stories, magnificence of its architecture and with the gaiety and merriment of its festivals and fares, and sometimes with the gravitas of an ascetic as well as with the sarcastic guffaw of an Aughar. The ancientness of Kashi, the medieval and premodern Banaras and the presentness of Varanasi have specific spans in the psyche of an average Banarasi. This patois is apparent in the general conversation to denote Kashi and Banaras. Varanasi per se continues to have a heavy intonation of officialese. Against this backdrop, let me mention some interesting typicality of Banaras.

Not many know that there is an entry tax when one enters Banaras. This is the continuation of an ancient pilgrims' tax that was levied since the days of the Mahajanapadas. Since the time of Tulsidas, Hanuman as a deity came into the pantheon of Hinduism. Earlier, Hanuman, in some animistic form, was already worshipped in the Kashi region and was a folk deity. Since Kashi was also called a Mahashamshan, death in the city, even of an animal, was considered liberation from the cycle of birth. There is a strange custom in Banaras that if a monkey dies, all the rituals, those that are prescribed for humans in the Hindu scriptures, are followed. It may sound hilarious, but the Banarasis take it very seriously. I have personally seen such a procession.

Another strange aspect of Banaras, despite being a riverine culture, is that it does not have a fishermen community that is dependent solely on the fish catch from the Ganga. For a Banarasi, fish caught in the Ganga cannot be consumed as it violates the religious doctrines. The fishermen community sells fish that have been hauled from the ponds and rainwater catchment areas. I heard an incident from a widow who lived adjacent to our house, a follower of the Jankipanth sect that worshipped Sita instead of Rama, which was perhaps the earliest form of feminism and defiance to patriarchy. We called her Buaji, and she was a regular visitor to our house and also served as a religious mentor to the ladies. She told us many mythical stories, which, in retrospect, seem to be related to the preservation of the biosphere. Leading scholar of Indian classical dance, art, architecture and art history, Kapila Vatsyayan, has articulated this well in her erudite treatise *Ecology and Indian Myth*, where she emphasizes the sustenance of the environment as a prerequisite for upholding the moral order of *rta* (biosphere) and dharma. Once, Buaji narrated a true incident in which a Bengali family was sold a fish that was trawled from the Ganga. Of course, there is no way to differentiate the fish from a pond and the Ganga, but there is an unwritten code of conduct, within the fishermen in Banaras, most of which is strictly adhered to. The women of the family, while gutting the fish for fillet, were stunned to find a thumb of a child that came out from the belly of the fish. This is not unusual, as in Banaras and the adjoining areas, under two circumstances, the dead body is floated in the Ganga and not cremated: death of a child and death by snake bite. The inherent belief being that the analeptic properties of the Ganga will bring back the dead.

Buaji also told us to pluck out the dead stalks from the tulsi plant because Tulsi Mata gets a headache from them. She emphasized on clearly pronouncing the mantras and ensured none of the birds' nests are disturbed during our yearly Diwali cleaning drive. I remember when a neem tree in front of her house was being cut to make space for construction, she was visibly disturbed, reminding me of a poem 'Ab Ye Chidiya Kahan Rahegi' by Mahadevi Verma.

In the lanes of Banaras, it is not uncommon to find very old earthen bowls as birdfeeders, identified by the accumulated bird droppings around them. People also hang flat bamboo baskets for the birds to shelter themselves during summers and sudden downpours, in the same manner as it was followed and mentioned in the Jatakas.

Another story in the Jatakas is where Kashiraj, the king of Banaras, was so impressed by the scholarship of the Bodhisattva born in an untouchable family that he removed the garland of red flowers from his neck and adorned the Bodhisattva with it. He also thereafter made him the Nagarguttika (mayor of the city). Since then, it has become a tradition in Banaras to honour the protector of the city with a red flower garland. Many English collectors and district magistrates were honoured by the delegates of various guilds in a similar manner, and perhaps some are still trying to continue this tradition.

I recently got an iron ring made for my wife, on the recommendation of an astrologer, for her *Shani dosha* (dominance of Saturn). I was surprised to find that, as per the scriptures, the prescribed ring was supposed to be made from the nail of an unused—preferably rotting—boat that has been ferrying on the river Ganga. I requested my friend Gajendra Pandey, whose ancestors have been residing near the Ganga in the Pakka Mahal area and are familiar with such peculiar sacerdotal procedures. It took nearly a month to first locate such a nail and then to find a karigar proficient enough in an age-old skill of making the ring. Unlike other metal rings, this was supposed to be made in the exact size and given a round shape without putting it in the *bhatti* (kiln) and without heating it. The skill lies in perfecting and moulding it into a ring only by hammering and twisting. Unfortunately, this skill is dying now, as the only ironsmith Nagina Lohar who practices this art in a quaint shop in Assi is the last one in his line of profession.

The *varna vyavastha* of the 'Rama Rajya' envisaged by Tulsidas is ironically tacitly followed in Banaras, even though an apparent egalitarianism holds sway. In Banaras, a Brahmin is never to be hurt; they should be fed, respected, and protected by the Thakurs and Rajputs. They should be treated like a mentor in life's affairs and a spiritual guide. I have an ethical story to narrate here. We, coming from the martial community, were traditional zamindars and petty chieftains of areas around Banaras. In our family value system, Brahmins were held in high esteem. Adjacent to our house was a maidan, and since childhood, it was our hunting ground, teeming with small birds, frogs, squirrels and many small creepy-crawlies, including a large number of snakes. This piece of land was gated, cultivated for seasonal vegetables and flowers by us, and had been in our possession since my grandfather purchased the land around it in the late forties. Unknown to us, it belonged to a Brahmin, who got it as a donation for his religious services. No one claimed the land, and the owner was unknown. In a city gasping for land, the plot size of around half an acre is a significant property in the heart of the city. My uncle, who knew this fact, was constantly in search of the rightful claimant—which, again, was unknown to us. He approached the city record office and the land record archives to find out the owner. Despite mockery and discouragement from most of our relatives, my uncle persisted in his search. He believed that, even though the owner hadn't come forward to claim it, it was essential to find the rightful owner. Through word of mouth he eventually came to know that a branch of the owner's family is now settled in Jhansi. He somehow managed to get the address and traced the inheritor, an old octogenarian widow. He not only facilitated the property transfer in her name but also ensured that her children and grandchildren came back to take possession of the land, after almost four-and-a-half decades of our family possessing it. This serves as a touching reminder to me that perhaps my uncle's belief system was inherently rooted in the Hindu religious doctrine of *paap* and *punya* (sin and benediction) and the role of being a protector, delivering the message loud and clear.

The first recorded strike in the country was organized on 24 August 1790 in Banaras in protest against unsanitary living conditions. Thereafter, in 1809–10, half of Banaras took to the streets to protest against the newly implemented House Tax, locking their houses and shops. People were pacified through the intervention of Raja Udit Narayan Singh, Nawab Sayyad Akbar Ali Khan, Moulvi Abdul Qadir Khan and Babu Jamuna Das, who assured and eventually got some amendments made in the original tax structure. There is an inherent rebel attitude in Banaras that, as mentioned earlier, comes from the mien of Shiva himself.

Ganga Pujaiya is another strange ritual only followed in Banaras. This practice is rarely seen anywhere else. After marriage, when the daughter-in-law comes to her *sasural* (in-laws' house), the women of the locality, following the dressing style as prescribed by the ritual, organize a procession from their house to the ghats. It involves the use of kettle drums locally called *dugdugi* and other musical instruments, along with singing the local wedding song, '*Sone ki thali mein jevna parosa*' (Offer tasty food in a golden plate). The ritualistic puja is then conducted at the ghats. There is a hilarious account of this in the travelogue of Ralph Fitch where he describes the rituals between the Brahmin along with the newly-wed and a cow that is performed at the ghats. The Brahmin covers the cow with a cloth and chants mantras holding its tail. He then asks the newlywed couple to complete the puja where 'the woman has a brass or copper pot full of water; the man takes hold of the Brahmin with one hand, and the woman with the other, all having hold of the cow by the tail, on which they pour water from the pot, so that it runs on all their hands'.[4] Another noteworthy custom is the Gaya Darshan declaration. When a couple returns from their pilgrimage from Gaya, it is referred to as Gaya Darshan. Though it is not that important, but in Banaras, it is supposed to be announced somewhat theatrically. Thus, the couple dresses in red, carries a bamboo stick on their shoulders, holds a pot of water in their hands, and proceeds to walk around their locality, sprinkling the water as they go.

There is another ritual that is elaborately planned, and is quite costly, called *aar-paar ki puja*, which is a way of expressing gratitude to Mother Ganga. In my family, my father and uncle had three more siblings who passed away soon after birth. The family priest conducted a wish fulfilment puja in which a vow was taken to perform the aar-paar ki puja. During this puja, when the Ganga river is swollen, a thick garland of flowers are stringed in a long rope with one of its ends tied to a sacred fulcrum of any temple at the ghat, usually Dashashwamedha, and the other carried and tied to a boat anchored across the river. The travelling time is sanctified by chanting mantras and paying obeisance to the Ganga.

While walking to school in the early mornings, I usually noticed day-to-day items consecrated and marked with vermilion, such as pumpkin, betel leaves, betel nuts, small paper dolls and their swings, marigold flowers, sugared candies, etc.—all placed either in the centre of the road or at a pedestrian crossing. We were strictly advised to skirt those objects or preferably wait for someone else to cross. Such items were called *utara* and were part of a black magic ritual to pass on ill luck or life-threatening diseases to someone else or to another locality. It is locally called *chalauva*, *totka* and *gothaee*. It was believed that the first person to cross such items would be affected by the purpose for which the chalauva was intended. To ward off such evils, services of the ojhas were called upon, who conducted a ritual called *Habuaana*. These rituals were endemic since the Mahajanapada periods and reached their peak during the Gupta era. The system of black magic is also an ancient ritual that existed in Banaras when the Yakshas were worshipped.

Banaras is the only place that had three kings; to some extent it still has—at least the Banarasis consider them to be. The real king, the Raja of Banaras, whose palace is across the river and not in the main city; the surreal, who is called the Dom Raja; and, of course, the ethereal who is Shiva himself. Dom Raja is an institution that even finds mention in the Kashi Khand. The Dom Raja is the chief of the great crematorium when Kashi was a Mahashamshan. He was the owner of all the cremation ghats located at the riverfront. Dom, as a community, belonged to low castes who were assigned duties pertaining to cremation. At the Harishchandra ghat, there is a prominent building with two statues of lions on its façade—this is the residence or the palace of the Dom Raja. Some interesting anecdotes pertaining to the then Dom Raja Kailash Chaudhary have been recorded by Hemant Sharma in his book *Dekho Hamari Kashi*. This concept of the chief of the Mahashamshan was established somewhere in the early eighteenth century, but its Puranic references are in the *Markandeya Purana* and Kashi Khand. Most of the earnings of the crematorium go to this institution and the family members. The Doms in Banaras consider themselves the representative of Yamaraj, the god of death. The present Dom Raja is Om Hari Narayan. This institution now is in the process of what the great sociologist M.N. Srinivas termed as 'Sanskritization' and is slowly losing its unique rituals that were a part of their profession. Many such practices, like the food in the palace of the Dom Raja being cooked from the half-burnt wood from the cremation pyre no longer exist because of the increasing use of electric crematorium. Interestingly, when asked who the king of Kashi is, the Dom Raja replies that he is the real king and represents Shiva. Shiva whispers the 'Tarak mantra'—the Rama naam—through him. He also compares the cosmic sound of 'Aum' with the resonations of 'Dom'. Thus, validating that Shiva is the deity of the Mahashamshan and is also called the Omkara or the cosmic lord of the primordial sound.

Nandi, the bull, the mount of Lord Shiva, holds an important place in the Banarasi tapestry. The Vrishabhdwaj, the bull emblem flag, as mentioned in the Puranic lore, symbolizes the grand entry of Shiva into Kashi. The Vrishabhdwaja festival and the seals from the Kushan era found from Rajghat bear the markings of a seated bull, as quoted by Vasudev Sharan Agarwal in *The Study of Rajghat Seals,*[5] further underscore the importance of Nandi in Banaras. Bulls are not just revered in this city; they are an essential concatenation in the religious and cultural life of Banaras. They are worshipped on the streets and are fed generously. While they are generally calm, they can be extremely dangerous and unpredictable in the narrow lanes and by-lanes of the city, especially if they are provoked to behave in the manner of the proverbial bull in a China shop. Bishop Reginald Heber, during his visit to Banaras in 1823–24, seems to have been quite amused on encountering them. He wrote: 'The sacred bulls devoted to Siva, of every age, tame and familiar as mastiffs, walk lazily up and down these narrow streets, or are seen lying across them, and hardly to be kicked up (any blows, indeed, given them must be of the gentlest kind, or woe be to the profane wretch who braves the prejudices of this fanatic population) in order make way for the tonjon.'[6]

In another account, when he visited the Vishwanath temple, Heber remarked: 'The temple-court, small as it is, is crowded like a farmyard with very fat and very tame bulls, which thrust their noses into every body's hand and pocket for gram and sweetmeats, which their fellow-votaries give them in great quantities.'[7]

Banaras has many anecdotes on the accidents caused by bulls. There is ritual in which people let the bulls loose in the holy city of Kashi that is called *Vrisotsarga*, literally meaning 'letting the bull loose'; it is a form of donation. It was similar to the popular *gaudan* (donating a cow). The bulls were cauterized and a fixed amount for fodder was offered to the two prominent citizens, Bhau Jaani and Vireshwar Jaani, whose intervention in the religious space of Banaras was highly respected. It was also a lucrative earning for them. The administration in 1852 once decided to end the bull menace and ordered that all such vagrant bulls be herded and put in a separate enclosure near the Commissionerate. The steady source of income for Bhau Jaani and Vireshwar Jaani dried up. They did not respond then but waited for an opportunity. Five years before the 1857 Revolt, Banaras again stands out for being a harbinger of a similar kind of revolt, fuelled by a rumour that the food being served in jail for the convicts is not in accordance with their religious practices. Coincidentally, the order to capture the bulls and this rumour came one after another. There was a huge protest and people took to the streets exhorted by Bhau Jaani, who perceived an opportunity for retribution.

The District Magistrate Mr Gravince asked the representatives of the various guilds and delegation for a meeting at Nati Imli. A huge crowd gathered to witness the negotiation. When it appeared that the negotiation is not going the way the people demanded, few antisocial elements started pelting the authorities with the clay hookahs from a nearby potter's shop locally called *gauraya*. Many officers were hurt. Eventually, the jail menu was revised and the order to herd the bulls also was withdrawn. This incident, in the annals of Banaras, is known as Gauraya Shahi. This time, I could not find a single bull in the Pakka Mahal area, which was ubiquitous just a few years back. Local people told me that the authorities have acted positively on the complaints of various tourists and have removed this menace once and for all, but a significant part of Banaras rituals have been compromised.

Another incident, on 1 May 1850, that marks a turning point in the early nineteenth century was an explosion in a boat near Rajghat, laden with pegs of gunpowder. Many were killed or wounded, and many houses were destroyed.[8] This was quite similar to the later Bombay docks explosion that occurred on 14 April 1944, in the Victoria Dock of Bombay, British India, when the British freighter *S.S. Fort Stikine*, carrying a cargo of cotton bales and explosives exploded, killing around 800 people.

As narrated earlier, our maidan was a mini forest with different types of reptiles, with a particularly daring one, which always slithered in our rooms, called *oatni* in the local dialect. It's a beautiful salamander with shimmering-coloured stripes of brown and dark yellow on the body with a bright orange tail—very agile and totally harmless. In Banaras, there is a belief that if one touches the tail of the oatni with the little finger, one will be rewarded with a windfall. We always tried to touch the tail but were never able to. It has disappeared now, probably extinct as I have not seen this in my house since last three decades now. Similarly, the red velvet beetle is elusive, which we would collect in dozens in our empty ink pots.

I cannot help but elaborate in great detail on what makes the Banarasi paan (betel quid) such a phenomenon and custom in Banaras. In its ritualistic beliefs and adherences, it can only be rivalled by the single-malt culture of Scotland and Ireland. The terms paan and *beeda* for the quid are derived from the Sanskrit words *parna* and *vida*, respectively, as well as Thambul. Chewing paan is mentioned in the *Jataka Tales* in 400 BCE and in the Sanskrit *dharmasutra*s. The Sultans of Delhi and Bengal adopted the Indian culture of chewing paan in their own Turkish variations. Ibn Battuta, in 1350, has described how it was served in Delhi by Muhammad Bin Tughlaq 'after an elaborate palace meal' and was very egalitarian; any subject of the Sultanate could help themselves with a betel quid. Writing in his travelogue, the traveller Niccolao Manucci, in 1654, has written that after trying to chew the betel quid for the first time, he nearly collapsed and was brought to senses by an English man who poured some salts in his mouth. I can assure that had Manucci tried the Banarasi quid, he would have become an addict of it because of the mild and lulling effect by the tempering of the leaves and ingredients. Banarasi paan is famous all over the world. There is no cultivation and plantations of betel leaves and its ingredients in Banaras. Still, offerings of a genuine Banarasi *Magahi* betel quid are like offering a rare vermouth or 100 years aged single malt. Almost all varieties arrive here from distant places like Bengal and Bihar. As the most dynamic cottage industry, it employs a chunk of day labourers, and its business is traditionally done by a caste called Baraee or the Chaurasias. The biggest business centre of betel is located near our mohalla, an area called Paan Dariba, and another one is near Thatheri Bazar in the downtown, the zarda factory is at

Misir Pokhra near Girija Ghar Chauraha. Bollywood has immortalized it in various popular numbers, with the salacious 'Paan khaye saiyan . . . humne to maanga surmedani, le aaya zalim banaras ka zarda' and the more argotic or sadak chhaap 'khaiyeke paan Banaras wala'. I have grown up with the acrid and sometimes fragrant smell of catechu, tobacco leaves and the decaying odour of rotten betel leaves. This business centre starts its operations since six in the morning and even before noon, all the daily produce are despatched in bulk or in small packets to the hundreds of retail outlets and betel vendors in the city and even to the other nearby cities. The processing and tanning of the green leaves are very laborious tasks, which are done by women of the Baraee community. Incredible as it may sound, by frequent spraying of the leaves with water and turning them over, they can remain fresh for over a year. The more it ages, the better a yellowish tan it develops, and this is the exclusive variety of the Banarasi betel leaves called Magahi. It is small and yellow in colour and melts in the mouth easily. Banarasis also sometimes relish other popular varieties called Jagnathi, Badka-patta and Sanchi-karpoori. The use of choona (slaked lime) and kattha (thickened extract of the heartwood of areca catechu) along with its panchsugandha (the five aromatic ingredients: cardamom, clove, nutmeg, mace and camphor) have been recorded in the *Charaksambinta* and by *Susubrutha.*[9] Raja Jai Narayan Ghoshal has marked the presence of Banarasi paan in his poem on Budhwa Mangal:

kono-kono nauka te taamboolee vaas kare,
divya paan saanchee chhoota keho beeda dhare

(Every boat carries the elaborate tobacco and betel quid with small boats carrying even the Bhang [cannabis leaves] and Ganja [cannabis])[10]

Although the speciality of the Banarasi paan is related to its tanning, the back-breaking and step-by-step vulcanization, refinement and cleaning of the ingredients used in the Banarasi paan are also no less important. Our neighbour Ganga, whose traditional family business is related to paan, has shared many procedures with me. Every leaf is thoroughly cleaned before applying, and then rubbed with a wet cloth to ensure it does not remain gritty due to dust. The betel nut is cut into a square shape; thereafter, it is soaked in water to remove its astringency. After a prolonged period of soaking, the softened betel dissolves immediately with Magahi or other betel leaves. Kattha is specially prepared to be used in the Banarasi paan by soaking it in water overnight. If its colour turns black, it is soaked in milk, which is then boiled and spread in a wide utensil and left to cool down. After a few hours, when the catechu solidifies, it is wrapped around in a thick cloth and pressed under a cob or a heavy stone to remove its astringency and heat. After this, it is buried in hot ash to bring out its typical petrichor aroma and to further remove its residual astringency. After this entire course of action, the catechu coagulates, turning whitish, which indicates that it is now ready to be used. This readily soluble clot of catechu is then rehashed with kevda or rose water. Kattha made in this manner is the essence of Banarasi paan. Along with the betel nut and the catechu, even the taken-for-granted choona that is offered at the paan shops and the plains tobacco leaves also goes under a stringent process of vulcanization quite unlike the other cities. Fresh lime is never used directly in paan. It is cleaned and slaked in water, and after three to four days of rigorous rehashing, it is filtered through a piece of cloth. After decanting the water, this fine lime residue is then used as one of the ingredients of paan. Some exotic shops also add a dash of milk and curd to remove its acidic content. The preparation of *surti* (plains tobacco leaves) involves thorough washing with water and the subsequent addition of green cardamom and peppermint powders, rose water and saffron. After being left to dry in sealed bottles, it subsequently absorbs the fragrance of the added aromatic ingredients. Importantly, this surti does not cause dizziness even if accidentally consumed in greater quantity. The factory-produced yellow surti is generally avoided by regular paan chewers. This step-by-step ritualistic process is unique to Banaras, contributing to the uniqueness and popularity of the

Banarasi betel quid. When you ask a paan shop owner to prepare a quid in Banaras, the first thing he will do is pinch the stalk of the leaf and throw it away, as it is believed that Yama, the lord of death, resides in the stalk.

The paan shops are an institution in Banaras, with bric-a-brac made of heavy brass. Depending on the ancientness of the shop, these items form much coveted family heirlooms—a life-sized mirror with a very attractive frame, gleaming brass utensils for supari, a heavy pot for kattha, a bowl for zarda or surti, and a small table covered with a wet red linen cloth. Though the table is made of wood, it is stapled with brass plates, the flat, heavy brass knife used to bedaub the leaves with kattha and lime—all of this has an old-world feel. The paan vends are also the place where no social taboos of purity and status, so endemic in the orthodox society, are observed. A day labourer or a low-caste cobbler will get his betel quid from the same hand that will offer it to a priest or a rich trader—the overwhelming camaraderie and warmth the paan vend owner displays go beyond the common business dealings the shop owners have with their customers. Recently, the Banarasi langda aam, Banarasi paan, Chandauli rice variety 'Adam cheeni chawal' and the Ramnagar aubergine 'bhanta' have received the GI tag. Chandauli and Ramnagar, which are part of the greater Banaras, have recently been separated as independent administrative units.[11]

The labyrinthine lanes and by-lanes of Banaras have always been a great topic of research and discussion amongst the visitors of this city. Prinsep's description conveys the essence of the narrow and confined lanes of Banaras: 'Some apology may be necessary for introducing so imperfect a sketch into our series: it will suffice, however, to explain the general features of a Benares Street, confined, crooked, and so narrow, that even narrow seems a term too wide!'[12] The heart and soul of Banaras is in these lanes. Since the Gahadavala times when the city limit shifted to the south, the medieval and premodern Banaras developed all along the river and was as cramped as it is today. In the architectural vocabulary of linearity, Banaras fits in perfectly. The narrow lanes are a byproduct of such an arrangement. It connects the northern part of the city to its south through its tangled and often teeming lanes that are proverbially known for its unhygienic living conditions, as also for spiritual and cultural enrichment. No wonder then that the most famous *shayar* (poet) of Banaras, Nazeer Banarasi, says:

har sant ke, saadhu ke, rishi aur muni ke
sapne hue saakaar banaaras kii galii mein

(Every saint, ascetic and learned men
have achieved their dreams in these lanes of Banaras)

shankar kii jataaon kii tarah saaya a figan hai
har saaya a-e-diivaar banaaras ki galii men

(It offers shelter and protection like the
matted locks of Shankar
There is contentment in the lanes of Banaras)

The gullies of Banaras are trading centres for specific items and also denote the community residing here. From the smallest Das-Putraiya gully to the longest and most popular Vishwanath gully, famous for wooden toys and glass bangles, there are a total of around forty-seven gullies that come under the category of popular and most visited gullies. It is not possible to name all but amongst the ones that are associated with food items, are Kachori gully, Khova gully, Nariyal gully and Gola Dina Nath gully. Similarly, the mohallas like Madanpura, Pandey Haveli and Sonarpura are famous for their saree manufacturing. Thatheri Bazar, Raza Darwaza and Ranikuan are known for the marriage-related trousseau and jewelleries. Most of the artists and courtesans stay and practise at the Dalmandi gully and mohalla. The centres of esoteric Hindu erudition are also such gullies. The residents in these gullies say that they get the pleasure of a hill station during summers and there is no effect of winter even though not a single ray of sun reaches the gullies. The construction of the Vishwanath Corridor has subsumed some popular gullies in its attempt to restore the ancient magnificence and outreach of the pilgrims from the stairs of the Vishwanath temple to the ghats.

The mohallas of Banaras have also adopted the names of their patrons, like the place where Dara Shikoh lived is called Dara Nagar, Aurangzeb set up Aurangabad, Nawab Ganj is named after Nawab Saadat Ali, Bhoju Beer and Lahurabeer are named so because of the Beer worship place, Chet Ganj owes its name to Chet Singh and Jagat Singh who established the mohalla of Jagat Ganj. It is infamous because he constructed many buildings with the stones from the ruins of Sarnath Dharma stupa. In 1553, Guru Nanak Dev, the first guru of the Sikhs, visited Kashi and stayed for a considerable duration of time. The place where he stayed is called the Gurubagh.

There is a lane in Kabir chaura that we always called the Padamshree gully. It has the house Kabir's parents, Neeru and Nima, the Kabirpanthis call this courtyard Moolgadi. Vyomesh's book *Aag aur Pani* lists them all. The founder of the Banaras Gharana-style of tabla playing, Pandit Ramsahay, tabla player Gudai Maharaj, Pandit Kishan Maharaj, dancer Sitara Devi, singers Sidhehwari Devi, Pandit Bade Ramdas, Pandit Rajan-Sajan Mishra, along with their now famous disciples and a large number of luminaries from the field of literature, all have their residences and conservatoires in this barely one sq. km area.

The first land settlement in town was conducted in 1787 by the District Magistrate, later the Commissioner, Jonathan Duncan. The houses of Banaras exhibit three distinct eras in their style and construction material. Till the eighteenth century, Banaras was densely forested and the earliest buildings were the Manmandirghat, Kumarswamy Math and the Bundi Mahal that have distinct Rajput architectural styles dating back to the early sixteenth century. Houses and buildings of the oldest Pakka Mahal areas of Chaukhambha, Tatheri Bazaar and the Sah Mohalla were built around 1765.

Reginald Heber, in his *Narrative of a Journey through the Upper Provinces of India,* described these houses as 'richly embellished with verandahs, galleries, projecting oriel windows, and very broad and overhanging eaves, supported by carved brackets'.[13]

By the early nineteenth century, Banaras was already a full-fledged urban centre with its sanitation department, policing and drinking water supply. The refined urbanity of the Banaras mohallas can be gauged from the fact that even at that time, it was a gated community and the remnants of those gates called *phatak* still exist. The mohallas derive their names based on them. Examples include Baans phatak, Sheikh Salim phatak, Rangeeledas ka phatak, Sukhlal Sahu phatak, Hathi phatak, Raja Darwaja and Hanuman phatak. Every mohalla had its own night watchmen who were compensated by the residents—a system quite similar to the one we have now in the modern cooperative group housing societies.

Many houses that appear to be magnificent from outside might actually be in a dilapidated condition if one steps in and vice versa. The houses and by-lanes of Banaras are a magical maze and entering them is tantamount to entering a tangled web of narrow corridors, steep and dangerously slippery stairs, with a tomb-like smell of pigeon perks and stale air. However, one can be stunned to find a sudden opening in a lush green courtyard or if one were to continue the climb, a spectacular, breezy, rooftop with a view of the Ganga greets you. The houses made of stones and Lakhori bricks are the oldest. Many brick houses date back to the East India Company era. In 1806, Viscount Valentia had given a vivid account of the Banaras houses: 'The houses are built of stone, some six stories high, close to each other, with terraces on the summit. They are whimsically painted, and the architecture is as extraordinary . . . . The windows are extremely small, probably . . . to prevent the opposite neighbours from overlooking the apart intents; and, secondly, to keep the houses more cool during the hot winds.'[14]

Beggars are ubiquitous in Banaras. The *Hindustan Times* has reported that a Varanasi-based start-up, Beggars Corporation, which has taken the responsibility of turning beggars into entrepreneurs, was recognized at the Entrepreneurs Global Start-up Contest in Nagpur in 2023. Chandra Mishra, the convener of the Common Man Trust and founder of Beggars Corporation, received the Best Social Impact Award.

Banaras saw its first metalled road in 1802, extending from Dalmandi via Rajadarwaja to G.T. Road. Immediately after the arrival of railways in the late 1850s, Varanasi Cantt railway station was built. Until the late nineties, the primary modes of conveyance for the Banarasis were the tonga and the ubiquitous and egalitarian cycle rickshaw. Although they still exist, most have been motorized or electrified, and the tonga has vanished from the streets of Banaras altogether. A huge tonga stand was once located at the Godowlia chauraha, and the area used to reek of horse urine and dung. Until the early eighties, the opulent class travelled in buggies or *taamjhaam*, from where the English word 'tomtom' originated. When I visited Bhartendu Harishchandra's haveli in Thatheri Bazaar, his great-great-grandson Dipesh Chandra showed me many memorabilia of the great poet, including his personal tamjhaam that still adorns the courtyard in his haveli. The youth of this opulent class indulged in a typical pastime called *gahrebaazi*. It was the race of the tongas, where the horses used were thoroughbred, and considered a status symbol. The race used to be organized on the empty streets, either early morning or late at night. Some trace elements of gahrebaazi can still be found in the fares of Ramnagar, Sarnath and Maduadeeh (stopped after the construction of the New Railway Station). Rickshaws and the rickshaw pullers of Banaras are like the Google Maps—they know every inch of Banaras but may feign ignorance if they don't wish to go to a particular place. Even if a customer offers a fortune, they won't budge if they are not interested either in the passenger or the locality where they are asked to go. The customers could be from the highest echelons of the society to the lowest. Banaras was electrified in 1928 and the first cinema theatre, Madan Theatre, was opened in 1918 by a rich merchant, Baijnath Shahpuri, whose descendants now run a mall in the city.

In 1923, in its very rudimentary form, a music festival was started on Hanuman Jyanti within the precincts of the Sankat Mochan temple. Later in the late fifties, three prominent artists and revered citizens of Banaras—the Mahant of Sankat Mochan temple Shree Amarnath Mishra, a Pakhawaj vadak, tabla maestro Pandit Kishan

Maharaj and Indian classical vocalist Pandit Harishankar Mishra—laid the foundation of a musical tradition that still continues. The Sankat Mochan Sangeet festival is held for a duration of five days in the month of April and ends with Hanuman Jayanti in the precincts of the temple. Artists of different genres and audiences from all over the country, cutting across religious and sectarian divides, throng to this festival. This is an open-to-all musical carnival where nearly all celebratory artists, along with their disciples, come and perform. No fee is paid to them; they are free to perform on any day. It starts from 7.30 in the evening and ends in the wee hours of the morning. I attended this festival for two years, in 1982 and 1983, and witnessed that contrary to the common belief of the Indian classical music being only for the elite, here one can see villagers and day labourers rubbing shoulders with university professors, prominent administrators and businessmen. Many young and aspiring singers, theatre directors and dancers are given a chance to perform in front of a large gathering of maestros and celebrities who keenly observe and appreciate them. This festival is perhaps the only place in the country to hold such a galaxy of thespians and virtuosos in a single span of five days. Young and budding theatre directors and singers like Vyomesh Shukla and Gajendra Pandey, respectively, have cut their teeth in this festival. The cultural scene in Banaras is still throbbing, thanks to the now growing popularity of this festival.

The Syncretic Traditions of Banaras

In the chapter on Sanatan Dharma, I posited that unlike Somnath and other northern Indian temples, the destruction caused to the temples of Banaras was purely driven by religious motives rather than mere plundering. Banaras temples never had jewels like the temple at Somnath. However, soon after Ghori's destruction of the temples in Banaras through his General Qutb ud-Din Aibak, he incorporated the Shaivite symbol of his arch-rival, the Hindu Shahi kings, on his coins.[15] This example of an attempt at cultural syncretism by someone who is a bête noire for all Hindus started unfolding very slowly in Banaras as well, albeit with some spurts of destructions of temples, as mentioned earlier. Hussain Shah Sharqi encouraged inter-theological exchanges and created an ecosystem where intellectuals could render the epics and scriptures de novo. He inaugurated translation workshops where Hindu epics such as the Mahabharata, the *Arthashashtra*, *Hitopdesh* and *Panchatantra* were translated. Manan Ahmed is spot on when he writes that: 'In fact, the vast corpus of nearly 300 million Sanskrit and Prakrit manuscripts extant in contemporary India dates from the Muslim medieval period.'[16] Banaras was indeed the epitome and harbinger of a vast amount of scriptural texts that were being redefined and reanalysed in the given sociocultural milieu. I would rather add here in the 'political' order of the day as well. Beginning with the Kritya Kalptaru and Tirthavivechana Khanda of Bhatt Lakshmidhar, Kashi Khand, Kashi Rahasya, Kashi Matamya, many portions of *Shiva Purana* with added emphasis on Kashi, Tulsidas's Ramcharitrmanas, Narayan Bhatt's own religio-literary contributions, including the Tristhalisetu, Girivan Patmanjari of Varadaraja and Girvana Vangamanjari of Dhundiraj and many more—all were creatively and dynamically being composed in the lanes and ghats of Banaras.

We have discussed the temple construction spree from the mid-fourteenth century till the early seventeenth century. I believe that the Muslim gentry, aristocracy and the converts were deeply influenced by the nuanced cultural and religious symbols, metaphors and analysis of Banaras since the early twelfth century. It took a while for them to evolve a version of the Islamic way of life that was truly subcontinental and emphatically Banarasi, gradually severing its ties from the overarching 'sword' metaphor of Islamic religious ideology. They coalesced and spawned a lifestyle and a Ganga–Jamuni tehzeeb (Ganga–Yamuna culture) that has almost become a cliché in the parlance of the sociological analysis. I often quote the famous social and political theorist Ashis Nandy, stating that, like elsewhere, in Banaras, this eclecticism was more like a 'melting pot' than a 'salad bowl'. It evolved into a separate genre in the realms of arts, cuisine, attire, architecture, philosophy and language that was inclusive and celebratory. When we observe this in the context of Banaras, it should not come as a surprise because earlier Kashi and later Banaras have always absorbed and evolved. Let me give some specific examples of such living continuities. Abdul Rahim Khankhana's famous friendship with Tulsidas was symbiotic, where both complemented each other's cognitive and poetic space. Not many know that there are close to 1200 Arabic and Persian words in the Ramcharitmanas. The festivals and fares at Lat Bhairava and the adjacent mosque named after Saint Salar Masood area are a living testimony of the ancient animist and medieval Islamic religious practices, layered by the Brahminical counterpane. The land grants to Brahmins for temple construction by many Muslim nobility, and the emperors at Delhi, have already been mentioned. Malik Mohammad Jayasi, writing in *Padmawat*, chooses the temple of Kasi Karwat (a temple where devotees cut their bodies) to amplify his angst.

The fascination of Dara Shikoh, as mentioned earlier, with the city was legendary. In 1750, Sheikh Ali Hazin Lahiji, an Iranian who visited Banaras and was so fascinated by the city that he dedicated few couplets to it and never left Banaras thereafter. He wrote: 'I will not leave Banaras for it is holy everywhere, Every Brahman here is a son of Lachman or Rama.'[17] The most prominent temple of Banaras, the Kashi Vishwanath temple, is emblematic of this very syncretism. The main temple was built by Rani Ahilyabai Holkar of Indore, the bell of the temple was installed by the king of Nepal, the golden plate on the *shikhar* of the temple was undertaken by a Sikh, Maharaja Ranjeet Singh. The Naubat Khana of the Vishwanath temple was constructed by Nawab Azimul Mulk Ali Ibrahim Khan Bahadur Khaleel of Doolighat, during his tenure as the Magistrate of Banaras, under the overall supervision of the Governor General Warren Hastings in 1785. I visited the newly constructed, very grand and spacious Vishwanath corridor but was not able to locate the Naubat Khana that I have been seeing since my childhood. This is the same Naubat Khana where Bismillah Khan also performed. Ibrahim Ali lies buried in the Fatman road graveyard, next to the tomb of Sheikh Ali Hazin Lahiji.

It is indeed something to take pride in that Ghalib expressed his obeisance for the sacred city in pure Persian, comprising 108 verses in the form of a Masnavi. The number '108' holds yogic significance and is sacred to both the Vaishnavites and Shaivites alike. The missionary writers Sherring, Kennedy and Heber, all came to preach and convert the heathens and idolators of Banaras, and all fell in love with the religio-metaphysical ancientness of the city, eventually setting aside their proselytizing zeal. They did criticize the deplorable conditions of the nineteenth-century Banaras but were also overwhelmed by the piety and sheer faith of the Hindus. Prinsep had manifested his enchantment and fondness for this city before them, through his sketches and as an administrator through a series of civic reforms.

Annie Besant was fascinated by the rich tradition of Hindu scriptures and religious treatise. She has used the word 'Hindu' in her educational institutions that were established by her. The use of the word 'Hindu' was not in the narrow sectarian sense but symbolized the pan synthesis and universal beliefs of Hinduism.

All the Muslims living in the vicinity of the Gopalji temple contribute significantly to all the celebrations. In the famous Ramlila of Banaras, the contribution and active participation of the Muslim artists is the result of such syncretism. Vyomesh has an interesting observation that the crown-makers of the characters in the Ramlila, the mandatory display of fireworks and effigy makers, are all Muslims. At the famous 'Mauni Baba' Ramlila, the role of Meghnath is played by a practising Muslim. I have mentioned Mohammed Ikram of Muslim Majlis, who played a pivotal role in launching a protest that led to the beginning of the tradition of Shiva Barat, following the gold robbery from the Kashi Vishwanath temple. Pandit Ghulam Dastagir Birajdar, who passed away at the age of eighty-seven, was a Sanskrit scholar and was the general secretary of the highly acclaimed and prestigious body Vishwa Sanskrit Pratisthan in Banaras. A Maharashtrian by birth, he was a regular invitee for delivering Sanskrit spiritual talks at Banaras Hindu University even after his retirement. His tradition is being continued by Firoz Khan of Banaras, appointed as a Sanskrit teacher, and Muhammad Mushtakeem Ahmad from Mirzapur, who sings bhajans in the temple of Vindhyavasini devi and is a regular visitor to Banaras to perform at the musical 'Bhajan Sandhya'. Heber has mentioned a Greek who was a Sanskrit scholar and was honing his skills in the gurukuls of Banaras when he visited the city in 1824. The creative calligrapher, Haji Irshad Ali, a saree seller by profession, expresses his love and connection to the spiritual city in an exceptionally emblematic manner. He has calligraphed, inter alia, the Hanuman Chalisa, Quran, Vishnu Sahastranama and is now calligraphing the Gita on sheets of white cotton Banarasi fabric, with an ink hand-made from the soil from the Ganga, and binds the sheets with the famous Banarasi silk brocade.[18] Let me conclude with a sher by Nazeer Banarasi:

Main vo kaashii kaa musalamaan hoon ki jisako ai najiir,
Apane ghere men lie rahate hain butakhaane kaii . . .

(I am that Muslim of Kashi,
who is protected by several temples . . .)[19]

Chapter 13

Perambulating the Idea of Banaras

Temples and Places of Worship

Banaras, the city of temples and places of worship, boasts a multitude of sacred sites, numbering in lakhs as per the scriptures. Even amidst all this divine atmosphere of Banaras, conversations often revolve around castes. In the early eighties, casteist descriptions were commonplace, detailing how a piece of land or public space was occupied by Rajputs, Bhumihars, Kayasthas, Ahirs and a Brahmin. For the Rajput and Bhumihars, might is right; a Kayastha would manipulate the papers in the land records; an Ahir would build a cow shed and start dairy farming; but for Brahmins, they say they will simply colour two bricks with vermilion, place a few garlands, and start a regular puja there, converting a huge area into a temple land. When land was plentiful, this manner of building a temple was highly venerated, and some even gave land grants for this very specific purpose. But now, it is more often resorted to for illegally encroaching on vacant pieces of land.

Most of the temple destruction started from 1194 and occurred sporadically till the final destruction of the Vishwanath temple in 1669. However, the construction of temples did not cease. The Kashmir kings, as per Kalhana's *Rajtarangini*, constructed many temples in Banaras from around tenth century CE. The mega ones included Padmeshwar, which was later destroyed by the Sharqi ruler of Jaunpur and Adi Vishweshwar, along with Bindu Madhav Temple, which was destroyed by Aurangzeb. Writing about the historicity of the temples, most historians date the present temples in Banaras to be not more than 400 years old.

The coming of age for this city as a temple town actually started only from the thirteenth century and culminated in the late nineteenth century with the phenomenal rise of pilgrimage sites along with the number of gods and their places of worship. This was also because most of the Puranas were being composed and rewritten. For example, the Puranas mentions the five 'Vinayaks' but in the Kashi Khand, the number goes up to fifty-six! If we see the general pattern from the Gupta era, many prominent Shivlings, including the Avimukteshwara, did exist, as testified from the Rajghat seals, even though the Gupta kings were Vaishnavs. The seals of Rajghat list nine temples of the Gupta era and a slightly later period. One of them, Gabhstishwar, and probably the only one, although in a highly dilapidated condition, still exists near Mangala Gauri temple. Despite Sherring's surface study analysis suggesting that the ruins of the large temples in Bakaria Kund are Buddhist Chaityas, there is now sufficient evidence to point to the existence of the Gupta era temples. Motichandra has found some idols of Krishna, from the Bakaria Kund, and along with the testimony of the Rajghat seals, he establishes the existence of a large Gupta era temple at the site. The Kashi Khand, while attributing all Vishnu places of worship to Shiva, narrates a story of a village girl, named Sulakshna, and her goat. Sulakshna, when blessed by Trilochan (another name of Shiva), requested immortality for her goat, leading to the renaming of the Ark Kund (pond where water offerings are made) to Bakaria Kund (*bakri* meaning goat).[1]

Lakshmidhar had mentioned about 350 temples in Banaras during the Gahadawala era around 1100 CE, and by the time Prinsep compiled his own database, the count exceeded 1000. When Sherring wrote his book in 1868, it further went up to 1654. Pandit Kubernath Sukul has listed nearly all the prominent temples but Diana Eck, in her book published in 1981, has listed only the major Hindu places of worship, that include fourteen Shivalingams, nine Durgas, nine Gauris, twelve Adityas, eight Bhairavas, eight directional guardians and fifty-six Vinayaks. Many more constellations of deities, along with other vegetative deities like the beers, Yakshas and Nagas, also find mention, with a host of them located on the Panchkroshi route. At present, the numbers of temples are mind-boggling, and most of them are revered with regular puja, but many have witnessed the flight of deities.

In addition to the Hindu places of worship, Banaras also has many Parshvanath Jain temples, nearby Buddhist sacred sites in Sarnath, major mosques, a huge gurudwara, ancient churches, Sufi shrines, and various other denominational centres that double up as places of worship and learning. Given the scope of this short sub-chapter, it's impossible mention all of them. So, the following section has a list of some of the most important ones, along with a few quaint ones that I recently revisited to update my narrations for this.

Exploring the Temples of Devon Ke Dev—Kashipuradhipati

The most important temple today—the Kashi Vishwanath—also carries a disturbing history. During the Gupta era, eight Shivalingams were listed: Harishchandra, Abhratkeshwar, Jaleshwar, Shree Parvat, Mahalay, Krimichandeshwar, Kedareshwar, and Avimukteshwar. Though, as per Kashi Khand, Shiva himself has elaborated on the fourteen main lingams and another fourteen lesser ones.[2] The three most revered ones are: Omkareshwar on the northern hill, Kashi Vishwanath on the central hill and Kedareshwar on the southern hill.

Omkareshwar is the first one mentioned in the Kashi Khand that was located at the ancient pilgrimage point of the Matsyodari Kund, where the Gahadawala ruler Govindchandra used to bathe during the peak flooding of the river Ganga, forming a Matsyodari Yog. The present Omkareshwar temple is located in the Adampura locality near the Machodari area and was renovated by Rani Bhabhani of Natore Estate Zamindari of Bengal in the early eighteenth century. It was originally situated on a hilltop, but now occupies a small portion surrounded by a Muslim graveyard. A thousand years back, along with the other two Shivalingams, it was a crucial temple, finding mention in many other Puranic sources long before the writing of the Kashi Khand. This almost-abandoned temple attracts only a handful of worshippers on occasions like Shivaratri or other auspicious days related to Mahadev. This is also the mythical place where the shaft of light appeared to Lord Brahma after he practised severe penance.

The Avimukteshwar, though mentioned as the thirteenth in the Kashi Khand, was and still is an important temple. The terminology for Shiva as Avimukteshwar was lost after the twelfth century. Till then, Shiva was also addressed as Devdev Swamy and was worshipped as a separate lingam. The divine names Vishweshwara and Vishwanath emerged and gained popularity for Shiva, only after the twelfth century CE. The original lingam is said to have been established by Shiva when he left Kashi to reside on Mount Mandara. As per the *Linga Purana*, it was dropped by the goblins from the sky.[3] The ancient Avimukteshwar is now only worshipped in the form of a stone near the Gyanvapi mosque. The Vishweshwar lingam is the last one as per the Kashi Khand but the most revered. This original temple has a hoary and a very disturbing past. Adi Vishweshwar was the same temple that was patronized by the Gahadavala kings, even though they were Vishnu worshippers, owing to its importance amongst the general masses. It was likely constructed around the seventh century CE. This temple was destroyed by Qutb ud-Din Aibak in 1194. Later, Razia Sultan decreed the construction of a mosque in 1238 on the same spot using the wreckage and building material of the destroyed temple, which still remains. I visited this mosque to find out about this old temple, and no one who has not studied the origin of the Vishwanath temple actually knows the place. Thanks to Eck, I was able to reach the same spot—situated in a lane behind the present Adi Vishweshwar temple that was built in the seventeenth century CE by a nobleman from the Amer royal family of Raja Jai Singh. From the Satyanarayan temple, a little ahead, a narrow lane climbs up and one is astonished to find a relatively open space in the midst of cheek by jowl buildings. This mosque is indeed located at the topmost places or the middle sacred hill of ancient Kashi. Sherring's surface study dates it to be of the Gupta era.

There was another Vishweshwar temple that was reconstructed in the same area where the present Kashi Vishwanath temple is located, during the Illtutmish reign in around 1280, by one Gujarati philanthropist merchant, Vastupal. Near this temple, the Padmeshwar temple was built in 1296 by one Padamsadhu. These temples were destroyed again by Firoz Shah Tughlaq in 1374 and by Sharqi rulers of Jaunpur in 1447, respectively. A third Vishwanath temple was constructed on a very large scale, inspired by the religious philosophy of Narayan Bhatt. The place chosen was near the ancient Gyanvapi well. During Akbar's secular and tolerant rule, Todar Mall—one of the ministers in the court of Akbar—directed his son Gobardhan Das, who was the Subedar of Jaunpur, to undertake this project in 1585. It was brought down by Aurangzeb in 1669, who constructed a mosque, ironically called the Gyanvapi mosque, at the same spot. The lingam was dropped in the Gyanvapi well to save it from desecration. In a recent interview, however, the descendant of the chief priest and the original mahant of the Kashi Vishwanath temple, Shree Rajendra Prasad Tiwari, disagrees. He asserts that the lingam was always in the custody of the family. To ensure the 'stubborn persistence of that glory' for the chief deity, another temple—the present one—was constructed by Ahilyabai Holkar in 1777, a little distance from the original site behind the Gyanvapi mosque. According to the former Mahant, Holkar was handed over the Shivling along with the small space where it was installed by his family. I have not been able to corroborate this claim through any available record, though. Another Kashi Vishwanath temple is located at Mir ghat, established in the early sixties by an orthodox Brahmin, Karpatri, who opposed the opening of the temple for Harijans after 1956. Yet another Vishwanath sits in the temple inside the Banaras Hindu University, built by the wealthy trader Ghanshyam Das Birla.

Many might not be aware, but the Marathas attempted to rebuild the Vishwanath temple by destroying the Gyanvapi mosque on three separate occasions. The first attempt in 1742 was attempted by Peshwa Balaji Bajirao. It was before Ahilyabai Holkar sponsored the new Vishwanath temple. However, this attempt was dissuaded by the already settled Panch Dravid Brahmins of Banaras, whose forefathers had made Banaras their home since the thirteenth century CE. On the second and third occasions, the Commissioner of Banaras, Jonathan Duncan, and the Viceroy, Lord Wellesley, in 1787 and 1798, respectively, refused to entertain any such petition. The Peshwa Balaji Bajirao desperately wanted to take the affairs of the important Hindu pilgrimage centres, like Allahabad, Banaras and Gaya, under his control. His main focus was on Banaras, which was then under the rule of the Awadh nawabs. By the time, Nawab Safdar Jung, the Nawab of Awadh, came to know of the plans of the Marathas, Bajirao had already camped in the Mirzapur area with the intention of capturing Banaras. Meanwhile, a delegation of Brahmin priests and mahants, under the sagacious leadership of Narayan Dixit, reached Mirzapur on 1 June 1742 and persuaded Bajirao to retreat. Peshwa's general diary and a letter dated 27 June 1742, from the office of Kaygawankar Dixit, mentions this historical event.

It is very clear that the Brahmins of Banaras were in great dilemma on the proposal of pulling down the Gyanvapi mosque to construct the temple, owing to serious threat to the general law and order and on their own life. On the second occasion, even after Ahilyabai Holkar had already built the temple at the present site, Mahadji Scindia in 1789 conveyed to the resident commissioner and the Viceroy's office in Calcutta to pay some compensation to the Muslims and convince them to let the Hindus construct a temple in place of the mosque. But the resident Commissioner Jonathan Duncan strictly refused to move ahead on any such proposal. On the third occasion, 'the Maratha Machiavelli', Nana Fadnavis, set a condition to support the British, in their campaign against Tipu Sultan in the Fourth Anglo–Mysore War (1798–99), only if they allow the Hindus to reconstruct the Vishwanath temple exactly at the same ancient site. However, even after the decisive victory of the British with support of the Marathas, they refused to keep up to their promise.[4]

The third Shivling, Kedareshwar, is placed seventh in the Kashi Khand and is located on the northern hill. This temple is located at the riverfront that is called Kedar ghat. This is a *swayambhu* (self-manifest) lingam and is supposed to be the oldest, as per the Puranic Shaivite corpus, that has survived the destruction inflicted upon other lingams by the Muslim heretics. An interesting story is that Aurangzeb's army did know about the sacred importance of Kedareshwar but were warned by a Muslim saint about the consequences of attacking Kedareshwar. When the commander attempted to attack the temple regardless, the moment he struck the Nandi bull at its entrance, it is said that real blood started oozing out from the idol and the armies of Aurangzeb got so petrified that they beat a hasty retreat. Unlike a perfectly rounded and smooth surface, it has rough top and is perfectly divided into two with a white line. The story goes that the ancient King Mandhatri decided to renounce his kingdom and proceeded to the Himalayas but even after spending many years there, he could not get the darshan of Mahadeo. He was then advised to go to Kashi, where it is possible to have his darshan. Mandhatri lived a frugal life in Kashi but, with his spiritual power, he returned to Kedar in the Himalayas every day, to have his only meal of the day. One day, after preparing his meal of khichri (lentils and rice porridge), as is customary, he went in search of someone to share his meal with but was unable to find anyone in the mountains. Later, in the guise of a vagrant, Shiva appeared. Mandhatri was overjoyed to offer his meal to the vagrant. He cut the porridge into half, but the porridge turned into a lingam. Since then, this lingam has a dividing white line and has small stones that resemble lentils. At present, it is run by the Kumarswamy Mutt and has a distinct south Indian temple architecture.

Nestled in the sacred alleys of Banaras is the Kashi Karvat, also known as the Bhima Shankar temple. It is located twenty feet below the bustling ground level in the Kachori gully, not very far from the present Vishwanath temple; it has an approach through a tunnel. Only the authorised priest can visit the sanctum sanctorum for the daily puja. The temple only opens once a week. In the past, it held sacred importance for people desiring moksha to cut themselves with a huge jigsaw by jumping on that. It later became a centre of huge fraud perpetrated by the Gangaputras on the innocent pilgrims. The rogue priests used to bring innocent travellers here and kill them. And after robbing them, they used to throw their dead bodies in the well of Kashi Karwat. It existed in the time of Akbar because Sher Shah's contemporary Malik Muhammad Jayasi has written in his *Padmavat: 'Karvat tapa hohi jimi chuh'*. In Sherring's words, it was a temple where fanatics would commit suicide.

Kashi Karvat was a leitmotif with most of the Bhakti-era poets such as Mirabai, Surdas and Raidas. The tradition of self-immolation was very common with Shiva bhakts since ancient times. Two more very important Shiva temples are located in Gowdolia area and in Maidagin. The Til Bhandareshwar, that grows every year equivalent to the size of a sesame seed, and Mahamrityunjay where rituals are performed by non-stop chanting of Shiva mantras for long life.

Afterword

For me, Banaras is *aah* (nostalgia) and *wah* (ecstasy). I no longer live in Banaras but it lives in me and constantly makes its presence felt: sometimes, subconsciously, in my Mother Tongue Effect (MTE) of the Banarasi dialect, which is always corrected by my daughter, or in the sudden strain of Girija Devi's thumri, at some vulnerable moment—in the choicest of Banarasi superlatives and swear words—in the notes of a distant temple bells in the calmness of the dawn when I am actually able to hear the low lapping burble of the Ganga . . . the aroma and the sound of the festivals activating my olfactory and salivary glands, and in many more of the simple human moments. The body of the city is ravaged in the global tourism mart. International tourism was always a significant source of earning for the city, but now it's become more of a vacation hub. The heart of the city is stunned. Banaras is waiting for those who can search its soul like the ancient seers did. It is yet to be seen how the juggernaut of the religious renaissance that is sweeping across the country is going to be perceived by the Banarasis. It is too early as they are in a state of a religious imagined community.

Notes

Introduction

1 Maaz Bin Bilal, trans. *The Temple Lamp: Verses on Banaras* (Delhi: Penguin Random House India, 2022).
2 Bilal, *The Temple Lamp*, p. xxix.
3 Rama Shankar Singh, *Nadi Putra: Uttar Bharat Mein Nishad Aur Nadi* (Setu Prakashan, 2022), p. 183.
4 Jawaharlal Nehru, *Glimpses of World History* (Penguin India, 2004), p. 31.
5 Eck, *Banaras: City of Light* (Penguin, 1993), p. 16 and 17.
6 M.A. Sherring, *Benares: The Sacred City of the Hindus* (Kathmandu: Pilgrims Publishing, 2016), preface.
7 George Viscount Valentia, *Voyages and Travels to India, Ceylon, The Red Sea, Abyssinia and Egypt* (London: William Miller, 1809), p. 104.
8 Reginald Heber, *Narrative of a Journey through the Upper Provinces of India* (J. Murray, 1828), Vol. 1, p. 371.
9 Mark Twain, *Following the Equator: A Journey around the World.* Chapters L–LIII (Harper and Brothers), pp. 158–478.
10 Vidula Jayaswal, ed. *Varanasi: Myths and Scientific Studies* (Aryan Books International, 2013), p. 91.
11 Jayaswal, *Varanasi*, p. 111.
12 Numair Atif Choudhury, *Babu Bangladesh!* (Fourth Estate India, 2019), p. 74; 'Tower of Brahma,' https://www.codechef.com/problems/CDWY02 (accessed 18 October 2023).

13 Eck, *Banaras*, p. 6.
14 Vertul Singh, *Bhopal Nama: Writing a City* (Manjul Publishing House, 2020), Foreword, p. xii.
15 Amitav Ghosh, *The Gun Island* (Penguin Random House India, 2019), p. 151.
16 J.S. Uberoi, *India: Timeless Splendour* (Media Transasia India Limited, 2011), pp. 1–2.
17 Gabriel García Márquez, *Strange Pilgrims* (Vintage, 2006).

Chapter 1: The Early Days

1 Kashi Khand, pp. 761–62.
2 U.K. Shukla, 'Varanasi and the Ganga River: A Geological Perspective', in *Varanasi: Myths and Scientific Studies*, ed. V. Jayasawal (New Delhi: Aryan Books International, 2013), p. 101.
3 K.N. Prudhvi Raju and Manish Pandey, 'Varanasi: Origin and Growth from a Geomorphic Perspective', in *Varanasi: Myths and Scientific Studies*, p. 135.
4 Dr Motichandra, *Kashi Ka Itihas* (Uttar Pradesh: Vishwavidyalaya Prakashan, 1985), p. 6; M.A. Sherring, *Benares: The Sacred City of the Hindus* (Kathmandu: Pilgrims Publishing, 2016), p. 219.
5 Kashi Khand, p.762.
6 Rana P.B. Singh and Pravin S. Rana, 'The Ganga ghats, Varanasi (Kashi): The Riverfront Landscapes', in *Banāras (Vārāṇasī): Cosmic Order, Sacred City, Hindu Traditions*, ed. Rana P.B. Singh (Varanasi: Tara Book Agency, 2018).
7 Dr Motichandra, *Kashi Ka Itihas* (Uttar Pradesh: Vishwavidyalaya Prakashan, 1985), p. 13.
8 M.A. Sherring, *Benares: The Sacred City of the Hindus* (Kathmandu: Pilgrims Publishing, 2016), p. 24.
9 Vidula Jayaswal, *Jataka Stories and Archaeology: A Case Study of Varanasi*, p. 86; Jayaswal, ed. *Varanasi: Myths and Scientific Studies* (Aryan Books International, 2013).
10 Diana L. Eck, *Banaras: City of Light* (US: Alfred A. Knopf, 1982), p. 27.

11 Svātmārāma, *Hatha Yoga Pradipika*, p. 162.
12 Hazari Prasad Dwivedi, *Banbhattaki Atmakatha* (Rajkamal Prakashan, 1946), p. 25 and 35.
13 Pandit Kubernath Sukul, 'Kashi ki Bhinn-Bhinn Vibhaagon ki Seemayein Tatha Parimar', in *Varanasi Vaibhav*, pp. 44–58.
14 Virag Sontakke, *Myths Related to Avimukteshwar*, pp. 91–92.
15 Eck, *Banaras*, p. xv.
16 K.N. Prudhvi Raju and Manish Pandey, 'Varanasi: Origin and Growth from a Geomorphic Perspective', in *Varanasi: Myths and Scientific Studies*, ed. Vayaswal Jayaswal (Aryan Books International, 2013), p. 140.
17 Rana P.B. Singh, *Banaras: The Heritage City of India* (Indica Books, 2009), p. 33.
18 Kapila Vatsyayan, p. xiii.
19 Kashi Khand, p. 719.
20 Kashi Khand, p. 723.
21 Hazari Prasad Dwivedi, *Banbhatta Ki Atmakatha* (Rajkamal Prakashan, 1946), pp. 123–24.
22 Dr Motichandra, *Kashi Ka Itihas*, p. 194.
23 Kashi Khand, pp. 717–23.
24 Max S. Shapiro and Rhoda A. Hendricks, *Dictionary of Mythology* (Paladin Books, 1981), p. 106.
25 In the Avesta, the devas are ironically malevolent spirits of evil but in the Vedas, they are the deities who are divine spirits of the good (Shapiro and Hendricks, *Dictionary of Mythology*, p. 53).
26 A sage who is well-versed in the scriptures and is known to be the 'mover of the mountains' or 'mover of the unmoving'.
27 Shinjana Sen, Parminder Kaur, Jaspreet Saini, Gurmeet Kaur and Meenal Mishra, 'Kaimur Sandstone of Vindhyan Supergroup: 'A Prevalent Prehistoric and Ancient Monumental Heritage Stone from Son Valley of Central India', *Geoheritage, Springer Nature*, June 2022.
28 K.T. Achaya, *The Illustrated Foods of India A-Z* (Oxford University Press, 2009).

29 It was called *Banaila* to distinguish it from the pork of suar or the domesticated pig, which was consumed by the 'untouchable' caste.

30 James Prinsep, *Benares Illustrated* (Uttar Pradesh: Vishwavidyalaya Prakashan, 1996), p. 39.

31 Kashi Khand, p. 801.

32 *Kashi Ka Itihas,* p. 2 and 3.

33 *Kashi Ka Itihaas*, p. 8.

34 *Kashi Ka Itihas,* p. 185.

35 Prinsep, *Benares Illustrated*, p. 10.

36 There is a map of Prinsep that has been displayed by Eck in her book on page no. 47.

37 Diana Eck, *Banaras*, p. 51.

38 James Prinsep, *Benares Illustrated* (Baptist Mission Press, Circular Road, 1831), p. 12.

39 Prinsep, *Benares Illustrated* (Uttar Pradesh: Vishwavidyalaya Prakashan, 1996), Introduction by O.P. Kejariwal, p. 13.

40 Prinsep, *Benares Illustrated*, 1831, p. 38.

41 U.K. Shukla, 'Varanasi and the Ganga River: A Geological Perspective', in *Varanasi: Myths and Scientific Studies*, ed. Vidula Jayaswal (Aryan Books International, 2013), p. 111.

42 Pranay Lal, *Indica: A Deep Natural History of the Indian Subcontinent* (Penguin Random House India, 2016), p. 273.

43 S. Singh, K. Prakash and U.K. Shukla, 'Decadal Scale Geomorphic Changes and Tributary Confluences within the Ganga River Valley in Varanasi region, Ganga Plain, India', *Quaternary International*, Vol. 507, 25 February 2019, pp. 124–33, https://www.sciencedirect.com/science/article/abs/pii/S1040618218301514

44 Lal, *Indica*, p. 273.

45 Kashi Khand: *Sanchhipt Skankpuran* (Geeta Press), p. 816.

46 Dr Motichandra, *Kashi Ka Itihas*, p. 14.

47 Meera Sharma, 'Ganga and Kashi: Myths and Scientific Enquiries', in *Varanasi: Myths and Scientific Studies*, p. 117.

48 Kapila Vatsyayan, 'Ecology and Indian Myth', in *Varanasi: Myths and Scientific Studies*, p. 15.
49 Ramashankar Singh, *Nadi Putra: Uttar Bharat mein Nishad aur Nadi* (Setu Prakashan, 2022), pp. 181–82.
50 Lal, *Indica*, p. 282.
51 Kalyan Ray, 'Scientists Take a Deep Dive to Get to the Bottom of Ganga Mystery', *Deccan Herald*, 12 January 2023, https://www.deccanherald.com/india/scientists-take-a-deep-dive-to-get-to-the-bottom-of-ganga-mystery-1180177.html (accessed 19 October 2023).
52 K.T. Achaya, *The Illustrated Foods of India A–Z* (Oxford University Press, 2008), p. 88.
53 Rana P.B. Singh and Pravin S. Rana, 'The Riverfront ghats: Cultural Landscapes', Cultural Heritage of Varanasi, https://culturalheritageofvaranasi.com/about_varanasi/the-riverfront-ghats-cultural-landscapes-special-highlights-of-the-manikarnika-ghat/ (accessed 19 October 2023).
54 A gathering of people for the performance of devotional activities.
55 Lal, *Indica*, pp. 331–32.
56 A popular winter speciality, it is a sweet made from lentils like moong dal and urad dal flours and desi ghee, i.e., clarified butter.
57 Pranay Lal, replying to my question in email dated 12 October 2022.
58 Introduction by Vasudeva Sharan Agrawala in Dr Motichandra, *Kashi Ka Itihas* (Uttar Pradesh: Vishwavidyalaya Prakashan, 1962), p. 14.
59 Dr Motichandra, *Kashi Ka Itihas*, p. 14.
60 Diana Eck, *Banaras*, p. 27.
61 *Skandpuran:* Kashi Khand (Geeta Press), p. 795.
62 James Prinsep, *Benares Illustrated* (Baptist Mission Press, Circular Road, 1831), p.14.
63 Maaz Bin Bilal, trans. *The Temple Lamp*, pp. 42–45.
64 Sauteed fresh green peas with powdered spices.

65 A double decker budgerow that is colloquially called a bujra.
66 Kashi Khand, p. 743.
67 Yuval Noah Harari, *Sapiens* (Dvir Publishing House Ltd. (Israel) Random House Harper, 2011), pp. 149–52.
68 Rahul Sankrityayan, *Volga Se Ganga* (Kitab Mahal, 1943), p. 84.
69 Dr Motichandra, *Prakritik Rachna aur Yatayat Ke Sadhan: Kashi Ka Itihas* (Uttar Pradesh: Vishwavidyalaya Prakashan 1962), p. 1.
70 Maaz Bin Bilal, trans. *The Temple Lamp*, verse 86, p. 88.
71 Romila Thapar, *The Past as Present: Which of Us Are Aryans?* (New Delhi: Aleph Book Company, 2014), p. 181.
72 Peggy Mohan, *Wanderers, Kings, Merchants: The Story of India through Its Languages* (New Delhi: Penguin Random House, 2021), p. 31.
73 Romila Thapar, *A History of India* (Penguin Books, 1966), p. 25.
74 Rahul Sankrityayan, *Volga se Ganga* (Kitab Mahal, 1943), p.80.
75 Kuber Nath Sukul, *Varanasi Down the Ages* (Kameshwar Nath Sukul, 1974), p. 17.
76 Tony Joseph, *Early Indians: The Story of Our Ancestors and Where We Came From* (Juggernaut Books, 2018), p. 208.
77 Joseph, *Early Indians,* pp. 186–87.
78 Mohan, *Wanderers, Kings, Merchants*, p. 19.
79 Marianne Keppens and Jakob De Roover, 'The Brahmin, the Aryan, and the Powers of the Priestly Class: Puzzles in the Study of Indian Religion, *Religions,* 2020, https://www.mdpi.com/2077-1444/11/4/181.
80 Romila Thapar, *A History of India* (Penguin Books, 1966), p. 53.

Chapter 2: Rajghat

1 M.A. Sherring, *Benares: The Sacred City of the Hindus* (Kathmandu: Pilgrims Publishing, 2016), p. 5.
2 Sherring, *Benares,* pp. 2–3.
3 James Tod, *Annals and Antiquities of Rajasthan,* Vol. I (Low Price Publications, 1990), Introduction, p. lvii.

4 K.N. Prudhvi Raju and Manish Pandey, 'Varanasi: Origin and Growth from a Geomorphic Perspective', in *Varanasi: Myths and Scientific Studies* (Aryan Books International, 2013), p. 137.
5 Vidula Jayaswal, ed. *Varanasi: Myths and Scientific Studies* (Aryan Books International, 2013), p. 72 and 78.
6 Vidula Jayaswal, 'Jataka Stories and Archaeology: A Case Study of Varanasi', in *Varanasi*, ed. Vidula Jayaswal, p. 76.
7 Dr Motichandra, *Kashi Ka Itihas*, p. 6.
8 James Fergusson, *Tree and Serpent Worship: Illustrations of Mythology and Art in India in the First and Fourth Centuries after Christ* (Hansebooks, 2017), p. 62.
9 James Prinsep, *Benares Illustrated* (Baptist Mission Press, 1831), pp. 7–8.
10 Dr Motichandra, *Kashi Ka Itihas*, pp. 12–13.
11 Vasudeva Sharan Agrawala, *The Study of Rajghat Seals* (Sahitya Akademi, 2012), p. 645.
12 Dr Motichandra, *Kashi Ka Itihas*, pp. 12–13.
13 Vasudeva Sharan Agrawala, *The Study of Rajghat Seals*, p. 645.
14 Pandit Kubernath Sukul, *Varanashi Vaibhav* (Bihar Rashtrabhasha Parishad, 2008), p. 268.
15 Sukul, *Varanashi Vaibhav*, p. 268.
16 Sherring, *Benares*, p. 214, 222 and 226.
17 Dr Motichandra, *Kashi Ka Itihas*, p. 59.
18 Dr Motichandra, *Kashi Ka Itihas*, p. 76; Diana L. Eck *Banaras: City of Light* (Penguin Books, 1993), p. 68.
19 Vasudeva Sharan Agrawala, *The Study of Rajghat Seals*, p. 653.
20 *Times of India*, 4 May 2023 and 8 May 2023.
21 Eck, *Banaras*, p. 132.
22 Sherring, *Benares,* p.137.
23 Agarwal, *The Study of Rajghat Seals*, p. 651.
24 Agarwal, *The Study of Rajghat Seals*, p. 648.
25 Agarwal, *The Study of Rajghat Seals*, p. 644.
26 Agarwal, *The Study of Rajghat Seals*, p. 655.
27 Dr Motichandra, *Kashi Ka Itihas*, p. 78.

28 Sherring, *Benares*, p. 221.
29 Dr Motichandra, *Kashi Ka Itihas*, pp. 75–76.
30 Agarwal, *The Study of Rajghat Seals*, p. 636.
31 Agarwal, *The Study of Rajghat Seals*, p. 646.
32 Agarwal, *The Study of Rajghat Seals*, p. 646. Dr Motichandra, *Kashi Ka Itihas*, p. 88.
33 Agarwal, *The Study of Rajghat Seals*, pp. 636–40 and Dr Motichandra, *Kashi Ka Itihas*, p. 93.
34 James Tod, *Annals and Antiquities of Rajasthan*, p. 139; and Dr Motichandra, *Kashi Ka Itihas*, p. 113.
35 Shivprasad Singh, *Neela Chaand* (Vani Prakashan, 1988), p. 518.

Chapter 3: Alluring Allusions

1 Dr Motichandra, *Kashi Ka Itihas* 1985 Vishavidyaalay Prakshan, p. 9 and 20, He has quoted Atharveda Paiplad Shakha 5|12||14.
2 Dr Motichandra, *Kashi Ka Itihas* (Uttar Pradesh: Vishwavidyalaya Prakashan, 1985), p. 9. He has quoted Atharveda Paiplad Shakha 5|12||14.
3 Dr Motichandra, *Kashi Ka Itihas,* p. 9 and 20.
4 Fitzedward Hall, *The Sacred City of the Hindus,* p. iii.
5 Maaz Bin Bilal, trans. *The Temple Lamp* (Penguin Classics, 2022), verse 86, p. 88.
6 Fitzedward Hall, *The Sacred City of the Hindus,* p. iii.
7 Kashi Khand: *Sanchhipt Skankpuran* (Geeta Press, p. 794).
8 M.A. Sherring, *Benares: The Sacred City of the Hindus* (Kathmandu: Pilgrims Publishing, 2016, p. xiv).
9 Diana L. Eck, *Banaras: City of Light* (US: Alfred A. Knopf, 1982), p. 24 and 26.
10 James Prinsep, *Benares Illustrated* (Baptist Mission Press, Circular Road, 1831), p. 9.
11 Eck, *Banaras*, p.45 and Dr *Motichandra, Kashi Ka Itihas*, p. 29.
12 1 yojana = 12.8 km/8 miles.
13 Sherring, *Benares*, p. xi.
14 Swami Muktibodhananda, *Hatha Yoga Pradipika,* pp. 12–13.

15 Sherring, *Benares*, p. 74.
16 M.A. Sherring, *The Scared City of the Hindus* (Pilgrims Book House, 2016), p. IX, Appendix to Introduction.
17 Rama P.B. Singh, *Banaras: The Heritage city of India Geography, History and bibliography* (Indica Books, 2008), p. 22
18 Vishwanath Mukherjee, *Bana Rahe Banaras* (Uttar Pradesh: Vishwavidyalaya Prakashan, 2017), p. 5.
19 Sherring, *Benares*, p. xix.
20 Ralph Fitch, *Journey to India Overland.*
21 Prinsep, *Benares Illustrated*, p. 23.
22 Kashi Khand, p. 794.
23 Dr Motichandra, *Kashi Ka Itihas*, p. 91.
24 Pandit Kubernath Sukul, *Varanashi Vaibhav* (Bihar: Bihar Rashtrabhasha Parishad, 2008), p. 54.
25 Dr Motichandra, *Kashi Ka Itihas*, p. 16.
26 In one of his interviews to a popular web newsmagazine NewsClick (28 September 2022).
27 *The Jatakas,* 3|226 (as quoted by Dr Motichandra, *Kashi Ka Itihas*, p. 17).
28 Prinsep, *Benares Illustrated*, p. 91.
29 Shiv Prasad Singh, *Neela Chaand* (Vani Prakashan, 1988), p. 111.
30 Sherring, *Benares.*
31 Sherring, *Benares*, p. 241.
32 Vyomesh Shukla, *Aag aur Paani* (Rukh Publication 2023), p. 40.
33 Srinath Sah and Vivek Sah, *Kashi ka Sah Gharana* (Piligrims Book House, 2007), p. 13.
34 Dr Motichandra, *Kashi Ka Itihas*, p. 313; Srinath Sah and Vivek Sah, *Kashi ka Sah Gharana,* p. 5.
35 Eck, *Banaras*, p. xvi.
36 Prinsep, *Benares Illustrated*, p. 15.
37 Reginald Heber, *Narrative of a Journey through the Upper Provinces of India* (Manohar Publishers and Distributors, 2022), Vol. 1, p. 381.
38 A periplus, or periplous, is an ancient manuscript document that lists the ports and coastal landmarks, in order and with

approximate intervening distances that the captain of a vessel could expect to find along a shore.

39 Kashi Khand: *SanchhiptSkankpuran,* p. 796.

40 Pandit Kubernath Sukul, *Varanasi Vaibhav,* 2008, Bihar: Bihar Rashtrabhasha Parishad, p. 55

41 Dr.Motichandra Kashi Ka Itihas 1985 Vishavidyaalay Prakshan,p.01 Preface by Dr.Vasudevsaran Aggarwal

42 Rana P.B. Singh, *Banaras: The Heritage city of India Geography, History, and Bibliography* (Indica Books, 2008), p. 23.

Chapter 4: Kashi

1 Nilima Chitgopekar, *Rudra: The Idea of Shiva* (Penguin India, 2007), p. xxxii.

2 V.S. Naipaul, *India: A Wounded Civilization* (Vintage, 2003).

3 Ananda K. Coomaraswamy, *Yaksas*, Museum of Fine Arts, Boston.

4 Vidula Jayaswal, ed. *Varanasi: Myths and Scientific Studies* (Aryan Books International, 2013), p. xix.

5 Diana L. Eck, *Banaras: City of Light* (US: Alfred A. Knopf, 1982), pp. 60–61.

6 Marianne Keppens and Jakob De Roover, 'The Brahmin, the Aryan, and the Powers of the Priestly Class: Puzzles in the Study of Indian Religion', https://www.mdpi.com/2077-1444/11/4/181

7 Jayaswal, *Varanasi*, p. 75.

8 Eck, *Banaras*, p. 35.

9 Yuval Noah Harari, *Sapiens* (Dvir Publishing House Ltd, 2011), p. 51.

10 Jayaswal, *Varanasi*, p. 34.

11 Jayaswal, *Varanasi*, p. 76 (Akhta as per her was a converted Brahmin settlement).

12 Jayaswal, *Varanasi*, p. 75

13 Pandit Kubernath Sukul, *Varanashi Vaibhav* (Bihar: Bihar Rashtrabhasha Parishad, 2008), p. 11.

14 Dr Motichandra,*Kashika Itihas*(Uttar Pradesh: Vishwavidyalaya Prakashan,1985), pp.19–20.

15 Rahul Saankrtyaayan, *Volga se Gang* (Kitab Mahal Agencies, 2018), p. 76.

16 Eck, *Banaras,* pp. 101–02.

17 Ushakiran Atram, The Protector: Ravan Was a Gond king', *Caravan,* November 2021, https://caravanmagazine.in/religion/ravan-gond-king (accessed 21 October 2023).

18 Pandit Kubernath Sukul, *Varanashi Vaibhav*, p. 11.

19 James Ferguson Esq., *Trees and Serpent Worship*, p. 70.

20 Dr Motichandra, *Kashi Ka Itihas*, p. 36.

21 Eck, *Banaras,* p. 36.

22 Marianne Keppens and Jakob De Roover, 'The Brahmin, the Aryan, and the Powers of the Priestly Class: Puzzles in the Study of Indian Religion', https://www.mdpi.com/2077-1444/11/4/181, Roth, 1847, pp. 80–81.

23 Weber, 1868, p. 4.

24 Müller, 1848, p. 348.

25 Uddalaka Aruni is a Vedic sage of Hinduism who preached and propagated the Upanishadic philosophy in Hinduism.

26 Romila Thapar, *History of India* (Penguin India, 2000), pp. 131–32.

27 Shivprasad Singh, *Neela Chaand* (Vani Prakashan, 1988), p. 517.

28 Allen Charles, *Ashoka: The Search for India's Lost Emperor* (Little Brown, 2012), p. xiii.

29 Kubernath Sukul, *Varanasi-Vaibhav* (Bihar: Bihar Rashtrabhasha Parishad, 2008), pp. 3–24.

30 *Caravan*, November 2022, p. 16.

31 *Book of Deuteronomy*, 12: 1–3. Elizabeth-Chalier Visuvalingam and Sunthar Visuvalingam, 'Between Mecca and Benares: The Marriage of Lat Bhairava & Ghazi Miyan', 1991.

32 Meenakshi Jain, *Flight of Deities and Rebirth of Temples* (Aryan Books International, 2019), pp. 1–3.

33 (Guillaume 1958: 10, 35–39, 151–153).

34 Jain, *Flight of Deities and Rebirth of Temples*, pp. 1–3.

35 Dr Motichandra, *Kashi Ka Itihas* (Vishavidyaalay Prakshan, 1985), p. 104; Munshi Premchand, ed. *Hans-Kashi Ank* (October–November 1933,) p. 19; Sukul, *Varanasi-Vaibhav*, p. 25.

36 Rahul Saankrtyaayan, *Volga se Ganga* (Kitab Mahal Agencies, 2018), p. 231.

37 M.A. Sherring, *Benares: The Sacred City of the Hindus* (Kathmandu: Pilgrims Publishing, 2016), p. 206.

38 George Viscount Valentia, *Voyages and Travels to India, Ceylon, the Red Sea, Abyssinia and Egypt* (William Miller, London, 1809), pp. 99–100, 105–06.

39 Sherring, *Benares,* p. 191 and 306.

40 Meenakshi Jain, *Flight of the Deities and Rebirth of Temples* (Aryan Books International, 2019), p. 3.

41 Bishambhar Nath Pande, *Aurangzeb Ke Farman* (Hindi Academy, 1991); Sukul, *Varanasi-Vaibhav,* p. 29.

42 Richard M. Eaton, 'Temple Desecration and Indo-Muslim States', *Journal of Islamic Studies*, Vol. 11, No. 3 (September 2000), pp. 283–319.

43 Jawaharlal Nehru, *Discovery of India*, p. 267.

44 A Shaivite monastic order in which the Aghoris usually engage in post-mortem-like rituals, often choosing the charnel grounds, human skulls and even bones for their ritualistic activities.

45 Hemant Sharma, *Dekho Hamari Kaashi* (Prabhat Prakashan, 2022), p. 158.

46 Vyomesh Shukla, *Aag Aur Paani* (Delhi: Rukh Publication, 2023), p. 24.

47 Mahasweta Devi, *Jhansi ki Rani* (Radhaakrishna Prakashan, 2000), p. 28.

48 Sandria B. Freitag, ed. *Culture and Power in Banaras. Community, Performance, and Environment, 1800–1980* (University of California Press, 1989), Introduction.

49 Dr Motichandra, *Kashi Ka Itihas* (Vishavidyaalay Prakshan, 1985), pp. 219–20.

50 K.T. Achaya, *The Illustrated Foods of India A-Z* (Oxford University Press, 2009), p. 87.

51 Sukul, *Varanasi-Vaibhav*, p. 25.
52 Diana L. Eck, *Banaras: City of Light* (US: Alfred A. Knopf, 1982), p. 92.
53 Sherring, *Benares*, p. 13.
54 Marianne Keppens and Jakob De Roover, 'The Brahmin, the Aryan, and the Powers of the Priestly Class: Puzzles in the Study of Indian Religion'. (Van Der Hey 1799, p. 2).
55 Keppens and Roover, 'The Brahmin, the Aryan, and the Powers of the Priestly Class'; Van Der Hey, 1799, p. 397.
56 Keppens and Roover, 'The Brahmin, the Aryan, and the Powers of the Priestly Class'; Van Der Hey, 1799, p. 406.
57 Suranjay Ganguly, *Allen Ginsberg in India: An Interview*, https://allenginsberg.org/tag/suranjan-ganguly/.
58 Shukla, *Aag Aur Pani*, 2023).
59 Amit Mazumdar, 'The Book of Vows', *Times of India,* 11 December 2022.
60 Mazumdar, 'The Book of Vows'.

Chapter 5: The Yakshas and the Nagas

1 Max S. Shapiro and Rhoda A. Hendricks, *Dictionary of Mythology* (Paladin Books, 1981), p. 166 and 211.
2 Shapiro and Hendricks, *Dictionary of Mythology*, p. 130.
3 James Fergusson, *Tree and Serpent Worship Esq.*
4 Sukul, *Varanasi-Vaibhav*, p. 22.
5 Vasudev Saran Agrawal, *Rachna Sanchayan*, ed. Kapila Vatsayan, pp. 531–32.
6 Agrawal, Rachna Sanchayan, p. 532.
7 Sarah Shaw, *The Jatakas: Birth Stories of the Bodhisatta* (Penguin Books, 2006), p. 57.
8 Dr Motichandra, *Kashi Ka Itihas* (Uttar Pradesh: Vishwavidyalaya Prakashan, 1985), p. 33.
9 Nilima Chitgopekar, *Rudra: The Idea of Shiva* (Penguin India, 2007), p. 170.

10 Jaishankar Prasad-Gunda, *Hans-Kashi Ank*, edited by Munshi Premchand (October-November 1933), p. 207.
11 Keppens and Roover, 'The Brahmin, the Aryan, and the Powers of the Priestly Class'; The City of God, 4.1; Augustine 1998, p. 143)
12 Vidula Jayaswal, *Varanasi,* p. 19.
13 James Fergusson, *Esq., F.R.S., M.R.A.S., Tree and Serpent Worship, LONDON : INDIA MUSEUM, 1868. W.H. ALLEN AND CO., 13, WATERLOO PLACE, S.W. Publishers To The India Office,* p. 62.
14 Dr Motichandra, *Kashi Ka Itihas*, p. 35.
15 Ananda Kentish, Coomaraswamy, *Yaksas: 1877–1947* (Freer Gallery of Art, 1928), Introduction.

Chapter 6: The Dichotomy of Shaivism and Vaishnavism

1 Hazariprasad Drivedi, *Banbhatta Ki Atmakatha* (Rajkamal Paperbacks, 2021), pp. 25–27.
2 Tony Joseph, *Early Indians: The Story of Our Ancestors and Where We Came From* (New Delhi: Juggernaut Books, 2019), p. 188.
3 Nilima Chitgopekar, *Rudra: The Idea of Shiva* (Penguin, 2007), pp. Xxiv–v; Joseph, *Early Indians,* p. 188; Eck, *Banaras*, p. 96.
4 John Marshall, *Marshall's Mohenjo-daro 1922–27* (Marshall, Vol. I, p. 52).
5 Catherine Johns, *Sex or Symbol? Erotic Images of Greece and Rome* (University of Texas Press, 1982), p. 14 and 60.
6 Joseph, *Early Indians*, p. 187.
7 Rahul Saankrtyaayan, *Volga Se Ganga* (Kitab Mahal Agencies, 2018), pp. 79–80.
8 Vasudev Saran Agrawal, *Rachna Sanchayan*, ed. Kapila Vatsayan (Sahitya Akademy, 2012), p. 547; Dr Motichandra, *Kashi Ka Itihas* (Uttar Pradesh: Vishwavidyalaya Prakashan, 1985), p. 21.

9 James Fergusson, *Tree and Serpent Worship Esq., F.R.S., M.R.A.S., LONDON : INDIA MUSEUM, 1868. W.H. ALLEN AND CO., 13, WATERLOO PLACE, S.W. Publishers To The India Office,* pp. 69–70.

10 *Esq., F.R.S., M.R.A.S., Tree and Serpent Worship,* LONDON: *INDIA MUSEUM, 1868. W. H. ALLEN AND CO., 13, WATERLOO PLACE, S.W. Publishers To The India Office,* pp. 70–71.

11 Chitgopekar, *Rudra,* p. 45 and 105.

12 Kashi Khand, *Skand Puran (Sankshipt)* (Uttar Pradesh: Gorakhpur Gita Press), p. 853.

13 Pandit Kubernath Sukul, *Varanashi-Vaibhav*, p. 281.

14 M.A. Sherring, *Benares: The Sacred City of the Hindus* (Kathmandu: Pilgrims Publishing, 2016), pp. 213–39.

15 Sukul, *Varanashi-Vaibhav* 2008, p. 281.

16 Dr Motichandra, *Kashi Ka Itihas*, p. 101.

17 Dr Motichandra, *Kashi Ka Itihas*, p. 31 and 50.

18 Elizabeth-Chalier Visuvalingam and Sunthar Visuvalingam, 'Between Mecca and Benares: The Marriage of Lat Bhairava & Ghazi Miyan', 1993, https://www.svabhinava.org/banaras/banaras-main.html

19 Eck, *Banaras*, p. 108.

20 Pandit Kuber Nath Sukul, *Varanasi Down the Ages* (Uttar Pradesh: Bhargav Bhushan Press, 1974), p. 187.

21 Chitgopekar, *Rudra*, p. 34.

22 (https://www.ancient-origins.net/unexplained-phenomena/falling-stars-and-black-stone-humanity-s-worship-meteorites-001901)

23 (https://www.ancient-origins.net/unexplained-phenomena/falling-stars-and-black-stone-humanity-s-worship-meteorites-001901)

24 Oliver C., The Worship and Folk-Lore of Meteoritesby Farrington, https://archive.org/details/jstor-533884/page/n3/mode/2up, pp. 202–03.

25 Pranay Lal, *Indica: A Deep Natural History of the Indian Subcontinent* (Penguin Random House India, 2016), p. 24.
26 George Viscount Valentia, *Voyages and Travels to India, Ceylon, the Red Sea, Abyssinia and Egypt* (William Miller, 1809), pp. 468–70.
27 Lal, *Indica*, p. 29.
28 Pranay Lal (email dated 12 October 2022, p. 111).
29 *Maheshwar Khand, Skanda Purana*, pp. 2–22.
30 *Maheshwar Khand, Skanda Purana,* pp. 5–26; Devdutt Pattanaik, *Shiva: An Introduction* (Vakils, Feffer and Simons Pvt. Ltd, 1997), p. 17; Chitgopekar, *Rudra*, pp. 100–01.
31 Kashi Khand, *Skand Puran (Sankshipt)* (Uttar Pradesh: Gorakhpur Gita Press), p. 897.
32 Dr Motichandra, *Kashi Ka Itihas*, p. 31.
33 Mahabharata: *Uddhog Parv 47–40*; Dr Motichandra, *Kashi Ka Itihas*, p. 25.
34 Eck, *Banaras*, p. 65.
35 Kashi Khand, *Skand Puran (Sankshipt)*, p. 862.
36 Kashi Khand, *Skand Puran (Sankshipt)*, p. 856.
37 Kashi Khand, *Skand Puran (Sankshipt)*, p. 850.
38 Kashi Khand, *Skand Puran (Sankshipt)*, p. 854.
39 Kashi Khand, *Skand Puran (Sankshipt)*, pp. 811–49.
40 Dr Motichandra, *Kashi Ka Itihas*, pp. 23–24.
41 Sherring, *Benares*, p. 28.
42 Eck, *Banaras.*
43 Dr Motichandra, *Kashi Ka Itihas*, p. 142.
44 James Fergusson, *Esq., F.R.S., M.R.A.S., Tree and Serpent Worship, LONDON : INDIA MUSEUM, 1868. W. H. ALLEN AND CO., 13, WATERLOO PLACE, S.W. Publishers To The India Office,*
45 James Fergusson, *Esq., F.R.S., M.R.A.S., Tree and Serpent Worship, LONDON : INDIA MUSEUM, 1868. W. H. ALLEN AND CO., 13, WATERLOO PLACE, S.W. Publishers To The India Office,* p. 71.
46 Visuvalingam and Visuvalingam, 'Between Mecca and Benares: The Marriage of Lat Bhairava & Ghazi Miya', 1993, https://www.svabhinava.org/banaras/banaras-main.html

47 'Nashik Kumbh Mela Hit by Conflict between Rival Sects', *Hindustan Times*, 13 July 2015, https://www.hindustantimes.com/india/nashik-kumbh-mela-hit-by-conflict-between-rival-sects/story-WwKgVlkWrL6o90sWxh7KmN.html

Chapter 7: The Ghats

1 Maaz Bin Bilal, trans. *The Temple Lamp* (Penguin Classics, August 2022), p. 28, Masnavi no. 26.
2 James Prinsep, *Benares Illustrated* (Baptist Mission Press, Circular Road, 1831), p. 9.
3 Pandit Kubernath Sukul, *Varanasi-Vaibhav* (Bihar: Bihar Rashtrabhasha Parishad, 2008), pp. 65–70.
4 William Foster, ed. *Early Travels in India: 1583–1619* (Munshiram Manoharlal Publishers Pvt Ltd., 1921), pp. 20–23.
5 Jean-Baptiste Tavernier, *Travels in India: 1605–1689*, Book iii, Chapter XI, p. 17.
6 Dr Motichandra, *Kashi Ka Itihas* (Uttar Pradesh: Vishwavidyalaya Prakashan, 1985), p. 279.
7 Anant Sadashiv Altekar, *History of Banaras: From the Earliest Times Down to 1937* (Culture Publication House, Benares Hindu University, 1937), p. 62.
8 William Hodges, *Travels in India* (1794), pp. 60–61.
9 George Viscount Valentia, *Voyages and Travels to India, Ceylon, the Red Sea, Abyssinia and Egypt*, p. 99.
10 Maaz Bin Bilal, trans. *The Temple Lamp* (Penguin Classics, 2022), pp. 59–62.
11 Diana L. Eck, *Banaras: City of Light* (US: Alfred A. Knopf, 1982), p. 4.
12 Dr Motichandra, *Kashi Ka Itihas* (Uttar Pradesh: Vishwavidyalaya Prakashan, 1985), p. 365; Munshi Premchand, ed., Hans-*Kashi Ank*; October–November 1933, p. 42.
13 Pandit Kubernath Sukul, *Varanasi-Vaibhav* (Bihar: Bihar Rashtrabhasha Parishad, 2008), p. 67.

14 Wiliam Dalrymple: *The Anarchy: The East India Company, Corporate Violence, and the Pillage of an Empire* (Bloomsbury, 2019), p. 191.
15 James Prinsep, *Benares Illustrated* (Baptist Mission Press, Circular Road, 1831), p. 35.

Chapter 8: The Weavers of Banaras

1 Dr Motichandra, *Kashi Ka Itihas* (Uttar Pradesh: Vishwavidyalaya Prakashan, 1985), p. 15; Pandit Kuber Nath Sukul, *Varanasi Down the Ages* (Uttar Pradesh: Bhargav Bhushan Press, 1974), p. 49.
2 Dr Motichandra, *Kashi Ka Itihas*, p. 47.
3 Dr Motichandra, *Kashi Ka Itihas*, p. 79.
4 Ralph Fitch, *Journey to India Over-land*, Merchant of London, and others, Volume 7, Chapter 9, Section 2 in 1583, p. 402.
5 Maaz Bin Bilal, trans. *The Temple Lamp* (Penguin Classics, 202), p. 8, verse 6.
6 Hemant Sharma, *Dekho Hamari Kaashi* (Prabhat Prakashan 2022), p. 85.
7 M.A. Sherring, *Benares: The Sacred City of the Hindus* (Kathmandu: Pilgrims Publishing, 2016), p. 7.
8 Sherring, *Benares*, p. 240.
9 James Prinsep, *Benares Illustrated* (Baptist Mission Press, Circular Road, 1831), p. 9.
10 Abdul Bismillah, *Jheeni-Jheeni Beeni Chadariya* (Delhi: Rajkamal Prakashan, 2018).
11 Bismillah, *Jheeni Jheeni Beeni Chadariya*, pp. 10–11.
12 Raman, *The World of the Banaras Weaver*, p. 81.
13 Raman, *The World of the Banaras Weaver*, p. 81.
14 Sandria B. Freitag, ed. *Culture and Power in Banaras. Community, Performance, and Environment, 1800–1980* (University of California Press, 1989,) p. 13.
15 Bismillah, *Jheeni-Jheeni Beeni Chadariya.*
16 Raman, *The World of the Banaras Weaver*, p. 141.
17 Elizabeth-Chalier Visuvalingam and Sunthar Visuvalingam, 'Between Mecca and Benares: The Marriage of Lat Bhairava and

Ghazi Miyan', 1993, https://www.svabhinava.org/banaras/banaras-main.html

18 Freitag, ed. *Culture and Power in Banaras.*

19 Freitag, ed. *Culture and Power in Banaras*, Introduction.

20 Nita Kumar, 'Work and Leisure in the Formation of Identity: Muslim Weavers in a Hindu City', in Freitag, ed. *Culture and Power in Banaras*, p. 155.

21 Nilosree Biswas and Irfan Nabi, *Banaras: Gods, Humans and Stories* (Niyogi Books, 2021), p. 138.

22 Raman, *The World of the Banaras Weaver*, p. 4.

23 Vasanthi Raman, *The World of the Banaras Weaver*, p. 258.

24 Rajeev Singh, *Kavita Mein Banaras* (Rajkamal Prakashan 2022), p. 133.

Chapter 9: Art at Heart

1 Mrinal Pandey, 'Kashi: City of Poets, Holy Men, Clowns and Courtesans', *Indian Express*, 12 April 2023.

2 Vishwanath Mukherjee, *Bana Rahe Banaras* (Uttar Pradesh: Vishwavidyalaya Prakashan, 2017), p. 106; Rajeev Singh, *Kavita Mein Banaras* (Rajkamal Prakashan 2022, p. 206).

3 Sandria B. Freitag, ed. *Culture and Power in Banaras: Community, Performance, and Environment, 1800–1980* (University of California Press, 1989); Kathryn Hansen, 'The Birth of Hindi Drama in Banaras, 1868–1885', in Culture and Power in Banaras: Community, Performance, and Environment, 1880—1980, ed. Sandria B. Freitag, pp. 63–64.

4 Pandey, 'Kashi: City of Poets'.

5 Allen Ginsberg in India: An Interview with Suranjan Ganguly, Allen Ginsberg, https://allenginsberg.org › tag › suranjan-ganguly

6 Ginsberg, India, and the holiness of dirt. Journal 176-78 Raymond-Jean Frontain, https://go.gale.com/ps/i.do?p=LitRC&sw=w&issn=&v=2.1&it=r&id=GALE%7CA297760668&sid=googleScholar&linkaccess=abs&userGroupName=anon%7Eaacf187d&aty=open-web-entry

7 Akshaya K. Rath, *Allen Ginsberg in India: Life and Narrative*, https://zbc.uz.zgora.pl/repozytorium/Content/60102/9_rath_allen.pdf
8 'The *kartal*, consists of two pairs of tapered metal rods, each approximately nine inches in length. The singer holds a pair in each hand, creating a high-pitched ringing sound by rhythmically hitting the two rods against each other.' (Scott Marcus, 'The Rise of a Folk Music Genre: Biraha', in *Culture and Power in Banaras: Community, Performance, & Environment, 1800–1980,* ed. Sandria B. Freitag (University of California Press, 1989), pp. 93–113).
9 Marcus, 'The Rise of a Folk Music Genre: Biraha.'
10 Mahasweta Devi, *Jhansi Ki Rani* (Ramakrishna Prakashan, 2000), p. 33.
11 Kashi Khand*, Skand Puran (Sankshipt)* (Gorakhpur: Gita Press), p. 828; Diana L. Eck, *Banaras: City of Light* (US: Alfred A. Knopf, 1982), p. 150.
12 The state of being a Buddha, the ultimate goal of a Buddhist Monk, *Arhat* means who has reached the stage of enlightenment.
13 Dr Motichandra, *Kashi Ka Itihas* (Uttar Pradesh: Vishwavidyalaya Prakshan, 1985), p. 89.
14 Dr Motichandra, *Kashi Ka Itihas,* p. 398.
15 Vishwanath Mukherjee, *Bana Rahe Banaras* (Uttar Pradesh: Vishwavidyalaya Prakashan, 2017), p. 23; Saba Dewan, *Twaifnama* (Context Publications, 2019), p. 313.
16 Dewan, *Twaifnama.*
17 Dewan, *Twaifnama*, p. 162.
18 A.N. Sharma, *Bajanaama: A Study of Early Indian Gramophone Records* (Kathachitra Prakshan, First edition, 2012), pp. 55–56.
19 Hemant Sharma, *Dekho Hamari Kaashi* (Prabhat Prakashan, 2022), p. 125; Dewan, *Twaifnama*, p. 162.
20 Dewan, *Twaifnama*, p. 42; James Prinsep, *Benares Illustrated* (Baptist Mission Press, Circular Road, 1831), p. 33.

21 Sharma, *Bajanaama*, p. 84.
22 Prinsep, *Benares Illustrated*, p. 33.
23 Dewan, *Twaifnama*, pp. 28–29.

Chapter 10: Saat Vaar, Nau Tyohaar

1 Diana L. Eck, *Banaras: City of Light* (US: Alfred A. Knopf, 1982), p. 123.
2 M.A. Sherring, *Benares: The Sacred City of the Hindus* (Kathmandu: Pilgrims Publishing, 2016), p. 160.
3 Kashi Khand, *Skand Puran (Sankshipt)* (Uttar Pradesh: Gorakhpur Gita Press), p. 867.
4 Vishwanath Mukherjee, *Bana Rahe Banaras* (Uttar Pradesh: Vishwavidyalaya Prakashan, 2017), p. 104; Pandit Kuber Nath Sukul, *Varanasi Down the Ages* (Uttar Pradesh: Bhargav Bhushan Press, 1974), pp. 244–45.
5 Vyomesh Shukla, *Aag Aur Paani* (New Delhi: Rukh Publication 2023, p. 102).
6 K.T. Achaya, *The Illustrated Foods of India A–Z* (Oxford University Press, 2009), p. 269.
7 Prinsep, *Benares Illustrated*, p. 27.
8 Prinsep, *Benares Illustrated*, p. 23.
9 Manan Kapoor, 'A History of Kite Flying in India', Sahapedia, 9 January 2020, https://www.sahapedia.org/history-kite-flying-india
10 M.A. Sherring, *Benares: The Sacred City of the Hindus* (Kathmandu: Pilgrims Publishing, 2016), p. 166.

Chapter 11: Banaras on My Palate

1 K.T. Achaya, *The Illustrated Foods of India A–Z* (Oxford University Press, 2009), p. 246.
2 Dr Motichandra, *Kashi Ka Itihas* (Uttar Pradesh: Vishwavidyalaya Prakashan, 1985), p. 223.

3 Vishwanath Mukherjee, *Bana Rahe Banaras* (Uttar Pradesh: Vishwavidyalaya Prakashan, 2017), p. 106.
4 Dr Motichandra, *Kashi Ka Itihas*, p. 91.
5 Achaya, *The Illustrated Foods of India*, p. 147.
6 Allen Ginsberg in India: An Interview with Suranjan Ganguly, Allen Ginsberg, https://allenginsberg.org › tag › suranjan-ganguly

Chapter 12: Living Continuities

1 Vyomesh Shukla, *Aag Aur Pani* (New Delhi: Rukh Publication, 2023), p. 105.
2 Kuber Nath Sukul, *Varanasi Down the Ages* (Uttar Pradesh: Bhargav Bhushan Press, 1974), p. 325.
3 Vyomesh Shukla, *Aag Aur Pani* (Rukh Publication, 2023), p. 9.
4 Ralph Fitch, *Journey to India,* Vol. 7, Chapter 9, Section 2, p. 402.
5 Vasudev Sharan Agarwal, *The Study of Rajghat Seals* (Sahitya Akademi, 2012), p. 636.
6 Reginald Heber, *Narrative of a Journey through the Upper Provinces of India,* Vol. 1, p. 372.
7 Heber, *Narrative of a Journey*, Vol. 1, p. 382.
8 Dr Motichandra, *Kashi Ka Itihas* (Uttar Pradesh: Vishwavidyalaya Prakashan, 1985), p. 353; Pandit Kuber Nath Sukul, *Varanasi Down the Ages* (Bhargav Bhushan Press, 1974), p. 282.
9 K.T. Achaya, *The Illustrated Foods of India* (Oxford University Press, 2009), p. 9.
10 Rajeev Singh, *Kavita Mein Banaras* (Rajkamal Prakashan, 2022), p. 206; Vishwanath Mukherjee, *Bana Rahe Banaras* (Uttar Pradesh: Vishwavidyalaya Prakashan, 2017), p. 106.
11 *Times of India,* 4 April 2023.
12 James Prinsep, *Benaras Illustrated* (Uttar Pradesh: Vishwavidyalaya Prakashan, 1996), p. 37.
13 Reginald Heber, *Narrative of a Journey through the Upper Provinces of India,* Vol. 1, p. 371.
14 Viscount Valentia, *Voyages and Travels in India, Ceylon, the Red Sea, Abyssinia and Egypt* (New Delhi: Facsimile Publisher, 2020) p. 104.

15 Manan Ahmed Asif, *The Loss of Hindustan: The Invention of India* (Harvard University Press, 2020), p. 54.

16 Asif, *The Loss of Hindustan*, p. 60.

17 Maaz Bin Bilal, trans. *The Temple Lamp*. Penguin Classics, August 2022, p. xxxiv, Dr Motichandra, *Kashi Ka Itihas.*

18 *Times of India,* 16 February 2023.

19 Nazeer Banarasi.

Chapter 13: Perambulating the Idea of Banaras

1 Kashi Khand, p. 831.

2 Kashi Khand, pp. 874–75.

3 Diana L. Eck, *Banaras: City of Light* (US: Alfred A. Knopf, 1982), p. 131.

4 Dr Motichandra, *Kashi Ka Itihas* (Uttar Pradesh: Vishwavidyalaya Prakashan, 1985), p. 303.

Scan QR code to access the
Penguin Random House India website